MOVING ON

Fourth Edition

MOVING ON

THE AMERICAN PEOPLE SINCE 1945

George Donelson Moss

With

Evan P. Thomas

Prentice Hall

Boston   Columbus   Indianapolis   New York   San Francisco
Upper Saddle River   Amsterdam   Cape Town   Dubai   London   Madrid
Milan   Munich   Paris   Montreal   Toronto   Delhi   Mexico City   Sao Paulo
Sydney   Hong Kong   Seoul   Singapore   Taipei   Tokyo

Publisher: Charlyce Jones Owen
Editorial Assistant: Maureen Diana
Director of Marketing: Brandy Dawson
Marketing Manager: Maureen Prado-Roberts
Marketing Assistant: Marissa O' Brien
Production Manager: Fran Russello
Manager, Visual Research: Beth Brenzel
Manager, Rights and Permissions: Zina Arabia
Image Permission Coordinator: Richard Rodrigues
Manager, Cover Visual Research & Permissions: Karen Sanatar
Art Director: Jayne Conte
Cover Designer: Bruce Kenselaar
Cover Art: Michal Czerwonka/AFP/Getty Images
Back Cover Image Credits (left to right): © JupiterImages, © Veer, © Monkey
   Business Images/Shutterstock, © Value RF/Corbis
Full-Service Project Management: Shiny Rajesh/Integra Software Services, Pvt. Ltd.
Printer/Binder: RR Donnelley & Sons, Inc.
Text Font: 10/12, Minion

Credits and acknowledgments borrowed from other sources and reproduced, with permission, in this textbook appear on appropriate page within text.

Library of Congress Cataloging-in-Publication Data
Moss, George
    Movin on : the American people since 1945/George Donelson Moss, Evan P.
Thomas. —4th ed.
        p. cm.
Includes bibliographical references and index.
ISBN-13: 978-0-205-69285-9 (alk. paper)
ISBN-10: 0-205-69285-0 (alk. paper)
    1. United States—History—1945-   I. Thomas, Evan P.   II. Title.
E741.M673 2010
973.92—dc22
                                                    2009042100

10 9 8 7 6 5 4 3 2 1

Prentice Hall
is an imprint of

www.pearsonhighered.com

ISBN 10:   0-205-69285-0
ISBN 13: 978-0-20569285-9

CONTENTS

PREFACE

Moving On: The American People Since 1945 covers sixty-plus years of American history from the summer of 1945 to the present; it endeavors to record the recent historical experiences that have shaped our nation and forged the culture and social character of our people. Recent American history is a compelling saga of human struggle, achievement, and failure; it is filled with irony, tragedy, and comedy.

We have enjoyed revising the book for a fourth edition because the recent American past has been supercharged with energy, conflict, and drama. And so much has happened in the last few years! While the nation has become embroiled in two wars thousands of miles from its shores, the domestic economy slid into its deepest recession since the Great Depression of the early 1930s. In the fall elections of 2008, more Americans than ever before went to the polls. They elected Barack Obama, who became the first African American president in the history of the republic. Not since Franklin D. Roosevelt took the oath of office in March 1933 has an incoming administration faced such a staggering array of challenging problems or been under such pressure to act.

Our revision for this new edition has been both thorough and extensive. Each chapter has been carefully reworked. In several instances we have divided longer chapters into two, separating cultural and social history from political history. The chapters dealing with cultural and social history have been enhanced and, with the exception of the final chapter concerned with the most recent events, the chapters covering political history have been reduced. The effect has been to create a book that gives comparatively greater attention to important cultural and social trends, and less attention to political developments. Also, the chapters are more cohesive and thematically unified. The bibliographical essays found at the end of each chapter have been revised and updated. Overall, we have shortened our story of recent America considerably. Without sacrificing anything substantial, we have brought forth a book that is approximately ninety pages (20 percent) shorter than its immediate predecessor.

The era that began amidst the storm of the planet's largest war and continues to the present global war against terrorism forms a coherent unit of study. It is no wonder that students have made recent U.S. history courses among the most popular of those currently being offered on the nation's college and university campuses. Paradoxically, most students who have had good high school survey courses in U.S. history are unlikely to know well the recent history of their country—even though it is the recent history that most usefully illuminates the present and suggests the shape of the future rapidly exploding upon us.

For most young people, Watergate and Iran-Contra are merely rhetorical labels, names for events that scarcely one in ten students can discuss meaningfully. They often know more about the Spanish–American War than they do about the Vietnam War. Having scant historical understanding of recent events, they have little sense of causation or consequences. They lack the experience of deriving structures of explanation and interpretation that create out of these recent events an intelligible, usable past.

Did the upheavals of the 1960s have an enduring impact on the status of minorities, women, and gay-lesbian people? How has the legacy of the Vietnam War influenced subsequent American diplomatic and strategic policies? Does the ongoing war against terrorism derive from a long U.S. involvement in the Middle East, and if so, what are the particular sources of this conflict? One of the most significant trends in recent political history has been the rise to power of the conservative movement. How to understand and explain the conservative ascendancy? One of the most significant sociocultural trend has been the emergence of a dynamic multicultural society during the past twenty years. How to understand and explain the rapid recent rise of multicultural America? How to connect it to the 1960s upheavals? How to connect it to the election of Barack Obama? Are there, in fact, connections? Two of the most significant and challenging questions to try to answer are how did the global economy evolve and how did the United States come to play a dominant role in the emergent global village. Only a close study of the recent past can provide answers to these and the myriad of other questions that thoughtful students raise.

During the past sixty years, Americans have developed a vital popular culture. Its most important forms reach most Americans through the mass media of radio, movies, television, and the Internet. Sections of many chapters of *Moving On* chart the rise of a commercial multimedia-saturated popular culture that is flourishing in the opening decade of the twenty-first century.

We have also devoted a good deal of space to the new social history with its focus on issues of class, gender, race, and ethnicity. Social history is often viewed from the perspective of those groups that in the past were either ignored or perceived as passive objects of more powerful historical agents. We have given much attention to immigration history, labor history, women's history, gay-lesbian history, African American history, Hispanic American history, Asian American history, and Native American history. The story of recent America includes the stories of all individuals and groups who have played active roles in the unfolding drama.

Our inclusive approach amounts to a work of restoration. We aim to restore to the recent past much of its diversity and complexity. If we have created the book that we intended, it will be the first study of the recent American past that you read, not the last. If historical study represents a kind of journey, consider *Moving On* a point of departure, not a destination.

ACKNOWLEDGMENTS

One of the many features of the historian's profession that makes it so rewarding is the incredible generosity of others who so willingly give their time, energies, talents, and knowledge. We are profoundly grateful for so much help from so many fine people: students, colleagues, and other scholars who have contributed in ways that improved the content, organization, and writing of this book and its several revisions over the past two decades. They are too numerous to cite individually, and we want to assert as emphatically as we can that our not mentioning them by name is not in the slightest way an indicator of ingratitude. We also want to thank the reviewers of this book: Julian M. Pleasants, University of Florida; Tracy S. Uebelhor, University of Southern Indiana; and Yanek Mieczkowski, Dowling College. Their critical comments and helpful suggestions significantly improved our book.

Special thanks go to Charlyce Jones-Owen, Publisher at Pearson Education, who provided us with an opportunity to produce this book. She provided expert guidance and support as needed, but she also left us free to create the book we wanted. Any flaws and limits remaining in the book are our responsibility, not hers.

George, as always, sends a special, special thanks to the lovely Linda. Evan wishes to extend special, special thanks to Majorie and Liz.

George Donelson Moss
Evan A. Thomas

Moving On

1

Postwar America

VICTORY!

On August 14, 1945, the Japanese government announced Japan's unconditional surrender, bringing history's largest war to a triumphant conclusion for the United States and its allies. Across America, its people erupted in frenzied victory celebrations. Tumultuous parades occurred in New York, Chicago, San Francisco, and other great cities. In small towns and cities everywhere, citizens joined in spontaneous, joyous victory parades. All Americans rejoiced at the final destruction of the Axis menace and the advent of peace throughout a battered world.

In one small town, Blythe, California, an agricultural community of perhaps 2,500 people, amidst the paraders, a ten-year-old boy astride his chestnut pony shouted, "We won! We won!" The high school marching band played "The Star-Spangled Banner," "America the Beautiful," and John Philip Sousa's rousing "Stars and Stripes Forever." Townspeople, lining the parade route, sang chorus after chorus of "God Bless America."

After the paraders had traversed Main Street, they turned onto a side road leading to the fairgrounds, which also served as a rodeo arena and high school football stadium. As it reached the fairgrounds, the parade dissolved. George Donelson Moss, weary but immensely proud to be an American on that long-ago, glorious summer day, his little boy's imagination fired by the sense that he had played a small part in a great historical drama, rode his chestnut pony home. It was dinner time.

LEGACIES OF WORLD WAR

At war's end, the United States was vastly changed from the nation that had been thrust suddenly into the cauldron of war by the Japanese surprise attack on Pearl Harbor on December 7, 1941. During the intervening years of fighting and winning World War II, America had undergone profound transformations that forever changed the social landscape and created new possibilities for its people.

FIGURE 1.1   Americans celebrating V-J Day in Times Square. All across the country, people erupted into spontaneous celebrations of victory.   *Source:* Corbis/Bettmann.

Important population shifts occurred in wartime that would shape the demographic contours of postwar America for decades. Population flowed from the rural interior of the country outward toward the cities along the Pacific, Atlantic, and Gulf coasts. People also left inland farms and villages for the cities of the Upper Midwest, because it was in the coastal and Midwestern cities that the major military installations, shipyards, aircraft assembly plants, and other war industries were located.

Population also made a major shift westward, particularly to California. California's population increased by 40 percent from 1940 to 1945, and millions of the military personnel and war workers who came to California in wartime remained or returned after the war to become permanent residents of the Golden State. The Sunbelt, that southern rim of states stretching from South Carolina to Southern California, also began to grow rapidly during the war years. The Sunbelt states, particularly Florida, Texas, and Southern California, would become the nation's most dynamic centers of population growth and economic expansion in the postwar decades.

Well-paying jobs in war industries lured over one million African Americans out of the Old South and on to New York, Chicago, Philadelphia, Detroit, and the rapidly growing cities along the West Coast. Most African Americans and their families would remain in these metropolises after war's end, becoming permanent residents.

Vast expenditures by the federal government during wartime revitalized the economy, extricated the American people from the lingering clutches of the Great Depression, and inaugurated a cycle of affluence that stretched into the 1970s. The gross domestic product more than doubled during the war years, from $95 billion in 1940 to more than $211 billion by 1946. During those years, economic expansion added ten million new jobs. By war's end, the nation's workers enjoyed full employment at the highest wages in history.

War transformed the American social structure. For the first time in its history, the United States became a middle-class nation in the sense that a statistical majority, more than half of its

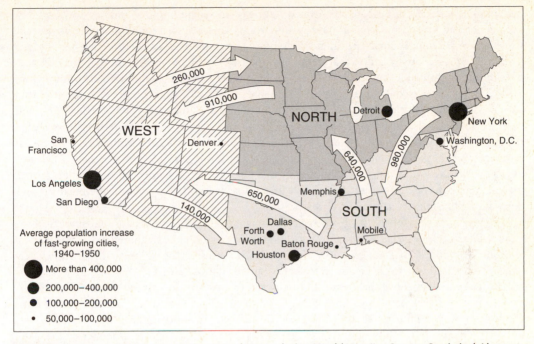

FIGURE 1.2 Internal migration in the United States during World War II. *Source:* Statistical Abstract of the United States, 1974 ed.

families, enjoyed middle-class incomes and lifestyles. The number of families earning less than $2,000 annually declined by 50 percent from 1941 to 1945, while the number of families earning $5,000 or more quadrupled during the same period. These wartime economic advances created the social foundations of the affluent society that flowered in the 1950s and 1960s.

Popular culture boomed during the war years and would continue to boom in the postwar era. Major league baseball games attracted large, enthusiastic crowds, and racetracks enjoyed historic high attendance and betting handles. Ballroom dancing flourished. The popularity of jitterbugging continued unabated, particularly among young people for whom it offered a distinctive world with its own clothes, language, and ritualistic behaviors. The major mass media—print journalism, radio, and movies—prospered. Radio became more popular than ever, and it continued to thrive in the postwar years. People read one or two daily newspapers, subscribed to several magazines, and went to the movies an average of twice a week. Sales of books, both fiction and nonfiction, increased sharply in wartime and again after the war. Building on their wartime experiences, most Americans would be eager participants in a vibrant postwar commercial mass culture.

A unified and powerful nation emerged victoriously from war. Its armed forces and industrial might had played decisive roles in destroying Fascism, militarism, and imperialism around the globe. America and its allies had won the largest war in human history. American civilians had been spared the devastations and terrors of a war fought outside of its continental boundaries.

The day the war ended, the United States strode the world as an international colossus; its armed forces, linked to its nuclear monopoly, made it the most powerful nation-state in the history of the planet. Its statesmen took the lead in creating a new international agency to preserve peace in the postwar era. Fittingly, the United Nations' permanent home would be New York City, the financial and cultural capital of the new imperium. Americans accepted involvement with the world beyond national boundaries; there would be no reversion to isolationism after 1945. The long Cold War with the Soviet Union that dominated international affairs for more than four decades after the war stemmed from the tensions and conflicts that strained the Grand Alliance in wartime.

The war restored America's optimistic sense of individual and national potential that would shape the national experience for decades. The Axis powers had been defeated—their power and wealth destroyed. Victorious America was strong, prosperous, and free. Its people felt ready for the "American Century" they believed lay ahead. America's economy was powerful. Its resources were abundant, and it had the scientific and technological talent to use them. Their war experiences gave Americans new confidence that they could solve all serious problems, both internal and external. They had proved that they possessed both the will and the means to lick depression at home and aggression abroad.

Americans also soberly confronted a future that they feared could bring a recurrence of the Great Depression. Could prosperity, growth, and full employment be sustained in the postwar era without the stimulus of a war economy? Could jobs be found for the millions of returning veterans and displaced war workers? Americans also worried about threats to their security posed by the Soviet Union, an expanding Communist power. Perhaps the war had not made the world safe for democracy. Perhaps there was not going to be an American Century. Most of all, Americans were alarmed by the nuclear shadow that they had cast over the postwar era.

Americans, in the summer of 1945, faced the future with a mixture of feelings: feelings of pride, confidence, and great expectations, as well as feelings of fear—of the return of depression, of expanding Soviet power, and of a nuclear Armageddon.

A PLURALISTIC SOCIETY

In 1945, approximately 140 million Americans inhabited the nation and its territories and served overseas in the armed forces. Of the approximately 38 million American households, two-thirds could be found in urban areas. Given that census takers defined as urban anyone living in a town having 2,500 or more residents and that the great explosion of postwar suburban development had only just begun, it would be more accurate to depict America at war's end as remaining primarily a nation comprising farms, villages, towns, and small and medium-sized cities. Most people focused on local life—on their friends and families, on their neighborhoods, and on civic issues. They were aware, of course, of the great war that had just been won, and most Americans understood that they inhabited the richest, freest, and most powerful nation in the history of the planet. But these were remote, abstract considerations. What was immediate and real to nearly all Americans was what happened on a daily basis as they lived their lives, went to school, worked, found time to have fun, and involved themselves in community affairs.

When the war ended in August 1945, over twelve million Americans, most of them young men between the ages of eighteen and thirty-five, over 90 percent of them conscripts, still served in the armed forces. Many of them had fought bravely and tenaciously for years, and they had fought in both the European and Far Eastern conflicts. With the war over and the Axis defeated, they yearned to come home and get out of the military. Above all, they wanted to return to normal life in America, and rejoin wives and girlfriends.

The federal government rapidly complied with the demands of the soldiers and their families. Within a year, most of the vast forces that had been mobilized for history's largest war were returned to civilian life. Within a year, the military had shrunk to 2.5 million, and by the summer of 1947, only about 1 million people remained on active duty. In the postwar years, millions of the veterans availed themselves of benefits under the GI Bill of Rights, a generous multibillion-dollar program, which enabled veterans to earn college degrees, acquire technical training, buy homes, and start their own businesses.

Contrary to the popular view of World War II as The Good War—in which all soldiers fought heroically to defeat powerful enemies threatening the American way of life, were welcomed home by a grateful civilian populace, and quickly got on with their civilian lives and careers—many veterans had difficulty readjusting to civilian life. Tens of thousands of veterans suffered from severely disabling wounds and psychological disorders. Other veterans were outraged and embittered by the rampant materialism, hedonism, and lack of patriotism they often encountered in postwar society. They sometimes wondered just what it was that they had fought and sacrificed for.

The approximately 140,000,000 Americans comprised one of the most ethnically and racially diverse national populations inhabiting the planet. Nearly 25 percent of the people were either foreign-born or had a parent who was foreign-born, and most of the foreign-born population were of European descent. African Americans (officially denoted as "Negroes" in the censuses) numbered about 14,000,000, 10 percent of the total population. About 2.7 million Hispanics, mostly of Mexican descent, inhabited the Southwestern states and Southern California. Asians, long excluded by racist immigration laws, numbered perhaps 250,000, mostly Han Chinese and Japanese. Perhaps 250,000 Pacific Islanders, mostly Filipinos, and 350,000 Native Americans (officially denoted as "Indians" in the censuses) also lived in the United States.

ASIAN AMERICANS

Some of these people were gravely harmed in wartime. During the spring and summer of 1942, about 120,000 Japanese Americans, two-thirds of them native-born American citizens, were uprooted from their homes along the Pacific Coast and taken to internment centers in remote, desolate interior regions of the country. There they lived in tar-paper barracks behind barbed wire for three years. The internment of Japanese Americans for the duration of World War II represented the worst violation of civil liberties in wartime in American history.

The initiative was taken by General John Dewitt, the military commander in charge of security along the West Coast. Dewitt and other officials claimed that the relocation of Japanese Americans was necessary to guarantee military security along the West Coast. They argued that if the Japanese Americans were not relocated, some of them would aid the enemy in case of attack. Their accusations were false. FBI agents admitted later that they never discovered a single proven act of disloyalty committed by any Japanese American. The real reasons for their removal included anti-Japanese prejudice, wartime hysteria, and greed. The claim of military necessity was based on unfounded suspicion, not on evidence.

Japanese American spokesmen asserted their loyalty to no avail. No political leaders or newspaper editors defended the Japanese. Earl Warren, California's attorney general in 1942, strongly advocated removal. The removal order, Executive Order No. 9066, came from President Roosevelt and could not be challenged. In 1944, the Supreme Court sustained the relocation of Japanese Americans. In the case of *Fred Korematsu v. the United States*, the Court accepted the claim of army lawyers that relocation was a wartime military necessity. A 5 to 3 majority ruled that in time of war, individual rights could be sacrificed to military necessity. Associate Justice Frank Murphy filed a powerful dissenting opinion, stating that the relocation of Japanese Americans fell "into the ugly abyss of racism."

Following the advice of their leaders, virtually the entire Japanese American population complied with the relocation order without resistance or protest. They submitted in accordance with the spirit of *shikata ga nai* (realistic resignation). Because they were given little time to gather at assembly centers and were allowed to take only what they could carry to the camps, families lost homes, businesses, farms, and personal property worth an estimated $400 million. They arrived at the camps to find hastily built tar-paper barracks amidst bleak desert landscapes that would be their homes for three years. The internment centers were *de facto* prisons. People were not free to come and go. The camps were under continuous surveillance by armed guards and enclosed by barbed wire fencing. During the war, some internees were allowed to leave the camps, provided that they agreed to settle in Eastern states. By the war's end, all were allowed to leave. A few fortunate families had non-Japanese friends who had saved their homes or businesses for them while they were incarcerated. But many internees had no homes or businesses to return to. They found that interlopers now resided in their former residences and owned their former businesses.

Even though their families were imprisoned in camps, thousands of young Japanese American men volunteered for military service. They were determined to prove their loyalty to a government that had betrayed them. Japanese American soldiers contributed much to the war effort. They fought in the European theater, and many served in the Pacific war as translators, interpreters, and intelligence officers. One Japanese American unit, the 442nd Regimental Combat Engineers, was the most decorated unit in American military history.

Congress authorized token restitution for Japanese Americans in 1948, and a total of about $38 million was paid to claimants during the 1950s. These payments totaled about 10¢ for each dollar of loss claimed. Years later, after much litigation and quiet political pressure, Japanese Americans belatedly received vindication and additional restitution. In 1983, U.S. District Court Judge Marilyn Hall Patel vacated Fred Korematsu's conviction. Judge Patel's action came after Korematsu's attorneys discovered secret government documents proving that government officials knew that Japanese Americans posed no dangers to national security in wartime, and they withheld this evidence from the Supreme Court. On August 10, 1988, President Ronald

FIGURE 1.3 U.S. soldiers uprooted about 120,000 Japanese Americans, most of them U.S. citizens, from their homes in early 1942 and imprisoned them in various internment centers. Here a family awaits a bus to haul them away. *Source:* National Archives and Records Administration.

Reagan signed legislation authorizing $20,000 in reparations to each of the estimated 60,000 survivors of wartime relocation. As he signed the historic legislation, President Reagan, speaking for all Americans, apologized to the Japanese American community: "We admit a wrong. Here we affirm our commitment as a nation to equal justice under the law."

Although some embittered victims dismissed the money as "too little, too late," others were grateful and appreciated the symbolic significance of the gesture. Ten years later, in the summer of 1998, after paying out over $1.6 billion to survivors, their heirs, and to some people whose property had been confiscated by the government, the United States closed the books on the matter of compensating the internees.

After the war, Japanese Americans did not protest the gross injustices that they were forced to endure in wartime. They internalized the anger, shame, and humiliation associated with the relocation experience and rarely talked about those experiences, even among close friends and family. Instead, Japanese Americans vowed to put their wartime experiences behind them and to go forward—to prove to the government and to the white majority that had abused them that they were good citizens and productive members of society.

Their postwar record of achievement has been astonishing. Japanese Americans, by any measure, are among the most successful groups in the country. They have integrated themselves into mainstream society and have achieved distinction in the sciences, the arts, medicine, law, engineering, academic life, business, finance, athletics, and politics. They are among the leaders in the amount of education attained and in annual per capita income.

In contrast to the brutal mistreatment of Japanese Americans during wartime, Chinese Americans fared comparatively well. Chinese Americans enjoyed the sympathy and goodwill of most Americans, because China was a wartime ally of the United States. Americans also felt much sympathy for the Chinese people, who were suffering terribly at the hands of Japanese soldiers during the war. Because of their status as allies and because of acute labor shortages in war industries, unprecedented opportunities for Chinese workers suddenly opened up. By the thousands, Chinese families streamed out of the Chinatown ghettos into the mainstream of American life. Most of these mobile families never returned to the ghettos, and in the years following World War II, they headed for the suburbs.

In 1943, Congress at long last repealed the Chinese Exclusion Act, that artifact of anti-Asian racism, which had been in place since 1882. For the first time in over sixty years, it was now possible for people to emigrate from China to the United States. In addition, the government finally extended citizenship to thousands of Chinese, many of them quite elderly, longtime residents of the United States who had hitherto been ineligible for citizenship.

There is a tendency to assume that the great task of mobilizing the vast human, financial, economic, and technological resources of the country for a maximal war effort brought all Americans together. However, long-established conflicts and tensions simmered just beneath the comparatively superficial wartime unity that to a considerable extent was imposed by the media and government spokesmen. Regional differences, particularly North versus South, remained profound. Ethnic feelings remained powerful; the great American melting pot had yet to melt millions of families. Racial animosities remained as American as apple pie during and after the war.

RELIGIOUS AMERICANS

Religious differences among Americans remained very strong in the 1940s. About half of the U.S. population in 1945 claimed church membership. Of these religious Americans, about forty-five million belonged to one of the numerous Protestant sects, twenty-five million were Catholic, and about five million identified themselves as Jewish. Church attendance was increasing in the postwar years even as the society and culture were becoming increasingly secular.

There was little evidence of any ecumenicalism among Americans who considered religion an important part of their lives. Theologically conservative evangelical groups gained in popularity at the expense of long-established mainline churches such as the Episcopalians, Presbyterians, and Congregationalists. Anti-Catholic feelings remained powerful. Highly-qualified Jews encountered systematic discrimination in gaining admissions to pretigious Ivy League universities. Many Catholics, Jews, and other first- and second-generation immigrants often embraced separate subcultures, which focused on neighborhood schools, churches, clubs, recreational sports, festivals, and a vibrant social life centered on extended families.

BIG LABOR

Trade unions had grown powerful in wartime. Congress created the War Labor Board in 1942, which set guidelines for wages, hours, and collective bargaining. Employers, unions, and government officials generally cooperated during the war. Union membership grew from 10.5 million in 1941 to over 15 million in 1945, enrolling one-third of the nonfarm workforce. During the war, trade union leaders consolidated their new status as members of the nation's elites.

There were some labor problems that the War Labor Board could not resolve. The American Federation of Labor and the Congress of Industrial Organizations (CIO) engaged in bitter, sometimes violent, jurisdictional disputes. Although organized labor had given a no-strike pledge for the duration of the war, it could not be enforced. In 1943, over three million workers went out on strike, although most work stoppages during the war years lasted only a few days. These strikes never caused serious production delays in the industries that cranked out the huge amounts of war materials required by the armed forces.

The CIO, the largest and strongest of the trade union federations, had created a political arm, the Political Action Committee (PAC), which was committed to working with the liberal factions of the Democratic Party to institutionalize the welfare state in America. Some liberal labor leaders such as Walter Reuther, head of the United Auto Workers (UAW), and David Dubinski, leader of the International Ladies' Garment Workers' Union (ILGWU), hoped to forge new labor–management industrial partnerships in the postwar era: Representatives from the unions and corporations would jointly determine workplace policies. But liberal labor aspirations soon foundered amidst economic dislocations and the more conservative postwar political climate. Trade unions found themselves on the defensive, trying to preserve wartime gains. Real industrial wages and consumer purchasing power fell during 1945 and 1946 because of skyrocketing inflation.

As runaway inflation degraded their incomes and purchasing power, frustrated workers went on strike. Waves of strikes swept through important industrial sectors. Over 200,000 General Motors workers walked off the job on November 20, 1945. They were soon joined by striking electrical workers and steelworkers. During the first year after the war, over five million men and women went on strike, tying up most of the nation's major industries. Reflecting their primary concern with inflation that was eroding incomes and living standards, strikers' demands focused on pay increases and job security.

Many of these strikes lasted for months, as management resisted union demands and the workers refused to back down. Eventually most were settled on terms that resulted in significant pay increases for workers and substantial price increases for companies' products. Corporations passed their increased costs of production onto their customers, thereby retaining high profit margins but adding to the inflationary spiral.

The settlement of the UAW strike against General Motors set the pattern for postwar industrial relations. After a bitter 113-day strike that hurt both sides, they agreed on a new contract, which granted workers substantial pay increases over the life of the contract and tied wage levels to increases in the cost of living. The new contract also strengthened job security for senior workers and contained more generous pension plans. In addition, the new agreements signaled that union leaders and management representatives in the postwar era would confine negotiations to the traditional issues of wages and hours, working conditions, fringe benefits, and job security. Union leaders quickly abandoned their social agenda for restructuring industrial relations or remaking society. Henceforth, they focused on "bread-and-butter" issues.

Strikes also threatened railroads and coal industries, which were primary. Walkouts in both of these industries could have paralyzed the U.S. economy. The railroad strike was averted, but not before President Truman had asked Congress to grant him authority to draft striking railroad workers into the Army. Congress refused. John L. Lewis took his coal miners off of the job in April 1946 over wage and pension fund disputes with mine owners. Industrial production dropped. Efforts to settle the strike failed. On May 21, with the nation's supplies of coal exhausted, President Truman ordered the federal government to seize the mines. The coal mines were administered by Julius Krug, Secretary of the Interior, who promptly began negotiations with Lewis. They reached an agreement within two weeks, and the coal strike ended. The mines were returned to their owners. Truman's bold actions hurt him politically; he and his party lost support among resentful workers, which affected the upcoming elections.

WOMEN

Between 1941 and 1945, over six million women entered the labor force, about half of whom worked in the manufacturing sector. Married women, many with children, made up three-quarters of working women in wartime. By 1945, more than half of working women had married, and their median age was thirty-seven. Before the war, women had been excluded from most manufacturing jobs. Employers considered women unsuitable for heavy labor amidst the masculine atmosphere prevailing in factories. Acute wartime labor shortages quickly changed those attitudes. Women learned skilled trades, joined unions, and earned high wages. They performed certain jobs better than men, such as those requiring close attention to detail and manual dexterity. Women worked in munitions factories and foundries. They also became riveters, welders, crane operators, tool and die makers, and ironworkers. They operated heavy equipment, drove trucks, and became train engineers.

Women increased their geographic and occupational mobility tremendously in wartime. Black women quit work as domestics to join the factory labor force. Millions of women moved from the rural South and Midwest to coastal cities where the war-generated jobs were located. In Southern California, hundreds of thousands of women went to work in aircraft assembly plants.

Traditional patterns of gender discrimination persisted in wartime. Surveys showed that women in manufacturing earned about 60 percent of what men received for comparable work. Factories offered limited promotional opportunities and supervisorial positions for women. Even though the war emergency opened up hitherto closed occupations to women, most jobs in the sex-segregated labor market remained classified as "male" or "female" work. Where women worked in factories, they often worked on all-female shop floors, under male supervisors. Women resented the unequal pay and working conditions, and the sexual harassment from chauvinistic males. But they loved the opportunity to do important work that contributed to winning the war, and they also enjoyed the camaraderie and support of their female coworkers.

FIGURE 1.4   Over six million women entered the labor force during World War II. Many of them worked in the aircraft industry such as these two "Rosie the Riveters."   *Source:* National Archives.

The most serious problem faced by working mothers in wartime was the almost complete absence of child care centers. During the war, juvenile delinquency, venereal disease, and teenage pregnancies rose sharply. "Latchkey children," those left alone while their mothers worked their shifts at a factory, became a national scandal. Children roamed the streets, were put in all-day movie houses, or were locked in cars outside of defense plants. Police arrested many teenage girls for prostitution and apprehended boys for theft and vandalism.

Because so many men went to war, millions of women found themselves the *de facto* heads of single-parent households. They had a much greater range of responsibilities than just working full-time shifts in factories and shipyards. They became the centers of family life. Many also found time for neighborhood volunteer work. They served on civil defense committees, attended club meetings, went to PTA meetings, gave blood, and worked as hostesses at USO (United Service Organizations) centers.

Increasing numbers of women got married at the same time they went to work in war industries. Many young couples got married to spend time together before the man got shipped overseas. The birthrate also climbed sharply. Many births enabled men to qualify for military deferments. Others conceived "good-bye babies" to perpetuate the family, even if the fathers were killed in the war. Returning prosperity provided the main reason for the increase in marriages and the rising birthrate. The baby boom that would be one of the most significant demographic trends of the postwar decades had begun.

Women's wartime factory work was considered only a temporary response to a national emergency. Once victory was achieved and the soldiers returned, women were expected to surrender their jobs to returning GIs. The president of the National Association of Manufacturers intoned, "Too many women should not stay in the labor force. The home is the basic American institution." But surveys showed that most women wanted to continue working after the war.

The postwar era proved disappointing to millions of women who had hoped to consolidate and build upon their wartime achievements in the nation's workforce. Women were subjected to tremendous pressures from industry, government, and influential media to surrender their well-paying jobs and to return to their "rightful" places in the homes of America. Ads placed in mass circulation magazines implied that any woman who resisted the propaganda campaigns aimed at driving her out of the workplace and back to the kitchen was being selfish, greedy, and a poor wife and mother as well.

As factories converted from war to peacetime production, women by the hundreds of thousands were fired. Under the provisions of the Selective Service Act, returning veterans had priority over civilian war workers in competition for factory jobs. In the auto industry, which during the war years made jeeps, army trucks, and tanks, women had constituted 25 percent of the workforce in 1944. A year after the war, as automakers began producing new cars for civilian consumers for the first time since 1942, only 7 percent of auto workers were women. Sometimes, older married women workers ran afoul of newly imposed, or reimposed, age requirements or restrictions on the hiring of married women. In the immediate postwar years, as women were swept out of jobs in the mass production industries, the percentage of women members in many industrial unions also declined sharply.

Overall, despite restrictions on opportunity, female employment did not decline in the postwar years. By 1950, women made up 32 percent of the workforce, compared to 27 percent at war's end. But women had been forced out of high-paying jobs in manufacturing to resume work in occupations traditionally reserved for women such as waitresses, maids, and service jobs. Women who had formerly been welders and riveters now washed dishes and scrubbed floors for a lot less money. Women's median earnings had reached 66 percent of what men were paid in wartime manufacturing jobs. Studies in the postwar era showed women earning 53 percent of what men earned for comparable work. Although more women than ever before were working in the postwar era, most found themselves back in low-paying jobs.

Professional opportunities for middle-class women also deteriorated in postwar America. The number of women doctors, lawyers, and college professors declined. Medical schools and law schools imposed quotas on women's admissions, usually in the 5–10 percent range. The Equal Rights Amendment, which had been introduced in every congressional session since the 1920s, did not come close to garnering enough votes for passage. Prominent women leaders continued to oppose the amendment on the grounds that retaining laws providing special protections for women in the workforce was more important than establishing a constitutional principle of equal rights.

Organized feminism did not exist in postwar America; no one challenged traditional definitions of masculinity and femininity. Neither the Truman administration nor any government agency showed the slightest concern about declining opportunities for women in the job markets. Women's issues were simply not part of the public discourse in the postwar era. Women's issues eventually reemerged stronger than ever in the 1960s.

AFRICAN AMERICANS

World War II proved a mixed blessing for African Americans: It provided both unprecedented economic opportunities and continuing encounters with the hardships of segregation and racism. About 1 million black men and women, nearly all of the men draftees, served in the armed forces during the war, entering all branches of military service. Even though the American military was still segregated during World War II, African Americans attained far more opportunities than had been available during World War I. The Army Air Corps trained black pilots who flew in all-black squadrons. African American Marines, fighting in all-black units, fought heroically in savage island battles in the Pacific war.

Black–white relations within the military reflected the racist society it served. Many race riots occurred on military bases. White civilians often attacked African American soldiers stationed in the South. The morale and motivation of black soldiers frequently suffered from encounters with racist whites. African American soldiers often found themselves serving in menial positions in wartime, and sometimes found enemy prisoners of war treated better than they were. But most black soldiers found reasons to fight the Axis powers, even if at times they could see little difference between German racism and the homegrown kind. They also kept up steady pressures for better assignments, fairer treatment, and improved statuses. African Americans planned to trade their wartime military service for improved educational and job opportunities after the war. Leading the war with its "Double V" campaign, the National Association for the Advancement of Colored People (NAACP) encouraged blacks to fight both the Axis powers abroad and Jim Crow at home. A more militant organization, the Congress of Racial Equality (CORE), founded by activist minister James Farmer in 1942, employed the "sit-in" tactic in demonstrations held in Northern cities that broke down racial barriers.

The war also opened up many new employment opportunities for African Americans. In January 1941, A. Philip Randolph, a powerful African American labor leader, angered because employers with war contracts refused to hire African American workers, threatened to stage a march on Washington to protest both employer discrimination and segregation in the armed forces. President Roosevelt, wanting to avoid the embarrassment of a protest march and possible violence, persuaded Randolph to call off the proposed march in return for an executive order establishing a president's Fair Employment Practices Committee (FEPC), which ordered employers in defense industries to make jobs available "without discrimination because of race, creed, color, or national origin." Although an important symbolic victory, the FEPC was understaffed and underfunded, and it had limited enforcement powers. Acute labor shortages far more than government policy opened up war employment opportunities for African Americans.

Over two million African American men and women left the South to find work in the industrial cities of the North and West. Many joined CIO unions. Black voters in Northern cities became an important constituency in local and state elections. Most African American families who left the South during the war remained a permanent part of the growing Northern urban population in the postwar era. Southern black migrants often encountered racist hostility as they struggled to adapt to their new lives in Northern cities. They discovered that there was little difference between Northern and Southern white racial attitudes. Many Northern whites hated blacks for competing with them for housing, jobs, and schools for their children. They resented coming into contact with African Americans at parks, beaches, and other public facilities.

These racial antagonisms flared violently during the summer of 1943. About 250 race riots occurred in nearly fifty Northern cities; the largest riots were in Detroit and Harlem. The worst violence occurred in Detroit, where it had been building for years. The immediate provocation had been an angry struggle for access to a public housing project demanded by both African American workers and white workers during a time of acute housing shortages for everyone. One hot night in June, things got out of control. A full-scale race riot exploded, which lasted several days. Before order could be restored, twenty-five African Americans and nine whites lay dead.

Despite these outbreaks of home-front racial violence, World War II proved to be a watershed for African Americans; the war experience aided the black struggle for civil rights and full citizenship. Military service gave most African American veterans greater self-esteem and a sense of empowerment. It also raised expectations. Many black veterans did not return to the rural South after the war but chose to settle in one of the Northern or Western states, perhaps one in which they had spent time while in the military. Others took advantage of the GI Bill to go to college, learn a skilled trade, or start a business after the war. These black professionals, technicians, and businessmen formed a new and much larger African American middle class. A combination of vastly improved economic opportunities and continuing encounters with racism generated a new militancy among black people. They were determined not to accept second-class citizenship after the war. African American veterans and their children took the lead in challenging Jim Crow and racism in the postwar era.

Despite significant wartime progress and heightened expectations for even greater progress in the postwar era, most African Americans still faced significant barriers to achieving anything like equal access to the American Dream. Two-thirds of the African American population resided in the states of the Old South. Perhaps two-thirds of this Southern black population lived in poverty. All African Americans living in the South encountered systematic segregation wherever they went and whatever they did, or tried to do. Virtually all white Southerners believed they belonged to a superior race and African Americans belonged to an inferior one. Southern blacks everywhere were denied any voice in politics at any level of government.

After the war, a few courageous black veterans dared to challenge the massive edifice of Southern segregation and discrimination. They won a few modest gains in some of the states of the Upper South, but in most places, whites violently suppressed their modest efforts at reform. Despite the violent repression, Southern African Americans remained determined to carry on the struggle against institutionalized discrimination. They also continued to build their own strong institutions—schools, churches, businesses, and voluntary associations. These strong community organizations, particularly the churches, would provide the foundation for the modern civil rights movement, which erupted in the 1950s.

Black protest in the North in the postwar era was much more open, dramatic, and successful than what Southern blacks were able to achieve. Several northern states enacted laws ending discrimination in public accommodations such as hotels, restaurants, and nightclubs. The Supreme Court in *Shelley v. Kraemer* (1948) ruled that restrictive covenants, private understandings whereby realtors and homeowners refused to sell homes to black people and other "undesirables," were not legally enforceable in the courts.

While the Supreme Court ruling provided some assistance to black families and others striving to overcome massive residential segregation, the federal government was playing a key role in enshrining residential segregation as public policy in the postwar era. The Federal Housing Administration (FHA) distributed billions of dollars in low-cost mortgage loans. FHA loan officers, who underwrote much of the suburban expansion of the late 1940s, screened out mortgage applications according to assessments of their "risk" or "undesirability." These risky undesirables turned out to be mainly African Americans and Jews.

The FHA's discriminatory mortgage lending policy hastened the development of large black ghettos, literally cities within a central city. Between 1940 and 1950, the white population of Chicago declined, while the black population massively increased. Black people, unable to buy homes in all-white neighborhoods or to move to the suburbs, were forced to rent or buy property in the increasingly all-black neighborhoods of southside Chicago.

Chicago's working-class whites, many of them first- or second-generation immigrants, who either could not afford to move to the suburbs or chose not to, lived in ethnically homogeneous neighborhoods. They often joined together to preserve their all-white neighborhoods, relying less on restrictive covenants than on direct action, which often included violence or the threat of violence. Chicago, which contained the largest African American population of any American city in the postwar years, featured an ongoing kind of urban guerrilla warfare in those sections of the city where black residents lived near all-white ethnic enclaves. Racially motivated bombings, arson, and housing riots were commonplace in Chicago during the 1940s and into the 1950s.

HISPANIC AMERICANS

Much of this predominantly rural population endured poverty, discrimination, and segregation. These people lacked decent jobs, housing, and educational opportunities and had no political influence. However, World War II created opportunities for Hispanics; thousands of Mexican Americans moved to urban areas to find work in war industries. About 350,000 went into the armed forces, nearly all of them draftees. Mexican American warriors joined elite units such as the airborne rangers, and they often volunteered for dangerous missions. Eleven Mexican Americans won the nation's highest military award, the Congressional Medal of Honor.

Because so many Hispanic Americans moved to the cities or went into the armed forces, farmers faced acute shortages of workers. American growers persuaded the government to make arrangements with Mexico to import farmworkers from Mexico. Under a program established in 1942, nearly two million Mexican *braceros* (laborers) entered the United States. Because of lax government supervision, employers often ruthlessly exploited these imported contract laborers.

Hispanics in the war labor force often suffered discriminations similar to those encountered by African Americans and women. They sometimes got paid less than "Anglo" employees for doing the same work. They found their problems most acute in the crowded cities. Many young Mexican Americans joined neighborhood gangs. They called themselves *pachucos* and favored a distinctive style of dress called a "zoot suit." The "zoot suit" consisted of baggy trousers that flared at the knees and fitted tightly around the ankles, complemented by a wide-brimmed felt hat. These costumes were an assertion of a distinct cultural identity and a defiance of Anglo values.

In June 1943, at a time when black–white racial tensions were erupting in cities, ethnic relations in Los Angeles also were strained. Hundreds of sailors and Marines on leave from bases in Southern California assaulted Mexican Americans on the streets of Los Angeles and tore off their "zoot suits." Police either looked the other way or arrested only Mexican American youths during these encounters. The local media supported the attacks on the *pachucos*. Only after the president of Mexico threatened to cancel the *bracero* program did President Roosevelt intervene to stop the violence.

Despite the zoot-suit incidents, Hispanic American wartime experiences brought some advances. As was the case for African Americans, military service gave thousands of Mexican Americans an enhanced sense of self-worth. They returned from the war with greater expectations and enlarged views of life's possibilities. Many Hispanic veterans took advantage of the GI Bill. In the postwar years, Mexican American veterans and their sons assumed leadership roles in organizations that challenged discrimination against Hispanic people in Southwestern states.

NATIVE AMERICANS

Approximately 25,000 Native Americans served in the armed forces during World War II. One group of Navajos performed invaluable service during combat operations against the Japanese. These "code-talkers," communicating via radio in their tribal dialect, transmitted crucial battlefield information about enemy operations that could not be decoded by the Japanese. Thousands more Native Americans left their reservations to work in war industries around the country. Most of these mobile people did not return to their reservations after the war. They remained in the cities and became part of the rapidly growing postwar urban and suburban population. Some of those who returned to the reservations brought with them new ideas, technologies, and plans for the future.

In 1944, in California, lawyers representing a group of Native Americans filed suit in federal court for $100 million as compensation for lands taken illegally from Native Americans' ancestors during the 1850s. Congress enacted legislation to pay them for their lands, but President Roosevelt vetoed the bill. Litigation on this matter continued on and off for the next thirty-five years, until finally, both parties reached a compromise. The Native Americans accepted a settlement that brought them about 47¢ per acre.

BIG GOVERNMENT

War moved the country toward the Right. Resurgent Republicans gained seventy-seven seats in the House and ten seats in the Senate in the 1942 midterm elections. A conservative coalition of Northern Republicans and Southern Democrats, which had emerged following the 1938 elections, consolidated its control of Congress. Roosevelt, sensing the political drift and preoccupied with the immense task of running history's largest war, put social reform on the back burner. Conservatives snuffed out many New Deal agencies in 1942 and 1943, on the grounds that wartime economic revival had rendered them obsolete.

Antitrust activity ceased. Businessmen poured into Washington to run new wartime bureaucracies. They regained much of the popularity and prestige that they had lost during the 1930s. Depression-bred popular resentment of business greed and social irresponsibility gave way to a new image of businessmen as patriotic partners providing the tools needed to win the war. Roosevelt, needing business cooperation for the war effort, cultivated a cordial relationship among his former adversaries. Populistic, antibusiness rhetoric vanished from public discourse. Many corporate leaders abandoned their bitter criticisms of Roosevelt and New Deal policies, having discovered that they could profit from the policies of the welfare state turned warfare state. Businessmen switched their political strategy from one of trying to dismantle big government to trying to use it to their advantage. Corporate executives would continue these new political strategies in the postwar era.

The war effort further centralized the corporate economy, because 90 percent of the billions of dollars the government spent on war contracts went to 100 large corporations. Big business got bigger in wartime, and most companies enjoyed historic high profits. Americans discovered that the positive state, erected by liberals to fight the Great Depression and to promote social reform, could be manned by conservatives who would use its power to promote business interests, curtail reform, and attack trade unions—while winning a war.

The huge increase in the size and scope of the federal government, particularly of the executive branch, represented the most important wartime political development. As government spent more and more money, it became far more centralized than ever before. Federal bureaucracies assumed many economic functions previously performed by the private sector. The number of federal employees quadrupled in wartime—from one million in 1940 to nearly four million in 1945. Wartime agencies proliferated. The most powerful politicians in the country, after Roosevelt, were the men he appointed to run the war agencies. The president recruited most of these "warlords" of Washington from the ranks of business.

As the executive branch made a quantum leap in size and power, Congress suffered a relative decline in power and prestige. Through his active participation in foreign conferences and various domestic agencies coordinating the gigantic war effort, Roosevelt significantly enhanced the powers of the presidency. He became by far the most powerful president in U.S. history and set an example followed by all postwar presidents. The "imperial" presidency had its origins in World War II.

In wartime, the Supreme Court enhanced the President's authority. Dominated by Roosevelt's eight liberal appointees, it refused to review any cases involving wartime extensions of federal power into economic affairs, an arena in which it had been especially active during the New Deal years. The Court also refused to intervene in cases involving wartime violations of civil liberties, except to affirm the relocation of Japanese Americans from the Pacific Coast. The FBI, in wartime, acquired enhanced authority to spy on Americans in national security cases.

The war multiplied the points of contact between the federal government and its citizens. Millions of names were added to the Social Security rolls, and everyone who worked had to pay federal income taxes. Wartime experiences strengthened the tendency of people to look to Washington for solutions to their problems. This trend weakened social bonds and undermined state and local governments. People traded some of their personal freedom for greater government control and an enhanced sense of social security. This trade-off, of liberty for security, carried into the postwar era.

Washington became the biggest of all war boomtowns. In 1942, the Pentagon, the world's largest office building, opened. Lobbyists stalked the corridors of political power seeking ever-larger shares of the vast wartime expenditures flowing outward from Washington into corporate coffers. The broker-state, a creation of New Dealers, was much refined and significantly expanded in wartime. The government also subsidized the creation of new industries required by the necessities of war.

Much basic research for new weaponry and war industries had come from universities and colleges, which became committed to meeting the needs of military research. Most colleges and universities suffered no loss of enrollment during the war, despite massive conscription, because the government utilized their campuses for training enlisted men and officers. After the war, the GI Bill, which paid for millions of veterans' college educations, ensured the continuing growth of higher education.

World War II created a wartime partnership among businesses, universities, Congress, and the Pentagon, engaged in the procurement of war contracts. This "military-industrial complex," as President Eisenhower would later call it during his famed farewell address, nurtured during the war, came of age during the Cold War. It became a powerful lobby for creating a kind of permanent war economy in the postwar decades. The military-industrial complex guaranteed that the vastly enhanced authority of government in American economic and scientific affairs would continue after the war.

ECONOMIC TRANSFORMATIONS

The New Deal had failed to find a cure for economic depression. On the eve of war, over seven million Americans were out of work, or 14 percent of the labor force. Real wages in 1941 were below 1929 levels. By New Year's Day in 1943, unemployment in America had vanished. Wartime economic expansion, fueled by unprecedented levels of government spending, combined with mass conscription to create severe labor shortages.

To help pay for these prodigious wartime expenditures, Congress broadened and deepened the tax structure. The Revenue Acts of 1942 and 1943 created the modern federal income tax system. Most Americans had never filed an income tax return before World War II, because the income tax, on the books since 1913, had been a small tax on upper-income families and corporations. Starting in 1942, anyone earning $600 or more annually had to file an income tax return. A withholding tax went into effect in 1943, which made employers the nation's principal tax collectors. Income tax revenues rose from $5 billion in 1940 to $49 billion in 1945, a tenfold increase. Even with the huge increase in federal income taxes, the largest federal tax increase in U.S. history, tax revenues paid only 41 percent of the cost of the war. The government paid the rest of the war bills by borrowing. War bonds, peddled by movie stars, war heroes, and professional athletes, added $135 billion. By war's end, the national debt had climbed to $280 billion, up from $40 billion when it began. The day World War II ended, the national debt had grown larger than the economy; that is, the debt exceeded the gross domestic product.

Vastly increased federal spending also unleashed powerful inflationary forces. The shift from peacetime to wartime production sharply reduced the amount of consumer goods available to buy just at the time when people had significantly more money to spend. By 1943, the production of new cars and other durable goods had ceased. A giant inflationary gap generated by too much money chasing too few goods threatened to drive prices way up and to rob Americans of their wartime economic gains. To clamp a lid on inflation, the government imposed price controls, joining them to a rationing system that used coupon allotments to consumers for scarce items such as sugar, butter, coffee, beef, tires, and gasoline.

Roosevelt created the Office of Price Administration (OPA) to administer the control apparatus nationally. The OPA had a daunting task. Business lobbyists, farm bloc politicians, and union leaders waged unceasing "guerrilla warfare" against the OPA for the duration of the war. Consumers chafed under rationing restrictions, particularly those on beef and gasoline. A ban on all "pleasure driving" and a 35-miles-per-hour speed limit accompanied gasoline rationing. Beef rationing caused the worst problems. Frustrated shoppers often abused butchers and occasionally rioted. Despite grievances and injustices, the universally unpopular OPA maintained a semblance of price stability and distributed scarce goods reasonably fairly. Most people complied with the system of controls, considering it both a wartime necessity and to their economic advantage. The cost of living rose only 3 percent in 1944 and 1945. Government controls and rationing effectively contained inflation in wartime.

Even as ordinary citizens chafed under the restrictions of rationing and price controls, a significant redistribution of income occurred. During the war years, real wages for workers employed in manufacturing rose over 50 percent, from $24 to $37 a week. The share of national wealth owned by the richest 5 percent of American families dropped from 23.7 percent to 16.8 percent.

Despite annoying shortages and rationing, people with money to spend in wartime found ways to spend it and enjoy it. Wartime prosperity strengthened materialistic values and revived consumerism, which largely had been suspended during the Depression decade. Americans spent money on entertainment, on going to the movies, and on going out to dinner. People resorted to black markets when rationed goods could not be found. Many people saved their money for new cars, new homes, new appliances, and new radios that they would buy after the war. Advertisers promised consumers new and better goods when civilian production patterns were restored following victory over the Axis powers. Consumerism, reborn amidst war, would become a powerful engine driving the postwar affluent economy.

The discovery that government spending could banish the specter of depression appeared to confirm the claims of the world's foremost economist, England's John Maynard Keynes. Keynes had contended that government spending could cure economic depression. If private sector investment proved inadequate, government could cut taxes and begin large-scale spending programs to stimulate demand and restore the business cycle. During the New Deal of the mid-1930s, government spending was not large enough and taxes were generally regressive, so Keynes's theories could not be tested until the war years.

Their wartime success in eliminating the depression also gave American political leaders a confidence that they could regulate the business cycle, a confidence that would last for the next thirty years. They believed that they now possessed the fiscal tools to monitor spending levels, maintain prosperity, keep unemployment low, and prevent the recurrence of recession, all the while controlling inflation. Americans also looked to government after the war to maintain a prosperous, growing, and full-employment economy. A new understanding of the role of consumerism in sustaining economic growth meant that government would promote spending rather than saving in the postwar years.

Economic growth was the most decisive force driving the postwar American society and popular attitudes. Prosperity broadened gradually during the late 1940s, accelerated in the 1950s, and climbed to even greater heights in the 1960s. Federal spending during World War II inaugurated a cycle of growth and prosperity that extended well into the 1970s! A former British prime minister, Sir Edward Heath exclaimed that Americans at the time were experiencing "the greatest prosperity the world has ever known."

Brief Bibliographical Essay

Many fine studies of America during World War II and the early postwar period are available. The following is a select list of those books that are especially well written and easily accessible. They will make informative, enjoyable reading for students who want to learn more about the prominent individuals and major events that influenced the course of recent American history. Most of these books are available in paperback editions and can be found in any good college, university, or public library. James T. Patterson, *Grand Expectations: The United States, 1945–1974*, is a magisterial synthesis of recent U.S. history from the end of World War II through the Watergate crisis. Several of the early chapters cover all aspects of American history for the early postwar period, 1945–1949. The best studies of the home front are Richard Polenberg's *War and Society: The United States, 1941–1945* and John Morton Blum's *"V"*

Was for Victory: Politics and American Culture during World War II. Susan M. Hartmann's *The Homefront and Beyond: American Women in the 1940s* is an account of women and the war. Neil A. Wynn's *The Afro-American and the Second World War* has recorded the crucial experiences of black people in wartime. Jeanne Wakatsuki Houston and James D. Houston's *Farewell to Manzanar* is a compelling story of a Japanese family interned for the duration of the war. James L. Baughman's *The Republic of Mass Culture* has an informative chapter about the major mass media—print journalism, radio, and movies—during the war years. John Brooks's *The Great Leap: The Past Twenty-Five Years in America* is an important book highlighting the immense changes brought about in this country by World War II that shaped the postwar era.

2

Wars: Cold and Hot

World War II had left a large part of Europe and many nations elsewhere in ruins, and it had shattered the old balance of power. Even most of the victors had fared badly. The Soviets had lost more than thirty million people, and much of their economy had been ruined by war. The British, depleted economically and militarily, faced the imminent loss of much of their empire. After 1945, Britain's ability to play a major role in world affairs would depend mainly on American support. France had been humiliated by defeat and occupation during the war. The French economy was weak, its government was unstable, and the French Communist Party was a rising force.

The war had so weakened the British, French, and Dutch nations that they could no longer control many of their rebellious colonies in Asia, Africa, and the Middle East. Throughout the postwar era, the decolonization process begun during World War II accelerated, presenting challenges to the United States in what became known as the Third World. In the Far East, China was sinking into the chaos of civil war. Only the United States emerged from the devastation of global war with its wealth and power enhanced, and with most of its citizens better off than they had ever been.

However, postwar celebrations of victory and expectations of a peaceful and prosperous world order dominated by the United States quickly gave way to conflicts between America and its erstwhile ally, the Soviet Union. A multitude of difficult postwar political problems generated decades of tension, ideological warfare, and a nuclear arms race that historians have labeled the Cold War. Its defining characteristic was an enduring warlike hostility under formal conditions of peace that made the conflict a *cold* war as opposed to a traditional violent and destructive conflict. The Cold War would remain the dominant international reality shaping the conduct of U.S. foreign policy for over forty years. Cold War preoccupations also exerted a powerful influence on American domestic politics and culture during this era.

ORIGINS OF COLD WAR

Immediately after the war, the United States funneled billions of dollars through various UN agencies for food, clothing, and medicines for needy people in Germany, Japan, China, and eastern Europe. The British borrowed $3.75 billion from the United States in 1946, much of which was used to pay for food imports. German industrial and agricultural production had shrunk to pitiful fractions of prewar levels. Germany's population had swelled by the addition of ten million "displaced persons," German refugees who had either fled or been expelled from various eastern European countries.

The United States shared occupation responsibilities in Germany with the Soviets, the British, and the French, but it had sole authority in Japan. In Germany, U.S. officials tried to eliminate all traces of Nazism. Special courts punished over 1,500 major Nazi offenders and over 600,000 minor Nazi officials. The most famous trials occurred at Nuremberg, the former site of Nazi Party rallies held during the 1930s. An international tribunal put twenty-two former high Nazi officials on trial. Nineteen were convicted, of whom twelve were hanged for "war crimes and atrocities." In Japan, U.S. officials under the command of General Douglas MacArthur staged a Tokyo equivalent of Nuremberg. Twenty-eight former high Japanese officials were tried, and all were convicted of war crimes; seven were hanged. To ensure Japanese cooperation during the U.S. occupation, U.S. officials spared the emperor from a trial. Stripped of any real political power and having renounced his claim of divinity, Hirohito remained a popular figurehead until his death in 1989.

Americans also completely remade Japanese society. They broke up industrial monopolies and abolished feudal estates. They introduced political democracy and established independent trade unions. They forced the Japanese to destroy all military weapons and to renounce war as an instrument of national policy. Ever since, the Japanese have depended on America's nuclear shield to protect their national security. Most important for the future of Japan, U.S. engineers modernized Japanese industry, introducing new management and quality control techniques. From the ashes of war, with help from their conquerors, the Japanese fashioned a working democratic and capitalistic system.

During 1945 and 1946, American and Soviet leaders clashed over many issues. Their wartime alliance deteriorated rapidly. Even before war's end, the Allies had quarreled over the opening of a second front in western Europe and the future political status of eastern European countries. The immediate origins of Cold War conflict lay in these wartime strains within the Grand Alliance. Historians have traced the roots of the Cold War to the U.S. response to the 1917 Bolshevik revolution and Lenin's profound hatred of Western liberal capitalist culture. From 1917 until 1933, a succession of U.S. presidents refused to recognize the Soviet state. Even after the normalization of Soviet–American relations in 1933, friendly relations between the two nations did not evolve. When Stalin concluded a nonaggression pact with Hitler in August 1939, most Americans equated the Soviet Union with Nazi Germany. It was the wartime alliance between the Americans and the Soviets, born of strategic necessity, that represented a departure from the historic norm of mutual distrust and ideological hostility.

In March 1945, President Roosevelt perceived Soviet efforts to impose a Communist regime on Poland to be a violation of the Yalta accords and protested to Stalin. But military force gave the Soviet Union control of Poland's and eastern Europe's political destinies. Between 1945 and 1948, the Soviet Union imposed Communist-controlled regimes on these nations. Stalin, determined to protect his empire and its Communist system from future security threats, erected a ring of submissive client states along the Soviet Union's vulnerable western periphery.

American political leaders strongly condemned Soviet domination·of Poland and other east European countries. They would not accept the new Soviet empire in eastern Europe as a legitimate "sphere of influence." Stalin resented America's refusal to accept Soviet domination of eastern Europe as legitimate, while excluding the Soviets from Italian and Japanese occupations.

American statesmen would not accept the new Soviet empire in eastern Europe for several reasons. Besides the sense of betrayal felt over Yalta, American statesmen had to reckon with domestic political considerations. Millions of Americans of east European background were enraged at the Soviet Union's brutal domination of their ancestral homelands. Americans also anticipated developing economic relations with eastern European countries in the postwar era until Communist control sealed them off. In addition, U.S. leaders felt a sense of righteous, missionary power: They felt they could move eastern Europe toward liberal capitalism. Soviet intrusions frustrated America's good intentions in the region and imposed an abhorrent system of political economy that many Americans equated with Fascism.

But there were clear limits as to what actions the Truman administration could take to prevent Soviet domination of eastern Europe. It could denounce Soviet actions; it could apply economic and diplomatic pressures; and it could even use its temporary atomic monopoly as a veiled threat, but the United States never directly threatened the Soviets with military action. When Stalin forcibly incorporated the eastern half of Europe into the Soviet empire between 1945 and 1948, the United States grudgingly accepted the creation of a *de facto* Soviet sphere of influence.

The Potsdam conference, held in late July 1945, the final wartime meeting of the Big Three, revealed the strains within the Grand Alliance. They often quarreled—over German boundaries and reparations, over the composition of the new Polish government, and over when the Soviet Union would enter the Pacific war against Japan. At Potsdam, the Soviets pressed their demand, made at Yalta, for $20 billion of reparations to be taken from the German occupation zones. The Americans and the British refused to affix a dollar amount for reparations but permitted the Soviets to remove some industries from their occupation zones.

However, in May 1946, the U.S. military governor halted all reparations shipments from the American zone. U.S. officials feared that the Soviets would strip their zone of resources that the Germans would need to rebuild their industrial economy in the postwar era. Angry Soviet officials denounced this unilateral action that cancelled an agreement the Soviets considered vital to Soviet postwar reconstruction. Continual conflicts between the Soviets and the Western powers over occupation policy in Germany were the core causes of the Cold War, which originated in the heart of Europe.

It was at Potsdam that President Truman learned of the first successful testing of an atomic device. The U.S. atomic bomb project was history's largest and costliest scientific undertaking. Between 1941 and 1945, American and British scientists, many of them émigré European Jews who had fled Nazi tyranny, labored intensively to build atomic bombs. General Leslie Groves headed the top-secret, highest-priority enterprise, code-named the "Manhattan District Project." A brilliant scientific team gathered under the direction of J. Robert Oppenheimer. Groves worked effectively with the scientific leadership of the project. Working at Los Alamos, New Mexico, Manhattan Project scientists solved the complex theoretical and technical problems involved in creating the immensely powerful weapons.

The Manhattan District Project was so secret that congressmen who appropriated the vast sums of money for the bomb had no idea what the money was for. Harry Truman came to the presidency ignorant of the project. He was astonished to learn in April 1945, from Secretary of War Henry L. Stimson, that the United States would soon have "the most terrible weapon ever known in human history, one bomb of which could destroy a whole city." On July 16, the world's first atomic device, nicknamed "the Gadget," was exploded in the desert near Alamogordo, New Mexico.

Before the weapon was completed, Stimson convened an Interim Committee that recommended unanimously to the president that the atomic bomb, when ready, be used without warning against Japan. Truman concurred. One day, for a few minutes over lunch, Interim Committee members discussed inviting Japanese observers to witness a harmless demonstration of the bomb's power, perhaps inducing their surrender. A letter in support of an atomic demonstration was also submitted to the Committee by Manhattan Project scientists at the University of Chicago. But Committee members unanimously rejected their recommendation. Other officials also urged holding back and trying to entice Japan to surrender without having to use atomic weapons. Truman consistently rejected such advice.

Meanwhile, a new government took power in Japan. A faction of its leaders sought a way to end the hopeless war. Unaware of the secret Yalta agreements that would soon bring the Soviet Union into the war against Japan, a member of the peace faction sought Soviet mediation. He hoped to get a modification of the unconditional surrender terms that would permit the Japanese to keep their emperor. The Soviets rebuffed the Japanese approach and informed Washington.

After discussions with his advisers, Truman issued a final warning to Japan before dropping the bombs. This "Potsdam Declaration," issued on July 26, urged Japan to surrender unconditionally or else face "the utter devastation of the Japanese homeland." But it made no mention of atomic weapons. The Japanese government ignored the ultimatum. Japanese leaders were irreconcilably divided between a peace faction that privately acknowledged Japan's defeat but hoped to modify the terms of surrender, and a war faction determined to defend the sacred Emperor and his homeland whatever the ultimate cost in Japanese lives.

Interpreting Japanese official silence as rejection, Truman saw no need to rescind an order given by General Thomas Handy on July 25 to proceed with atomic bomb attacks on Japan. Early on the morning of August 6, 1945, three B-29s lifted off the runway at Tinian bound for Hiroshima. The lead aircraft, the *Enola Gay*, carried a five-ton atomic bomb in its specially configured bomb bay. The other two planes carried cameras and assemblages of scientific recording instruments.

At 8:45 A.M. local time, the sky exploded over Hiroshima. The world's first atomic bomb struck with the force of 12,000 tons of TNT. It killed some 80,000 people instantly, many of them vaporized by the intense heat. By the end of the year, 60,000 more people had died from burns, wounds, and radiation poisoning. A city of 350,000 inhabitants was reduced to rubble.

A few hours after the bombing, Truman announced to the world the existence and first use of the bomb. He also warned the Japanese that unless they surrendered unconditionally, immediately, "they may expect a rain of ruin from the air, the like of which has never before been seen on earth." The Japanese did not surrender. Their refusal provided the Soviets an opportunity that Stalin quickly seized, to enter the war against Japan on August 8, launching surprise attacks in Manchuria and Korea.

Bad weather delayed the dropping of the second bomb for a few days. But on August 9, an even more powerful atomic bomb was dropped on Nagasaki. It yielded about 20,000 tons of TNT and destroyed large sections of the city, killing about 45,000 people immediately. Dropped under conditions of poor visibility, by an airplane running low on fuel, the Nagasaki bomb fell off target and did not inflict its ultimate destructive potential on the city.

Even after the second atomic bombing and the Soviet entry into the war, Japanese military leaders devoted to the Emperor wanted to fight on. Only the personal intercession of Hirohito induced them to accept defeat. On August 10, the Japanese offered to surrender if the emperor was allowed to retain his sovereignty.

Truman and his advisors rejected this peace feeler, refusing to let Japan dictate the terms of surrender, and perceiving that denying the emperor his exalted status was essential to eradicating Japanese militarism. The "Byrnes Note," a reply crafted by Truman's secretary of state, declared that following Japan's surrender the emperor would be subordinate to the supreme commander of the Allied powers, and that Japan's ultimate form of government would be determined by the Japanese people. This left the future of the imperial institution uncertain, but did not call for its abolition. On August 14, Emperor Hirohito reaffirmed his decision to surrender, and made a formal announcement that was broadcast to the Japanese people and the Allied governments the next day. Surrender ceremonies occurred on September 2 aboard the battleship USS *Missouri*, anchored in Tokyo Bay, with General Douglas MacArthur presiding.

Since the conclusion of World War II, historical research on the atomic bombing of Japan has generated much controversy regarding President Truman's reasons for letting the attacks proceed. Most Americans have accepted Truman's justification for using the atomic bomb: "We have used it in order to shorten the agony of war, in order to save the lives of thousands and thousands of young Americans." But critics have contended that the Japanese, perceiving their cause as hopeless, would have surrendered soon without the atomic bombings. This claim has been demolished by research demonstrating that the Japanese made extensive plans to defend their home islands to the bitter end.

Critics also assert that Truman had other motives for using nuclear weapons besides ending the war. He wanted to enhance U.S. postwar diplomatic leverage against the Soviet Union. They also accuse Truman of using the bombs on the already beaten Japanese to hasten their surrender in order to keep the Soviets from sharing in the postwar occupation of Japan and to make the Soviets more agreeable to U.S. diplomatic initiatives. There is no doubt that Truman was wary of Soviet intentions in the Far East. But the charge that he used the atomic weapons primarily to frighten or impress the Russians has also been demolished by subsequent research.

In attempting to fathom President Truman's motives, it should be understood that there was very little discussion of whether or not to use the atomic bomb. From the beginning, when President Roosevelt authorized the Manhattan Project, it was understood that the bomb, when available, would be used on the Germans and the Japanese if the wars were still raging. Since Germany surrendered on May 8, 1945, it was assumed that atomic bombs would be used on Japan as soon as they became available.

Truman and his advisers could not know in advance that these two bombs would end the war; they discussed where, when, and how to use atomic weapons; they did not debate whether or not to use them. Truman himself later said, "I regarded the bomb as a military weapon and never had any doubt that it should be used." There were additional considerations. Political leaders feared *post hoc* criticism if they did not use the weapons. Suppose it came out after the war that they had wasted $2 billion on a giant atomic boondoggle that was developed and never used? Suppose it came out that they had developed a powerful weapon that might have shortened the war and saved thousands of U.S. soldiers' lives and they failed to use it?

Truman's primary concern always was to shorten the war and to save American soldiers' lives. He wished to avoid a protracted and bloody campaign to conquer the Japanese home islands. Intelligence reports available to U.S. military leaders exposed a huge military buildup on the island of Kyushu, the planned site for the first U.S. invasion of a Japanese home island scheduled to occur on November 1. The battered Japanese military could still field a formidable force consisting of ten Imperial Army divisions, and the Japanese air force could provide between 6,000 and 10,000 aircraft.

No doubt Truman hoped that U.S. use of the powerful new weapon might give the United States additional bargaining leverage with the Soviets. He also hoped that use of the bombs might induce the Japanese to surrender before the Soviet Union entered the war, but the Soviets intervened between the dropping of the bombs. Some scholars have argued that even the atomic bombings were insufficient to induce the Japanese to surrender; it required also the news of Soviet forces moving rapidly southward toward Japan. Whatever their relative importance, the combined impacts of the Hiroshima bombing on August 6, the Russian offensive on August 9, and the Nagasaki attack on August 9 compelled Emperor Hirohito to decide at last that Japan must surrender without further attempts at negotiation.

U.S. willingness to use the atomic bombs in war, coupled with Washington's failure to keep Stalin informed of the progress of the Manhattan District Project, and the American refusal to share any broad scientific information about nuclear weaponry with the Soviets, contributed to the development of the Cold War. At a recess one evening following a Potsdam conference session, Truman told Stalin that the United States had recently tested an extremely powerful new weapon. He did not tell the Soviet dictator that it was a nuclear device. Stalin merely smiled and said that was fine and that he hoped that it would soon be used on Japan. Truman did not have to tell Stalin that the United States had developed an atomic bomb; the Soviet leader understood instantly what Truman was talking about. Stalin decided on the spot to speed up a Soviet atomic weapons project that had been curtailed during wartime. He vowed that the American atomic monopoly would not change his plans for postwar Europe. The Soviet–U.S. nuclear arms race began at that moment.

FBI files, subsequently made public, revealed that a spy ring working for the Soviet Union, whose most prominent members included a German-born English physicist, Klaus Fuchs, and Americans David Greenglass, Harry Gold, and Julius Rosenberg, had penetrated the Manhattan District Project. By the time Americans had atomic bombed the two Japanese cities, the spy ring had already delivered about 10,000 pages of classified government documents to their Soviet masters. These secret data significantly shaped the Soviet atomic bomb project. Experts have estimated that espionage may have accelerated the Soviet bomb project by as much as two years.

Perhaps the Japanese should have been forewarned. Perhaps a demonstration explosion should have been made. Perhaps the unconditional surrender terms should have been modified before the bombs were used in order to strengthen the peace party within the Japanese government. Any or all of these measures might have induced Japanese surrender before the bombs were used, although no one can know for sure how the Japanese would have responded to any of these initiatives, or when they might have surrendered.

It also is important to remember that even if Japan could have been induced to surrender without having to endure the horrors of two atomic bombings, the conceivable alternative scenarios would have in all probability been worse. Had the war gone on even for a few weeks more, the continuing firebomb raids over Japanese cities would have killed more people and destroyed more property than did the two atomic bombs. U.S. historian Robert Newman has calculated that between a quarter million and 400,000 Asians, mostly noncombatants, were dying each month that the war continued. And had invasions by U.S. forces been necessary, there would have been devastating losses on both sides. While continued fighting went on in Japan between the Americans and Japanese, Soviet soldiers would have annihilated the Japanese armies in Korea, Manchuria, and northern China.

Despite its great wealth and power, the United States could not prevent the growing division of Europe nor bring stability to the Far East. When American, British, and Soviet foreign ministers met in London in September 1945, they quarreled bitterly over who threatened whom. Mutual suspicion and hostility rendered traditional diplomacy impossible. The Western powers demanded that the Soviets ease their control of eastern Europe. In response, the Soviet leaders accused the West of capitalist encirclement and atomic blackmail.

The former allies appeared to be on collision courses: The Soviets were determined to dominate the lesser states of eastern Europe in order to erect a security sphere around their nation. The United States was determined to break down international trade barriers and rebuild Germany. In the postwar era, Americans intended to build a prosperous new world order, a world order based on free governments and free trade. America, having launched itself on a mission to build a brave new world in its own image, with an atomic bomb in the holster hanging on its hip, enraged and frightened the Soviet leaders.

From the American perspective, neither its great wealth nor its atomic monopoly guaranteed U.S. security in the postwar era. The destruction of German and Japanese power had removed historic barriers to Soviet expansion in Europe and northeastern Asia. Anticolonial rebellions against lingering Western imperialism also gave the Soviet Union opportunities to expand its influence. Expanding American influence in Europe and Asia alarmed the Soviet leaders. They were fearful of the vastly superior American wealth and military power. Stalin tried to isolate the Soviet Union and its newly acquired empire in eastern Europe from contact with the Western powers.

In early 1946, both sides escalated their rhetoric. On March 5, 1946, former prime minister Winston Churchill, visiting in the United States, declared "From Stettin in the Baltic to Trieste in the Adriatic, an iron curtain has descended across the continent." He called for an Anglo-American effort to roll back the Soviet iron curtain. Stalin accused Churchill of calling for war against the Soviet Union. Stalin also had given a speech in February in which he reasserted the Leninist doctrine of the incompatibility of capitalism and socialism, and the necessity of revolutionary conflict in the world. Following Stalin's belligerent speech, the Soviets rejected an American offer to join the World Bank and International Monetary Fund, the two principal agencies for promoting free trade and stable currencies in the postwar world.

In an atmosphere of growing hostility and suspicion, Truman and his advisers tried to work out a plan for the international control of nuclear weapons through the United Nations. Bernard Baruch, the American delegate, proposed a plan calling for international control of atomic weapons to be achieved in stages, during which the United States would retain its nuclear monopoly. His plan called for inspections within the Soviet Union by a UN commission to ensure compliance. The Soviets, working feverishly to develop their own nuclear weapons, rejected onsite inspections within their territory. They proposed an alternative plan calling for the destruction of American nuclear weapons before any control system would be devised. The Americans rejected the Soviet plan. The United States then opted for its own internal control mechanisms; Congress created the Atomic Energy Commission (AEC) to control all atomic energy research and development within the nation.

Thus vanished the world's only chance, admittedly a slim one, to prevent a nuclear arms race between the superpowers. The nuclear arms race added a terrifying dimension to the Soviet–American rivalry, making it unlike any previous great power conflict in history. From about 1955 on, both sides possessed the technical capability to destroy the other. But nuclear weapons also functioned to keep the Cold War cold. Had it not been for nuclear weapons, the Americans and the Soviets would probably have had a war, for there was enough provocation on both sides. But neither side dared attack because it knew the other would resort to nuclear weapons before it would accept defeat. Mutual terror deterred both nations from combat for the duration of the Cold War. The great redeeming irony of the Cold War era was that the most destructive weapons ever developed by the technological genius of humankind prevented World War III between the United States and the

Soviet Union. What deterred the leaders of both sides was the certain knowledge that igniting World War III in the thermonuclear age amounted to a mutual suicide pact.

The failure of Washington and the Kremlin to find a mutually acceptable formula for controlling atomic weapons technology highlighted the dawn of the atomic age. The United States conducted a series of atomic bomb tests in the South Pacific at Bikini atoll. Radio accounts and dramatic photos of the tests forced Americans to the horrific realization that humankind had produced weapons of mass destruction that could destroy cities in an instant. Fear of a nuclear

FIGURE 2.1   Division of Europe, 1945–1955.   *Source:* George D. Moss, *Moving On*, 1st ed. (Englewood Cliffs, N.J.: Prentice Hall, 1994), p. 38. Public Domain Map.

holocaust took root in the American collective psyche. American imaginations in the postwar era were haunted by twin symbols of catastrophe—the mushroom cloud and nuclear missiles striking America's great cities. According to historian Paul Boyer, "A primal fear of extinction pervaded all society." The atomic age ushered in the age of anxiety that continuously undercut celebrations of the affluent society.

The disputes between the United States and the Soviet Union grew out of the power vacuum created by the smashing of German power, a vacuum into which rushed the two expansionist powers: the United States, a global power, its leaders motivated by a sense of righteous power based on America's prosperous economy and atomic monopoly, by strong ideological convictions, and by important economic interests; and the USSR, a strong regional power, its leaders motivated by Communist ideology, an urgent desire to protect vital security interests, and a pressing need to rebuild its shattered economy. The two superpowers collided at many points in central and eastern Europe. Given their fundamental differences, the intrinsic difficulties of their many problems, the pressures and antagonisms inherent in their many disputes, and their clashing goals and ambitions, in retrospect, it appears that conflicts between the Americans and Soviets were inevitable.

The Cold War was also probably inevitable. It occurred because of the failure of the two most powerful nations emerging from World War II to resolve their conflicts of interest through diplomacy. Instead, the leaders of the two nations, quick to read the worst intentions into the actions of their rivals and to habitually anticipate worst-case scenarios, believed themselves compelled to resort to over four decades of ideological warfare. They also felt compelled, "like two apes on a treadmill," in Cold War analyst Paul Warnke's phrase, to engage in a costly and dangerous nuclear arms race without precedent in human history. The Cold War became an interlocking, reciprocal process, involving genuine differences of principle, clashes of interest, and a wide range of misperceptions and misunderstandings.

THE TRUMAN DOCTRINE

To Washington in early 1947, the world appeared to be sinking into chaos. A nearly bankrupt Great Britain prepared to abandon India, Palestine, and Greece. The Vietnamese refused to accept the return of French colonialism, and Indochina was engulfed in war. Likewise, the Indonesians refused to accept the return of the Dutch and ignited a war. In China, a civil war raged between the Nationalists and Communists. Amidst rubble-strewn cities and ruined economies, the Japanese and Germans struggled to avoid famine. American leaders feared that the Soviet Union would try to exploit the severe political and economic problems of Europe and Asia.

Meanwhile, crises arose in the Balkan region involving Greece and Turkey. Greece was engulfed in a civil war that pitted Communist insurgents against a Rightist government backed by the British. Simultaneously, the Soviets were pressuring the Turkish government to grant them joint control of the Dardanelles, a vital link between the Black Sea and the Mediterranean. The Turks rebuffed the Soviets, and Stalin threatened to take action against them. The British also backed the Turks in their dispute with the Soviets over control of the waterway. On February 21, 1947, citing economic problems, the British government informed Washington that it could no longer provide support to the Greek and Turkish governments.

President Truman wanted to help the Greeks and Turks, but he had to convince the Republican-controlled Eightieth Congress that his initiative served the national interest. The principal architect of the U.S. aid program to Greece and Turkey was Undersecretary of State Dean Acheson. Acheson evoked an early version of the "domino theory" to stress the need for

U.S. aid to the two countries: If Greece fell to the Communists and the Soviets gained control of the Dardanelles, North Africa and the Middle East would be endangered. Morale would sink in Italy, France, and western Germany; all would become vulnerable to a Communist takeover. Three continents would then be opened to Soviet penetration. Acheson's presentation persuaded Senator Arthur Vandenberg, Chairman of the Senate Foreign Relations Committee, to support Truman's proposed aid bill for Greece and Turkey. George Kennan, a brilliant State Department Soviet expert, also furnished arguments supporting Truman's interventionist policy. Kennan wrote of the need to develop a policy of firm containment, designed to confront the Russians with unalterable counterforce at every point where they show signs of encroaching upon the interests of a peaceful and stable world.[1]

Kennan's analysis coincided with Truman's views of Soviet behavior. His recommendations accorded with the president's desire to get tough with the Soviets. Containment, stopping the spread of Communist influence in the world, became the chief operating principle of American foreign policy in the postwar era. It remained the cornerstone of U.S. Cold War foreign policy for forty years.

In the most important speech of his presidency, Truman appeared before a joint session of Congress on March 12 to ask Congress to appropriate $400 million for Greek and Turkish aid. Truman told the American people that the Communist threat to Greece and Turkey represented Hitler and World War II all over again. Truman then spoke the famed words that became known as the Truman Doctrine.

> At the present moment in world history, nearly every nation must choose between alternative ways of life.
>
> One way of life is based upon the will of the majority, and is distinguished by free institutions . . . and freedom from political oppression. The second way of life is based upon the will of a minority forcibly imposed on the majority . . . and the suppression of personal freedom.
>
> I believe that it must be the policy of the United States to support free peoples who are resisting attempted subjugation by armed minorities or by outside pressures . . . If we falter in our leadership, we may endanger the peace of the world—we shall surely endanger the welfare of our own nation.[2]

Truman's speech depicted a world engaged in an apocalyptic struggle between the forces of freedom and the forces of tyranny. The political fate of humankind hung on the outcome. In this mortal struggle, U.S. aid to Greece and Turkey would serve the American mission of preserving freedom in the world and preventing World War III. Polls, which had been negative before his speech, soon showed a large majority favoring the U.S. aid program.

Not everyone accepted Truman's fervent invitation to join the anti-Communist crusade. Both liberal and conservative critics opposed aid to Greece and Turkey. But after a brief debate, large bipartisan majorities in both houses of Congress passed the aid bill. Truman's powerful rhetoric had carried his cause.

---

[1] George Kennan, *American Diplomacy* (New York: New American Library, 1952), p. 104. (Reprinted with permission of the editor of *Foreign Affairs*, XXV, no. 4 [July, 1947], pp. 566–582.)
[2] Excerpted from a copy of Truman's speech in Armin Rappaport, ed., *Sources in American Diplomacy* (New York: MacMillan, 1966), pp. 329–330.

The Truman Doctrine defined a new U.S. foreign policy direction. Isolationism had been abandoned and the United Nations bypassed. Truman had committed the United States to actively resist Soviet expansionism in southern Europe. The era of the containment of Communism had begun. Although the first application of the new containment policy was limited, the doctrine justifying it was unlimited. During the early 1950s, U.S. foreign policy based on the containment of Communism would expand to become a global commitment to contain Communism everywhere.

Congress created several new governmental agencies to implement the containment policy more effectively. The National Security Act (1947) created the Department of Defense and established the Joint Chiefs of Staff. The act also made the Air Force a separate branch of military service and put the administration of the Army, Navy, and Air Force under a single department. The National Security Act also created the National Security Council (NSC), a cabinet-level advisory body to coordinate military and foreign policy for the president. Creation of the NSC indicated the growing influence of military considerations in the conduct of American foreign policy. The National Security Act also created the Central Intelligence Agency (CIA) as an agency directly under the authority of the NSC. The CIA, a child of the Cold War, became a covert arm of American foreign policy during the late 1940s.

THE MARSHALL PLAN

In 1947, European recovery from the devastation of war was flagging. Washington feared that continuing hardships could force cold and hungry Europeans to turn to Communism, particularly in France and Italy, which had popular Communist parties. A prostrate Europe also endangered American prosperity because of a huge "dollar gap" that had emerged. The dollar gap, totaling about $8 billion in 1947, represented the difference between the value of U.S. exports and the amount of dollars European customers had on hand to pay for them. The dollar gap threatened to undermine overseas trade and erode U.S. postwar economic growth and prosperity.

Europeans could not buy U.S. products unless they received dollars from the United States. To offset the lure of Communism and to pump dollars into the impoverished European economies, U.S. officials drafted a comprehensive European aid program. On June 5, 1947, Secretary of State George Marshall announced the plan directed against "hunger, poverty, desperation, and chaos," which came to bear his name. Truman urged Congress to back the proposed Marshall Plan with a $27 billion appropriation.

The Marshall Plan called for a cooperative approach in which Europeans would plan their recovery needs collectively and the United States would underwrite a long-term recovery program. All European nations were invited to participate in the Marshall Plan, including the Soviet Union and the east European nations. With the British and French leading the way, Europeans responded enthusiastically. A general planning conference convened in Paris on June 26, 1947, to formulate a European reply. But the Soviets walked out of the conference, denouncing the Marshall Plan as an American scheme to dominate Europe. Stalin may also have feared that U.S. economic aid would undermine his control of eastern Europe, so he forced these nations to abstain from the recovery program. On July 16, Europeans established a Committee on European Economic Cooperation, which drew up plans for a four-year recovery effort.

Within the United States, Senator Vandenberg led a bipartisan effort to obtain congressional approval for the plan. Support for the aid program increased when Americans learned of a Communist takeover in Czechoslovakia, which occurred as Congress debated the bill. Stalin apparently ordered the Czech coup as a response to the increasing integration of the West German economy into the liberal capitalist order. Congress appropriated $5.3 billion to implement the Marshall Plan in the summer of 1948. When the Marshall Plan ended in 1952, the United States had provided over $13 billion for European economic recovery.

The Marshall Plan worked. European industrial production increased 200 percent from 1948 to 1952. The foundations for the West's later affluence were firmly laid. The appeal of Communism in the West diminished. The program worked because of its planned, long-term, cooperative approach. It succeeded also because Europe possessed the industrial base and skilled manpower needed to use the aid funds effectively. European economic recovery restored a region of crucial importance to the United States. It also proved to be a major stimulus to American economic activity, and it accorded with Cold War ideological goals. George Marshall expected American economic aid to permit the "emergence of political and social conditions in which free institutions can exist." The Marshall Plan gave the U.S. policy of containment of Communism in Europe a sound economic foundation.

NATO

While furnishing the means for Europe's economic reconstruction, the United States also concerned itself with rebuilding western Germany. With the rise of Soviet power in eastern Europe, there was a power vacuum in central Europe that America wanted to fill with a democratic and capitalistic Germany. Near the end of 1946, the Americans and British merged their German occupation zones and began to assign administrative responsibilities to German officials. By mid-1947, the effort to rebuild Germany's industrial economy had begun.

The Soviets reacted to Western efforts to rebuild the German economy and incorporate it into the European recovery plan by tightening their control of eastern Europe. Perceiving that he had failed to prevent the economic restoration of western Germany, Stalin tried to squeeze the Western powers out of Berlin. In June 1948, the Soviets suddenly shut down all Western access routes to their Berlin sector, which lay deep inside the Soviet zone.

The Berlin Blockade confronted Washington with a serious crisis. Truman ordered U.S. strategic bombers with the capability of hauling nuclear weapons to targets within the Soviet Union to fly to bases in England. The Western powers also devised an Anglo-American airlift that flew food and fuel to 2.5 million West Berliners. The Soviets, not wanting war, did not interfere with the airlift. After 324 days, the Soviets canceled the blockade. It had failed to dislodge the Allies, and it had failed to prevent the integration of the West German economy into the European recovery program.

In American eyes, the Berlin airlift symbolized Western resolve to maintain an outpost of freedom in the heart of Soviet tyranny. Truman had outmaneuvered the Soviets and forced them to rescind the blockade. The Western powers created the Federal Republic of Germany (West Germany) soon after the blockade ended. In retaliation, the Soviets erected the Democratic Socialist Republic of Germany (East Germany). For the next forty years, there would be two German states. The Berlin Blockade represented the first major American–Soviet conflict of the Cold War. It was also the paradigmatic conflict that established the pattern of U.S.–USSR confrontations that would periodically recur until the Cold War ended.

The Czech coup, the Berlin Blockade, and other Soviet actions hostile to Western interests convinced Washington officials that containment required military as well as economic measures. The germ of the North Atlantic Treaty Organization (NATO) appeared in a Senate resolution passed in 1948, expressing America's resolve to defend itself through collective security if necessary.

FIGURE 2.2 Beleaguered West Berliners eagerly await the arrival of an airplane carrying precious food and fuel during the Berlin Airlift. *Source:* Getty Images/Time Life Pictures.

NATO came to life on April 4, 1949; ten European nations, Canada, and the United States signed the treaty. The heart of the mutual security pact could be found in the language of Article 5: "an armed attack against one or more members . . . shall be considered an attack against them all." Attack any NATO member, and you have to fight them all. With the creation of NATO, Soviet aggression against any western European nation would mean World War III. The Senate ratified the treaty, 82 to 13, on July 21, 1949, with little debate.

Congress followed its approval of American membership in NATO by voting to grant military aid to its allies and to contribute U.S. troops to NATO defense forces. U.S. forces stationed in Europe would function as a "tripwire" in case of Soviet aggression, guaranteeing that American strategic bombers would attack the Soviet Union if western Europe were invaded. The Soviets responded to the creation of NATO by creating the Warsaw Pact among eastern European countries.

Because U.S. forces were not sent to Europe until 1952, the creation of NATO did not immediately alter the strategic balance of power in that critical region. At the time of NATO's creation, there was no imminent threat of war in Europe. America appeared to be winning the Cold War in western Europe and Japan. The Marshall Plan nations and the Japanese were both well on the road to economic recovery. The new state of West Germany had been firmly established. Soviet efforts to keep Japan and Europe weak and isolated from the United States obviously had failed.

Given the geopolitical realities in Europe, it is evident that NATO had other uses besides giving containment of Communism in Europe military muscle. NATO gave these nations the confidence to combat internal subversion and the will to resist Communist pressure. NATO conveyed a sense of security that encouraged western European economic recovery under the Marshall Plan. It also served as a means to bind western Europeans more tightly into an American sphere of influence. Ironically, NATO later proved useful in providing a way to rearm West Germany. By integrating the new West German military forces into NATO, the United States could allay French alarm at a rearmed Germany.

From 1947 to 1949, American leaders made many crucial decisions that shaped American Cold War policy for decades. First came the formulation of containment ideology, embodied in the Truman Doctrine. The Marshall Plan offered economic aid enabling western Europeans to stay clear of the Iron Curtain and rebuild their war-shattered economies. NATO added a strategic component. It also represented a historic departure for the United States: America joined its first binding military alliance in modern history. In the nuclear age, foreign entanglements now appeared necessary to ensure U.S. security.

Soon after Senate ratification of NATO came the alarming news that the Soviets had developed an atomic bomb. The American nuclear monopoly, which had functioned as a security blanket to dampen Cold War anxieties, had vanished. Soviet possession of nuclear weapons prompted President Truman to consider ordering the development of a hydrogen fusion weapon, a "superbomb" many times more powerful than atomic fission weapons. In January 1950, an intense secret debate occurred between scientific supporters of the H-bomb, led by Edward Teller, and its opponents, led by J. Robert Oppenheimer. Teller carried the debate with his argument that

FIGURE 2.3   On October 31, 1952, the first hydrogen bomb exploded over the Pacific Ocean with a force of 10 megatons—more than 800 times the power of the atomic bomb that destroyed Hiroshima.   *Source:* U.S. Navy News Photo. Photo by Joint Task Force One.

if the United States failed to develop the weapon and the Soviets did, they could blackmail the United States. Truman ordered the hydrogen bomb to be built.

U.S. scientists exploded a hydrogen bomb in November 1952. But the American technological edge in the arms race against the Soviet Union proved to be short lived. The Soviets tested their own hydrogen bomb in August 1953. These thermonuclear weapons were a thousand times more powerful than the bombs that had destroyed Hiroshima and Nagasaki in August 1945. Experts in both nations ruefully observed that a handful of hydrogen bombs could destroy any of the world's greatest cities and kill millions of its inhabitants. With the advent of the hydrogen bomb, the potential threat to world survival had taken a quantum leap.

THE CHINESE REVOLUTION

Since the Cold War began, the Truman administration had pursued a Europe-oriented foreign policy. But the collapse of the Chinese Nationalist government in 1949, after years of civil war between its forces and Communist troops, brought U.S. Asian policy to the fore. As the Communist leader Mao Zedong established the People's Republic of China, the American people were disheartened at the loss of a favored ally. Conservative critics of the Truman administration's China policy went on the warpath.

America's China policy had been in disarray since the end of World War II. The long civil war between the Nationalists and the Communists, suspended during the war with Japan, resumed soon after the Japanese surrendered. Between 1945 and 1949, the United States had provided the Nationalist government with $2 billion in economic and military aid. In 1946, Truman had sent General George Marshall to China on a futile mission to arrange a political compromise between the warring parties. Both sides, each believing that it could win a military victory over the other, refused to share power.

In 1947, Nationalist leader Jiang Jieshi, aided by U.S. logistical support, launched a major offensive designed to destroy his Communist foes. His armies captured the major cities of China, but in doing so, Jiang's forces spread themselves thin. The Communists controlled the countryside, which contained over 85 percent of the vast Chinese population and provided food for the cities. Maoist armies besieged the Nationalist troops in the cities. By the summer of 1949, Nationalist forces had lost their will to fight and surrendered en masse. As 1949 ended, Jiang, with a remnant of his government, fled to the island of Formosa (Taiwan).

Washington cut itself loose from the failing Nationalist government in August 1949, a few months before Jiang fled China. A State Department White Paper insisted that the United States had done all it could for the Nationalists. The Nationalists had lost the civil war because they had not used U.S. assistance properly.

The Communist victory in China triggered an intense debate within the United States over foreign policy in general and Asian policy in particular. Bipartisanship, which had prevailed during the years of containing Communism in Europe, disintegrated as Republican leaders attacked Truman's Far Eastern policy. The Asia-first wing of the Republican Party and the China Lobby, led by Senator Styles Bridges and Congressman Walter Judd, charged the Democratic-controlled Congress and the Truman administration with responsibility for Jiang's fall. They insisted that U.S. military involvement in the Chinese civil war could have saved Jiang's government.

If anyone could be saddled with the responsibility for losing China, it would be Jiang and his corrupt, inept government. The American failure in China was not due to insufficient aid or lack of concern. However, U.S. leaders never understood the dynamic force of a peasant society ripe for change and the strong appeal of the Maoist land reform program among the Chinese peasants.

Millions of Americans believed the charges brought by the Asia firsters and the China Lobby. Such beliefs stemmed from a false assumption that many Americans made about U.S. foreign policy during the early Cold War era—that the rich and mighty United States could control political events around the globe if only the right leaders took the right actions. They could see no limits to American power. In their view, China had fallen to Communism because U.S. leaders had blundered, or worse, as Senator Joseph McCarthy and others charged, because disloyal American officials, secretly favoring the Communist forces, had subverted America's China policy.

If the Chinese revolution could have been thwarted, it would have taken a massive and sustained U.S. military intervention. In 1949, the United States lacked the ground troops to intervene in China. Truman tried to hide the declining status of the Nationalist regime until near the end; hence its collapse came as a sudden shock. His own actions left him vulnerable to Republican accusations that he had lost China. Containment of Communism had worked in Europe; it had failed in China. The Maoist victory in China was a devastating diplomatic defeat for the United States and a political disaster for the Truman administration.

After the Maoist victory, the United States implemented a policy of diplomatic nonrecognition and clamped a trade boycott on the world's most populous nation. American officials insisted that Jiang's government, now ensconced in Formosa, constituted the legitimate government of China. Nonrecognition of mainland China would be the official U.S. policy for the next twenty years, until Richard Nixon made his dramatic journey to Beijing in February 1972.

NSC-68

Truman, responding to the Soviet development of atomic weapons and the success of the Chinese revolution, directed Secretary of State Acheson to conduct a full-dress review of U.S. foreign policy. Under Acheson's guidance, the review was carried out by the State and Defense departments, and coordinated by the NSC. Six months later, analysts produced National Security Council Document Number 68 (NSC-68), an important top-secret paper that would shape American Cold War policy for the next twenty years.

Truman received NSC-68 in April 1950. It assumed perpetual conflict in the world between the United States and the Soviet Union. It depicted this struggle in stark terms—the survival of America, its free institutions, and its ideals were at stake. It assumed that the Soviets would achieve the nuclear capability to destroy the United States within a few years. In order to forestall that ultimate disaster, NSC-68 called for a massive buildup of U.S. military forces to resist the Soviet menace anywhere in the world that it might arise. It recommended defense budgets of $50 billion a year, a fourfold increase over the $13 billion appropriated for 1950. The outbreak of the Korean War would give President Truman the opportunity to implement many of the recommendations contained in NSC-68, which militarized the policy of containment and transformed it from a regional to a global policy.

THE KOREAN WAR, 1950–1953

In the wake of the Chinese revolution, the Truman administration forged a new Asian policy. Secretary of State Acheson delineated a new defensive perimeter in the Far East, incorporating Japan, Okinawa, and the Philippines. It excluded Formosa, Korea, and Southeast Asia. The new line suggested that nations located within the excluded regions would have to defend themselves against Chinese aggression, or they would have to seek help from the United Nations. Republican leaders vigorously attacked Truman's Asian policy.

As controversy over U.S. Asian policy continued, the Truman administration confronted another Far Eastern crisis—North Korea's invasion of South Korea. The invasion was rooted in divisions within the country stemming from World War II. As the war ended, Soviet and U.S. troops had occupied Korea. The two nations hastily arranged for Soviet soldiers to accept the surrender of Japanese troops north of the thirty-eighth parallel of north latitude and for U.S. soldiers to accept the surrender of Japanese forces south of that line. Efforts to unify Korea failed, and the nation remain divided at the thirty-eighth parallel. North of the boundary, the Soviets helped Kim Il-Sung create a Communist state and trained an army to defend it. South of the border, the United States supervised the creation of a government headed by Syngman Rhee. The Soviet Union and the United States removed their troops from the divided land in the late 1940s. Both Rhee and Kim Il-Sung sought to unify Korea—one under capitalism and the other under Communism.

Kim moved first. With direct assistance from the Soviets, North Korean forces invaded the South on June 25, 1950, in an effort to destroy Rhee's government and unify Korea under Communist control. Kim expected to win an easy victory, having calculated that the United States would not intervene. Kim had received Stalin's permission to invade South Korea,

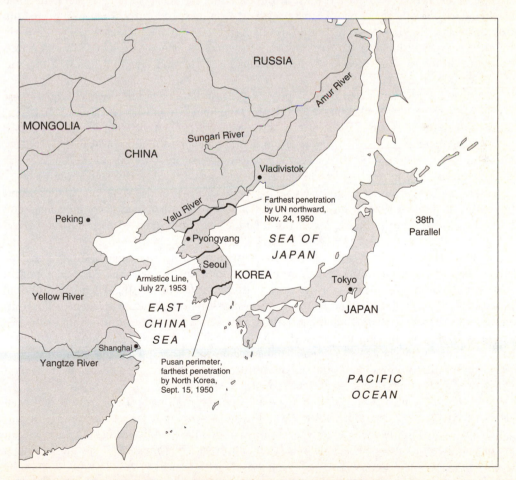

FIGURE 2.4 The Korean War, 1950–1953. *Source:* Public Domain Map.

and Mao Zedong concurred. Stalin and Mao both approved Kim's invasion because they anticipated a quick victory for the North Koreans and saw the move as one that advanced their national interests. By approving the attack, these Soviet and Chinese Communist leaders turned an internal Korean conflict into an international war that involved the United States and the United Nations.

President Truman, surprised by the invasion, hastily conferred with his senior advisers. They assumed immediately that Kim had not acted alone, that the Soviets had masterminded the attack. They perceived North Korea's attack as Communist aggression and reacted accordingly, within the context of the Cold War. The threat, in their judgment, was global; they believed that U.S. national security and world peace were threatened. They understood that if the United States did not intervene quickly, North Korea would surely overrun the South. Truman quickly decided to send U.S. troops to try to save South Korea from Communism.

The President compared Communist aggression in Korea with Fascist aggression during the 1930s and said that if the United States let aggression go unchallenged, as the democracies had done in the 1930s, "it would mean a third world war." Truman was also concerned that the Soviets might be using the invasion as a feint to draw U.S. troops into Korea, leaving western Europe vulnerable to Soviet attack, just at the time that NATO was being implemented. He further shared a concern about Japanese security. Conquest of South Korea would give the Communists airfields within thirty minutes flying time of Japanese cities. Finally, domestic political realities influenced Truman's decision to send U.S. armed forces to Korea. He dared not serve up the loss of Korea to the Republicans in an election year that followed so soon after the "loss" of China.

When Truman committed U.S. troops to the Korean War, he did not seek a declaration of war from Congress. He claimed that he lacked time, and he relied on what he called his "inherent war-making powers" as commander in chief of the armed forces. But the United States did obtain UN endorsement for its Korean intervention. The Security Council approved U.S. military intervention because the Soviet delegate was absent from its sessions. Officially, the Korean War was a UN "police action" to repel aggression against South Korea. In reality, UN sanction furnished a cover for what was mainly an American effort. The United States provided 90 percent of the ground forces, and all of the sea and air power aiding the South Koreans. All battlefield commanders came from the United States. General MacArthur, whom Truman appointed to head the Korean campaign, took orders from the U.S. Joint Chiefs of Staff.

Tough, battle-hardened North Korean troops, many of whom had fought in China alongside the Maoist forces, overran most of South Korea, except for a small area around Pusan, a seaport at the southern tip of the peninsula. For a time, Washington feared that the defenders would be pushed into the sea. But U.S. and South Korean forces finally halted the invaders at Pusan in August 1950. General MacArthur then dramatically turned the war around with a brilliantly executed amphibious landing at Inchon, 150 miles north of Pusan. U.S. forces moved south from Inchon as other forces broke out at Pusan and headed north. They caught the North Koreans in a giant pincers and a rout was on. By the end of September, the UN forces had pushed the retreating North Koreans back across the thirty-eighth parallel.

Within three months, the UN mission had been accomplished. The aggressors had been cleared from South Korea. But with the North Korean army in disarray, and the USSR and China apparently not inclined to intervene, Truman decided to go north across the thirty-eighth parallel. The Joint Chiefs and General MacArthur enthusiastically approved. Polls showed that a large majority of the American people also supported the action. Truman's decision to cross the border transformed the Korean War. Containment became rollback, an effort to liberate North

Korea from Communism. The UN forces set out to destroy a Communist satellite and to unify Korea under a pro-Western government. As the Soviet delegate was still absent, the UN Security Council obediently endorsed Truman's decision.

The UN forces drove their foes north. Meanwhile, the general U.S. military buildup, in accordance with NSC-68, accelerated. The draft had been reinstated. Congress doubled the Pentagon's budget, from $13 billion to $26 billion. Additional troops were earmarked for NATO. The Seventh Fleet was stationed between the Chinese mainland and Formosa to shield Jiang's forces from a possible Communist attack. The war effort enjoyed broad popular approval. The UN forces appeared headed for victory.

As the UN forces advanced northward, Chinese leaders issued a series of warnings. When U.S. leaders ignored their warnings, Chinese officials stated publicly that if UN forces continued to advance northward, they would intervene. On October 15, 1950, President Truman flew to Wake Island in the mid-Pacific to confer with General MacArthur. MacArthur assured the president that the Chinese would not intervene, and if they did, they would be slaughtered.

Truman accepted MacArthur's assessment and discounted the Chinese warnings. MacArthur launched what he intended to be the final Korean offensive on November 24. The UN forces advanced along two widely separated routes toward the Yalu River border with China and toward Pyongyang, the North Korean capital. Two days later, the Chinese sent more than 300,000 troops swarming across the frozen Yalu. The Chinese armies split the UN forces and sent them reeling backwards. They drove MacArthur's forces back across the thirty-eighth parallel and down the Korean peninsula.

U.S. officials, who had walked into disaster together, were now divided over how to respond to it. MacArthur wanted to expand the war and strike at China. He was supported by many Republicans and some Democrats. He believed the Chinese made the decision to invade Korea on their own. However, Truman and Acheson assumed the Chinese were carrying out Soviet policies. If they were correct, going to war with China meant going to war with the Soviet Union in Asia. President Truman opted for a return to the original limited UN mission of restoring the prewar status quo in Korea and for continuing the U.S. military buildup in accordance with NSC-68.

In December, a new U.S. field commander in Korea, General Matthew Ridgway, brought in reinforcements and rallied the American forces. Heavy artillery slaughtered the Chinese forces, advancing in massed formations. U.S. naval and air forces helped blunt the Chinese drive. Ridgway's Eighth Army fought its way back to a point near the thirty-eighth parallel and held that line for the rest of the war. Truce negotiations began on July 10, 1951, but they were unproductive for a long time. A seesaw war of trenches and fortified hills would continue for two more years.

During the first months of 1951, as Ridgway's troops held the line in Korea, Truman continued his implementation of NSC-68. Annual military spending reached $50 billion. The United States committed additional forces to NATO and obtained additional overseas bases. The U.S. Army expanded to 3.6 million men, six times its size when the Korean War began. Military aid was sent to Jiang's Nationalist forces on Formosa. The United States also began to supply military aid to French forces fighting in Southeast Asia. Washington signed a peace treaty with Japan that ended the occupation and restored Japanese sovereignty. However, the treaty permitted the United States to maintain military bases in Japan. The Truman administration embraced the general strategy of ringing China and the Soviet Union with U.S. military might. Containment had grown into a global commitment and now packed potent military muscle.

The rapid U.S. military buildup did not satisfy Republican critics supporting General MacArthur's proposal to take the war to China. MacArthur did not want to hold the line at the

FIGURE 2.5   U.S. soldiers in the 2nd Infantry Division, fighting in Korea near the Chongchon River, December 1950. The Korean War was the first war in American history in which soldiers fought together in racially integrated combat units.   *Source:* Moss, *America in the Twentieth Century*, 3rd ed. Corbis. Photo by Department of Defense/Acme/UPI.

thirty-eighth parallel and negotiate; he wanted a military victory over China and a unified, pro-Western Korea. Ordered by Truman to make no public statements, he defied his commander in chief. On April 5, House Republican leader Joseph Martin read a letter from MacArthur to Congress calling for an alternative foreign policy. If victory in Asia required bombing Manchurian bases, blockading Chinese ports, and using Nationalist forces from Taiwan, so be it: "In war there is no substitute for victory." MacArthur repudiated Truman's Europe-first orientation, his effort to achieve limited political goals in Korea, and his containment policy. He had issued a fundamental challenge to the administration's Cold War foreign policy.

Truman dismissed MacArthur from his command and ordered him home. Truman's actions provoked one of the great emotional events of modern American history. The White House was swamped with letters and phone calls, mostly supporting MacArthur. Polls showed that 75 percent of the people supported him. MacArthur's Republican supporters heaped abuse upon the embattled Truman. Many newspaper and magazine editors called for his impeachment.

Much of the uproar over Truman's firing of MacArthur reflected popular disenchantment with the war. Many Americans neither understood nor accepted the concept of limited war for particular political objectives. After all, when an easy military victory appeared possible, Truman himself had tried to take all of Korea, only to revert to the original, limited objective following Chinese intervention. The president wanted to avoid a major war that he feared could escalate into World War III. But MacArthur's contempt for half measures and his stirring call for victory appealed to a nation of impatient idealists. The United States had the power to destroy North Korea and China. Why not use it?

MacArthur returned to America to a hero's welcome. About 500,000 people turned out to greet him when he arrived in San Francisco on April 16, 1951. Three days later, he addressed a joint session of Congress. His moving speech was interrupted thirty times by applause. After he spoke, he rode triumphantly down Pennsylvania Avenue to the acclaim of hundreds of thousands of cheering citizens. He traveled to New York where he received the largest, most tumultuous ticker-tape parade in the city's history. An estimated three to five million people turned out to catch a view of MacArthur.

As MacArthur basked in public acclaim, Congress investigated the circumstances of his removal. Hearings were held before the combined Senate Armed Services Committee and Foreign Relations Committee. The testimony of the Joint Chiefs, particularly of General Omar Bradley, made the case for containment in Korea forcibly and clearly: The Soviet Union, not China, was America's main enemy; Europe, not Asia, was the most important region of American interest. General Bradley insisted that fighting China in Asia "would be the wrong war in the wrong place at the wrong time against the wrong enemy." There also was MacArthur's refusal to follow orders and his efforts to make foreign policy over the president's head. The constitutional principle of civilian control of foreign policy and military strategy was at stake. Truman, the Commander in Chief of U.S. armed forces, had fired an insubordinate general. Rather quickly the tumult subsided, and MacArthur faded into quiet retirement.

Meanwhile, in Korea, the truce talks between the Americans on one side and the North Koreans and Chinese on the other side dragged on inconclusively, the fighting continued, and thousands more U.S. soldiers would die. The main reason for the impasse at the talks was the Chinese insistence that captured North Korean and Chinese soldiers be returned to them, even though these soldiers wanted to remain in South Korea. The United States refused to return them against their will. An armistice was finally reached on July 27, 1953, when President Eisenhower threatened the Chinese with an expansion of the war. The Chinese yielded, and the prisoners remained in the South. The thirty-eighth parallel was restored as the boundary between North and South Korea. To appease Syngman Rhee, who was unhappy with the settlement, the United States furnished his government with military aid and stationed 50,000 American troops in South Korea.

Although it has been forgotten by many Americans, Korea was a major land war in Asia. It lasted three years and involved over three million U.S. military personnel. Its costs exceeded $100 billion. A total of 36,516 Americans died in Korea, and another 150,000 were wounded. Millions of Koreans and Chinese perished during the war. Korea proved to be an unpopular war, which ended in a draw. No celebrations greeted its end. Returning Korean veterans melted into society, to become part of the 1950s "silent generation."

The Korean conflict reshaped the Cold War. Containment was transformed from a regional policy to a global stance. U.S. foreign policy shifted from its Eurocentric focus toward increasing concern with the Far East. War with the People's Republic ensured that the United States and China would remain bitter Cold War adversaries for decades. The image of an aggressive Soviet Union commanding a centralized, worldwide Communist movement fastened itself on the American mind. China and North Korea were seen as extensions of

Soviet power. Viewing developments in Asia from this perspective, Truman incorporated the defense of Formosa and French interests in Southeast Asia into the larger framework of U.S. containment of Communism in the Far East.

The Korean War also militarized the Cold War. Prior to the war in Korea, containment primarily represented an effort to eliminate the political and economic conditions that spawned Communism. After Korea, containment consisted of setting up military frontiers behind which free societies could develop. The United States committed itself to maintaining a huge permanent military force in peacetime, although given the crisis atmosphere that prevailed during much of the Cold War, the traditional distinction between peace and war often blurred.

From a broader perspective, the Korean War can be seen as a turning point in which, unlike the 1930s, the United States and Western Europe avoided appeasement and faced the challenges of an aggressor in a manner that averted a world war. The Korean War also positioned the Western powers advantageously in the ongoing Cold War vis-à-vis the Soviet Union and China. In that sense, the Korean War could be considered a strategic success for the United States despite its failure to reunite the Korean peninsula under a pro-western government.

THE COLD WAR CONSENSUS

From the end of World War II to the spring of 1947, containment of Communism evolved as the major U.S. foreign policy response to the rise of the Cold War. Beginning as a response to perceived Soviet threats to the security of small nations in southern Europe, containment expanded to include the periphery of East Asia and Southeast Asia in 1950, following the Maoist triumph in China, the U.S. decision to support the French in Indochina, and the outbreak of the Korean War.

As the global split between the former allies widened, most Americans came to support President Truman's "get tough" approach to the Soviet Union. Influenced by the media, Americans increasingly viewed the Soviet Union as the aggressive successor to the destroyed Third Reich. Communism was equated with Fascism, and Stalin was seen as a "Red" Hitler, a despotic ruler with megalomaniacal ambitions to dominate the new postwar world order. Soviet leaders were depicted as Marxist-Leninist zealots in the service of a master plan for imposing Communism on the world. The great lesson of World War II appeared to be that aggressors must not be appeased. As the Soviet leaders came to be seen as the New Nazis in the world, American leaders vowed to contain them, to prevent aggression, and to ensure that there would be no World War III.

Some prominent Americans dissented from Truman's new foreign policy approach. They opposed the enormous costs of rearmament and foreign aid. They disliked the new internal security controls clamped onto American life, the complexities and tensions of great power rivalries, and the domination of public life by foreign policy issues. Some idealistic Americans did not relish having to support reactionary governments just because they appeared to be threatened by Communism.

But the dramatic events of the early Cold War years—the Soviet takeover of eastern Europe, Soviet pressures on Turkey, the civil war in Greece, the Communist coup in Czechoslovakia, the Berlin Blockade, Soviet acquisition of nuclear weapons, the "fall" of China, the French effort to retain possession of Vietnam, and the Korean War—collectively worked on the American public consciousness to create a consensus supporting the Truman administration's policy of containment of Communism.

During World War II, cooperation with the Soviets had been a strategic necessity. By 1947, the world had changed dramatically. The transformation in world affairs brought about by World War II necessitated a transformation in U.S. attitudes and approaches to foreign policy. Containing the expansionist tendencies of the Soviet Union everywhere in the world had become the new American geopolitical imperative.

Despite continuing criticism from both the Left and the Right, a bipartisan consensus in support of the main direction of U.S. foreign policy had emerged in this country by 1947. There was broad agreement that the major objective of U.S. foreign policy would be the containment of Communism. The U.S. bipartisan foreign policy consensus in support of this objective would remain intact until the Vietnam War cracked it during the late 1960s and brought about the first major debates over U.S. foreign policy goals in nearly twenty years.

Brief Bibliographic Essay

See Patterson, *Grand Expectations*, Chs. 4, 5, & 8 for general treatments of the origins of the Cold War and the evolution of post–World War II U.S. foreign policy into a global commitment to contain Communist expansion everywhere, which culminated in the Korean War and in time a war in Southeast Asia. Stephen Ambrose's *Rise to Globalism: American Foreign Policy, 1938–1980* contains an excellent account of the origins of the Cold War. Another fine study of the genesis of the Cold War is John L. Gaddis's *The United States and the Origins of the Cold War*. Gaddis, America's most eminent diplomatic historian, has produced another study of the origins of the Cold War, *Now We Know: Rethinking Cold War History*. On the basis of materials he accessed in Soviet archives, he makes a convincing case that Stalin was primarily responsible for provoking the Cold War. Gaddis's *The Cold War: A New History* is the best recent general history of the Cold War. Walter LaFeber's *America, Russia,* *and the Cold War* is a classic account of the Cold War conflict between the United States and the Soviet Union. A magisterial recent account of the Cold War is Melvyn Leffler's *For the Soul of Mankind: The United States, the Soviet Union and the Cold War*. Problems in Germany that were the major causes of the Cold War are carefully analyzed in John Gimbel's *The American Occupation of Germany: Politics and the Military, 1945–1949*. Thomas Parrish's *Berlin in the Balance, 1945–1949: The Blockade, the Airlift, the First Major Battle of the Cold War* is an excellent recent study of the first major U.S.–USSR confrontation of the evolving Cold War. Akira Iriye's *The Cold War in Asia* is a good account. See also Michael Schaller's *The American Occupation of Japan: The Origins of the Cold War in Asia*. The late David Halberstam's last book, *The Coldest Winter: America and the Korean War*, is the most recent and one of the finest studies of the Korean War ever done.

CHAPTER

3

Postwar Politics

With the end of World War II, most Americans believed that they were entering a new era, that postwar America would be a very different nation from the one that had gone to war on December 7, 1941. At the same time that they looked ahead to new opportunities and new experiences, Americans yearned for a return to the normal routines and rhythms of everyday life. They wanted to put the disruptions and dangers of the wartime crisis behind them. But for many Americans, the road back to normality in the years immediately after the war proved rocky. The immediate postwar years were dominated by hyperinflation, bitter strikes, continuing shortages of housing and consumer goods, fierce partisan political divisions, and racial conflict. Compounding the many problems inherent in adapting to the new postwar world, the Cold War struck home with a special fury: America was convulsed by a Second Red Scare and the rise of the politics of anti-Communism that reached intense levels during the Korean War.

HARRY WHO?

Harry S. Truman had come to the presidency on April 12, 1945, ill prepared and nearly unknown.

Many Americans knew nothing about him when he suddenly inherited the presidency from a fallen titan. He had difficulties early in his presidency because of his inexperience and because he inherited an administration, many of whose members viewed him as an inferior successor to Roosevelt. Prominent New Dealers departed, and Truman replaced them with more conservative advisers recruited from the ranks of big business, corporate law firms, Wall Street brokerage houses, and the senior ranks of the military. Honest himself, Truman tolerated a crowd of political hacks who had followed him to Washington. Most of these camp followers belonged to the "Missouri gang," led by Harry Vaughn.

During his campaign for reelection in 1944, Roosevelt had promised the American people that after the war he would craft an economic bill of rights for all Americans, including jobs, decent housing, adequate health care, and a good education. Roosevelt's proposals convinced many of his liberal followers that the president planned to revive the New Deal reform tradition that had been placed on hold for the duration of the war. Truman appeared to share his predecessor's reform commitments when he proposed to Congress in the fall of 1945 a sweeping program of social legislation. Truman called upon the legislators to enact a national housing program, to raise the minimum wage, to extend Social Security benefits, and to pass a full employment bill.

The proposed full employment bill was the centerpiece of Truman's reform package. It called for the federal government to assume responsibility for full employment by enhancing purchasing power and spending for public works. As the nation demobilized its military forces and shut down its war industries, most Americans shared a persistent fear that the American economy, no longer stimulated by war spending, would regress to massive unemployment and even depression. They feared that millions of suddenly released war workers and discharged veterans could not be absorbed by a peacetime economy.

After making his bold proposals, Truman vacillated, allowing Congress to enact a measure in 1946 called the Employment Act. It called for "maximum employment" rather than full employment. It established the government's responsibility for maintaining prosperity without prescribing the means to achieve it. It was more a statement of principles than a program of action. The act's most significant reform was the creation of a Council of Economic Advisers (CEA) to provide policy recommendations to the president and to assist in long-range economic planning. Congress failed to enact any of Truman's other reform proposals.

With the creation of the economic council, the Truman administration and all subsequent U.S. presidencies committed themselves to relying on economic theory and quantifiable measurements for direction. Economists became the nation's high priests. Henceforth, the starting point of every administration's economic policies would be growth: how to achieve it and for whose benefit. Generally, Democratic administrations focused on demand-side economics and Republican administrations focused on supply-side economics. Democratic presidencies generally used tax cuts to accelerate growth in order to expand the size of the middle classes and to reduce poverty. Republican presidencies generally used tax cuts to promote growth in the private sector, undermine the welfare state, and limit the reach of government.

The economy shrank during the first year after the war, mainly because the federal government abruptly canceled $35 billion in war contracts. The gross domestic product (GDP) for 1946 was slightly smaller than for 1945, the last year of the war. Unemployment, which had vanished in wartime, rose to 4.5 percent in 1946. But the feared reversion to depression never happened; most war workers and veterans were absorbed into the postwar economy.

Many factors accounted for the economy's unexpected resiliency. The GI Bill provided low-interest loans to help veterans buy homes, farms, and businesses. It granted billions of dollars of educational benefits, permitting millions of veterans, many with families, to attend colleges and trade schools. Tax cuts strengthened consumer purchasing power and stimulated business activity. Government also aided the business sector by transferring over $15 billion worth of government-owned plants to the private sector, adding some 20 percent to industrial capacity. Further, government spending, although much reduced from wartime levels, remained far higher than prewar levels.

The main reason the economy transitioned from war to peace without recession or depression lay in an unforeseen powerful force. American consumers came out of the war with billions of dollars in savings and with long-frustrated desires to buy new clothes, homes, cars, radios, and appliances. Unleashed consumer spending kept factories humming and people working after the war ended, and it staved off recession or depression.

However, unleashed consumer demand ignited hyperinflation as the economy was decontrolled. By early 1946, the Office of Price Administration had removed most rationing restrictions, but it had kept wage, price, and rent controls. Inflation soared. Desired commodities like new cars and refrigerators remained scarce. Businessmen, farmers, and trade unionists demanded the removal of all remaining restrictions on their economic activity. A rash of strikes broke out in the auto, meatpacking, electrical, and steel industries, idling productive capacity and delaying fulfillment of consumer demands. President Truman tried and failed to ensure a gradual, orderly phaseout of controls by restraining all interest groups.

In the spring of 1946, the bipartisan conservative coalition controlling Congress battled the President over extending the life of the OPA. Congress enacted a weak control measure that Truman vetoed, causing all controls to expire on July 1. There followed the worst surge of inflation since 1919. Congress, deluged with angry complaints, hastily passed another, even weaker bill, which Truman signed. Consumer prices continued to soar amidst the politics of confusion. Thereafter, the OPA lifted all remaining controls and faded away. The cost of living rose 20 percent in 1946, and acute shortages persisted as did populist anger and frustration.

THE ELECTION OF 1946

As the 1946 midterm elections approached, Truman and his party faced serious political trouble. The Democrats had split into their Northern and Southern wings, with Southern Democrats often joining Northern Republicans to block administration measures. Many liberal Democrats still yearned for Roosevelt, dismissing Truman as an inept successor. Truman and his party were damned for both shortages and skyrocketing prices. Organized labor, sullen over the Truman administration's and the Democratically controlled Congress's failure to strongly support workers when they struck several of the nation's major industries in 1945 and 1946, made only token efforts to support Democratic congressional candidates.

Republican congressional candidates attacked the failures of Truman's price control program. They jeered, "To err is Truman." When beef disappeared from meat markets, housewives rioted. When beef was back on the shelf a week later, the women were shocked to discover that prices had doubled. "Had enough?" chorused Republicans. On the eve of the elections, polls showed that Truman's popularity had dropped to 32 percent. Many Democrats stayed home on election day.

The election results mirrored the popular mood. Republicans scored substantial victories, winning control of the new House of Representatives by 246 to 188, and they would hold a 51 to 45 majority in the new Senate. For the first time since before the Great Depression, the Republicans won control of both houses of Congress. Many working-class voters deserted the Democrats, shattering the labor bloc that had been solidly Democratic since 1932. The election results also confirmed the new conservative mood of the electorate and doomed liberal hopes for a revival of the New Deal spirit or the enactment of social reforms in the postwar era.

THE EIGHTIETH CONGRESS

Many new faces appeared in Washington as members of the Eightieth Congress. They were war veterans, representing a new generation of politicians who had come of age. One congressional rookie, Republican Richard Nixon, hailed from Southern California. Another, Democrat John F. Kennedy, represented a working-class district of the south side of Boston. To the Senate came Joseph McCarthy, a Republican from Wisconsin. McCarthy would soon propel himself into the center of the Communists-in-government controversy that rocked Washington and made his name a household word.

The Republicans took charge of the new Congress. So long out of power, the GOP set out to reassert the authority of Congress and to trim the powers of the executive branch. One of their first items of business was to propose a Twenty-second Amendment, which would limit future presidents to two elected terms. They wanted to ensure that there would be no more presidential reigns such as Franklin Roosevelt's. The Eightieth Congress tore to shreds Truman's domestic program to extend the welfare state. It rejected all his important proposals. Although it did not abolish basic New Deal programs, the Eightieth Congress certainly trimmed their edges.

Senator Robert Taft of Ohio, son of a former president, spearheaded the Republican assault on the New Deal. Taft, who had been in the Senate since 1938, hoped to create a record that would vault him into the White House one day. He believed that the voters had given the Republicans a mandate to eradicate the New Deal. He said that most Americans wanted lower taxes, less governmental interference in business, and especially curbs on the power of organized labor.

Twice in 1947, Congress enacted tax cuts. Truman vetoed both measures. A third tax cut was passed over his veto. Taft also led the fight to enact a measure, passed over Truman's veto, modifying the National Labor Relations Act, the nation's basic labor law. The new law, the Labor Management Relations Act, popularly called the Taft–Hartley Act, which went into effect in 1947, made many changes. It extended the concept of "unfair labor practices," previously confined to management, to unions. Among forbidden union practices was the closed shop, which mandated that a worker join a union before working. The new law also required unions to file annual financial statements with the Department of Labor. Cold War concerns could be seen in the requirement that all union officials file affidavits showing they were not members of the Communist Party or any other subversive organization. The act also prohibited union contributions to national political campaigns, and it forbade strikes by federal employees. In cases of strikes that "affected the national welfare," the Taft–Hartley Act empowered the attorney general to seek a court injunction ordering an eighty-day delay in the strike. During this eighty-day "cooling-off period," federal mediators would try to settle the conflict. If, after eighty days, union members rejected the mediator's final offer, the strike could occur. One section of the new law, Section 14(b), permitted states to legalize the open shop, making union membership voluntary.

Organized labor fiercely attacked the Taft–Hartley Act. William Green, head of the American Federation of Labor (AFL), charged that the bill was forged "in a spirit of vindictiveness against unions." President Truman claimed that it was both unworkable and unfair. In addition to general denunciations, labor leaders attacked particular provisions of the new law, such as the mandatory eighty-day strike delay feature. Repeal of the new law became the major political goal for organized labor.

The Taft–Hartley Act was the most important social legislation enacted during Truman's presidency. It did not undermine the basic strength of American trade unions, which conservatives hoped and liberals feared might happen. The Communist registration requirement was nullified by the Supreme Court. Union membership increased from fourteen million at the time of passage to sixteen million five years later. During the 1950s, collective bargaining between teams of labor and management representatives generated wage increases and improved fringe benefits, enough to make American workers members of the most affluent working class in history. Later Congresses never repealed the Taft–Hartley law, nor amended any of its major provisions.

CIVIL RIGHTS

A dramatic breakthrough for African Americans occurred in an unlikely venue in 1947, when Branch Rickey, the general manager of the Brooklyn Dodgers, broke the color line of major league baseball by adding a gifted black athlete, Jackie Robinson, to his team's roster. Robinson quickly became an all-star player and future Hall of Famer on a team that won six National

FIGURE 3.1 Jackie Robinson in action during a World Series with the New York Yankees. Robinson was the first African American to play major league baseball in modern times.   *Source:* Corbis/Bettmann.

League pennants in the next ten years. His success paved the way for other gifted African American athletes, previously confined to segregated baseball leagues, to play major league ball, including Larry Doby, Henry (Hank) Aaron, and the legendary Satchel Paige.

The Cold War brought additional pressure for integrating African Americans and other nonwhite minorities into the mainstream of American life. The United States was now seeking the support of African and Asian nations whose leaders resented American mistreatment of its racial minorities. "Jim Crow" laws mandating systemic segregation throughout the South also made the United States vulnerable to Soviet propaganda that sought to highlight the inequities of American democracy in order to win influence among Third World people of color.

Truman was the first modern president to promote civil rights causes. His involvement came from both moral and political considerations. He passionately felt a strong need for justice for African Americans. He also was aware of the growing importance of the black vote in Northern cities, and he wanted to offset efforts by Republicans to regain African American support that they had enjoyed before the Great Depression.

Responding to the concerns of African American leaders, Truman created a Committee on Civil Rights in December 1946. The committee issued a report entitled "To Secure These Rights," in which it recommended a series of actions to eliminate racial inequality in America. Among its recommendations were the following: the creation of a civil rights division within the Justice Department, the creation of a Commission on Civil Rights, the abolition of the poll tax, the desegregation of all government agencies, the desegregation of the armed forces, and the enactment of a permanent Fair Employment Practices Commission (FEPC). In a special message to Congress, Truman endorsed the committee's recommendations. Black leaders, delighted by Truman's statements, lavishly praised him.

But the president's rhetorical support for civil rights did not produce any positive legislative results. Congress rejected all of the committee's proposals. Republicans generally ignored them, and Southern Democrats denounced them. The Justice Department did not investigate Southern efforts to prevent African Americans from registering to vote, although Justice Department attorneys began to submit friends-of-the-court briefs on behalf of civil rights cases involving public schools and housing. Truman became the first president ever to address a civil rights organization when he spoke at an NAACP convention in 1948.

In February 1948, the president made an important contribution to the cause of racial equality when he issued an executive order barring discrimination in all federal agencies. In July of that year, Truman also ordered the desegregation of the armed forces. At first the pace of desegregating the military, particularly the Army, which had more African Americans than the other branches of military service, was glacial. Segregation persisted in the Army until the Korean War. Integration of the Army occurred during that conflict when Army officers discovered that African American soldiers fought more effectively in integrated units than in segregated ones. It was Truman's most important civil rights victory. Within a few years, the Army became the most integrated American institution, and during the 1950s and 1960s, many African Americans found opportunities in the military that were not available to them in civilian life.

THE ELECTION OF 1948

As the 1948 election approached, Truman appeared to have no chance. At times he was discouraged by his inability to lead the country as well as his low ratings in the polls. In the fall of 1947, he even sent a member of his staff to talk to General Eisenhower, then Army chief of staff, to see if he might be interested in the Democratic nomination for 1948. Eisenhower was not. Truman then decided to seek reelection. At the Democratic Convention held in Philadelphia in July, delegates, convinced that Truman could not win, tried to promote a boom for Eisenhower—it fizzled. Disappointed Democrats then held up signs that read, "I'm just mild about Harry."

To add to his woes, Truman's party was fragmenting. Splinter groups formed on the Left and the Right. At the Convention, Northern liberals forced the adoption of a strong civil rights plank over the furious objections of Southern leaders. When it was adopted by a floor vote after a raucous debate, delegates from Mississippi and Alabama marched out in protest. These renegade Southerners later formed their own party, the States' Rights Party. At their convention, delegates from thirteen states nominated South Carolina Governor J. Strom Thurmond as their candidate for president. These Southern defections appeared to remove any remaining Democratic hopes for success. The Solid South, a Democratic stronghold since the end of Reconstruction, had bolted.

The liberal wing of the Democratic Party also threatened to split off. Back in 1946, Truman had fired Secretary of Commerce Henry Wallace for publicly criticizing his "get tough" foreign policy toward the Soviet Union. In 1948, Wallace became the presidential candidate of a Leftist third party, the Progressive Party. Many New Dealers considered Wallace, whom Truman had replaced as Roosevelt's vice president in 1944, the true heir to the Roosevelt legacy, and they supported his candidacy. Polls taken that summer showed that Wallace could cost Truman several Northern industrial states. It appeared that the remnants of his party had given Truman a worthless nomination. But the gutsy leader told the assembled Democrats, "I will win this election and make those Republicans like it—don't you forget that." Few believed him at the time.

The confident Republicans, eager to regain the White House after a sixteen-year Democratic hold on the presidency, again nominated New York Governor Thomas E. Dewey and adopted a moderate program. Dewey, soundly beaten by Roosevelt in 1944, was determined to avenge that defeat this time around. All polls showed him running far ahead of Truman. Dewey opted for a safe, restrained strategy to carry him to the executive office. He raised no controversial issues, and he never mentioned his opponent by name.

Truman, aided by former Roosevelt adviser James Rowe, devised an electoral strategy he believed could win. He would stress his adherence to the New Deal tradition by advocating an advanced program of liberal reform. As soon as he got the nomination, he called the Eightieth Congress into a special session and reintroduced all of his reform programs that Congress had failed to pass in regular sessions. Again, the Congress rejected them. This bold move set the tone for the campaign.

Truman took off on a transcontinental train tour in search of an electorate. He traveled over 32,000 miles and made hundreds of speeches, talking directly to about twelve million people. He repeatedly blasted what he called the "do nothing, good for nothing" Eightieth Congress, blaming all of the ills of the nation on the Republican-controlled legislature. He called the Republicans "gluttons of privilege" who would destroy the New Deal if elected. He depicted Dewey as Hoover *redux* and insisted that a Republican administration would bring back the grim days of depression. Speaking in an aggressive populist style, he delighted his crowds. "Give 'em hell, Harry!" they yelled. "I'm doin' it!" Truman yelled back.

Despite his strenuous campaign, he apparently faced certain defeat. Two weeks before the election, fifty political experts unanimously predicted that Dewey would win. Pollsters stopped interviewing a week before the election, assuming that Dewey already had it wrapped up.

On election day, Truman scored the biggest upset in American political history. It was not close. He beat Dewey in the popular vote, 24.2 million to 22 million, and 303 to 189 in the electoral college. His party also regained control of Congress by a 54 to 42 margin in the Senate and a whopping 263 to 171 margin in the House. Wallace's campaign failed. Most liberals ended up voting for Truman. The Dixiecrats carried only four Deep South states. A trend toward

FIGURE 3.2 How sweet it was! A jubilant Harry Truman holds up a newspaper whose prediction of victory for Thomas Dewey was, to say the least, a bit premature. *Source*: St. Louis Mercantile Library. Used with permission.

Truman had surfaced in the final week of the campaign, but the pollsters missed it since they had already quit taking opinion samples.

How could Truman score such a surprising victory and confound all of the experts? Republican overconfidence helped. Many Republicans, assuming victory, did not bother to vote. Truman's spirited, grassroots campaign effort was a factor. But Truman won mainly because he was able to hold together enough of the old New Deal coalition of labor, Northern liberals, blacks, and farmers to win. Black voters provided Truman with his margin of victory in key states such as California, Ohio, and Illinois. Many independent voters opted for Truman, blaming an obstructionist Republican-controlled Congress rather than the president for the legislative gridlock. Many Southern whites, although offended by Truman's advocacy of civil rights, nevertheless voted for Truman out of party loyalty and because they did not want to waste their votes on a protest candidate who had no chance to win.

Truman successfully pinned an anti–New Deal label on the Republicans and identified them with Depression memories. He effectively identified the Progressives with Communism and support for the Soviet Union at a time of rising Cold War tensions. A commentator suggested that "Roosevelt had won a fifth term." The splits within his party worked to Truman's advantage. They sheared off the Democratic Left and Right and allowed Truman to concentrate on the political center, where most of the votes were.

The 1948 election had a long-term significance. It was a transitional election during which American liberalism was reconfigured. Party-based voting declined, and issue-based voting increased. Two relatively new issues became prominent in the election, as Truman embraced both civil rights and anti-Communism. With the Democratic Party victory, the South and the Left both shrunk in importance to the Democrats nationally. The party gravitated from the Left toward the Center. Henceforth, Democratic Party leaders would abandon New Deal liberalism and embrace a more Centrist variety.

A FAIR DEAL

In the fall of 1945, President Truman had sent an ambitious package of legislative proposals to Congress, only to see them shunted aside during the political scrambling over decontrol and inflation. Now president in his own right, his January 1949 program began thus: "Every segment of our population and every individual has a right to expect from our government a fair deal." Truman's Fair Deal proposals included price controls, tax increases, improving civil rights, expanding public housing, raising the minimum wage, expanding Social Security, repealing the Taft–Hartley law, supporting farm prices, providing federal aid to education, and implementing national health insurance.

The Eighty-first Congress enacted only a small portion of the Fair Deal. They rejected his proposals for tax hikes and price controls, refused to repeal the Taft–Hartley law, and refused to implement his agricultural program embodied in Secretary of Agriculture Charles F. Brannan's plan for high fixed supports for commodity prices. Truman's civil rights proposals were thwarted by the threat of a Southern filibuster in the Senate. Federal aid to education was opposed by the Catholic Church for not including funds for parochial schools. Truman's controversial proposal for compulsory health insurance provoked opposition from the American Medical Association (AMA), a powerful doctor's lobby that defeated what it called "socialized medicine."

Nevertheless, the president succeeded in getting some Fair Deal measures passed during his second term, although most of the measures enacted only extended existing programs. The minimum wage was raised from 40¢ to 75¢ an hour. Social Security coverage was extended to 10.5 million additional workers, and benefits were increased on an average of 77 percent.

The most important Fair Deal measure to pass in 1949, with the help of Senator Taft, was the National Housing Act, which provided funds for slum clearance and the construction of 810,000 units of low-income housing over a period of six years.

Truman's efforts to expand the boundaries of the welfare state were defeated by a combination of lobbyists, the congressional bipartisan conservative coalition, an apathetic citizenry, and his own ineffective leadership. But he succeeded in updating and expanding many existing programs, and Truman thereby helped assimilate the New Deal into the vital center of American life. The Fair Deal was a centrist variant of liberal reformism that presaged the New Frontier and Great Society reforms of the 1960s.

During the midterm elections of 1950, the Republicans picked up twenty-eight seats in the House and gained five senators. Although still nominally controlled by the Democrats, the Eighty-second Congress saw the bipartisan conservative bloc grow more powerful than it had been in the Eighty-first. The Fair Deal lost momentum, and no new social legislation of any consequence was enacted in 1951 or 1952. Social reform was submerged by Cold War concerns and growing public complacency about domestic institutions. Truman spent much of the last two years of his presidency focused on foreign policy and the Korean War. He also was on the defensive much of the time, trying to defend his floundering government against mounting Republican charges that his administration had been infiltrated by Communists and was riddled with corruption.

Republican charges that corruption was rampant in the Truman administration stemmed from irregularities unearthed in several government agencies that involved minor officials. The "mess in Washington" never reached Truman personally, but one of the accused "influence peddlers" turned out to be Harry Vaughn, the head of the notorious Missouri gang and military aide to the president. Vaughn had been given a home freezer allegedly for using his influence on behalf of clients who had business with federal agencies. The wife of an official with the Reconstruction Finance Corporation (RFC), which loaned money to banks and insurance companies, was given a mink coat. The coat was a gift from an executive with a company that borrowed funds from the RFC on very favorable terms. Scandals in the Internal Revenue Service (IRS) forced several officials to resign from their positions and led to an administrative overhaul of the agency.

The corruption infesting Truman's administration appeared to be confined to a handful of low-level officials at the periphery of power and influence. Nevertheless, when the wrongdoing was exposed, many American were shocked and angry. Republicans got a lot of partisan political mileage out of the Truman scandals. In the wake of these damaging exposés, public support for the Truman administration, never very high, plummeted to historic lows. One Gallup Poll gave Truman an approval rating of only 23 percent, the lowest rating ever given to a sitting president.

RED SCARE

As a result of the growing hostility between the United States and the Soviet Union, frustrations, tensions, and anxieties gripped the American people. The Cold War hit home in early 1950, when millions of Americans were alarmed by charges that Communists had infiltrated their government and many other institutions. Fears of internal threats posed by Communists long preceded the Cold War era. They first surfaced in the decade of the 1850s and flared periodically during times of social tension and political upheaval. Following World War I, jittery Americans worried that a Bolshevik-style uprising would occur in America. The Red Scare of 1919 and 1920 had culminated in government raids on the homes and meeting places of suspected revolutionaries, followed by mass deportations of radical aliens. In 1938, Southern opponents of New Deal agricultural policies established the House Committee on Un-American Activities (HUAC), chaired by Martin Dies. Dies and his colleagues accused New Deal farm officials of marching to Moscow's beat. In 1940, Congress enacted the Smith Act, which made it a federal crime for anyone to advocate the overthrow of the government.

Neither the Palmer raids nor HUAC's accusations of the late 1930s were justified, but fears of government subversion by Communists arising after 1945 had a basis in reality. During the late 1930s and early 1940s, U.S. government security procedures had been lax. Communists had infiltrated virtually all important federal agencies, and hundreds actively spied for the Soviets. Unfortunately, during this Second Red Scare, opportunistic politicians exploited the popular fear of Communism to enhance their power. They exaggerated the Communist menace, harmed innocent people, confused and divided Americans, and threatened basic political freedoms.

The drive to root Communists out of government agencies began in 1945. The Office of Strategic Services (OSS), a wartime intelligence agency, discovered that some of its classified documents had been delivered to Soviet agents. In February 1946, a Canadian investigating commission exposed the operation of Soviet spy rings within Canada and the United States that had given the Soviets military and atomic secrets. Investigators documented subversion that had occurred during the war.

These spy revelations, coming at a time when U.S.–Soviet relations were deteriorating, energized Washington. President Truman issued an executive order on March 21, 1947, establishing a loyalty program for federal employees. Truman also directed the Attorney General to publish a list of ninety organizations that were considered disloyal to the United States. Truman's efforts resulted in 2,900 resignations and 379 dismissals from various federal agencies. Although federal investigators found no spies, the Truman loyalty program heightened rather than calmed public fears of subversion.

Congress also actively hunted subversives. In October 1947, HUAC, with rookie congressman Richard Nixon as its junior member, launched a sensational two-week-long investigation of Hollywood to see whether the film industry had been subverted by Reds. The actor Ronald Reagan, president of the Screen Actors Guild (SAG), appeared before the committee to defend the loyalty of the film industry. For anyone familiar with the ways of Hollywood, the notion that Communist Party members had inserted Communist propaganda into movies that brainwashed the children of America as they sat innocently in their corner neighbor theaters munching popcorn on Saturday afternoons was absurd. No doubt, a few Communists and fellow travelers were working in Hollywood during the 1940s, but they worked for studio heads, not for Moscow. As writer Murray Kempton observed, it was Hollywood that corrupted the Communists, not vice versa.

Nevertheless, HUAC's investigation of the movie colony made for great political theater, and it generated tremendous national attention. Although they found little evidence of celluloid Communism, HUAC subpoenaed a group of ten writers, directors, and actors who were or had been members of the Communist Party USA. They refused to answer any questions about their political beliefs and lectured committee members about civil liberties.

The "Hollywood Ten's" confrontational tactics confirmed committee suspicions that they were disciplined Stalinists determined to disseminate agitprop through the movies. The studio heads, already worried about dropping box office receipts for their films, panicked. They considered the congressional investigation and the performance of the Hollywood Ten a public relations disaster. The moguls blacklisted the ten radicals. No studios would hire them until they agreed to cooperate with HUAC. They refused, and all went to jail for contempt of Congress.

During the early 1950s, the blacklist grew dramatically and extended to Broadway, radio, and television. For several years, government investigators, private vigilante groups, and political conservatives working within the entertainment industry continually accused various actors, writers, and directors of past membership in the Communist Party or in Communist front organizations. Fearing box-office disaster, loss of advertising revenue, and drops in audience ratings, Broadway producers and network executives were no more willing than the film bosses had been to resist political pressures and protect the accused performers.

Those who were accused came under tremendous pressure to repudiate their radical pasts. They confronted a painful choice: They could defy their inquisitors and risk being blacklisted, or they could cooperate with the authorities by recanting their radical beliefs and naming names, that is, providing investigators with the names of individuals they had known from party or front activities. Some defied the committee and were blacklisted. Others such as Elia Kazan and Burl Ives named names and continued to work in the entertainment business. Altogether, about 250 people were blacklisted; many of these blacklistees never worked again in show business.

In the aftermath of Truman's loyalty program and HUAC's Hollywood investigations, a great fear of anyone who was thought to be disloyal spread across the land. In such a paranoid atmosphere, teachers and professors were fired for expressing dissenting views. Books were removed from library shelves. Parent-Teacher Association (PTA) leaders were attacked as subversives. The Boy Scouts and Campfire Girls came under suspicion for their advocacy of world peace and understanding. Liberal ministers were harassed. School districts required teachers and administrators to sign loyalty oaths. Many states enacted legislation denying public employment to Communists or to anyone affiliated with any organization that showed up on the attorney general's list.

Those who waged the domestic Cold War in the name of national security often undermined the democratic rights and intellectual freedoms for whose sake the United States waged the Cold War against the Soviet Union. The idea that a free society, tolerant of wide-ranging discussions and rigorous criticism of American institutions might be the best defense against the spread of Communism in the United States appeared to be an alien notion to those engaged in the quest for internal security. During the early 1950s, to many an enthusiastic Red hunter of that era, it became necessary to destroy freedom in order to save it.

The domestic Cold War also engulfed the trade union movement. Within the ranks of the CIO, Communist Party members or individuals supportive of the Communist Party program held leadership positions in many of the affiliated unions. Often these Communist labor leaders had been skilled organizers who had helped build the CIO unions. The Communists had risen to positions of power within the ranks of labor because they were committed trade unionists. Most of the rank-and-file members of these Communist-led unions were either indifferent or hostile to Communism.

In 1948, Philip Murray, head of the CIO, fearing his organization's vulnerability to attack by powerful antiunion forces for having Communist leaders, began to purge the CIO of its Communist influences. Within a year, eleven unions had been expelled from the CIO, and its membership fell from 5.2 million to about 3.7 million.

In 1949, the Truman administration went after the leadership of the American Communist Party. The Justice Department put the top leaders of the party on trial for allegedly violating the Smith Act. They were convicted, and the Supreme Court upheld the verdicts. After the Court had sustained the convictions of the top leaders, the Justice Department prosecuted dozens of lesser figures within the Communist movement over the next several years.

Truman's loyalty program did not quiet popular fears of Communist subversion, nor did it prevent Republicans from exploiting the Communists-in-government issue. One event severely damaged the reputation of the Truman administration. In 1949, after the most famous political trial in American history, Alger Hiss was ostensibly convicted of perjury, but in reality, he was convicted for having been a Communist spy.

Hiss, allegedly a participant in a Soviet espionage ring during the late 1930s, had risen to become an assistant secretary of state. He had been an adviser at Yalta and had chaired the founding sessions of the United Nations in San Francisco. He left the State Department in 1947 to become president of the Carnegie Endowment for International Peace. Outwardly, Hiss's public career had been that of a model New Deal bureaucrat. However, prior to leaving the government, he had already come under suspicion.

Hiss's downfall came in 1948, when Whittaker Chambers, a confessed former courier in the same spy ring to which Hiss had allegedly belonged, appeared before the HUAC. In a closed session he accused Hiss of having been a Communist spy while working for the State Department in 1937 and 1938. He offered no evidence to substantiate his charges. In a later HUAC session, Hiss confronted Chambers and threatened him with a libel suit if he dared to make his accusations public. Chambers appeared on the television show *Face the Nation* and repeated his charge that Hiss was a former Communist spy. Hiss denied the charge and filed his libel suit. Many prominent public figures backed Hiss and dismissed the charges against him. Among HUAC members, only Richard Nixon, who believed that Hiss was lying, initially backed Chambers' unsubstantiated charges.

To defend himself against Hiss's libel suit, Chambers produced evidence: microfilm copies of sixty-five classified State Department documents, which Chambers claimed Hiss had passed to him in 1937 and 1938 to give to Soviet agents. A federal grand jury could only indict Hiss for perjury because the statute of limitations on espionage had expired. Hiss was tried twice, his first trial having ended with a hung jury. During the second trial, the prosecution established that many of the documents had crossed Hiss's desk at the State Department and had been copied on Hiss's typewriter by his wife Priscilla. Hiss was convicted and sentenced to five years in prison.

Hiss was HUAC's greatest catch and vaulted Richard Nixon into national prominence. Many liberals believed that Hiss was innocent, framed by a conspiracy of vindictive conservative politicians. But the Hiss conviction, more than any other event of the domestic Cold War, convinced millions of Americans that there was truth to the oft-made Republican charges that Roosevelt and Truman had not been sufficiently alert to the dangers of Communist espionage. Americans worried about

FIGURE 3.3 The Red Scare of the late 1940s gave Richard Nixon, an obscure young congressman from California, his chance to become nationally prominent. He is shown here with Robert Stripling, chief investigator for the House Committee on Un-American Activities, examining some of the microfilm evidence that led to Alger Hiss's perjury convictions. *Source:* Corbis/Bettmann.

other undetected Communist agents who might still be working at the State Department and other government agencies.

Other events shook the Truman administration. The FBI caught Judith Coplon, a Justice Department employee, passing information to a Soviet agent. In 1949, the Soviets exploded an atomic device, ending the U.S. nuclear monopoly. Soon after this shock came the Communist victory in China. The stage was set for the emergence of a demagogue: widespread fear of a hidden enemy thought to be everywhere, and frustration that victory in the World War II had brought not eternal peace but Cold War and the possibility of a nuclear holocaust.

Enter Senator Joseph McCarthy. In 1950, casting about for an issue that might get him reelected, he decided to see if he could get any political mileage out of the Communists-in-government issue. Although he was something of a latecomer to the issue, McCarthy quickly became the political star of the domestic Cold War. He retained his top billing until his Senate colleagues destroyed him politically in late 1954.

McCarthy opened his anti-Communist campaign on February 9, 1950, in Wheeling, West Virginia. He told the Ladies' Republican Club of Wheeling that the United States found itself in a weak position in the Cold War because of the actions of disloyal officials in the State Department. Holding up a piece of paper in his right hand, he apparently told his fascinated audience that "I have in my hand" a list of 205 names of Communists working at the State Department. Further, he charged that some of them were in policy-making positions, and their names were known to the Secretary of State. The media carried McCarthy's sensational charges of Communists working in the State Department. Quickly, the obscure young politician captured the limelight; soon the entire nation knew of his accusations.

The Democratic leadership in the Senate, responding to McCarthy's charges, convened a subcommittee headed by one its most powerful members, Maryland senator Millard Tydings, to investigate McCarthy's accusations. The Tydings committee quickly demonstrated that McCarthy not only did not have 205 names, he did not have even the name of one Communist employed in the State Department. Undaunted, McCarthy then accused Owen Lattimore, a prominent expert on Far Eastern affairs, of being the leader of "the espionage ring in the State Department." At the time McCarthy accused him, Lattimore did not work for the State Department. Lattimore denied under oath that he was or had ever been a Communist or had ever espoused the Communist line. McCarthy's charges against Lattimore also collapsed. In a public report issued in July 1950, the Tydings committee dismissed McCarthy's charges as a "fraud and a hoax."

Such setbacks at the outset of his campaign might have derailed a less nervy politician, but McCarthy persisted. Most Republican members of Congress backed McCarthy. They sensed that the "Communists in government" issue could pay political dividends. Frustrated and embittered by their losses in the 1948 elections, Republicans hoped that the politics of anti-Communism could be the vehicle that would carry them to power in 1950 and 1952. Conservative Democrats from the South and the West also took up the politics of anti-Communism.

Congress enacted the McCarran Internal Security Act in September 1950 over President Truman's veto. The act required that all Communist and Communist-front organizations register with the Attorney General's office. It also forbade Communists from working in defense factories and prohibited them from traveling abroad on an American passport. Congress enacted another strong anti-Communist measure in 1952, again, over Truman's veto, the McCarran–Walter Act, which forbade Communists and other "undesirables" from entering the country.

The 1950 elections confirmed the Republicans' hunch that they had found a popular issue. In California, Richard Nixon won a seat in the Senate by calling his liberal Democratic opponent,

Helen Gahaghan Douglas, "the pink lady." Several prominent liberal Democrats went down in defeat, including Senator Tydings. McCarthy quickly became one of his party's most popular campaigners.

McCarthy and his fellow practitioners of the politics of anti-Communism soon acquired a vast following among a public primed by the Hiss case and frustrated by the Korean War. McCarthy stayed on the political offensive. He kept making unsubstantiated charges and naming names. He implied guilt by association, and he told outright lies. It was impossible to keep up with his accusations or to pin him down. He could never be put on the defensive. If one set of charges was dismissed as bogus, he was soon back with another. He called Secretary of State Acheson the "Red Dean of the State Department." He denounced George Marshall, a man with a distinguished record of public service, as a liar and a traitor. McCarthy was always careful to make his charges when shielded by his senatorial cloak of immunity, which prevented his victims from suing him for libel. His smear tactics and his use of the "big lie" technique added a new word to the American political lexicon—"McCarthyism."

Several factors accounted for McCarthy's spectacular success. The ground had been prepared by years of Cold War conflict with the Soviet Union, and by politicians who had dramatized the issue, frightening Americans with their accounts of the hidden enemy within.

Alarms raised by politicians were seconded by prominent media editorials. McCarthy's sense of timing, his ruthless tactics, and his demagogic ability to voice the fears of many ordinary American citizens all strengthened his cause. He made skillful use of the news media. Radio and television newscasts carried his charges. Newspapers headlined his accusations. Millions of Americans, frightened by revelations of real espionage, found McCarthy's lies plausible.

McCarthy's popularity also came from his being the man with a simple, plausible explanation for America's Cold War setbacks: Communists and liberals who secretly supported the Communists had undermined American foreign policy from within. Traitors working within the State Department and other government agencies were responsible for Communist Cold War triumphs. Millions of Americans believed him.

Events also played into McCarthy's hands. Two weeks after his Wheeling speech, British intelligence agents discovered an Anglo-American spy ring that had penetrated the atomic bomb project in New Mexico during 1944–1945. The key man in the ring had been a nuclear physicist, Dr. Klaus Fuchs, a German-born, naturalized British citizen assigned to the bomb project. He was arrested, and he confessed everything. He told the British that he had succeeded in delivering complete information on the bomb to Soviet agents. Using information from Fuchs's confession, FBI agents arrested his American accomplices, Harry Gold and David Greenglass. They in turn implicated Julius and Ethel Rosenberg. The Rosenbergs were tried for espionage, convicted, and executed in 1953. The stalemated Korean War also aided McCarthy significantly. As American morale sagged, he attacked those whom he called "the traitors and bunglers in the State Department who were losing the Cold War to the Communists."

When the Republicans regained control of the Senate as a result of the 1952 elections, McCarthy, now more powerful than ever, became the chairman of his own investigating committee. He continued his rampages in the State Department and other federal agencies. But in 1954, he overreached when he attacked the U.S. Army for allegedly harboring subversives. It was the beginning of the end for the nation's most formidable practitioner of the politics of anti-Communism.

Brief Bibliographic Essay

Alonzo L. Hamby's *Beyond the New Deal: Harry S. Truman and American Liberalism* is the most comprehensive account of postwar politics. Eric Goldman's *The Crucial Decade and After: America, 1945–1960* is a lively account of the Truman and Eisenhower years. William Berman's *The Politics of Civil Rights in the Truman Administration* is the most complete account of Truman's civil rights policies. An excellent recent study, Thomas Borstelmann's *The Cold War and the Color Line: American Race Relations in the Global Arena*, convincingly demonstrates that from 1945 to 1960 government officials working to end white supremacy were driven more by geopolitical considerations than by a quest for social justice. An excellent recent study of postwar economic policy is Robert M. Collins's *The Politics of Economic Growth in Postwar America*. David Brody's *Workers in Industrial Society* is the best account of postwar labor history. Richard Freeland's *The Truman Doctrine and the Origins of McCarthyism* is a good account of the origins of the Second Red Scare. The best account of the general issues of anti-Communism during the domestic Cold War is Earl Latham's *The Communist Controversy in Washington*. By far the best biography of the controversial senator from Wisconsin is *A Conspiracy So Immense: The World of Joe McCarthy* by David Oshinsky. Stephen J. Whitfield's *The Culture of the Cold War* recreates the atmosphere of the 1950s, when fear of international Communism pervaded American culture. Allen Weinstein's *Perjury: The Hiss-Chambers Case* is a brilliant study that argues persuasively that Hiss was a secret member of the Communist Party and was guilty of espionage. In recent years, a flood of books by researchers who have had access to the archives of the KGB and other agencies of the former Soviet Union, as well as recently declassified decryptions released by the U.S. National Security Agency (NSA), have been published. These studies demonstrate beyond argument that the Soviet penetration into American life, government, science, and industry during the 1930s and 1940s was deep, thorough, and hostile. The NSA decryptions, also known as the "Venona Papers," also show that hundreds of members of the American Communist Party (CPUSA) spied for their Soviet masters. The most informative of these books is *Venona: Decoding Soviet Espionage in America* by John Earl Haynes and Harvey Klehr.

4

The Affluent Society

At mid-twentieth century, a majority of American families enthusiastically participated in a culture of abundance and leisure. The world's most productive economy generated a cornucopia of consumer goods that crowded the shelves and display racks of supermarkets and stores everywhere. Millions of working-class families owned those twin symbols of American affluence—a home in the suburbs and a gleaming new automobile. Americans at mid-century were the most mobile people on the planet. By the millions, families moved from the cities to the suburbs. From the Northeast and the Upper Midwest, they moved to the dynamic states of the Sunbelt region.

DEMOGRAPHIC PATTERNS

The postwar "baby boom" caused a tremendous population increase, as returning veterans and their wives made up for lost time. The American population grew from 153 million in 1950 to 179 million in 1960, the second-largest decennial increase ever. In 1957, 4.3 million births were recorded, the highest one-year total in American history. That year, demographers discovered that over fifty million Americans were age fourteen or younger. These young baby boomers created powerful demands for new houses, appliances, bicycles, toys, and diapers. During the decade of the 1950s, the number of youngsters enrolled in schools grades K–12 increased from twenty-eight million to forty-two million. More new schools were constructed during the 1950s, mostly in the burgeoning suburban communities surrounding central cities, than had been built during the first fifty years of the twentieth century. As the U.S. birthrate shot up, the death rate fell. Americans added five years to their median life expectancy during the 1950s, and death rates among young people declined dramatically as well. New "miracle drugs" such as penicillin and cortisone took much of the pain and misery out of life. Polio vaccines tamed a cruel childhood disease that often left its victims crippled and helpless for life.

Suburban growth, underway in the late 1940s, exploded during the 1950s. Millions of families seeking new homes and jobs or just fleeing from myriad urban problems moved from metropolitan centers to outlying communities. By the end of the decade, the suburban population of sixty million equaled that of the rest of urban America. During the 1950s, most large cities within the United States lost population. Of cities with more than one million people, only Los Angeles grew significantly during the decade. The flight to the suburbs transformed living patterns for millions of middle-class families at mid-century.

Americans in the 1950s were not only the richest and healthiest generation ever, they also were the most mobile. Regionally, the American population continued its shift west and south. Families poured into the South, the Southwest, and the West. California, Florida, and Texas added millions of new residents. Soon the Sunbelt encompassed most of the southern rim of the nation, from Southern California to Florida. Americans moved in search of better jobs and business opportunities and the more spacious lifestyles that were possible in Sunbelt suburbs. The economic foundations of the Sunbelt's spectacular population boom included agribusiness, aerospace, electronics, oil, real estate, and a large infusion of military spending. Low taxes and right-to-work laws also attracted industry to the southern rim. Rural America continued to lose population during the 1950s. The depopulation of the countryside, a demographic trend that had accelerated during the years of World War II, continued into the 1950s.

AN ECONOMY OF ABUNDANCE

Federal subsidies stimulated economic growth during the 1950s and enabled millions of working-class families to achieve middle-class status. Washington dispensed billions of dollars annually as welfare payments, Social Security checks, and payments to farmers. Congress funded over half of the nation's industrial research and development and over half of all university scientific research. The Federal Reserve Board regulated the money supply and interest rates. Other government bureaucracies regulated the securities and communications industries, interstate transportation, and aviation. During the 1950s, military budgets pumped $40 billion to $50 billion a year into the economy, and government spending as a percentage of the GDP increased steadily. The number of Americans working for government at all levels increased by 50 percent during this decade. The prosperity of many locales became dependent on government purchases or government payrolls.

Americans during the 1950s celebrated what they were fond of calling the "American free enterprise system." But economic reality was more complex than what their simplistic rhetorical labels implied. Out of their efforts to battle the Great Depression and to produce the materials needed to win World War II, Americans had fashioned a mixed economy that blended public and private enterprise. Government spending and regulatory activities had become integral elements of the U.S. economy. The mixed economy conformed to no economic model or theory. Most Americans did not understand its nature or how it worked, but they were delighted with its prime creation—an affluent society.

Between 1945 and 1960, the GDP doubled. During the 1950s, the American economy grew at an average rate of 4.0 percent per year, despite enduring periodic recessions. Between 1946 and 1960, the American workforce grew from 54 million to 68 million jobholders. Median wages in manufacturing industries rose 60 percent, and median family income rose from $3,000 to $5,700 during that same period. Since the rate of inflation remained low, about 2 percent per annum for the decade of the 1950s, wage increases translated into significant gains in purchasing power and rising standards of living. Unemployment rates remained low, averaging around 4 percent in the

1950s. During this decade, millions of Americans could afford goods and services that would have been beyond their means previously. The rapidly growing American economy generated a widespread abundance that became the envy of the world. During the 1950s, the United States, with about 5 percent of the world's population, consumed over one-third of its goods and services.

Credit significantly enhanced consumer purchasing power. Short-term installment credit, mainly for new cars, increased fivefold from 1946 to 1960. A revolution in spending patterns got underway in 1950, when the Diners' Club introduced the general credit card, soon followed by American Express. During this decade, oil companies and department stores issued millions of revolving credit cards. Private debt within the affluent society climbed from $73 billion to $200 billion during the decade of the 1950s. Consumer demand stimulated huge private sector investment in new plant capacity and new technology, an average of $10 billion per year. Automation, the use of self-regulating machines to control manufacturing operations, enhanced the nation's industrial productivity and improved the quality of products.

Big business grew bigger during the postwar era. Another wave of mergers swept the industrial economy. By 1960, America's 200 largest industrial corporations owned over half of the nation's industrial assets. But unlike the merger waves of the 1890s and 1920s, which joined businesses within the same economic sectors, the 1950s' mergers brought together businesses in unrelated fields. Conglomerates such as International Telephone and Telegraph (ITT) linked a car rental company, a home construction company, a retail food outlet, a hotel chain, and an insurance company under the same corporate roof.

The manufacture of automobiles remained the most important American industry during the 1950s. New car and truck sales averaged seven million units annually during the decade. By 1960, there were seventy million vehicles on the nation's roads and highways. Two-thirds of the nation's employees commuted to work by car. The number of service stations, garages, motels, and the size of the oil industry all expanded with autos.

The growth of suburbia and the automobile boom occurred together. Suburbia required automobiles. Mothers driving station wagons, piled full of kids on their way to school, shopping centers, or team practice, became the reigning symbol of the 1950s' suburban lifestyle.

Congress enacted the National Interstate and Defense Highways Act of 1956. By the 1970s, the program had become the largest single public works program in American history, building over 10,000 miles of highways at a cost of approximately $75 billion. New taxes on gasoline, oil, tires, buses, and trucks funded the road-building projects on a pay-as-you-go basis. Federal subsidies for instate highway construction provided a powerful stimulus to both the auto and suburb-building industries. The social landscape of America was transformed during the 1950s and 1960s with motels, fast-food restaurants, and other businesses serving an increasingly motorized consumer public. The new social networks also accelerated the decline of urban mass transit and of older cities. They also provided Americans with the world's finest roads and one of the worst public transit systems.

As the numbers of cars on the roads multiplied, they became longer, wider, more powerful, and gaudier. Detroit reached its pinnacle in the late 1950s. Automakers outdid themselves, creating chromium ornaments, two- and three-tone color combinations, soaring tail fins, and gas-guzzling V-8 engines. The buying public was delighted with Detroit's offerings, which also included wraparound windshields, power steering, automatic transmissions, air conditioning, and hi-fi radios.

Advertisers stressed the power, the flashiness, and even the sex appeal of these elaborate machines. Dinah Shore appeared on television to sing, "See the U.S.A. in your Chevrolet." What was more American than apple pie, mom, and your new Chevrolet? Domestic automakers had

FIGURE 4.1   A big gleaming new car was one of the supreme status symbols of the affluent society. Here a 1954 Buick Super Riviera shines in all of its glory.   *Source:* National Archives and Records Administration.

the American market all to themselves; imports accounted for less than 1 percent of sales in 1955. Gas was cheap and plentiful at 25¢ to 30¢ per gallon. A big, gleaming new car was one of the supreme status symbols of the affluent society, a shining testament to America's technological world supremacy. Subsequent generations would have to deal with the decay of mass transit, the decline of smog-choked inner cities, and freeway gridlock.

The chemical industry grew even faster than the auto business during the 1950s. Du Pont's slogan, "Better things for better living through chemistry," became known to every television viewer. Du Pont, Dow, and the other chemical giants turned out a never-ending feast of new synthetic products—aerosol spray cans, Dacron, and new plastics like vinyl and Teflon.

Electricity and electronics also grew rapidly in the postwar era. A horde of new electric appliances sprang forth—air conditioners, electric blankets, automatic clothes washers, clothes dryers, and hair dryers. The electronics industry expanded mainly because of the advent of television. By the early 1950s, dealers were selling six million new TV sets each year. Other popular electronic products enjoyed wide sales during the 1950s. Almost every one of the nearly sixty million new cars sold in the decade had a radio. Transistors made possible the development of new computer technologies. International Business Machines (IBM) marketed its first mainframe computers, inaugurating the postindustrial age. In 1960, the Xerox corporation marketed its 914 copier, thereby inaugurating a revolution in document copying. The aerospace industry kept pace with other growth industries, stimulated by multibillion dollar contracts to supply the Pentagon with sophisticated military hardware. Air travel increased rapidly after 1945 and took a quantum leap forward in 1958 with the introduction of regularly scheduled commercial jet travel.

Although postwar growth industries flourished, some traditional heavy industries and manufacturing declined, such as railroads, coal mining, and textiles. Long-haul trucking and air travel cut heavily into railroad freight and passenger business. Coal could no longer compete with oil, natural gas, and electricity. Cotton and woolen manufacturers succumbed to synthetic fibers spun out by the chemical companies. Americans increasingly wore clothes made of nylon, orlon, and polyester. Industrial decline brought permanent depression to New England mill towns and Appalachia, creating pockets of poverty amidst general affluence.

Agriculture changed drastically in the postwar years. Farmers produced more food than consumers could buy, and commodity prices dropped. Profits could be made in farming only by reducing unit costs of production through intensive use of fertilizers, pesticides, expensive farm machinery, and sophisticated managerial techniques. Larger farms prospered from a combination of greater efficiency and government subsidies. Small farmers got squeezed out and joined the rural exodus to the cities. The nation's farm population dropped from twenty-five million at the end of the war to fourteen million in 1960. The number of agricultural workers dropped to just 6 percent of the workforce. In regions of Arizona, Florida, and California, huge corporate farms replaced family farms.

LABOR AT MID-CENTURY

Organized labor prospered during the 1950s, as trade unions won significant wage increases and new fringe benefits from corporate employers. The United Auto Workers and General Motors agreed to a clause in their contract calling for automatic annual cost-of-living adjustments in wages. That agreement set a pattern soon copied in other industries and occupations. Corporate managers discovered that it was more profitable to negotiate wage increases with union representatives and to pass their increased costs on to consumers than to engage in lengthy strikes with strong unions.

Organized labor remained a powerful force within the Democratic Party that normally controlled Congress during the 1950s. George Meany declared in 1955, "American labor never had it so good." Labor's major achievement was to bring about the merger of the AFL and CIO in 1955. The creation of the AFL-CIO brought 90 percent of America's eighteen million trade unionists into a single national labor federation, headed by Meany.

Although unions generally prospered during the 1950s, they also faced serious problems. Corruption riddled several of them. Senator John McClellan of Arkansas chaired a senate committee that investigated union racketeering in 1957. The McClellan committee exposed widespread corruption in the Teamsters Union. Robert "Bobby" Kennedy served as chief counsel for the committee, and his brother Senator John F. Kennedy also served on the committee. They found that Teamster officials had involved themselves in a wide range of crooked activities, including the misappropriation of union funds, rigged elections, extortion, and association with members of organized crime. Committee investigations led to the enactment of the Landrum–Griffin Act in 1959. This moderate labor reform measure imposed new legal restrictions on unions, and expanded the list of union unfair labor practices. It also contained anticorruption provisions to safeguard democratic election procedures within unions and to make misuse of union funds a federal crime.

Trade unions also confronted a more fundamental problem than racketeering during the late 1950s. Union membership peaked in 1956 at 18.6 million and declined thereafter. The proportion of the workforce that belonged to unions declined mainly because of the loss of jobs in heavy industry. The American economy continued to grow and prosper after 1958, but organized labor could not keep pace. Many industries moved to the South to take advantage of lower wage levels and a nonunion workforce. But even where unions remained strong, workers were less inclined to join them than before, primarily because, without joining, they received the higher wages and benefits that union negotiators had obtained. Most important, the economy was shifting from a production orientation to a service orientation, which meant a shift from blue-collar occupations to white-collar jobs.

Most of the new job growth in the 1950s economy occurred in the service, clerical, and managerial sectors. In 1956, for the first time in American economic history, white-collar workers outnumbered blue-collar workers in the workforce. White-collar workers generally resisted the efforts of union organizers in the 1950s. As white-collar jobs multiplied in the growth sectors of the economy, technological innovations eliminated jobs in mining, manufacturing, and transportation.

A few unions did organize categories of white-collar employees, the most successful being the American Federation of State, County, and Municipal Employees (AFSCME), whose members worked for various state and local government agencies. Since the 1950s, the most dynamic sectors of the trade union movement have been the public employee unions. By the early 1970s, over four million civil service employees, postal employees, teachers, police, and firefighters had joined public employee unions. Public employee union leaders constituted one of the most important power blocs within the Democratic Party during the early years of the twenty-first century.

POVERTY AMIDST PLENTY

Although the majority of American families were eager participants in the economy of abundance, millions of their fellow citizens were mired in poverty. In 1960, according to the Bureau of Labor statistics, forty million Americans representing approximately 25 percent of the population were poor. The elderly, people over sixty-five, made up one-fourth of the poor. One-fifth were nonwhite, including nearly half of African Americans. Two-thirds of the poor inhabited households headed by a person with an eighth-grade education or less. One-fourth of poor people lived in a household headed by a single woman.

The poor congregated in the inner cities, as middle-class people fled to the suburbs. Between 1945 and 1960, over three million black people, most of them unskilled and many of them illiterate, moved to Northern and Western cities from the rural South. Poor whites from Appalachia joined blacks in this migration from the country to the cities. Many poor people also inhabited rural America in the 1950s. Both white and black tenant farmers and sharecroppers remained trapped in a life cycle of poverty and hard work. A famous television documentary shown in 1960, *The Harvest of Shame*, narrated by Edward R. Murrow, depicted the poverty and hopelessness of migrant farmworkers.

One of the major causes of poverty in America lay in the fact that wealth remained highly concentrated. In 1960, the richest 1 percent of the population owned one-third of the national wealth. The wealthiest 5 percent of America's families owned over half of the nation's wealth. Some of the poverty in mid-century America could be attributed to the failure of the welfare state forged during the New Deal era to provide for poor people. Its benefits had mostly gone to groups that were organized to make demands on Congress. The Wagner Act did nothing for nonunion workers. Minimum wage laws and Social Security benefits did not extend to millions of low-income workers in dozens of occupations.

Women made up a large percentage of poor Americans at mid-century. Few well-paying jobs were open to them in the 1950s. A greater portion of women's jobs than men's jobs was not covered by minimum wage or Social Security protection. Also, divorced women usually were saddled with major child-rearing responsibilities. Ex-husbands often failed to make child support payments, and many divorced women with children slipped into poverty.

Few people showed much interest in the plight of poor Americans during the 1950s. Publicists focused on celebrating the achievements of the affluent majority. The poor themselves lacked organizations and articulate leaders to call attention to their problems. They inhabited another America outside the boundaries of affluence.

SUBURBAN SPRAWL

America experienced the greatest internal population movement in its history in the fifteen years following World War II, when forty million Americans fled the cities for the suburbs. Young white middle-class people led the flight to the suburbs. They fled traffic jams, high taxes, contact with racial minorities, overcrowded schools, high real estate prices, and high crime rates. Suburbia beckoned for many reasons: the obvious attraction of open country, where spacious houses could be built for a fraction of what big-city construction would cost, and the lure of homes with yards where, as one father put it, a kid could "grow up with grass stains on his pants." Suburban homes also promised the privacy and quiet not found in crowded noisy city apartments. Many suburban-ites also sought a community of like-minded people and accessible local government.

The rapid rise of suburbia in the postwar era occurred because of an alliance between the federal government and the private sector. Low-interest mortgages requiring little or no down payments and tax subsidies produced a postwar housing boom. A burst of federally funded highway construction connected the central cities with surrounding bedroom communities.

Across the country, developers busily tossed up new housing tracts, wiping out forests, bean fields, fruit orchards, and grazing lands. By 1960, over 60 percent of American families owned their homes, the most significant accomplishment of the affluent society. Businesses also moved to the suburbs in response to the growing suburban markets. Suburban shopping centers multiplied. The first fully enclosed shopping mall, Southdale Center, opened in a suburb of Minneapolis on October 8, 1956. By 1960, there were 3,840 such centers sprawled across the nation, transforming shopping patterns throughout the country.

Using mass-production and mass-merchandising techniques, William Levitt built Levittown on Long Island, 30 miles east of New York City. Between 1947 and 1951, Levitt built 17,000 homes, along with 7 village greens and shopping centers, 14 playgrounds, 9 swimming pools, 2 bowling alleys, and a town hall—on 1,500 acres where farmers had only recently grown potatoes. Other Levittowns soon appeared in Bucks County, Pennsylvania, and Willingboro, New Jersey.

The Levittowns were immediate successes; tens of thousands of young families, many of them headed by veterans, left their rented city apartments and joined the rush to the suburbs. But social critics made the Levittown concept stand as a metaphor for the postwar failings of American suburban society. According to urbanist Lewis Mumford, Levittown represented a culture of "ticky-tacky." It was inhabited by people of the same class, the same tastes, who watched the same pallid fare on television and ate the same bland prefabricated foods.

Mumford's indictment of Levittown was not so much inaccurate as beside the point. Levittown appealed to the mass of ordinary American families precisely because it was reassuring as well as affordable. Levitt observed, "Critics don't live in Levittowns, people do." Although suburbs tended to be internally homogeneous, they were typically differentiated along social and economic lines. Suburbs were identified as working class, middle class, or enclaves of upper middle-class fami-lies. Analysts of suburban culture observed that ethnic identities attenuated in suburbia; in that sense suburbs tended to make people more homogeneous. Suburban community identities were based more on shared styles of consumption than on ethnic ancestry or cultural background.

Suburbanization separated Americans racially. Most African American and Hispanic families were left behind in big cities as white families headed for the suburbs. The developer of Levittown initially put a whites-only clause in both his lease and his sales contracts. The national metropolitan pattern became one of predominantly black cities encircled by white suburbs. The 1960 census showed suburbia to be 98 percent white; it also showed that some of the nation's larger cities—Washington, D.C., Newark, Richmond, and Atlanta—had black majorities. As white middle-class

FIGURE 4.2 Levittown, Long Island, New York, U.S.A., during the 1950s. *Source:* National Archives and Records Administration.

people moved out of the central cities, tax bases shrunk, social services shriveled, and crime rates soared. Suburban sprawl represented the geography of inequality. One consequence of the white flight to suburbia that left African Americans trapped in deteriorating inner cities was the fiery urban riots during the long hot summers of 1965 to 1968.

WOMEN: FAMILY AND WORK

During the 1950s, the family was the most rapidly growing American social institution. These new families held down well-paying jobs, purchased suburban homes, and made the consumer purchases that kept the mighty U.S. economy growing. American families became more child-oriented during the 1950s. Dr. Benjamin Spock advised women to make child rearing their most important task, to put their children's needs first. Early editions of Spock's book also advised women to stay at home and not to work outside of the home so that they would be available to meet all of their babies' needs.

Some psychiatrists, influenced by Sigmund Freud's writings, criticized working women. To these writers, the independent woman was an oxymoron. They claimed that women could be fulfilled and happy only through domesticity. Dr. Marynia Farnham's influential *Modern Woman: The Lost Sex* considered women who held jobs outside the home to be neurotic feminists trying to be "imitation men." Farnham and other writers assumed that a woman's gender determined her role in life. Anatomy was destiny. At the core of this "feminine mystique" was the idea that women constituted the foundation of society. Women made the home a haven from the stress of the competitive business world. Women in their roles as wives and mothers did necessary and noble work, and in the process they fulfilled their feminine destinies.

In 1956, *Life* published a special issue on American women. It profiled housewife Marjorie Sutton as a successful woman who fulfilled her feminine potential. She was mother, wife, home manager, and hostess. She was active in the PTA, the Campfire Girls, and charity work. Sutton had four children, and she did all of the cooking, cleaning, and sewing for her family. She chauffeured her large brood of children wherever they needed to go. She also helped her husband's career by entertaining his business clients. Marjorie Sutton fulfilled the official feminine ideology of the 1950s, the suburban wifely counterpart to her husband, the organization man.

Films of the 1950s highlighted sex symbols such as Marilyn Monroe or wholesome heroines such as Doris Day. Both movie stars served as role models for women. Women's fashions stressed femininity at the expense of practicality or comfort. There were strong pressures on women to conform to the prevailing sexual stereotype. During the decade, no organized feminist movement existed to challenge the prevailing feminine mystique.

Mid-century women were caught in a dilemma. According to the prevalent ideology, the ideal role for a woman was found in the home. Her fulfillment lay in creating an island of love and security for her children and husband, with scant regard for her own needs. But studies of women, especially college-educated women, showed that many were unhappy with the constraints and lack of fulfillment in their lives, as defined by domesticity. They especially resented the lack of mental stimulation, the lack of any outlet for their academic skills and intellectual energies. The rise of social pathologies—of alcoholism and anomie among women who had fulfilled the cultural ideal of wife and mother—furnished additional evidence of their widespread stress and confusion.

Compounding the confusion over women's roles in mid-century society was the fact that millions of middle-class women had entered the labor markets. The female labor force expanded from seventeen million in 1946 to twenty-two million in 1958. By 1960, 40 percent of women were employed full-time or part-time. During the decade of the 1950s, female employment increased at a rate four times faster than male employment. By 1960, 30 percent of married women worked outside of the home. Despite the burgeoning cult of motherhood, most new entrants to the female job market during the 1950s were married women with children. Most of these married women workers were not pursuing full-time careers, were not competing with men, and were certainly not seeking equality in the workplace. Many worked part-time, and most took positions in clerical and other white-collar fields traditionally reserved for women, where pay and status were low and the prospects for promotion were slim.

In many instances, these married, middle-class women worked to supplement their families' incomes. Their contributions ensured a status and lifestyle for their families that was not attainable from their husbands' earnings alone. A sizable proportion of middle-class family incomes in the $12,000 to $15,000 per annum range during the 1950s was made possible by having two income earners. The wife's income made possible the purchase of a split-level suburban home in a fashionable neighborhood and the purchase of a second car or station wagon. These hardworking 1950s' middle-class women did not see a conflict between working outside of the home and maintaining their duties as wives and mothers. Most worked for a few years until their children were born, then quit their jobs until their children had become teenagers. They then reentered the workforce. These women, of course, deviated from the norms prescribed by the feminine mystique, from the roles played to perfection by the Marjorie Suttons of the 1950s.

Another factor strongly influencing family life and the roles of women during the 1950s was a consequence of American social history. Millions of American families during the 1950s were headed by men and women who had grown up amidst the economic deprivations of the Great Depression of the 1930s. They had been young adults during World War II, experiencing the

FIGURE 4.3   An office in New York City. Women at work during the 1950s.   *Source:* Brown Brothers.

loneliness and physical separation from friends and family inherent in military service in wartime. After experiencing fifteen years of economic and emotional insecurity, they were determined to enjoy the material security of the affluent society, and they were equally determined to have the emotional security found in a cohesive family life. These men and women made the baby boom and championed "togetherness." The term "togetherness" first appeared in a 1954 *McCalls* article. It meant a happy family melded into a team, specifically the woman fusing herself with her husband and children. Family life was oriented around shared activities—television watching, backyard barbecues, outings to parks and beaches, and traveling vacations.

CLASS AND STATUS

Sustained postwar economic growth allowed millions of Americans to increase their incomes, advance their occupational statuses, and improve their standards of living. During the 1950s, most Americans believed that their society offered hardworking individuals abundant opportunities—a better job, more profitable business ventures, or a college education. They also believed that enhanced occupational and social mobility operated to diminish social distinctions and to distribute income more evenly in mid-century America.

While it was undoubtedly true that 1950s American society was highly mobile and that many people found opportunities to enhance their wealth, status, and influence, it also remained in many important ways a class society. Wealth remained concentrated in the hands of a relatively small number of families at the top. Below the elite classes, Americans aligned themselves in strata markedly differentiated by wealth, culture, ethnoracial identities, political clout, legal protections, education, health, and patterns of recreation and leisure. At the bottom rungs of American society were the tens of millions of poor people, who had little formal education, money, status, or power, and only meager opportunities to acquire them.

Champions of the affluent society believed that it provided the ultimate counter to the ideological challenge posed by Communism during the Cold War. These pundits believed that Americans had eliminated class conflict, that ancient problem that had riven capitalistic societies for centuries. In the America of the 1950s, they argued, the "bourgeois" society included nearly everyone. Industrial workers were members in good standing of that vast middle class that constituted nearly the entire American society. By becoming a nation of middle-class families, Americans had attained social equality and had done so while maintaining an unprecedentedly high level of material well-being. Within America, it had not been necessary to dispossess the wealthy or to redistribute wealth, merely to let the solvents of economic growth and social mobility work their magic. The pie was so large that all could share in the abundance.

It was certainly true that unionized workers employed in the mass production industries made striking gains in job security and economic well-being during the 1950s. Many senior skilled workers earned larger incomes annually than many traditional middle-class office workers, teachers, and those in the service trades. Yet achieving middle-class incomes, buying a new car, and moving into Levittown did not necessarily mean that industrial workers adopted middle-class manners, attitudes, and values. The great American middle class remained split, if no longer along class lines, then along cultural lines. Working-class lifestyles in many instances remained distinct from middle-class suburban lifestyles.

Brief Bibliographic Essay

There are many fine books written about American economic and social history during the 1950s. Landon Y. Jones's *Great Expectations: America and the Baby Boom Generation* is the best study of one of the most important demographic development of postwar America. David Halberstam's *The Fifties* is a fine recent general study of the 1950s. John Kenneth Galbraith's *The Affluent Society* is a good analysis of postwar prosperity. John B. Rae's *The American Automobile* describes the car culture of the 1950s. Kenneth Jackson's *Crabgrass Frontier: The Suburbanization of the United States* provides a broad historical context for understanding postwar suburbanization. For women's roles during the 1950s, see Betty Friedan's famed *Feminine Mystique*. Elaine T. May's *Homeward Bound: American Families in the Cold War Era* is a thoughtful study linking family life with the tensions of living in the shadow of Cold War.

The Consumer Culture

Americans had evolved into an affluent middle-class society, based on consumerism fueled by credit buying on an unprecedented scale. The children of affluence created their own teen variant of the consumer culture, buying adolescent staples such as chewing gum, Cokes, hamburgers, clothes, and phonograph records. During the 1950s, television quickly established itself as the vital center of the new consumer culture.

During the 1950s, journalists, writers, and scholars developed a scathing critique of the culture of affluence: Many young people were growing up alienated and rebellious. They did not fit easily into the niches of the consumer society. As to the large majority who did fit in, critics found them to be suffering from a herd mentality; America had reared a generation of mindless conformists. Looking through the picture windows of suburban homes, critics could see that millions of middle-class Americans, displaying all of the outward trappings of affluence, found achieving the 1950s' version of the American Dream insufficient. Some of these troubled souls sought solace and meaning in religion, which enjoyed a major revival. America remained the most religious nation in the Western world. Others sought escape in popular music, sports, alcohol, and a frenetic social life. Many, worried about the possibility of nuclear annihilation, continued to live lives of quiet desperation. For millions of Americans in the 1950s, the age of affluence generated much tension, insecurity, and anxiety.

THE "TEEN CULTURE"

According to the *Dictionary of American Slang*, the United States is the only country that has a word to define young people between the ages of thirteen and nineteen, and is also the only country to consider it a distinct subculture having fads, fashions, influence, and purchasing power distinct from the world of grown-ups. Adult Americans paid unprecedented attention to teenagers during the 1950s. Teenagers themselves were often caught between the desire to carve out their own separate sphere and pressures to become an adult as quickly as possible. Teenagers during the 1950s were often in a hurry, a hurry to get in all the partying and rebelling they could before having to settle down, get married, and start raising families of their own in a culture that idealized domesticity in a suburban community.

Advertisers and merchandisers responded synergistically to these affluent teenagers who often had large disposable incomes and clear consumer preferences. Ray Kroc, a traveling salesman from Chicago, observed a drive-in restaurant in San Bernardino, California, that was doing a thriving business. It sold only hamburgers, french fries, and milk shakes, and it sold them cheap and fast. Its owners, Dick and Mac McDonald, had applied assembly-line, mass production technology to the preparation of food, and while doing so had invented the fast-food restaurant. With borrowed money, Kroc concluded a business arrangement with the McDonald brothers that permitted him to establish a chain of fast-food restaurants using their name and modeled on their format. The first McDonald's, complete with twin golden arches, sprang out of the prairie soil of Des Plaines, Illinois, a suburb of Chicago, on April 15, 1955. By the end of the decade, there were hundreds of McDonald's restaurants rapidly spreading across the country selling hamburgers for 15¢, french fries for 1 dime, and milk shakes for 20¢.

In the same year that Ray Kroc opened the first McDonald's fast-food restaurant in the Midwestern heartland, Walt Disney offered Disneyland, the first theme park, to American consumers. Disney sponsored a lavish telecast the night before Disneyland opened to the public. One of the emcees of the telecast was screen actor and television host Ronald Reagan. Disneyland, located in Anaheim, a suburb of Los Angeles, immediately attracted hordes of visitors, mostly families with children. It featured combinations of fairy-tale images derived from Disney's earlier animated masterpieces and sanitized historical images from his live-action films.

FIGURE 5.1 Affluent Americans at mid-century had more money to spend and more leisure time to enjoy than any previous generation. Here people flock to the beach at Coney Island for a day of sun and surf. *Source:* National Archives and Records Administration.

The Autopia ride was meant to be the major magnet when Disneyland first opened. Autopia was a miniature freeway with small cars for child drivers. Disney believed that it would not only be fun for kids but also would teach youngsters to be responsible adults behind the wheel. Within six weeks after opening, only six of the cars were drivable, the rest battered wrecks. Rather than drive safely and responsibly, young scofflaws had turned their vehicles into bumper cars, happily chasing and slamming into one another at high speeds. Autopia was shut down and redesigned. When it reopened, the cars could only go slow and were fastened to tracks.

Some areas of the park—Main Street, Frontierland, and Adventureland—featured a vast display of the icons of Americana. Young people could take a Jungle Cruise and conquer Africa, the "dark continent." They also could take a cruise on the steamboat Mark Twain down a man-made river, and they could be inspired by a larger-than-life robotic Abraham Lincoln who, in a deep, rumbling voice, declaimed the virtues of constitutional democratic governance.

ROCK 'N' ROLL

Teen culture centered around fads and pop music. Affluent teenagers constituted a vast new market that the recording companies and record stores hastened to exploit. Before rock music made its appearance in the mid-1950s, mainstream pop music was a mélange of somewhat bland musical styles. Novelty songs, ballads, waltzes, celebrations of teenage love, and an occasional significant song such as Les Paul and Mary Ford's beautifully rendered "Vaya Con Dios" topped the charts. African American music, although supercharged with religious and sexual energies, remained largely unknown to white audiences and off of the pop charts.

In the early 1950s, a white Cleveland disc jockey, Allen Freed, began airing African American music, which he called "rhythm-and-blues." In 1954, Freed moved to New York, where he continued to promote rhythm-and-blues recordings. That same year, a white band, Bill Haley and the Comets, recorded "Rock Around the Clock," the first rock 'n' roll hit.

In 1956, a sullenly handsome nineteen-year-old truck driver from Tupelo, Mississippi, Elvis Presley, living in Memphis, became the first rock 'n' roll superstar. Presley, who developed his unique blend of black rhythm-and-blues and country-and-western idioms, shot to the top of the hit parade in 1956 with a series of monster hits, including "Heartbreak Hotel," "Blue Suede Shoes," and "Hound Dog." Crowds of teenage girls screamed hysterically at Presley's highly suggestive stage performances, particularly his gyrating hips keeping time with the frenetic chords he banged out on his acoustic guitar. He made a famous appearance on the *Ed Sullivan Show*, where the cameras focused discreetly on Presley's midsection to conceal his suggestive pelvic thrusts from the huge television audience. Over the next two years, Presley released an amazing string of fourteen consecutive hit recordings.

Presley reinvented American popular music, and he revitalized popular culture. Presley's performing style became a symbol of youthful rebellion. His concerts provoked criticism from parents, teachers, and ministers, who encouraged youngsters to listen to the recordings of Pat Boone, a devoutly religious, wholesome performer with a rich baritone voice. The Presley rebellion was implicit in his music, in its rhythms, which excited youngsters and provoked sexual fantasies. Presley himself was anything but a rebel. He was an artist and a showman, a champion of traditional values and a political conservative. When the Army drafted Presley in 1958, he dutifully served his two-year stint without fanfare or incident. Student radicals of the 1960s outraged him.

In his wake came a host of rock 'n' rollers, many white Southerners like him, including Jerry Lee Lewis, Buddy Holly, and the Everly Brothers. The incredible popularity of these white rock 'n' rollers helped bring African American music into the pop mainstream and also helped win white acceptance of African American recording artists such as Little Richard, Ray Charles, and Fats

FIGURE 5.2   Elvis Presley with fans.   *Source:* St. Louis Mercantile Library. Used with permission.

Domino. Probably the best songwriter and guitarist to emerge from this first era of rock 'n' roll was Chuck Berry, an African American artist from St Louis. Berry was attuned to the world of teenagers. He sang about the trials and tribulations of school ("School Days"), about young love ("Memphis"), about cars ("Maybellene"), and about making it as a rock 'n' roller ("Johnny B. Goode").

Controversy over the moral threat to young people posed by rock 'n' roll music in the late 1950s was closely linked to a taboo subject, sexual behavior. An Indiana biology professor, Dr. Alfred Kinsey, had published *Sexual Behavior in the Human Male* (1948) and its sequel *Sexual Behavior in the Human Female* (1955). Kinsey interviewed thousands of subjects and used statistical analyses to produce the first scientific study of American sexual behavior. The picture of American sexual behavior that emerged from his research shocked many. He found that 10 percent of American males were homosexuals and about half of American women had engaged in premarital sex. His studies firmly established that each new generation of Americans were sexually more active than their predecessors. Subsequently, investigators would discredit many of Kinsey's findings, particularly his use of statistical data that significantly exaggerated the number of homosexuals inhabiting American society. Other critics refuted his claim to objectivity and his effort to reduce sexual experience to statistics.

Paralleling the rise of rock 'n' roll music was a growing concern about an increase in juvenile delinquency. Violent gangs of brawling teenagers staged gang fights in the streets of New York and Chicago. Bands of motorcyclists roamed the streets of big cities, back roads, and highways. The media focused on the gang fights, drug and alcohol abuse, and sexual offenses. The U.S. Senate established a special subcommittee to investigate juvenile delinquency, which held highly publicized hearings in 1955 and 1956 and found that youth crime had indeed risen, especially in the suburbs.

Some commentators have suggested that public concern about juvenile criminality in the 1950s was probably exaggerated; it reflected anxieties over family life and the erosion of adult authority. Teenagers in the 1950s increasingly defined themselves by their peer culture rather than the culture of their parents. Much of the teen behavior—their speech patterns, styles of dress, and the music they listened and danced to—appeared alien, even threatening to adults. The role played by the mass media, particularly movies, in defining the youth culture of the 1950s magnified the anxieties of parents, teachers, and ministers. In a famous movie, *Rebel Without a Cause* (1955), James Dean, Natalie Wood, and Sal Mineo played troubled young people in an affluent Southern California suburb. The movie suggested that parents are responsible for juvenile delinquency when they fail to provide proper role models and fail to enforce firm and fair rules.

TELEVISION TAKES OVER

The most remarkable aspect of television was how quickly it became a mass medium. Regularly scheduled telecasts began in this country in 1947. As late as 1948, fewer than two million households owned a television set. That year, most people watched television in bars and taverns, or perhaps stood in front of a department store window gazing in wonderment at the new electronic marvel that broadcast pictorial imagery. Some skeptics were unimpressed by the new electronic gadgetry called television. They dismissed it as "radio with pictures" and predicted it would be merely a passing fad. But within five years, half of America's households had a television set, and by 1960, 90 percent of homes had at least one black-and-white set. No new household technology had ever spread so widely or so fast nor acquired such a tight hold on the entire culture. By the mid-1950s, studies revealed that the average American spent more time watching television than he or she spent in school or on the job.

Prime-time evening television viewing became the social focus of family life during the 1950s. It displaced listening to the radio, playing records, attending movies, reading magazines and books, playing cards and board games, and conversation. A comedian joked that after-dinner conversation in the typical television-saturated American household of the 1950s consisted of two phrases: "What's on the tube tonight?" and "Good night."

As television fastened itself onto American popular culture during the early 1950s, programming was dominated by the "Big Two," NBC and CBS. The prime-time television fare that Americans watched during the 1950s was mostly dictated by a bicoastal duopoly: NBC's programs produced in New York and CBS's shows emanating from Television City in Los Angeles. Both national networks owned many of the nation's 240 television stations, especially those broadcasting in the larger metropolitan markets. By the mid-1950s, those stations earned a high return on their investments, often in the 30 percent to 35 percent per annum range. So lucrative had television broadcasting become by the mid-1950s that getting a license from the Federal Communications Commission (FCC) to operate a television station amounted to getting a government permit to print money.

Initially the producers of television shows borrowed from all established popular cultural forms for their programs, particularly vaudeville and radio. Many of the early television stars such as Jack Benny, Burns and Allen, Red Skelton, Groucho Marx, and Arthur Godfrey had previously been popular performers on radio. Some TV performers reached heights of stardom in the new visual medium, far surpassing anything that they had achieved in radio. Milton Berle, a second-rate nightclub comedian, became NBC's biggest TV star. As the star of the variety show *The Texaco Comedy Hour*, "Uncle Miltie," often appearing in drag, became known as Mr. Television. Another top variety show host, CBS's Ed Sullivan, could neither sing nor dance. A New York newspaper's gossip columnist, Sullivan's awkward posture, mechanical gestures, and slurred speech became the standard fare of nightclub impressionists for twenty years. Sid Caesar, Carl Reiner, and Imogene Coca starred in another popular offering, *The Show of Shows*.

As radio and Hollywood had done previously, 1950s' television programming relied on standard formats or genres. In addition to variety shows, popular TV genres included thirty-minute situation comedies (sitcoms), dramatic series, musicals, and Westerns. The most popular TV sitcom of the 1950s, *I Love Lucy*, starred Lucille Ball. She played Lucy Ricardo, the bubble-headed wife of Cuban-born bandleader Ricky Ricardo, played by Desi Arnaz, Ball's real-life husband. *Ozzie and Harriet* was a sitcom that featured Ozzie and Harriet Nelson and their two teenage sons Ricky and David, a real-life family playing themselves on TV. Another popular situation comedy, *The Honeymooners*, starred Jackie Gleason as bus driver Ralph Cramden and his good buddy, sewer-pipe repairman Ed Norton, played by Art Carney. Other 1950s' sitcom stars included Phil Silvers as *Sergeant Bilko* and Eve Arden as the quick-witted schoolmarm in *Our Miss Brooks*.

In the late 1950s, Westerns became the most popular television genre. At one time there were thirty-nine Westerns on each week. CBS showed most of these top-rated shows, including *Have Gun Will Travel*, which starred Richard Boone as "Palladin," a hired gunman from San Francisco who killed wicked men in the Old West. The most durable of the 1950s' television Westerns turned out to be *Gunsmoke*, starring James Arness as U.S. Marshall Matt Dillon, enforcing the law in Dodge City, Kansas.

Many factors accounted for the enormous popularity of the 1950s' TV horse operas. Children, especially young boys, loved to watch them. They afforded viewers the opportunity to watch gunplay and violence. The charismatic actors who starred in the leading shows had vast appeal. More important, Westerns evoked the frontier myth of national origins. Each show recapitulated, in melodramatic style, a chapter in the saga of how the West was won—the taming of the wild frontier, the suppression of the Indians, and the triumph of law and order over villainy and anarchy. Westerns were a highly romanticized, didactic genre that celebrated the triumphalism of America's democratic national culture.

The appeal of Westerns also connected with America's Cold War with the Soviets, which raged with great intensity during the 1950s. Westerns reaffirmed the American national identity in a time of ideological conflict with Communism. Just as Marshall Dillon's steady hand maintained the rule of law and morality in a violent frontier cattle town, so too would America's nuclear-carrying bombers maintain law and order in the violent world frontiers of the 1950s. Westerns reigned supreme in the late 1950s, while the Cold War consensus remained intact. During the late-1960s, the genre vanished suddenly amidst the cultural crisis catalyzed by the American disaster in Vietnam. As disillusioned Americans rejected the frontier as a viable national myth, Westerns quickly disappeared from the nation's television screens.

In addition to the programs produced in studios, television covered many live events during the 1950s. Sporting events quickly became a staple of live television: Professional wrestling, auto races, boxing, and roller derby were early favorites. Football, baseball, and basketball, all of which had been covered extensively on radio, also received television coverage. Initially, because of technological limitations, neither National Football League games nor major league baseball games telecast particularly well. An innovation that greatly increased the size of the audience for televised football games was the introduction in 1960 of instant replay. In the early years of TV, baseball was an especially difficult game to telecast. One camera stationed behind home plate tried to cover all of the action. The single camera gave a static, one-dimensional aspect to the game; it also foreshortened the distances that balls were hit and players had to run. Owners of professional sports franchises in the early years resisted television coverage. They claimed that it cut into their attendance. Many minor league baseball teams and entire leagues folded during the 1950s, in part the victims of the advent of television coverage of major professional sports.

During television's early years, many hours were devoted to live coverage of public affairs and news features. United Nations sessions at Lake Success, New York, received extensive live coverage. Starting with the 1948 conventions, television quickly established the tradition of live coverage of the major political parties' quadrennial presidential nominating conventions. Controversial Congressional hearings were telecast during the 1950s, the most famous being the Army–McCarthy hearings of 1954. The major networks all inaugurated nightly newscasts of a fifteen-minute duration. In retrospect, it appears that during the 1950s television had limited impact on American politics. There was no evidence that television altered political behavior in any significant way or had any impact on voting patterns. Millions of Americans continued to rely on radio for political commentary, for news, and for listening to presidential speeches.

During the mid-1950s, quiz shows that awarded winning contestants large cash prizes became very popular. The *$64,000 Question* and *Twenty-One* were the two most popular shows. *Twenty-One* was especially dramatic. Contestants, sweating in isolation booths under the glare of studio lights, answered lengthy, complex, and very difficult questions about a wide range of topics. In 1956, Charles Van Doren, a young English instructor at Columbia, and the bearer of a distinguished literary pedigree, became a celebrity performer on *Twenty-One*. Week after week, Van Doren demonstrated encyclopedic knowledge, a phenomenal memory, and grace under pressure, winning a total of $129,000. He was celebrated in the media and became a role model. *Time* featured him on its cover. Educators hailed Van Doren's inspiring example for young people and contrasted his influence with the supposedly baneful influence of rock 'n' roll stars such as Elvis Presley and Chuck Berry.

Alas, Van Doren turned out to be a fraud. One of the contestants that Van Doren had defeated complained that Van Doren had been fed answers to questions in advance. A congressional subcommittee investigated *Twenty-One* and other game shows. Van Doren admitted under oath that he had cheated. He claimed that he had been corrupted by the lure of wealth and fame. He also admitted that he had even been given acting lessons to appear more convincing as he feigned to struggle to answer questions. Disgraced, Van Doren lost his academic job and quickly faded from public view. The networks canceled the big-money quiz shows. A wave of angry disillusionment swept the nation. The print media devoted much space to soul-searching and to asking rhetorical questions about the sources of corruption in American life. Critics of television used the quiz show scandals to indict the new mass medium as a cultural wasteland and corrupter of youth.

Corrupt wasteland or not, television had surely become an all-encompassing cultural force as the 1950s ended. An estimated two-thirds of the nation's sixty million households watched television on an average of six hours a day. Network executives aimed their fare at the largest possible audiences, treating their viewers as though they were an undifferentiated mass with identical tastes and preferences. In reality, the mass audience consisted of diverse viewing groups, differentiated by age, lifestyle, gender, class, education, ethnicity, and race. Although no one was interested in studying them during the 1950s, these distinctive groups presumably had different perceptions of and ascribed different meanings to the programs they watched. Their particular understandings and preferences simply got overridden during the heyday of crude demographics and mass-marketed national network shows.

Television programming during the 1950s generally reinforced official values and established hierarchies of power, wealth, and status. Popular programs such as *Father Knows Best* portrayed the warm inner life of an idealized white suburban family. It celebrated togetherness and the domestic destinies of women. Television functioned as a conservative cultural instrument. It never challenged the powers that be nor their official views. Racial minorities hardly appeared on television; when they did, they were cast in traditional servile roles and depicted as demeaning stereotypes. Television mostly served up popular entertainment and commercials. It functioned primarily as a commercial instrument, an advertising conduit, the most intrusive yet invented. Television quickly became the vital center of the consumer culture. It was a vast educational enterprise teaching Americans about the latest styles of consumption and creating desires to purchase the vast array of goods and services offered up to consumer civilization.

RELIGION REVIVED

Religion enjoyed a revival during the 1950s. President Eisenhower tied religion to patriotism when he observed that recognition of God was "the first, the most basic, expression of Americanism." With America locked in a Cold War with godless Communists, religious worship became one of the defining characteristics of Americanism. Atheism was associated in the popular mind with Communism and disloyalty; a mix of religious worship, free enterprise, and political democracy epitomized the American way. Religion was also promoted as bonding family members together in worship: "The family that prays together stays together." The Bible topped the best-seller charts every year during the 1950s. Congress inserted the words "under God" in the Pledge of Allegiance to the American flag recited in classrooms, and it put the motto "In God We Trust" on paper money.

Thousands of new suburban churches appeared during the 1950s. From 1945 until 1960, church attendance in this country increased by 50 percent. The Baptist evangelist Billy Graham emerged as the major leader of a mass movement back to Bible fundamentalism. A Catholic prelate, Bishop Fulton Sheen became a prominent television personality, speaking to millions of people about ethical and spiritual issues. A minister with training in psychology, Dr. Norman Vincent Peale wrote a book, *The Power of Positive Thinking*, which sold millions of copies. Blending religion with pop psychology, Peale preached a gospel of reassurance. He told his anxious listeners that God watched over Americans, assuring individual success in careers and ultimately national victory over Communism in the Cold War.

A public opinion poll taken in 1955 showed that 97 percent of Americans believed in God and that two-thirds of the population claimed to attend church regularly. America remained the most religious nation in the West. Religion played a serious role in the lives of millions of American families. Most Americans appeared unconcerned over doctrinal differences among the various religions or with serious theological issues. Nor was there any serious interest in ecumenicalism. For most Americans, religious commitments had little, if any, intellectual content. Rather than reorient their lives to God, many Americans considered religious observances essentially a social activity. For others, religious belief got intermixed with patriotism, family togetherness, and Thursday night bingo. High school and college athletic events began with a prayer or a moment of meditation. Religion could also serve as a means of establishing one's social identity, of becoming a member of a suburban community. Religion in the 1950s suffused most American social and public affairs, adding a sense of goodness and appropriateness to these activities.

CULTURE CRITICS

Although the decade of the 1950s is remembered mainly as a time of conformity and complacency, an era of pervasive intellectual blandness when Americans took a holiday from thinking to indulge in the pleasures of affluent consumption, it also produced a number of independent thinkers who espoused a lively critical discourse about the foibles and failures of mid-century Americans. While most 1950s' culture critics agreed that Americans had created an affluent society, that most Americans no longer needed to concern themselves with basic questions of economic survival, they also observed that pockets of poverty, concentrations of wealth and power, class distinctions, and social injustice persisted in mid-century America. Others raised questions about the lack of meaning in lives based on work, consuming, and social conformity.

William Whyte, author of the best-selling *Organization Man*, claimed that Americans no longer followed the traditional individual success ethic. They embraced what Whyte termed an "organizational ethic," which stressed belonging to a group and being a team player. Corporations employed more and more Americans. Within these large companies, bureaucratic management styles prevailed. Businesses encouraged their employees to look, dress, and act alike. Each appeared to be *The Man in the Gray Flannel Suit*, the title of a best-selling 1950s' novel by Sloan Wilson. Whyte raised serious questions about the energy, drive, and productivity of corporate executives whose highest ambition was to belong to a group and "fit in."

The urge to conform spread to the general society. David Riesman's *Lonely Crowd*, a classic study of the postwar social character, highlighted the lonely individual lost within mass society. Riesman observed that mobility had uprooted people from their traditional ethical moorings. Old values no longer offered guidance or meaning. People were cast adrift morally. Young people adapted to the new social environment by embracing peer group norms and turning to television for guidance. They consumed their values as they did their breakfast cereals. Unpopularity with peers was more to be feared than violations of personal standards, which often were confused. People valued success in the personality market more than retaining their integrity.

Riesman called this new American character type "other-directed" in contrast to the traditional "inner-directed" American who internalized individualistic success values early in life from his parents and thereafter followed his destiny. Other-directed men preferred to join the lonely crowd, not lead it. They would rather fit in than stand out. Other-directed workers were better adapted to fill the niches of the 1950s' consumer economy. The American workforce at mid-century was predominantly white collar. New jobs were mostly generated in the service sectors—sales, advertising, customer service, clerical, accounting, and the like. Organization men, whose tickets to employment were high school diplomas or college degrees instead of union cards, proliferated.

Critics of the 1950s also attacked the rampant consumerism of the age; they questioned whether a fulfilling life could be based on earning money only to spend it on the proliferating goods and services churned out by the productive American economy. Other mid-century critics raised serious questions about the quality of suburban life. They wrote about hastily built, shoddy developments teeming with haggard men, frustrated women, and demanding children. Author John Keats wrote a satirical novel about suburbia called *The Crack in the Picture Window*. Keats's fictional suburb Rolling Knolls featured a family, John and Mary Drone, whose neighbors included the Fecunds and the Amiables. The economist John Kenneth Galbraith, in *The Affluent Society*, while praising the triumphs of the private sector, wrote about the squalor of the public sector and the persistence of poverty. One radical critic of the 1950s, Columbia sociologist C. Wright Mills, argued in his book *The Power Elite* that American political democracy was a facade. In reality, a small group of powerful military, political, and corporate leaders controlled America within a political framework that left most Americans relatively powerless. The anarchist Paul Goodman, in *Growing Up Absurd*, leveled a withering criticism at public schools for stifling the individualism and creativity of America's children. Probing beneath the bland surface of 1950s' complacency about society, perceptive culture critics understood that America's problems had not disappeared. They were just being ignored by the nation's political leaders, influential mass media, and most of its people.

REBELS

Not everyone was caught up in the culture of conformity during the 1950s; rebels, especially young people, rejected the manners and mores of the affluent society. Some middle-class youngsters dropped out of the college-career "rat race." They joined Bohemian enclaves in Greenwich Village and in San Francisco's North Beach district. Herb Caen, a San Francisco columnist, dubbed these dropouts "beatniks"; they preferred to call themselves the "beat generation." "Beats" confronted the apathy and conformity of American society; they went out of their way to defy prevailing norms of respectability. They abandoned materialistic values to embrace poverty; and they lived in cheap flats, did not work or study, listened to jazz, smoked marijuana, and indulged in a casual sexuality. The Beats were harbingers of the hippie rebellion of the 1960s.

Beat writers wrote poems and novels espousing the values of their rebellious generation. Jack Kerouac wrote the best Beat novel, *On the Road* (1958), which told the tale of two young men, Sal Paradise and Dean Moriarty, who had no money, traveling across America and into Mexico in frantic search of emotionally engaging adventures, what Kerouac and his buddies called "kicks." Poet Allen Ginsberg wrote the most famous beat poem, "Howl," which scathingly indicted a materialistic age that destroyed sensitive souls:

> I saw the best minds of my generation destroyed by madness, starving hysterical naked, dragging themselves through the negro streets looking for an angry fix, . . . burned alive in their innocent flannel suits on Madison Avenue amid blasts of leaden verse & the tanked-up clatter of the iron regiments of fashion.[1]

In addition to the Beat writers, individual authors expressed their alienation from the conformist culture. J. D. Salinger expressed the theme of personal alienation in *Catcher in the Rye.* Salinger's hero, Holden Caulfield, was a schoolboy trapped in a world populated by adults with whom he could not communicate and who did not understand him. Holden rebelled, ran away, and had a weekend fling in New York, desperately trying to find an island of integrity amidst a sea of conformity. His efforts failed, and he returned to home and school. Salinger's novel was especially popular among 1950s' college students, for he expressed their discontent with a culture that masked a painful reality—not everyone easily fit into the society of would-be organization men and women.

---

[1] From George Donelson Moss, *America in the Twentieth Century* (Englewood cliffs, N.J.: Prentice Hall, 1987), p. 282.

Brief Bibliographic Essay

Teenagers: An American History is a lively recent account of the emergence of teenagers as a new social class in the 1950s. *All Shook Up: How Rock 'N' Roll Changed America* is a fine recent social history of rock 'n' roll. Erik Barnouw's *Tube of Plenty* is the classic study of television during its "golden age." James L. Baughman, *Same Time, Same Station: Creating American Television, 1948–1961* is an excellent new study of the emergence of television as the nation's dominant mass medium. Will Herberg's *Catholic-Protestant-Jew* stresses the important role of religion in mid-century American society. The role of churches in suburban America is well treated in Gibson Winter's *The Suburban Captivity of the Churches*. C. Wright Mills's *White Collar: The American Middle Class* and *The Power Elite* are two critical analyses of the affluent society by a radical sociologist. For two classic studies of the social and cultural history of the 1950s, see *The Lonely Crowd: A Study of the Changing American Character* by David Riesman *et alia* and *The Organization Man* by William H. Whyte Jr. The popular culture of the 1950s is analyzed critically in *Mass Culture* by Bernard Rosenberg and D. M. White, eds. Bruce Cook, in *The Beat Generation*, writes about the "beat" writers who flourished in the late 1950s.

CHAPTER

6

Consensus at Home and Abroad

In the larger world, the Cold War conflict between the United States and the Soviet Union raged unrelentingly throughout the 1950s. The focus of the U.S.–Soviet rivalry shifted to the Third World, to those nations of Africa and Asia emerging from long periods of colonial domination by fading European imperial powers. At home, a bipartisan consensus spanning the American political spectrum supported the American global commitment to contain Communism.

The domestic Cold War climaxed in 1954, when the Eisenhower administration working with the Senate leadership joined forces to destroy the power of Senator Joseph McCarthy. After 1954, the Cold War at home receded; fears and tensions calmed. As the domestic Cold War cooled, the drive by African Americans for full citizenship and dignity in America intensified. In a historic decision, the Supreme Court nullified school segregation and undermined the legal basis of the entire segregationist regime. Heartened by the Court's decision, black people accelerated their drive for inclusion in the mainstream of American life.

President Dwight D. "Ike" Eisenhower was the dominant political leader and icon for the 1950s. He projected an image of confidence and optimism. Ike was also a determined anti-Communist, committed to maintaining American preeminence during continuing Cold War conflicts with the Soviets. Most Americans embraced a consensus in the 1950s, that America was the greatest nation in the world, and the American Dream required thermonuclear defenses in the Cold War era.

THE ELECTION OF 1952

As the Republican presidential race shaped up in 1952, Senator Robert Taft, leader of the conservative heartland, appeared to have the inside track to the nomination. But the powerful Eastern, internationalist wing of the party promoted the candidacy of the war hero, General Eisenhower, currently commanding NATO forces in Europe. At the Republican Convention held in Chicago in July, Eisenhower won a close first ballot nomination. He chose Richard Nixon, a rising political star from California who had nailed Alger Hiss, to be his running mate.

When Truman chose not to seek reelection, the Democrats selected Illinois governor Adlai Stevenson to challenge Eisenhower. Eisenhower launched the Republican drive for the White House by announcing a "great crusade" for honest, efficient government at home and for freedom abroad. Nixon and Senator Joseph McCarthy turned their rhetorical siege guns on the Democrats. They convinced millions of voters that Communist infiltration of government agencies, for which the Democrats were mainly responsible, posed a serious threat to internal security. Eisenhower's most dramatic move came when he took up the Korean War, the chief issue of the campaign. He declared that "an early and honorable" peace required a personal effort, and he pledged to go to Korea.

In September, a hitch developed that threatened briefly to derail the Republican campaign. Reporters discovered that Richard Nixon had benefited from a secret fund raised by wealthy Southern California businessmen to pay his political expenses. The party that had been scoring points from its moral crusade against its scandal-plagued opposition suddenly had a scandal of its own. Eisenhower appeared to be considering dumping Nixon from the GOP ticket.

The Republican National Committee purchased airtime, and Nixon went on television and radio to defend himself before the bar of public opinion. He convinced most of his huge television audience that he had not broken the law or done anything wrong. The emotional high point of his speech came when he referred to a cocker spaniel puppy a supporter had sent the family, which one of his daughters had named "Checkers":

> And you know the kids, like all kids, love the dog, and I just want to say this right now, that regardless of what they say about it, we're going to keep it.[1]

His "Checkers" speech generated a massive outpouring of popular support. Nixon stayed on the ticket, and the Republican campaign rolled on.

On election day, Eisenhower scored a landslide victory. It was in large measure a personal triumph for the popular general. In defeat, the Democratic Party showed considerable strength. The Republicans managed only a narrow majority in the House and broke even in the Senate. Eisenhower ran far ahead of his party. Issue differences between the parties appeared slight. The politics of consensus prevailed.

DYNAMIC CONSERVATISM

President Eisenhower projected an image of moderate nonpartisanship. He came across as a disinterested leader serving the nation, who appeared happy to leave the details of government to energetic subordinates. In reality, Eisenhower embraced a strong conservative philosophy. He believed in fiscal restraint, balanced budgets, and devout anti-Communism. Beneath the affable mask was an able, effective chief executive who controlled his administration and its policies. Eisenhower was also a skilled, precise writer. His writing stands in sharp contrast to the rambling, incoherent utterances characteristic of his press conference responses to reporters' questions. Liberal pundits made fun of Eisenhower's apparent muddleheadedness without realizing that they

---

[1] Quoted in Stephen Ambrose, *Nixon, The Education of a Politician, 1913–1962* (New York: Simon & Schuster, 1987), p. 289.

had fallen for one of his ploys. Eisenhower often feigned ignorance or resorted to gobbledygook to avoid premature disclosures of policy decisions.

His administration tried to implement conservative policies in several important areas. Income taxes and federal spending were both cut by 10 percent. Interest rates were raised and credit tightened to reduce inflation, which had averaged 10 percent between 1950 and 1953. Republicans tried hard to balance the budget but usually failed. Republican efforts to reduce the role of the federal government and strengthen local and state governments also failed. For agriculture, the administration pushed for more flexible and lower price supports for farmers. Crop production increased, farm income dropped, and farmers protested the new policies.

It soon became evident that Eisenhower had no interest in repealing the New Deal. He accepted the expansion of several New Deal programs. Congress expanded Social Security coverage, raised the minimum wage, and extended unemployment insurance. It also created a new Department of Health, Education, and Welfare to coordinate government social programs. The federal government continued to expand during the Eisenhower years. When Eisenhower proposed and Congress enacted the National Interstate and Highways Act of 1956, it set in motion the largest and most expensive public works project in American history.

Eisenhower's moderation accorded with the public mood of the 1950s. Many Americans believed that economic growth would solve all social problems, gradually enlarging the economic pie until poverty vanished. There was no need for higher taxes, special programs, or sacrifices by anyone. The 1950s were a time for holding the line against inflation, recession, and social disorder—of balancing liberty and security within a moderate framework acceptable to most everyone.

The New Deal was legitimated during Ike's reign. It became the status quo undergirding consensus politics. The pragmatic accommodation that the conservative Eisenhower made by protecting and expanding the welfare state signaled the breakdown of traditional political categories. Politicians no longer battled one another over fundamental issues; they merely quarreled over which interest group got how much. Previously, big government had been linked to liberalism, and limited government tied to conservatism. In the 1950s, except for a few traditional ideologues on the Left and the Right, the real issue was no longer whether government was large or small but whose interests it served. Conservatives often voted for huge spending programs like defense budgets, highway programs, and Social Security extensions. Liberals often voted for huge defense budgets in the name of Cold War bipartisanship and to protect national security in the nuclear age.

McCARTHY DESTROYED

National alarm over Communist infiltration of government agencies persisted well into Eisenhower's presidency. Joseph McCarthy continued his investigations of alleged subversion in various government agencies. A 1954 poll showed that 50 percent of Americans approved of his activities and only 29 percent opposed them. Many of his Senate colleagues, knowing that he was a fraud, despised him. But they refused to challenge him openly, having seen what McCarthy could do to an opponent at election time. Eisenhower also refused to confront him because he did not want a party rupture over the controversial demagogue.

In 1954, McCarthy went too far when he went after the U.S. Army. His subcommittee investigated alleged Communist subversion at Fort Monmouth, New Jersey, the site of sensitive communications technology. The Army mounted a counterattack against McCarthy, accusing him of trying to blackmail the Army into giving preferential treatment to a former McCarthy staffer who had been assigned to Fort Monmouth. McCarthy retorted that the Army was holding his former staffer hostage to keep his committee from investigating the Army. McCarthy's subcommittee voted to hold hearings on the charges made by the two adversaries, with Senator Karl Mundt of South Dakota temporarily assuming the chairmanship. On April 22, 1954, the famed Army–McCarthy hearings began. For six weeks they were telecast daily to 15 million viewers.

McCarthy starred in the televised political drama. The hearings also made a star out of Joseph Welch, a soft-spoken trial lawyer who was the Army's chief counsel. At one point, Welch left McCarthy temporarily speechless by asking rhetorically, "Have you no sense of decency, sir, at long last? Have you left no sense of decency?" Although the hearings made for great political melodrama, they ended inconclusively. It is a myth that television exposure and Welch's dramatic remark undermined McCarthy's popularity. Polls taken shortly after the hearings showed McCarthy still retained his 50 percent approval ratings.

McCarthy's methods and his unruly behavior provoked his downfall. In August 1954, the Senate established a committee to study a set of censure charges brought against McCarthy by Ralph Flanders of Vermont. The committee recommended that the Senate censure McCarthy. After noisy hearings, the full Senate voted to "condemn" McCarthy for contempt of the Senate and for abuse of committee members. The vote was 67 to 22.

Senate condemnation destroyed McCarthy. He still made accusations, but his attacks no longer made headlines. His health failed, and he did not live out his Senate term. He died in May 1957 of infectious hepatitis aggravated by heavy drinking. McCarthy could perform only as long as his senate colleagues were willing to tolerate his behavior. Anti-Communist liberals have always insisted that McCarthy's greatest disservice to the nation was to give anti-Communism a bad name, thereby enabling the Old Left and the New Left in later years to claim that any concern about American Communism was just another McCarthyite smear.

THE POLITICS OF CONSENSUS

Anti-Communism as a major issue in American domestic politics died with McCarthy. But anti-Communism remained a staple of American political culture, far outliving its foremost practitioner. Most Americans regarded as axiomatic the notion that the Soviet Union headed an international conspiracy unrelentingly hostile to the United States. The Cold War bipartisan consensus on the conduct of U.S. foreign policy remained intact.

Political alignments during the 1950s remained unstable. Eisenhower's 1952 victory signaled the breakup of the Roosevelt coalition of labor, farmers, ethnics, and Southerners forged during the 1930s; but the Republicans could not form a majority coalition to replace it. As traditional political allegiances declined during the 1950s, a large independent "swing" vote emerged, varying in size with each election. Millions of citizens voted a split ticket, supporting a man or an issue instead of a party, and shifted sides in response to particular situations. The two major parties attained a rough equality for the first time since the early 1890s. An unstable equilibrium prevailed.

The 1956 election was a dull replay of 1952. Ike was at the peak of his popularity and almost immune to criticism. Stevenson campaigned tentatively, groping for an issue and never finding one. He tried to make issues of Ike's age and health. Eisenhower had suffered a serious heart attack in September 1955 and had been incapacitated for weeks. But he recovered, and in 1956 he enjoyed good health, and he was obviously fit to run again. The Democratic Party had nothing to match the Republican slogan of "four more years of peace and prosperity." Eisenhower won reelection by a larger margin than his 1952 victory. But the Democrats carried both houses of Congress.

However, the nominal Democratic congressional majorities were undercut by the bipartisan coalition of Southern Democrats and Northern Republicans who could gut or block most liberal legislation. During the 1950s, moderate Texas politicians led the Democrats in Congress. Speaker Sam Rayburn led the House, and his protégé, Lyndon Johnson, led the Senate. Both leaders pursued a strategy of compromise and cooperation with the Republican White House.

CIVIL RIGHTS

Soon after taking office, President Eisenhower appointed Governor Earl Warren of California as chief justice of the Supreme Court. The Court had been chipping away at the constitutional foundations of racial discrimination since the 1940s in two areas: denial of voting rights and school segregation. It was in the realm of education that the Court chose to nullify the "separate but equal" principle that had provided the constitutional basis for segregation.

Several cases challenging school segregation were before the Court. The justices decided a representative case, *Brown v. the Board of Education of Topeka, KS*, on May 17, 1954. A unanimous Court ruled that *de jure* (legal) public school segregation was unconstitutional under the Fourteenth Amendment, reversing the "separate but equal" doctrine established in *Plessy v. Ferguson* (1896). The Court's decision incorporated much of the legal brief filed by Thurgood Marshall, chief counsel for the NAACP:

> In the field of public education, the doctrine of "separate but equal" has no place. Separate educational facilities are inherently unequal.[2]

A year later, the Supreme Court instructed federal district courts to order school desegregation to begin in their areas and to require "good faith compliance with all deliberate speed." Having destroyed the legal basis of school segregation, the courts proceeded to undermine Jim Crow everywhere. Federal court decisions nullified segregation in public housing, recreational facilities, and interstate commerce. The *Brown* decision was the most important Supreme Court decision of modern times.

The South defied the *Brown* decision. In 1956, a group of 101 congressmen and senators from eleven Southern states that had comprised the Confederacy almost a century before signed the Southern Manifesto. It pledged to "use all lawful means to bring about a reversal of this decision which is contrary to the Constitution." The Southern Manifesto also encouraged Southern officials to try to prevent implementing desegregation. All across the segregated South, white officials called for "massive resistance" to prevent the integration of public schools.

In some Southern states, the *Brown* decision changed the dynamics of local politics. Arkansas is a case in point. The crucial confrontation between federal and state authority over school desegregation came at Little Rock, Arkansas, in September 1957. The Arkansas chapter of the NAACP endeavored to implement the *Brown* decision by enrolling nine African American students in Central High School.

Governor Orville Faubus, who was the son of a socialist labor organizer, had been elected on a race-neutral moderately liberal platform. He was the first governor in Arkansas history to appoint blacks to the state Democratic Central Committee. Faubus had also ordered the desegregation of

---

[2] Quoted in Anthony Lewis, *Portrait of a Decade: The Second American Revolution* (New York: Bantam Books, 1965), p. 26.

public transportation. It was only after it became clear that a large majority of the white citizens of Arkansas passionately opposed even the token integration of Central High that Faubus moved to prevent integration by ordering National Guardsmen to block the school entrance.

A federal court ordered the troops to leave, and the African American students enrolled. But white students threatened them, and they were removed from the school. Faced with clear defiance of the law, Eisenhower acted. For the first time since Reconstruction, a president sent federal troops into the South to protect the rights of African Americans. Paratroopers entered Central High, and the National Guardsmen were placed under federal command. Guarded by soldiers, the nine teenagers enrolled. Governor Faubus then ordered all Arkansas public schools to close rather than allow further integration.

There is a close interrelationship between the Supreme Court decision outlawing segregation and the Southern civil rights campaigns of the mid-1950s. Civil rights activists were tremendously encouraged by the Court's ruling. They responded by escalating their attacks on racial injustice. When state and local jurisdictions refused to obey the *Brown* decision, activists took to the streets in an effort to pressure white Southerners into compliance with the law or else provoke federal interventions to enforce it. Civil rights activists used radical tactics such as civil disobedience and boycotts to bring about enforcement of federal law.

Eighteen months after the *Brown* decision, in Montgomery, Alabama, Rosa Parks refused to surrender her seat at the front of a bus to a white man and ignited the modern civil rights

FIGURE 6.1 A fifteen-year-old black student, Elizabeth Eckford, is shown outside Central High School in Little Rock, Arkansas, being jeered by a white student, Hazel Massery. Massery later apologized to Eckford and spoke out publicly against racism. *Source:* Arkansas Democrat Gazette.

movement. A charming myth has risen about Parks as the seamstress who was simply too tired to move to the back of the bus and whose arrest set off a spontaneous demonstration that ended happily with integrated bus service. Such an account misrepresents a carefully planned and well-organized movement for social change. It also omits Parks's long prior career as a community leader and social activist. The boycott was initiated by the Montgomery chapter of the NAACP working closely with the Women's Political Council in which Rosa Parks had long been a leader. These organizations brought a young Baptist minister on board to lead the boycott, Reverend Martin Luther King Jr. who for the rest of his tragically short life, would be the foremost leader of the civil rights revolution. King declared:

> Integration is the great issue of our age, the great issue of our nation, and the great issue of our community. We are in the midst of a great struggle, the consequences of which will be world shaking.[3]

Helped by a Supreme Court decision declaring bus segregation unconstitutional, and after an arduous campaign lasting 381 days, the boycott eventually forced the city to integrate its bus service. The company also agreed to hire African American drivers and mechanics.

At the same time, the NAACP mounted an intensive legal campaign against segregation everywhere African Americans encountered it. Victorious in forty-two of forty-six appeals to the Supreme Court, the NAACP advanced voting rights and integrated housing, transportation, public accommodations, and schools in many parts of the South. While Thurgood Marshall and the NAACP fought their civil rights battles in the federal courts, King and his followers fought theirs in the streets of Southern towns and cities.

A drive to guarantee African American voting rights also started. The Senate majority leader Lyndon Johnson shepherded the Civil Rights Act of 1957 through the Senate. It created a Civil Rights Commission and gave the attorney general the power to take local officials to court in cases in which they denied African Americans the right to vote. Congress enacted a stronger civil rights law in 1960; it provided legal penalties against anyone interfering with the right to vote.

The civil rights movement made a powerful start during the 1950s. Most progress came from efforts by African Americans themselves, and they were aided considerably by Supreme Court decisions that nullified the legal foundations of segregation. These actions set the stage for the spectacular gains of the early and mid-1960s.

THE NEW LOOK

During the 1952 campaign, Republicans charged that the Truman-Acheson policy of containing Communism had failed, especially in Asia, with the loss of China and the stalemated war in Korea. John Foster Dulles, who would become secretary of state, insisted that the United States, instead of pursuing containment, should make it "publicly known that it wants and expects liberation to occur."

Once in power, Republicans continued the containment policies that they had condemned during the 1952 campaign. They had no choice. The logic of liberation led inescapably to one conclusion—Americans would have to fight to free the captive nations, because the Communists would never voluntarily set them free. Freedom for eastern Europe meant war with the Soviet Union. Republicans hid their failure to liberate anyone from Communism behind tough talk.

---

[3] *Ibid.*, p. 62.

They called their foreign policy the New Look. It relied on strategic air power to destroy the Soviet Union with nuclear bombs if Communist aggression occurred anywhere in the world. Dulles believed that the threat to obliterate the Soviets would "deter" them from hostile actions. The New Look strategy allowed the administration to reduce outlays for conventional forces. Dulles described their approach as "massive retaliation." Secretary of Defense Charles E. Wilson observed that the New Look provided "more bang for the buck."

Critics of the New Look strategy charged that "massive retaliation" locked America into an all-or-nothing response to Communist aggression. A Communist-led uprising in a small country would not warrant an attack on the Soviet Union, hence such a revolution would probably succeed. The Soviets could also see the limitations of massive retaliation and would not be deterred from supporting small insurrections. Freedom would be nibbled away at the periphery.

Ike defended his foreign policy by contending that the United States could not afford to police the entire world; it must concentrate on defending its vital interests. If NATO nations or Japan were attacked, the United States' response would be swift and overwhelming. Dulles also tried to compensate for the limitations of the New Look strategy by forging regional security pacts with allies in which the United States would furnish the military hardware and its allies would furnish the troops if the Communists attacked. By 1960, the United States had committed itself to defend forty-three countries.

VIETNAM

Dulles described his diplomatic method as the willingness to go to the brink of war to achieve peace. "Brinkmanship" was more threatening as rhetoric than as action. Dulles never used brinkmanship on the Soviets, nor did the United States become embroiled in any major wars during the Eisenhower–Dulles tenure. Brinkmanship was tried mainly in Asia, with mixed results. It worked in Korea. Dulles warned the Chinese that if they did not accept a settlement, the United States might use nuclear weapons in the war. That threat broke a two-year-old deadlock and ended the conflict on American terms.

Dulles then applied brinkmanship to Southeast Asia where, since 1946, the French, trying to reimpose colonialism in Indochina, had been fighting Vietnamese guerrillas. In 1950, the Truman administration began sending economic and military aid to support the French efforts to contain Communism in Asia, following the Maoist triumph in China. Eisenhower expanded American aid to the French. By 1954, the United States was paying 78 percent of the cost of the war. Eisenhower, like Truman before him, applied Cold War ideology to this struggle between Asian nationalists and European imperialists. Washington viewed the Indochina War as part of the global conflict between Free World forces and Communism.

Despite U.S. help, the French were losing the war. By 1954, Viet Minh forces held most of Vietnam. French generals tried to retrieve the military initiative, putting 11,000 of their best troops in a remote fortress deep within guerrilla-held territory at Dien Bien Phu and daring the Viet Minh to fight an open battle. The French believed that Asians could not defeat European forces in a conventional battle. Vietnamese forces besieged the garrison. Within weeks, it was on the verge of surrender. With war weariness strong in France after eight years of war, the fall of Dien Bien Phu would mean victory for the Vietnamese and the end of French Indochina.

Facing imminent defeat in Southeast Asia, the French made an eleventh-hour appeal to the Americans to save them. President Eisenhower considered air strikes to relieve the siege around Dien Bien Phu, but he insisted that America's allies join the effort and that Congress support it.

Prime Minister Winston Churchill rebuffed Dulles's efforts to enlist British support. Senate leaders told the president that without British involvement the Senate would not approve U.S. military intervention. Lacking support from allies or Congress, Eisenhower rejected the French request. On May 7, 1954, Dien Bien Phu fell to the Communists.

Meanwhile, an international conference had convened in Geneva to find a political solution to the Indochina War. Conferees worked out a settlement in July 1954. The French and Viet Minh agreed to a cease-fire and a temporary partition of Vietnam at the 17th parallel of north latitude, with French forces withdrawing south of that line and Viet Minh forces withdrawing to the north. Free elections were to be held within two years to unify the country. During the interim, the French were to help prepare southern Vietnam for independence and then leave.

The United States opposed the Geneva Accords but could not prevent them from being adopted by the conferees. The U.S. delegate refused to sign them, but he agreed to accept them and pledged not to use force to upset the arrangements. But at the time, President Eisenhower announced that the United States "has not been party to nor is bound by the decisions taken by the conference." Vietnamese Communist leader Ho Chi Minh, whose forces verged on taking all of Vietnam, settled for just the northern half of the country at Geneva because he was confident of winning the forthcoming elections over the French-backed regime in the south.

After Geneva, Dulles salvaged what he could from what Washington regarded as a major Communist victory that threatened all of Southeast Asia. In September 1954, Dulles arranged for Great Britain, France, Australia, New Zealand, Thailand, Pakistan, and the Philippines to create the Southeast Asia Treaty Organization (SEATO). Members agreed to "meet and confer" if one of them were attacked. A separate agreement covered Laos, Cambodia, and "South Vietnam," that is, Vietnam south of the seventeenth parallel.

The United States also supported a new government emerging in southern Vietnam, headed by Ngo Dinh Diem. The Eisenhower administration promoted the diplomatic fiction that the seventeenth parallel had become a permanent national boundary separating two states, "South Vietnam" and "North Vietnam." America also backed Diem when he refused to allow the scheduled elections to unify the country to take place in 1956.

Eisenhower believed that if southern Vietnam fell to the Communists, all of Southeast Asia would be imperiled. He compared the nations of Southeast Asia to a row of dominoes: Knock one over and the rest would fall quickly. After Geneva, America committed its resources and prestige to building a nation in southern Vietnam that would "serve as a proving ground for democracy in Asia."

With strong U.S. backing during the late 1950s, Diem attempted to suppress all opposition to his regime. His repressive actions provoked violent opposition. Local officials and Diem informers were assassinated by Communist and non-Communist opponents, all of whom Diem called the "VietCong," meaning Vietnamese who are Communists. The North Vietnamese infiltrated men and supplies south of the seventeenth parallel to take control of the anti-Diem insurgency. Small-scale civil war had begun. By 1959, the second Indochina War was underway. It would eventually involve the United States in full-scale war.

THE CHINA CRISIS

While Americans were trying to build a nation in Southeast Asia, they faced a crisis with mainland China over Formosa (Taiwan). Nationalist Chinese pilots flying U.S. planes had bombed mainland shipping and ports since 1953. The U.S. Seventh Fleet patrolled the waters between China and Taiwan, protecting the Nationalist Chinese from Communist reprisals. In September 1954,

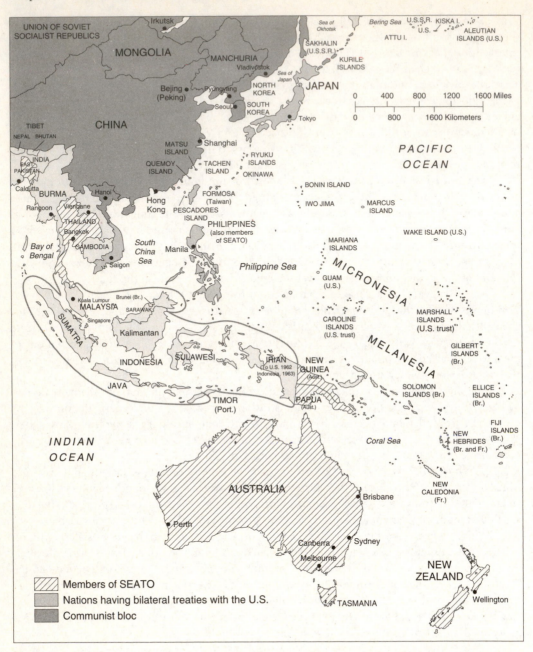

FIGURE 6.2 The Alliance System in the Far East. *Source:* George D. Moss, *Moving On,* p. 119.

Communist Chinese artillery began shelling Quemoy and Matsu, two small islands situated in the mouths of two mainland ports about 100 miles from Taiwan. These islands were held by Nationalist forces. Eisenhower was determined to hold these islands because he believed that they were essential to the defense of Formosa.

Washington reacted to the shelling by increasing the American military presence in the Taiwan Strait, strengthening Nationalist defenses, and issuing stern warnings to Beijing. In December 1954, Washington and Taiwan signed a mutual defense treaty. The following year, Congress gave President Eisenhower the authority to use military force if necessary to defend Taiwan and the offshore islands. The Chinese, lacking nuclear weapons and getting no help from the Soviets, reduced the shelling and offered to negotiate "a relaxation of tensions." The United States, which did not recognize the mainland Chinese government, refused to negotiate with Beijing. However, it stopped its war preparations, and the situation calmed. Beginning quietly at Geneva in the summer of 1955, Chinese and U.S. officials held talks about Taiwan, trade, and other topics.

U.S. problems in Asia highlighted the emergence of Third World nations as a major force in world affairs during the 1950s. A conference of twenty-nine African and Asian nations, many of them former colonies of European imperial powers, convened at Bandung, Indonesia, in April 1955, during the height of the Quemoy-Matsu crisis. Leaders of these Afro-Asian nations wanted to form an alternative to the two superpowers and their alliance systems. Chinese Premier Zhou En-lai played a prominent role at Bandung; China assumed leadership of the emerging Third World nations.

AT THE SUMMIT

Continuing Cold War tensions and conflicts of the mid-1950s highlighted a frightening strategic peril. Both the Soviets and Americans possessed thermonuclear bombs, and both were developing intercontinental missiles. Both sides had to face the possibility of a nuclear exchange if they went to war. They agreed to hold a "summit conference" to try to reduce the possibility of nuclear catastrophe.

The conference was convened at Geneva on July 18, 1955. President Eisenhower, Premier Nikolai Bulganin of the Soviet Union, Prime Minister Anthony Eden of England, and Premier Edgar Faure of France attended the conference. Geneva signaled a turning point in the Cold War. Both sides conceded in effect that the Cold War could not be won militarily. The atmosphere at the summit was cordial. A "spirit of Geneva" emerged, symbolized by a photograph of Eisenhower shaking hands with Bulganin. The conference yielded no substantive agreements, and the arms race continued after the summit ended. But a thermonuclear stalemate had forced a relaxation of tensions. Both sides agreed to start arms control negotiations, and they later suspended atmospheric testing of nuclear weapons.

THE CIA IN COVERT ACTION

In 1953, Ike appointed Allen Dulles, younger brother of the secretary of state, as director of the CIA. Allen Dulles recruited Cold Warriors eager to fight Communism, many of whom were liberal intellectuals from Ivy League universities. Under his leadership, paramilitary covert operations became a secret arm of U.S. foreign policy. The CIA's first major triumph came in Iran in 1953. A nationalist government led by Mohammed Mossadegh had nationalized oil fields controlled by the British and had forced the young Shah of Iran into exile. The United States, fearing that Mossadegh might sell oil to the Soviets and align himself with Iranian Communists, sent CIA operatives to Iran. Working with British and Iranian army officials, they overthrew Mossadegh and restored the Shah to power. Iran then made a deal that sold U.S. oil companies 40 percent of Iranian oil production, the British 40 percent, and the Dutch 20 percent.

The CIA also helped overthrow a Leftist government in Central America. Jacob Arbenz Guzman had been elected president of Guatemala in 1951. Arbenz was not a Communist, but Communists supported his government and held offices within it. In 1953, the Arbenz government expropriated 234,000 acres of land belonging to a U.S. corporation, the United Fruit Company, for a land reform program. The company claimed that Latin America was being threatened with Communism.

The United States cut off economic aid and sent CIA forces to Guatemala to help overthrow Arbenz Guzman. They recruited an army of exiles in neighboring Honduras, led by Colonel Carlos Castillo Armas. When Armas's forces were ready for attack, CIA pilots airlifted their supplies and bombed the Guatemalan capital. Arbenz Guzman, facing military defeat, fled into exile. Armas established a military dictatorship and returned the expropriated lands to the United Fruit Company. Buoyed by their success in toppling a Leftist government perceived to be hostile to U.S. economic and strategic interests in Guatemala, CIA officials would try to replicate their efforts in Cuba in 1961 with disastrous results.

TROUBLE IN SUEZ

The Arab–Israeli conflict dated from the end of World War II. Most of the European Jews who survived the Holocaust wanted to go to Palestine where a sizeable Jewish population had been built up since 1900. Palestine was administered by the British who tried to prevent Zionist refugees from entering Palestine in order to safeguard their Anglo-Arabian oil interests. But the British, weakened by losses in World War II, withdrew from Palestine in 1947, turning it over to the United Nations. At that time, the United States and the Soviet Union united to carve an Israeli homeland out of the western portion of Palestine. The UN partitioned Palestine to create a Jewish state, Israel, along the Mediterranean coast. On May 14, 1948, Israel proclaimed its independence. America recognized Israel immediately and the Soviet Union soon afterward.

Instantly, Arab armies attacked, determined to drive the Jews into the Mediterranean Sea and preserve all of Palestine for the Palestinian Arabs. At first, the outnumbered Israelis were driven back. They asked for a truce; the Soviets and Americans imposed one. During the cease-fire, the Soviets flew in quantities of heavy arms, violating the truce. When fighting resumed, the Israelis routed the Arab forces. Israeli forces also advanced far beyond the original boundaries assigned by the UN partition. The defeated Arabs sued for peace in 1949.

An African American diplomat, Ralph Bunche, arranged an armistice ending the first Arab–Israeli war. Israel survived because of Soviet arms and U.S. diplomatic support. Its inflated borders included thousands of Palestinians. Another 700,000 Palestinians fled or were driven from their homes by the advancing Israeli forces, creating a Palestinian refugee problem that has never been solved.

Israel's leaders recognized in 1949 that to allow the return of the Palestinian refugees would have been suicidal, just as Israel's leaders in 2009 understand the consequences of acceding to a Palestinian "right of return." The Arab–Israeli conflict is a tragic story of two peoples, each with reasonable claims to the same small patch of arid land, evidently fated for endless conflict because their aspirations are not amenable to compromise.

With U.S. assistance, Gamal Abdul Nasser came to power in Egypt in 1952, the first of a new generation of Arab Nationalists. America offered him $270 million to build a huge dam on the Upper Nile to control flooding and generate hydroelectric power. The aid money for the Aswan Dam represented an American effort to tilt its Middle East policy in an increasingly pro-Arab direction. In 1955, Dulles arranged the signing of the Baghdad Pact, linking Britain, Turkey, Iran, Iraq, and Pakistan. The pact's main objective was to keep the Soviets out of the Middle East. The pact angered Nasser, who viewed it as an effort to bring the Cold War to the Middle East and to strengthen Iraq, Egypt's rival for Arab leadership. The USSR reacted to the signing of the Baghdad Pact by becoming more active in Arab affairs, particularly in Egypt and Syria.

Egyptian and Israeli forces clashed along the Gaza Strip, territory that both nations claimed, inhabited mainly by Palestinian refugees. The Israelis suddenly attacked in force in 1955, inflicting a major defeat on the Egyptians. Nasser, angry and humiliated, asked the United States for arms. Washington refused him. Nasser then turned to the Soviet bloc and concluded an arms deal with the Communists. Dulles, fearing that Egypt was becoming a Soviet client, withdrew U.S. aid for the Aswan dam. Nasser responded by nationalizing the Suez Canal. He used its $30 million annual revenues to finance the Aswan Dam. He also closed the canal to Israeli shipping.

Britain and France, dependent on Persian Gulf oil shipped through the Suez Canal, proposed overthrowing Nasser and returning the canal to its former owners. The United States, afraid such actions would involve the Soviets and lead to war, rejected the Anglo-French proposal. The British and French decided to overthrow Nasser and incorporated the Israelis into their plans. On October 29, 1956, Israeli forces invaded Egypt. A week later, the French and British landed troops in Egypt to seize the canal. Nasser's army collapsed. French paratroopers and tanks were poised to roll into Cairo.

But with U.S. support, UN secretary Dag Hammarskjold intervened. A UN resolution condemned Western imperialism. Hammarskjold arranged a cease-fire and called for a British, French, and Israeli withdrawal. The U.S. also cut off oil shipments to France and Britain, and threatened to wage financial war against the British pound sterling. The French and British, reeling from a combination of U.S. and UN opposition, Soviet threats to intervene, and an Arab oil boycott, withdrew without occupying the canal. The Soviets used the occasion to provide funds for the Aswan dam project; in return, the Egyptians granted the Soviets the use of a former British military base at Suez.

American efforts to avoid war in the Middle East yielded mostly negative consequences for U.S. foreign policy interests. Administration efforts weakened NATO, humiliated America's major European allies, alienated Nasser, angered the Israelis, helped the Soviets get a military base in Egypt, and failed to improve relations with other Arab countries. Nasser eventually paid the French and British $81 million for the Suez Canal, and Middle Eastern oil supplies remained in Western hands.

While the Suez crisis raged, crises erupted in eastern Europe. Early in 1956, the new Soviet leader, Nikita Khruschchev, promised to ease Soviet restrictions in satellite countries. Ferment spread quickly throughout eastern Europe. Riots in Poland forced the Soviets to grant the Poles substantial concessions. Hungarian students and workers overthrew a Stalinist puppet. He was replaced by Imre Nagy. Nagy demanded removal of Red Army forces and implementation of democracy; the Soviets conceded to both of these demands. Dulles promised the Hungarians economic aid if they broke with the Soviets. On October 31, Hungary announced that it was leaving the Warsaw Pact. Liberation appeared at hand; a captive nation was freeing itself from Communist tyranny.

Soviet leaders, unwilling to let the Warsaw Pact disintegrate, crushed the Hungarian revolution and killed 30,000 Hungarians. Radio Budapest pleaded for help, but none came from America or elsewhere. Eisenhower had never considered sending troops, nor would he have, had there been no Suez crisis. Neither he nor any other U.S. president would ever risk World War III to help liberate an eastern European country from Soviet clutches. American talk of liberation for eastern Europe had always been a sham. U.S. forces were not strong enough to defeat the Red Army in Hungary, except with the use of nuclear weapons that would have ruined the country and killed millions of people.

After the Suez crisis, America announced the Eisenhower Doctrine to try to offset Soviet influence and militant Arab nationalism in the Middle East. It offered military aid to any country requesting it to resist Communist threats. The Eisenhower Doctrine extended containment to the Middle East region. It was implemented twice. In 1957, U.S. troops were sent into Jordan to protect its government from Egyptian threats. In 1958, about 14,000 Marines landed in Lebanon to protect its government from an insurgency supported by Nasser. In neither intervention did U.S. troops engage in combat, and they were quickly withdrawn.

As the 1950s ended, the United States enjoyed good relations with traditional Arab states like Saudi Arabia, the region's major oil producer, which had become a U.S. client through economic aid and arms sales. But U.S. influence in the Middle East was declining. Arab nationalism and Soviet influence were growing. American efforts to balance Arab and Israeli interests largely failed during the 1950s.

FIGURE 6.3 Postwar alliances: Europe, North Africa, and the Middle East in the 1950s.   *Source:* Litwack & Jordan, *The United States: Becoming a World Power,* Vol. 2, 7th ed. (Englewood Cliffs, N.J.: Prentice Hall), p. 416.

SPUTNIK

In September 1957, the Soviets test-fired an intercontinental ballistics missile (ICBM), over a year ahead of the United States. A month later, they launched the first space satellite, which they called *Sputnik*. It was small, about the size of a beachball, but it circled the earth every 90 minutes, traveling at a speed of 18,000 miles per hour. Its ominous strategic implications frightened Americans. Soviet rocket science appeared to be well ahead of American efforts. Perhaps they would conquer space. Initial American efforts to catch up failed badly. Critics scoffed at "Stay-putnik," "Flopnik," and "kaputnik." Popular pressure mounted for increased spending for research and development of U.S. rockets and missiles. Democrats complained of a "missile gap," a phrase they used against Republicans in the 1958 and 1960 elections.

Americans need not have worried. At the time *Sputnik* was beep-beep-beeping its way around the heavens, President Eisenhower knew that the United States retained a huge and growing advantage over the Soviets in missile development and nuclear weaponry. He had seen the evidence gathered by U-2s, aircraft capable of overflying the Soviet Union at altitudes of up to 80,000 feet equipped with powerful cameras that enabled U.S. analysts to lay out in sequence what the Soviets were doing. Eisenhower knew that if the Soviets were to attempt a nuclear attack on the United States, American forces would have adequate warning of their preparations and could unleash a devastating counterattack that would destroy Soviet military and industrial power, and kill tens of millions of their people.

However, since the U-2 flights were top secret, Eisenhower could not tell the American people their fears that the Soviets had surpassed the United States in missile and space technology were groundless. He refused to be pressured into ordering vast increases in defense or space spending, which he knew were unnecessary. With only partial success, he tried to play down Soviet achievements and reassure Americans that they were safe.

Popular concerns about falling behind in the space race were reinforced by the sluggish performance of the economy, which slipped into recession, and by the revelation of a scandal in the administration. Eisenhower's special assistant, Sherman Adams, was forced to resign for accepting favors from a businessman who wanted help from a federal agency.

Ostensibly the Soviets had scored a tremendous ideological victory over their rivals. U.S. technological superiority over the supposedly backward Soviets, a source of security during the Cold War, had been wiped away. Senator Lyndon Johnson conducted a thorough investigation of the nation's missile and space programs, thereby establishing the Democrats as favoring stronger national defense and space efforts than the Republican administration.

Critics faulted American public schools for not demanding excellence from students and for stinting on math and science training. There had been persistent criticisms of public schools preceding *Sputnik*. After *Sputnik*, educational shortcomings became a national security issue. Educators insisted that Americans must put greater emphasis on mathematics, foreign language study, and science in order for the United States to regain its technological edge over the Soviets. Congress responded in 1958 by enacting the National Defense Education Act (NDEA), which funded high school math, language, and science programs. The NDEA also offered fellowships and loans to college students entering those fields.

CUBA AND CASTRO

In the 1950s, U.S. economic interests dominated the Cuban economy, a result of the neocolonial relationship between the countries that had evolved in the aftermath of the Spanish–American War. U.S. companies owned Cuba's oil industry, 90 percent of its mines, 80 percent of its utilities,

50 percent of its railroads, 40 percent of its sugar plantations, and 40 percent of its cattle ranches. Most of Cuba's major export crop, sugar, was sold on U.S. markets, and two-thirds of Cuban imports came from the United States.

At the end of 1958, Fidel Castro overthrew Fulgencio Batista, a corrupt dictator who had protected U.S. economic interests in Cuba. Castro quickly implemented a social revolution. He broke up the large cattle ranches and sugar plantations, giving the land to peasants. He established summary courts that condemned former Batista supporters, thousands of whom were shot or imprisoned. Communists took over Cuban trade unions and infiltrated Castro's army.

Although alarmed by Castro's radical actions, the United States quickly recognized his government. Castro had considerable support within the United States; he was viewed as a liberal reformer who would restore Cuban democracy. He visited the United States in April 1959. In meetings with U.S. officials, he spoke reassuringly about future relations with the United States. He promised that any future expropriations of U.S. property would be legal and the owners compensated. He then returned to Cuba and began nationalizing more U.S. property without compensating the owners.

Relations between the United States and Cuba continued to deteriorate as Castro's revolution continued its left-wing tack. Cuban liberals, many of whom were former Castro supporters, fled Cuba for Florida. Castro had come to power with only vague notions about implementing an economic program. Once in power, he joined the Communists. By the end of 1959, his government had confiscated about $1 billion in U.S. properties. In February 1960, Castro signed an agreement with the Soviet Union in which the Soviets traded oil and machinery for sugar. The Soviets also loaned Cuba $100 million. Washington responded by sharply cutting the import quota on Cuba's sugar.

Eisenhower decided by mid-1960 that Castro would have to be removed from power. The president preferred to work through the Organization of American States (OAS), but Castro had supporters among OAS members; they admired him as a nationalist who had defied the United States. Others were afraid to oppose Castro lest he foment unrest among their people. Frustrated by OAS inaction, Ike approved a CIA project to train Cuban exiles for an invasion of Cuba to overthrow Castro. The CIA established a training camp at a remote site in Guatemala and began preparations. The United States then embargoed all trade with Cuba and severed diplomatic relations.

Cuban agents meanwhile spread Castroism elsewhere in Latin America, and Washington tried to blunt Castro's appeal by promoting social reform. Administration officials, working through the OAS, promoted a reform agenda including tax reform, improved housing and schools, land reform, and economic development. Congress appropriated $500 million to launch the ambitious program.

CONTROVERSY IN EUROPE

The Cold War in Europe intensified in November 1958 when Khrushchev, unhappy with the integration of West Germany into NATO, announced that within six months he would sign a separate peace treaty with East Germany. Such action would nullify Western occupation rights in West Berlin. Ike refused to abandon West Berlin, but he also avoided a confrontation with the Soviets. Eisenhower invited Khrushchev to visit the United States. The Soviet premier extended the Berlin deadline following Eisenhower's invitation.

Khrushchev spent two weeks in the United States in the summer of 1959, the first Soviet leader ever to set foot in America. Following meetings with Eisenhower at Camp David, an ebullient Khrushchev announced the cancellation of his Berlin ultimatum. At the same time, Ike suggested that the troubling question of West Berlin ought to be speedily resolved. A month after

FIGURE 6.4 One of the dramatic moments of the Cold War occurred on July 7, 1959, when Vice President Richard Nixon and Soviet Premier Nikita Khruschev staged their famous "kitchen debate" in front of the American pavilion at an exhibit in Moscow. They argued over the merits (and demerits) of their rival systems of political economy. *Source:* National Archives and Records Administration.

Khrushchev's American tour, Eisenhower announced that there would be another summit meeting in Paris scheduled for May 1960, and he invited the Soviet leader to attend. Khrushchev accepted and invited the president to visit the Soviet Union following the summit. Ike accepted Khrushchev's invitation. The Cold War appeared to be thawing once again.

But the Paris summit never occurred. On May 1, 1960, a Soviet V-750 surface-to-air missile shot down an American U-2 spy plane over Soviet soil. Initially Eisenhower lied; he stated that a weather reconnaissance plane had flown off course and had inadvertently violated Soviet air space. An angry Khrushchev then revealed that the aircraft had been shot down 1,200 miles into the Soviet Union and that the Soviets had captured the pilot, Francis Gary Powers, who admitted that he had been on a spy mission.

When Eisenhower took full responsibility for the flight and refused to repudiate it, Khrushchev angrily canceled the summit. He subsequently withdrew his invitation to the American president to visit the Soviet Union. Eisenhower deeply regretted the breakup of the summit, seeing all of his efforts for peace dashed because of the U-2 incident. A few months later, U.S. spy satellites equipped with high-resolution space cameras began to overfly the Soviet Union. The need for the U-2 vanished. Powers was the last man to fly as a spy over Soviet territory.

END OF AN ERA

The U-2 incident, the launching of *Sputnik,* and the seemingly endless crises of the Cold War all took their toll on the American people. A sense of declining power to control events in the world spurred a rising debate over national purpose. Social critics wondered if Americans retained the same drive to achieve goals that had motivated previous generations. Did they have the will to face future Soviet challenges?

In the spring of 1960, *Life* magazine and the *New York Times* published a series of commentaries on the national purpose. All agreed that something was lacking in the national spirit.

President Eisenhower established a National Goals Commission to develop national objectives. The commission produced a book, *Goals for Americans*, in which it recommended an increase in military spending to meet the Soviet challenge, a government commitment to an expanding economy, a college education to be made available to all, the promotion of scientific research and the arts, and a guaranteed right to vote for all citizens.

On January 17, 1961, Ike spoke to the American people for the last time as president. His farewell address consisted of a series of warnings, as had George Washington's famed address of 1797. Eisenhower warned of the Communist menace, of squandering the nation's resources, and of spending too much on either welfare or warfare. The most famous part of his valedictory warned of the power of the military establishment and its corporate clients:

> We must guard against the acquisition of unwarranted influence, whether sought or unsought, by the military-industrial complex.[4]

In light of Vietnam and Watergate, his warnings proved to be prophetic. Eisenhower understood more clearly than any other modern president the potential dangers that the Cold War posed to the American people's wealth and freedom. Eisenhower presided over a peaceful, prosperous interlude in U.S. history. But as he exited public life, the nation faced many foreign crises and unsolved domestic problems. The civil rights movement was gathering momentum, and other disadvantaged groups would soon challenge the status quo. American prosperity and power had suffered relative decline in the late 1950s. Soviet military power and influence were expanding. Anti-Western nationalism had intensified among Third World countries.

Brief Bibliographic Essay

The political history of the 1950s is generally well covered in Charles C. Alexander's *Holding the Line: The Eisenhower Era, 1952–1961*. Stephen E. Ambrose's *Eisenhower the President* is the best account of the Eisenhower presidency. Robert A. Divine's *Eisenhower and the Cold War* is the best diplomatic history of the Eisenhower years. A recent study, Robert R. Bowie and Richard Immerman's *Waging Peace: How Eisenhower Shaped an Enduring Cold War Strategy*, makes a strong case for Eisenhower's devising the strategy for eventual victory over the Soviet Union in the Cold War. Using recently released documents and records, Keith Kyle's *Suez* is an informative account of that crucial episode in U.S. Middle Eastern diplomatic history.

---

[4] Quoted in Charles C. Alexander, *Holding the Line: The Eisenhower Era, 1952–1961* (Bloomington, Ind.: Indiana University Press, 1975), p. 289.

CHAPTER

7

New Frontiers at Home and Abroad

In the early 1960s, Americans regained the confidence in their national destiny that had faltered in the late 1950s, when the economy went slack and the Soviets appeared to have gained a strategic advantage in the Cold War. The economy revived. Most middle-class American families enjoyed unprecedented affluence, and their children's prospects never looked brighter. An energetic, articulate young president kindled this resurgent optimism. John Fitzgerald Kennedy voiced national goals in language that Americans, particularly young Americans, could understand and accept. He told Americans that they could face the challenges of mid-century life, hold their own in world affairs, beat the Soviets in the space race, and solve nagging social problems at home. Civil rights activists, building on their victories in Montgomery and Little Rock, directly challenged the system of segregation still in place everywhere in the South, thereby provoking the most serious domestic crisis of the Kennedy presidency.

THE ELECTION OF 1960

A Democratic resurgence began with the 1958 midterm elections. A series of events had shaken public confidence in the Eisenhower administration: *Sputnik* and the apparent missile and space race gaps, crises in the Middle East, and a sharp recession at home, which had driven unemployment above 7 percent, the highest level since 1941. Also, the Sherman Adams scandal tarnished the antiseptic image that the Republicans had enjoyed since coming to office. The Democrats increased their majorities in the Senate, sixty-four to thirty-four, and in the House, 283 to 153. These were their largest majorities since the New Deal heyday of 1936. In Massachusetts, Senator John Kennedy won a lopsided reelection victory. His impressive performance made him the Democratic front-runner for 1960.

Many Democratic leaders entered the race for their party's 1960 presidential nomination. With the popular Ike forced to resign because of the Twenty-second Amendment, prospects for a Democratic victory looked better than any time since the glory days of FDR. Other candidates

FIGURE 7.1 Presidential candidate John F. Kennedy and Jackie. *Source:* Getty Images, Inc.—Taxi. Photo by Peskin HY.

included Senators Hubert Humphrey, Stuart Symington and Senate majority leader Lyndon Johnson. Adlai Stevenson was still a contender, even though he had lost twice to Eisenhower.

Two obstacles blocked Kennedy's path to his party's presidential nomination. First, he would have to dispel the myth that a Catholic could never be elected president. The second obstacle was the candidacies of his powerful rivals, all of whom had longer, more distinguished political careers than he. Kennedy was an upstart among seasoned veterans of the political wars.

Victories in the early primaries gave him momentum that carried him to the nomination. Kennedy chose Lyndon Johnson, who had come in second to him in the convention balloting for president, to be his vice presidential running mate. He needed Johnson to win Texas and to hold the South if he were to have any chance of winning the presidency in November.

When the Republicans gathered in Chicago a week later, Richard Nixon had the nomination sewn up. The nearest thing to a challenge came from Nelson Rockefeller, governor of New York. He had no chance and withdrew long before the convention. But Rockefeller influenced the drafting of the party platform. The Republican platform came out similar to the Democratic one and amounted to an implicit indictment of Eisenhower administration policies for stinting on defense spending and allowing the economy to nosedive. Conservative Republicans reacted angrily to the Rockefeller platform. Arizona senator Barry Goldwater called it "the Munich of the Republican Party."

The candidates shared similar political views. Nixon was a moderate conservative with liberal tendencies. Kennedy was a moderate liberal with conservative tendencies. Both were Cold Warriors. Both accepted the basic structure of the New Deal welfare state. Both advocated civil rights and believed in a strong presidency. Because they shared similar political views, the campaign featured few substantial debates over the issues. Because the electorate perceived their views to be so similar, the outcome of the election turned on personal image and the voters' feel for one or the other.

Nixon began the campaign with some liabilities. The sagging economy was the most serious. The Cold War setbacks that the Eisenhower administration suffered also hurt the candidate's chances. Even so, the early advantage clearly lay with Nixon. He was far better known to the American people because of his active role in Eisenhower's administration. September public opinion polls gave Nixon the lead. The election appeared to be Nixon's to lose.

Kennedy's religious affiliation was an important campaign issue, and he met his detractors forthrightly. He clearly stated his views: There was nothing in his religion that would prevent him from obeying his constitutional oath and governing the nation; he supported the First Amendment's separation of church and state; he opposed federal aid to parochial schools; and he favored birth control. He appeared before a gathering of prominent Protestant leaders in Houston, and he told the ministers, "I am not the Catholic candidate for president, I am the Democratic Party's candidate for president, who also happens to be a Catholic." At the conclusion of his speech, the ministers gave him a warm, standing ovation. His performance defused the religious issue and freed Kennedy to concentrate on attacking Nixon and the Republican record.

The highlight of the campaign occurred when the candidates staged four nationally televised debates between September 26 and October 21. They were the first televised debates between presidential candidates, and they reflected the growing influence that television was now playing in the nation's political life. The first debate was decisive, and Kennedy won it. Nixon looked haggard; he was weakened by a knee infection and tired from a long day of campaigning. He was victimized by a poor makeup job that did not hide his dark stubble. On camera, under hot lights, the makeup powder streaked as Nixon sweated noticeably. He faltered when answering some of the questions.

Kennedy, in contrast, was fresh and primed for the encounter. He had rested that day, poring over his notes like a college student cramming for an examination. He exuded cool, cheerful confidence and displayed a sure grasp of the issues, an agile intelligence, and a sharp wit; Kennedy dispelled any lingering doubts about his maturity or ability to be president. Nixon did much better in the three subsequent debates and had a slight advantage overall, but he could not completely overcome the disadvantage of his appearance and performance during that crucial first debate.

October polls showed Kennedy taking the lead for the first time. In the final month of campaigning, Kennedy attracted large, excited crowds. He appeared along a beach in Southern California and was mobbed by excited followers who behaved like rock 'n' roll or movie star fans. Kennedy had momentum, and the Democrats could smell victory.

But in the final week of the campaign, Nixon strongly defended the Eisenhower record and hammered away at Kennedy's inexperience in international affairs. Republicans staged a media blitz across the nation. Eisenhower finally entered the fray and campaigned energetically for Nixon. Kennedy's advantage in the polls vanished.

Kennedy's 303 to 219 edge in electoral votes masked the closest presidential election in American history. Kennedy, by narrowly winning populous states such as New York, Pennsylvania, Michigan, and Texas, squeezed out victory. Out of a record sixty-eight million votes cast, Kennedy's margin of victory was 118,574. Kennedy received 49.7 percent of the popular vote to Nixon's 49.5 percent. In congressional elections, Republicans picked up twenty-two seats in the House and two seats in the Senate.

It is impossible to say precisely what factor determined Kennedy's hairline victory. In such a close election, any of the many variables could have determined the outcome. Kennedy's religious affiliation cut both ways: In rural Protestant areas of the South, Southwest, and West, it cost him votes, but in Northeastern, Midwestern, and Western urban states, it gained him votes. On balance, he may have gained more than he lost because of his religion, for the states where people voted for him because of his religious affiliation contained the largest clusters of electoral votes. Kennedy benefited from the televised debates, particularly the first. The winner also ran well among black voters. Kennedy had followed a bold strategy during the campaign of relying on Johnson to hold white Southerners while he appealed for black voters. He responded to an appeal to help Dr. Martin Luther King Jr. gain release from a Georgia jail, where his wife feared he would be killed. Kennedy also promised to sign an executive order forbidding segregation in federally subsidized housing. Black votes provided his winning margin in Texas and North Carolina, and he received most of the Northern black inner-city vote. Personal charisma was another factor that contributed to his victory. Many people, including the writer of this account of the 1960 election, who met the candidate during his electoral campaign, were dazzled by his incandescent personality. And without Lyndon Johnson on the ticket, Kennedy would have not carried key states of the South, Southwest, and West.

The 1960 election demonstrated that regional, class, and party loyalties continued to erode. Many voters split their tickets in 1960. Millions of Republicans, many of them Catholics, voted for Kennedy. Millions of Democrats, mostly Protestants, voted for Nixon. The 1960 election further blurred the distinctions between the major parties and their candidates. Both candidates ran pragmatic, centrist campaigns. The center held. The politics of consensus still prevailed.

SOCIAL REFORM

Kennedy's thin electoral victory in 1960 carried with it no mandate whatsoever for social reform. He failed to persuade Congress to enact most of his ambitious New Frontier program, which included medical care for the elderly, tax reform, federal aid to education, housing reform, aid to cities, and immigration reform. In Congress, the bipartisan conservative coalition could block any effort to expand the welfare state and could often dilute measures designed to broaden existing programs. Public opinion in the early 1960s reflected the complacency toward unsolved social problems that had characterized the 1950s.

Kennedy also failed to assert effective legislative leadership. Congress questioned the depth of his commitment to social reform, understanding that he gave higher priority to foreign policy, military matters, world trade, and strengthening the economy. Kennedy also wanted to maintain bipartisan support for American foreign policy initiatives, and he was reluctant to strain the unity of Congress with divisive battles over reform measures.

A major defeat came early when Congress rejected Kennedy's $2.3 billion education bill, which foundered over the issue of federal aid to parochial schools. A Catholic himself, Kennedy knew that he would be accused of showing favoritism toward his coreligionists if he favored federal aid to Catholic schools. His bill excluded federal aid for private schools with a religious affiliation. He claimed that such aid would violate the First Amendment principle of separation of church and state. Opposition to the bill from the Catholic lobby was intense. The education bill never got out of the House Rules Committee. The failure of the education bill foreshadowed the defeat of the rest of the New Frontier agendum.

Although Kennedy did not come close to achieving his broad program of social reform, he scored a few victories. Congress enacted an Area Redevelopment Act in 1961 to provide funds for economically depressed areas. The Manpower Retraining Act of 1962 provided $435 million over three years to train unemployed workers in new job skills. Congress raised the minimum wage from $1.00 to $1.25 per hour and extended coverage to 3.6 million more workers.

THE ECONOMY

When Kennedy took office, the American economy was suffering from a lingering recession. The new president tried to work with the business community to restore prosperity. He held meetings with corporate leaders to obtain their policy suggestions. He tried to reassure them that he was a pragmatic centrist, not a liberal ideologue, and was committed to a stable price structure. Corporate leaders refused their cooperation, rejecting his reliance on academic economists rather than men with practical business experience.

A major confrontation with business came in the spring of 1962 when Roger Blough, the head of United States Steel, announced that his company was raising the price of steel $6 a ton. Other major steel producers promptly announced identical increases. Kennedy denounced the steel companies and promptly mobilized major agencies of the federal government to force the steel companies to rescind their price hikes. The Federal Trade Commission announced that it would investigate the steel industry for possible price-fixing. Under an all-out assault from the White House, the steel companies canceled their price increases. Kennedy had won; however, the business community remained intensely hostile toward his administration.

Kennedy proposed innovative economic policies to end the business slump of the early 1960s. In June 1962, he proposed a deliberately unbalanced budget to promote economic growth. Six months later, he asked Congress to enact a $13.5 billion cut in corporate and personal income taxes over the next three years. The tax cuts, coupled with increases in spending for military and space programs already in place, would guarantee budget deficits. Kennedy insisted that these applied Keynesian economic strategies would generate capital spending that would stimulate economic growth, create new jobs, and provide increased tax revenues—all without rampant inflation. But Kennedy's tax bill never cleared Congress during his presidency.

Even though Kennedy failed to get his new economic policy enacted, the economy recovered from recession, and in 1962 began an extended period of growth. Recovery mainly occurred because of powerful, preexisting developments, including low-cost energy, continuing technological innovation, and increased productivity. The Kennedy administration sharply increased military and aerospace spending. Kennedy's first defense budget called for spending $48 billion, a 20 percent increase over Eisenhower's final budget. Most of Kennedy's foreign aid requests were approved, including increased spending for technical assistance and economic development for Third World countries.

The Senate ratified a treaty in 1961, making the United States a member of the newly created Organization of Economic Cooperation and Development (OECD), made up of the United States,

Canada, and eighteen European nations. Congress also enacted Kennedy's proposed Trade Expansion Act in 1962, his most important legislative victory. This legislation enabled the United States to establish closer ties with European Common Market countries. The Trade Expansion Act also allowed the president to reduce tariffs on commodities in which the United States and European nations accounted for most of the world's trade. American overseas trade increased significantly during the years of Kennedy's presidency.

LET FREEDOM RING

In order to maintain the momentum of the civil rights struggle during the late-1950s, Martin Luther King Jr. brought together nearly 100 black religious leaders to found the Southern Christian Leadership Council (SCLC). The SCLC called upon African Americans to continue their nonviolent resistance to segregation and disfranchisement. The creation of the SCLC also signaled that henceforth the Southern black churches would lead the fight, replacing the Northern elite that had focused on legal action and judicial directives.

However, the next great surge in the civil rights struggle came not from activist ministers, but from courageous black college students. Four freshmen from North Carolina Agricultural and Technical College in Greensboro, North Carolina, sat down at the whites-only lunch counter in Woolworth's and ordered coffee and doughnuts. They were refused service, but they stayed until closing time. News of their actions spread quickly. The next day they returned with dozens of supporters. Within a few days scores of supporters, including a few white people, clogged the counters at Woolworth's and other stores in the downtown area. The sit-ins continued for months. The events in Greensboro made the national news. When police arrested forty-five students for trespassing on April 25, outraged African Americans boycotted major downtown businesses. Merchants, losing money, pressured Greensboro city leaders to reach a settlement with the protesters. On July 25, 1960, the first African American ate lunch at the now famous Woolworth's lunch counter.

The victorious Greensboro sit-in activated young African Americans all across the South. During the next eighteen months, thousands of college students, most of them black, staged sit-ins against segregation in dozens of cities. The most significant of these sit-in campaigns occurred in Atlanta, Georgia, the South's largest city. Beginning in March 1960, students from the all-black colleges comprising Atlanta University staged large-scale sit-ins in department stores; they also picketed and boycotted downtown merchants. The campaign went on for more than a year, during which hundreds of protesters were jailed. The city's white establishment finally conceded defeat; Atlanta was desegregated in September 1961.

During the 1960 presidential campaign, civil rights had not been a central issue, although Kennedy praised the sit-in movements as an example of the revival of a national reform spirit. He also promised to issue an executive order ending racial segregation in federally funded housing. During the campaign, he helped to get Dr. King released from jail. African Americans appreciated these gestures from the candidate and gave Kennedy a large black majority in 1960, which helped him win his narrow victory.

But the very closeness of his victory imposed limits on Kennedy's support of the civil rights struggle. He proved to be a cautious leader on civil rights for most of his presidency. He delayed introducing civil rights legislation, fearing that it would fail and also that it would alienate Southern Democrats, whose votes he needed on other measures. He appointed dozens of African Americans to federal offices, the first president to do so. Robert Weaver became head of the Housing and Home Finance Agency, and Thurgood Marshall became a Circuit Court judge. But

Kennedy also appointed many segregationist judges to Southern courts, and he delayed issuing his promised housing desegregation order for nearly two years.

At the beginning of his administration, the lead in civil rights was taken by the president's brother, Attorney General Robert Kennedy. Robert Kennedy energized the Civil Rights Division of the Justice Department, which had been created by the Civil Rights Act of 1957. He recruited a team of committed attorneys headed by Burke Marshall. They worked to end discrimination in interstate transportation and supported the voting rights of African Americans in the South. But the Kennedy administration could not solve the central political dilemma: how to move forward on civil rights issues without alienating powerful Southern Democratic Congressional leaders.

From the outset of his presidency, Kennedy had to respond to pressures created by confrontations between civil rights activists and their violent segregationist foes. In the spring of 1961, the Congress of Racial Equality (CORE) sponsored "freedom rides." Groups of black and white travelers rode through the South deliberately entering segregated bus terminals and restaurants. Local mobs often attacked the "freedom riders." In Anniston, Alabama, the Greyhound bus in which one group had been riding was burned. Black and white passengers fleeing the burning bus were attacked by a white mob. A newly formed civil rights organization, the Student Nonviolent Coordinating Committee (SNCC), also sponsored "freedom rides." On May 20, 1961, a Greyhound bus carrying SNCC "freedom riders" pulled into the bus station at Montgomery, Alabama. As the passengers got off the bus, they were attacked by hundreds of whites. People were clubbed to the ground and beaten with chains. A journalist and a Justice Department official observing the violent scene were also beaten.

Responding to the freedom riders and their violent encounters, the Interstate Commerce Commission (ICC) ordered bus companies to desegregate all of their interstate routes and facilities. The companies complied, and black passengers began entering previously "whites-only" restaurants, waiting rooms, and restrooms. The Justice Department persuaded thirteen of the nation's fifteen segregated airports to desegregate and filed suits against the two holdouts.

The following year, Mississippi became a civil rights battleground. In September 1962, an African American, James Meredith, attempted to enroll at the all-white University of Mississippi. Although he met the university's entrance requirements, university officials refused to admit him. Meredith then obtained a court order from Supreme Court Justice Hugo Black enjoining the university to admit him, whereupon Governor Ross Barnett personally intervened to prevent his enrolling.

President Kennedy responded to Barnett's defiance of federal authority by sending 500 federal marshals to the university. They were met by a mob of several thousand whites, many of them armed with rifles and shotguns. On the night of September 30, violence reigned on the university campus. Two men were killed, and 160 marshalls were injured. Vehicles were burned, and the stench of tear gas covered the campus. President Kennedy ordered 5,000 U.S. Army troops onto the campus to restore order. A contingent of troops remained on campus to protect Meredith after the riots were suppressed.

Another violent confrontation occurred on April 12, 1963, Good Friday, when Martin Luther King Jr. and the SCLC led demonstrations in Birmingham, Alabama. Birmingham was the most segregated big city in America. African Americans endured total segregation in schools, restaurants, movies, city parks, and shopping. Although they constituted over 40 percent of the population, they represented only about 10 percent of the registered voters. The SCLC sought to end segregation and end discrimination in employment and hiring policies.

Their protests were nonviolent; the city's response was not. City leaders directed Public Safety Commissioner Eugene "Bull" Connor to forcibly put an end to the demonstrations. During the next month, Birmingham police arrested over 2,000 African Americans, many of them schoolchildren. Connor ordered his police force to use high-pressure fire hoses, electric cattle prods, clubs, and police dogs to break up the demonstrations. Newspapers and television news broadcasts conveyed to a shocked nation the brutal white police assaults on nonviolent black people. King himself was jailed. While locked up in solitary confinement, he composed his famed *Letter from Birmingham Jail*, an eloquent defense of the tactic of nonviolent civil disobedience.

The Justice Department intervened during the Birmingham demonstrations. On May 10, federal officials and city leaders worked out an agreement. The SCLC agreed to end the protests. City leaders agreed to desegregate municipal facilities and hire African Americans. A biracial committee was formed to keep open the channels of communication between the races. King claimed victory, but Governor George Wallace denounced the agreement. A thousand Ku Klux Klansmen burned a cross in a Birmingham park. Bombs rocked the local headquarters of the SCLC.

A few months after Birmingham, two young African Americans, Vivian Malone and James Hood, tried to enroll at the University of Alabama. Governor George Wallace stood at the entrance to Carmichael Hall on the campus of the university. With television cameras rolling and over 200 reporters looking on, Wallace raised his hand and refused to allow the two black students to enter the school. Two hours later, the crisis was over. President Kennedy, hoping to avoid a replay of the Mississippi violence, federalized the Alabama National Guard. He confronted Wallace with an overwhelming show of force, using native Alabama white and black soldiers. Wallace had stood in the doorway only long enough to have his picture taken for the papers and

FIGURE 7.2 Dr. Martin Luther King Jr. led demonstrations into the heart of the segregated South—Birmingham, Alabama—in April 1963. Firemen use high-pressure fire hoses to disperse civil rights demonstrators. *Source:* AP/Wide World Photo.

to ensure that his actions made the nightly television and radio news. He then stepped aside. Malone and Hood enrolled at the university, peacefully.

That night, on June 11, 1963, John Kennedy gave the first civil rights speech ever delivered by a president. Part of his speech was extemporaneous, and he conveyed a sense of moral urgency, an emotional concern for civil rights:

> One hundred years of delay have passed since President Lincoln freed the slaves, yet their heirs, their grandsons, are not fully free. They are not yet free from the bonds of injustice; they are not yet freed from social and economic oppression. And this nation will not be fully free until all its citizens are free.[1]

A week later, Kennedy proposed his long-delayed civil rights bill. It had been crafted carefully so as to secure the backing of moderate Republicans without whose votes the bill could never pass. It focused on eliminating racial discrimination in public accommodations. It also called for eliminating *de jure* segregation of public schools, thus ignoring widespread *de facto* segregation in the North. Its voting rights section excluded state and local elections. A section on employment would create an Equal Employment Opportunity Commission. The bill did nothing to protect activists from police brutality.

To show support for the pending legislation, civil rights leaders organized a march on Washington. Such a demonstration alarmed Kennedy and his aides who worked very hard to limit it and to tone it down. Approximately 250,000 people, including 50,000 whites, gathered on the mall in front of the Washington monument on August 28. Black and white people joined in a peaceful, festive occasion. With most people holding hands in an extraordinary show of interracial unity, folksinger Joan Baez led the massive crowd in singing the anthem of the civil rights struggle, "We Shall Overcome." Marian Anderson and Mahalia Jackson sang movingly during the official program at the Lincoln Memorial. The highlight of an exhilarating day of speeches came when the last speaker, Martin Luther King Jr., passionately affirmed his faith in the decency of humanity and in victory for his cause:

> I have a dream that one day this nation will rise up and live out the true meaning of its creed: We hold these truths to be self-evident; that all men are created equal. I have a dream that one day on the red hills of Georgia, the sons of former slaves and the sons of former slaveowners will be able to sit together at the table of brotherhood.[2]

Liberals celebrated the march and Dr. King's magnificent peroration as a mighty outpouring of egalitarian and interracial ideals, which it surely was. But black people throughout the nation gained nothing substantial from the march or the speeches. They continued on a daily basis to confront the frustrating and galling reminders of their second-class status in America. The march failed to change a single vote on Capitol Hill on the civil rights bill that was bottled up in the House Rules Committee. Even if the bill eventually cleared the House, it would certainly encounter a filibuster in the Senate. In September, a powerful bomb blew up in a Birmingham church, killing four little black girls. Kennedy himself was killed on November 22; his civil rights bill still bogged down and going nowhere.

---

[1] From the transcript of Kennedy's televised speech over the three major networks on June 11, 1963.
[2] Quoted in Anthony Lewis, *Portrait of a Decade* (New York: Bantam Books, 1965), pp. 218–219.

FIGURE 7.3   On August 28, 1963, supporters of the pending civil rights bill staged a march on Washington to show their support. Around 250,000 people rallied in front of the stately Washington Monument to sing songs and hear speeches.   *Source:* National Archives and Records Administration.

COLD WARRIOR

Kennedy believed in a strong, centralized presidency that operated free of the restraints of Congress, public opinion, and the media. He also believed that managerial competence was more important than dedication to a cause or commitment to ideological dogma. He thought that the major problems he had inherited from the outgoing administration—a sluggish economy at home and Cold War crises abroad—stemmed from Eisenhower's failure to assert his power and to streamline the executive office for action. Kennedy was determined to energize the presidency. He would be at the center of action.

Kennedy gave top priority to the conduct of American foreign and military policy, which centered on America's global rivalry with the Soviets. His administration sought to contain the Soviet Union and prevent revolutionary change in the Third World. Cold War ideology shaped Kennedy's view of the world. He viewed the Communist system itself as the Free World's main enemy. He viewed the Third World as the primary arena and the key to winning the Cold War. It was among the underdeveloped countries of Asia, Africa, and Latin America where the battle against Communism would be joined and won.

THE BAY OF PIGS

The new administration encountered its first Cold War crisis in Cuba. Kennedy no more than his predecessor could tolerate the existence of a Communist state in the Caribbean. The CIA project to overthrow Castro, begun by Eisenhower six months earlier, readied for action.

Anti-Castro Cuban exiles, many of them former liberal supporters of the Cuban dictator, had been training for an amphibious assault on Cuba at a secret camp set up in the Guatemalan mountains. CIA officials believed that an invasion of Cuba would activate a general uprising within Cuba that would overthrow Castro. Kennedy, after consultations with senior advisers, all of whom assured him that the planned invasion would succeed, gave the operation the green light.

About 1,450 invaders, debarking from a Nicaraguan port in ships provided by the CIA, landed before dawn at the Bay of Pigs, a remote area on the southern Cuban coast. Castro quickly deployed his army to meet them. Cuban gunners sank many of the landing craft. Attackers who made it ashore were hit by tanks and tactical aircraft. Lacking adequate artillery support and air cover, the invaders were quickly overwhelmed. Within three days, the Cuban army had captured 1,189 of the invaders and killed 114. (About 150 were able to escape.) The invaders never made contact with Cuban underground elements, and the expected anti-Castro uprising never occurred.

The Bay of Pigs disaster humiliated the Kennedy administration. The United States' European allies sharply criticized its actions, and Third World spokesmen took turns condemning the United States at the United Nations. Within the United States, liberals attacked Kennedy for undertaking the invasion, and conservatives condemned him for failing to overthrow Castro.

The U.S.-backed invasion had violated the OAS charter that prohibited any Western Hemispheric nation from intervening in another's affairs. Latin American nations, resenting the thinly disguised American reversion to gunboat diplomacy, refused the U.S. request to quarantine Cuba from inter-American affairs. Both Soviet aid to Cuba and the pace of Cuban Sovietization accelerated in the aftermath of the failed invasion.

The invasion project had been ill conceived and mismanaged from the start. The CIA underestimated Castro's military strength and exaggerated the extent of anti-Castro sentiment in Cuba. Kennedy ensured the mission's failure when he curtailed CIA air strikes preceding the landings and then refused all requests for naval air support as Castro's forces overwhelmed the invaders. Kennedy did not want a war with Cuba, and he tried to preserve the fiction that the invasion was an all-Cuban affair.

The President assumed full responsibility for the fiasco, but afterward he ordered an investigation of the CIA. He forced its director Allen Dulles, into retirement, and he replaced him with John McCone, a conservative California oilman. Kennedy also made an aggressive speech before a convention of newspaper editors in which he made it clear that he remained determined to get rid of Castro despite the spectacular failure of the invasion.

According to the findings of a special Senate investigating committee that later examined CIA covert operations, Kennedy ordered the CIA to "eliminate" Castro following the failure of the Bay of Pigs invasion. Robert Kennedy took charge of Operation Mongoose, which included efforts to disrupt the Cuban economy and to support anti-Castro elements. During 1961 and 1962, CIA operatives tried to kill the Cuban dictator; their efforts included cigars laced with explosives and deadly poison and an attempt to spear him with a harpoon while he was snorkeling at a Caribbean resort. CIA agents also plotted with Mafia elements to get rid of Castro, but they had to abandon the project because of opposition from FBI director J. Edgar Hoover. Castro knew about Operation Mongoose and was aware of some of the CIA plots to assassinate him. He appealed to his allies in Moscow for help. The Soviets responded by sending troops. Later they would try to station nuclear-capable, intermediate-range missiles in Cuba, which provoked the most dangerous crisis of the Cold War.

ALIANZA PARA PROGRESO

To blunt the appeal of Castroism and foreclose Soviet opportunities in Latin America, the Kennedy administration developed a multifaceted assistance program called the *Alianza para progreso* (Alliance for Progress), which expanded Eisenhower's previously announced aid program. Congress appropriated $500 million to start the program, designed to eradicate poverty and social injustice in the Western Hemisphere. Over the life of the program, billions of dollars in loans and grants from both public and private sources were fed into the Alliance for Progress.

In most Latin American countries, the results were disappointing. Governments refused to reform their tax systems, to grant land reform, or to democratize their politics. Economic growth rates remained sluggish. Unemployment rates, mortality rates, and literacy rates did not improve in most Latin American countries. The elite classes that held power in these lands feared the appeal of Castro's revolution, but they preferred to rely on repression rather than implement social reforms.

In the summer of 1961, the Kennedy administration launched the Peace Corps, a successful initiative to help people in Latin American and other Third World countries. The Peace Corps derived from the same Cold War concern to involve the United States more directly in Third World countries, and from a desire to give idealistic young Americans an opportunity for public service. Over the next two years, about 7,500 Peace Corps volunteers were sent to forty-four nations in Asia, Africa, and Latin America. Most of them worked as teachers; others found jobs in health care, agricultural reform, and community development.

BERLIN

At the beginning of his presidency, Kennedy and Secretary of Defense Robert McNamara began a crash program to expand and diversify America's military forces. They believed that Eisenhower's reliance on massive retaliation and his refusal to engage the Soviets in a missile race had set dangerous limits on the American ability to counter Soviet-backed insurgencies in Third World countries. The United States rapidly increased its strategic nuclear forces, which included ICBMs, missile-launching Polaris submarines, and long-range bombers. They also built up conventional war capabilities, adding a Kennedy favorite, counterinsurgency forces. The president sought strategic versatility, which he termed "flexible response"—the ability to intervene anywhere in the world with flexible force levels in response to Soviet or Soviet-backed initiatives.

The Kennedy military buildup had broad bipartisan congressional and popular support. At the same time the United States expanded its military capacities, Kennedy repeatedly urged the Soviets to join in arms limitation talks aimed at reducing the arms race. But Khrushchev responded by increasing Soviet military spending for more ICBMs, the backbone of the Soviet strategic system. The American arms buildup had triggered another upward spiral in the nuclear arms race.

Having been burned badly by the Bay of Pigs fiasco, Kennedy was more determined than ever to respond strongly to Communist threats. Three months after the invasion, he met for a series of private talks with Khrushchev in Vienna in June 1961. The two leaders exchanged views on a wide range of issues and used the occasion to size each other up. Kennedy was calm, rational, and polite in these conversations. Khrushchev's moods varied. At times he talked warmly of peaceful coexistence between Communism and capitalism. At other times he became angry, even threatening. He turned into an ideologue, asserting the inevitable triumph of socialism in the world. He came away from these meetings with the mistaken impression that Kennedy could be pressured. Khrushchev misread Kennedy's civility as weakness. His misjudgment would later contribute to the most dangerous moment in modern history.

The major issue discussed in Vienna was the long-standing problem of Berlin. The German question had never been formally settled after World War II because of Cold War conflicts. At war's end, Germany had been divided into occupation zones by the victorious nations. In 1948 and 1949, the Western zones were merged into one zone, which became the Federal Republic of Germany (West Germany), a Western liberal state. The Soviet zone in Eastern Germany became the Socialist Democratic Republic of Germany (East Germany), on which the Soviets imposed a Communist system. By 1950, there existed two *de facto* German states.

Berlin, lying deep within East Germany, also remained divided between East and West, causing periodic crises during the Cold War. Tensions had flared in 1948, when the Soviets had tried to drive the Western nations out of Berlin and Truman had thwarted them with the Berlin airlift. Khrushchev had pressured Eisenhower in 1958 about Berlin and then backed off when Ike stood firm. Now, with Kennedy in office, the Soviet leader pressed for a peace treaty between the two German states that would legitimate the *de facto* division of the country, remove the possibility of reunion, and deprive the West of any legal basis for its occupation of West Berlin. Khrushchev told Kennedy that he wanted the Berlin issue settled by year's end; if it was not settled, he threatened to conclude a separate peace treaty with East Germany, forcing the West to negotiate with a government that none of the Western states recognized. Khrushchev and the East German rulers also wanted to stop the flow of East Germans into West Berlin. Thousands of East Germans fled poverty and tyranny each month to enter free and prosperous West Germany through West Berlin.

Kennedy rebuffed Khrushchev's proposals and reaffirmed the Western presence in West Berlin. He also asked Congress to increase military appropriations by $3 billion, tripled draft calls, called up reserves, and extended enlistments of military personnel on active duty. He also asked for $207 million from Congress to expand civil defense fallout shelters, dramatizing the terrifying implications of the Berlin crisis.

The Soviet response came on August 13, when East German workers suddenly erected a concrete, barbed wire wall across Berlin, which stanched the flow of refugees into West Berlin. Nearly three million East Germans had escaped to the West since 1945. During the first twelve days of August 1961, about 46,000 had fled Communism.

To reassure West Berliners that accepting the wall did not presage eventual Allied withdrawal from the divided city, Kennedy sent an additional 1,500 combat troops to West Berlin. In June 1963, he visited West Berlin and told a huge crowd, "Ich bin ein Berliner" ("I am a Berliner") to dramatize the United States' determination to stay. The Berlin Wall quickly became a potent Cold War symbol of the impasse between East and West, and of the division of Germany and its major city.

But the Wall also provided a practical solution to the Berlin question. It stopped the flow of refugees, which was Khrushchev's immediate goal, and it allowed West Berlin to remain in the Western orbit, which was Kennedy's main goal. German reunification was deferred to the indefinite future. Khrushchev announced in October that he would no longer insist on Western withdrawal from West Berlin. The crisis ended, and Berlin was never again a major source of Cold War conflict.

MISSILE CRISIS

Following the Bay of Pigs, the Soviets sent technicians and weapons to Cuba to protect it from U.S. hostility. Castro also supported guerrilla actions in other Latin American countries. Republicans attacked the Kennedy administration for allowing the Soviet arms buildup in Cuba. Kennedy opposed attacking Cuba as long as the Soviets placed only defensive weapons in that country, which posed no threat to the United States or any other Western Hemispheric nation. But Khrushchev decided on a daring move to deter any further U.S. action against Cuba. The Soviets secretly tried to install medium-range and intermediate-range nuclear missiles and bombers in Cuba, offensive weapons that had the capability of carrying nuclear payloads to U.S. cities and military installations.

On October 14, 1962, a U-2 reconnaissance plane photographed a launching site for an intermediate-range missile nearing completion in western Cuba. Kennedy immediately determined that the missiles must be removed from the island. But how to get the missiles out of Cuba without triggering a nuclear war? The most dangerous crisis of the Cold War had begun.

Kennedy convened a special executive committee of thirteen senior advisers. Their assignment was to propose tactics that would force the Soviets to remove the missiles from Cuba without igniting World War III. The president's brother and closest adviser, Robert, chaired the committee sessions.

Beginning with their initial session, all members of the committee agreed that the missiles had to be removed, but they disagreed on the tactics. Army General Maxwell Taylor proposed taking out the missile sites with air strikes that would likely kill both Soviet technicians and Cuban soldiers. Robert Kennedy rejected that idea, saying he wanted "no Pearl Harbors on his brother's record." Taylor then proposed an invasion to get rid of both the offensive weapons and the Castro regime. The president rejected this suggestion as being too risky. It could provoke a Soviet attack on West Berlin or even bring nuclear war. Secretary of Defense McNamara proposed a naval blockade to prevent further shipments of weapons to Cuba. The United States could decide to attack or negotiate later, depending on the Soviet response to the blockade. President Kennedy accepted the blockade tactic.

On Monday morning, October 22, the blockade began. That evening, Kennedy went on television to address the American people and the Soviet leaders. He described the naval blockade, which he called a "quarantine," that was in place around Cuba. He demanded that the Soviets dismantle and remove all missile bases and bombers from Cuba immediately, and he stated that the quarantine would remain in place until all offensive weapons had been removed. Then he spoke these chilling words:

> It shall be the policy of this nation to regard any nuclear missile launched from Cuba against any nation in the Western Hemisphere as an attack by the Soviet Union on the United States, requiring a full retaliatory response upon the Soviet Union.[3]

Kennedy's speech alarmed millions of Americans. He confronted Khrushchev with the risk of nuclear war if he did not remove the missiles. For the next five days, the world hovered on the brink of catastrophe. The first sites would be operational in a few days. The U.S. Air Force prepared strikes to take them out before they would be capable of launching missiles at targets in the United States. Soviet merchant ships hauling more weapons continued to steam toward Cuba. The U.S. Navy positioned its blockade fleet to intercept them. U.S. invasion forces gathered in Florida. B-52 strategic bombers took to the air with nuclear bombs on board. U.S. strategic missiles went to maximum alert. The moment of supreme danger would come if a Soviet ship tried to run the blockade, for U.S. ship commanders had orders to stop it.

---

[3] Quoted in Elie Abel, *The Missile Crisis* (New York: Bantam Books, 1966), p. 106.

The first break came on October 24. Soviet ships hauling offensive weapons turned back. Two days later, Khrushchev sent a letter to President Kennedy offering to remove all offensive weapons from Cuba in exchange for a U.S. pledge not to invade Cuba. Kennedy accepted the offer, but before he could send his reply, Khrushchev sent a second letter raising the stakes: America would have to give a no-invasion-of-Cuba pledge plus remove its Jupiter missiles stationed in Turkey and Italy, which were targeted at the Soviet Union. Kennedy refused to bargain. It was his view that Khrushchev's reckless initiative had triggered the crisis, and it was his responsibility to remove the missiles from Cuba quickly.

As the most perilous day of the Cold War if not in all of human history approached, Kennedy, heeding the advice of his brother, made one last try to avert the looming catastrophe. The president sent a cable to Khrushchev accepting the offer in the first letter and ignoring the second letter. The next night, Robert Kennedy met with the Soviet ambassador to the United States, Anatoly Dobrynin, to warn him that that the United States would have to have a commitment by the next day that the missiles would be removed. He told Dobrynin either remove the missiles or the U.S. military would remove them. Kennedy also indicated to Dobrynin that the U.S. missiles in Turkey and Italy, although not part of any *quid pro quo* agreement, would be removed soon after the Cuban missiles were removed.

While these tense negotiations were in progress, a U-2 spy plane was shot down over Cuba, and the pilot was killed. Angry Hawks on the executive committee wanted to launch air strikes and invade Cuba, not only to destroy the missile sites but to overthrow Castro's regime and send the Soviet troops back home. Robert Kennedy, McNamara, and others restrained them, pleading that a few more days were needed to allow the president to work out a diplomatic solution to the crisis.

U.S. officials learned years later that their restraint may have avoided nuclear war with the Soviet Union. Unbeknownst to Washington at the time, the Soviet field commander in Cuba had six tactical nuclear surface-to-surface missiles in his arsenal. He is on record as having stated that if the Americans had invaded, he would have used the nuclear missiles on them. Secretary of Defense McNamara has stated that if any U.S. troops had been killed by Soviet nuclear missiles, "it is a 100 percent certainty" that the United States would have retaliated with its nuclear weapons.

The next morning, on October 28, Khrushchev agreed to remove the missiles and bombers in return for the president's promise not to invade Cuba. He claimed that he had achieved his goal of protecting Cuba from U.S. attacks. The United States suspended its blockade. The United Nations supervised the dismantling and removal of the Cuban bases. The U.S. missiles were removed from Turkey and Italy a few weeks later. While Kennedy was showered with praise for his handling of the missile crisis, it proved humiliating to Khrushchev. The Soviet leader was removed from power in October 1964; his actions during the crisis contributed to his demise.

Why had Khrushchev tried to put the missiles in Cuba? Historians who have examined documents in Soviet archives believe that Khrushchev hoped to use the missiles placed in Cuba as bargaining chips. He would offer to withdraw them in exchange for U.S. concessions on Berlin. He hoped to extract a German peace treaty from the West and possibly an Allied withdrawal from West Berlin.

Khrushchev had not expected Kennedy's strong response, having sized him up as being weak under pressure. During the Bay of Pigs invasion, Kennedy had backed off from a war with Cuba, let the invasion fail, and allowed Castro to consolidate a Communist revolution right in America's backyard. These acts of restraint sent the wrong signals to the adventurous Soviet ideologue. Khrushchev was not looking for a confrontation with the United States over Cuba, and he certainly did not want a nuclear war.

The missile crisis forced both sides to tone down their Cold War rhetoric and begin to reduce tensions. Direct communication, a "hotline," was established between Moscow and Washington so the two leaders could talk to each other in time of crisis to reduce the chances of miscalculation and war. A mutual desire to limit nuclear testing gave the two nations an opportunity to improve relations. A treaty, signed on July 25, 1963, banned all atmospheric, aboveground, and underwater testing of nuclear weapons. The Nuclear Test Ban Treaty imposed a measure of control on the nuclear arms race. The United States and the Soviet Union also concluded an agreement for Soviet purchases of U.S. wheat.

VIETNAM: RAISING THE STAKES

During Kennedy's presidency, the United States significantly increased its involvement in Indochina. The president first turned his attention in that region to Laos, which had been the scene of conflict for years. Neutral under the terms of the 1954 Geneva Accords, Laos was engulfed in a three-way civil war among pro-Western, pro-Communist, and neutralist forces. Kennedy sought a political solution involving the Soviets that guaranteed a neutral and independent Laos. On June 12, 1961, leaders of the three Laotian factions formed a neutralist coalition government.

In southern Vietnam, Kennedy significantly escalated U.S. involvement in response to the Communists' stepped-up efforts to overthrow the American-backed government of Ngo Dinh Diem. Kennedy and his senior foreign policy advisers believed it was imperative to contain Communist expansionism in Southeast Asia. The legacy of McCarthyism also stalked the Democrats in power. Since the early 1950s, they had been politically vulnerable to charges that they were "soft on Communism" at home and abroad. Further, the Kennedy team shared a faith in American power, technical expertise, and national goals. They believed that the Americans would succeed in southern Vietnam where the French had failed. To them, Vietnam furnished a bright opportunity for nation building. Kennedy also deployed the Army Special Forces, the Green Berets, in Southeast Asia. Kennedy believed that the Special Forces, using counterinsurgency techniques, would win the hearts and minds of the Vietnamese people for Ngo Dinh Diem.

When Kennedy assumed office in January 1961, there were about 600 U.S. military advisers in South Vietnam assisting Diem's forces. During the next eighteen months, Kennedy sent some 16,000 U.S. troops to South Vietnam. Even though the soldiers went officially as advisers, some units occasionally engaged VietCong forces in combat. Despite the huge increase in U.S. support, Diemist forces were losing the civil war to the VietCong insurgents and their North Vietnamese backers. U.S. officials tried to persuade Diem to implement social reforms and to curb his repressive security forces. Diem refused to do either. Diem's decline stemmed mainly from the inability of his military forces to fight effectively and his failure to win the loyalty of the peasants, who constituted approximately 85 percent of the South Vietnamese population.

Diem provoked a political crisis in June 1963 that led to his downfall when he ordered Buddhists to obey Catholic religious laws. When they refused and took to the streets to protest, Diem's police, led by his brother Nhu, brutally crushed their rebellion. In response to this repression, an elderly Buddhist monk immolated himself by fire at a busy intersection in downtown Saigon. Other monks followed suit as opposition to Diem's government escalated. Observing that Diem's political base had been reduced to family members and a few loyal generals and bureaucrats, and fearing that his army would lose the civil war, officials in the Kennedy administration decided that Diem had to go. On November 1, an army coup, acting with the foreknowledge and support of the CIA, overthrew Diem. U.S. officials quickly backed a directorate of generals who formed a new government and pledged to continue the war.

At the time of Kennedy's death, U.S. Vietnam policy was in disarray and his advisers divided over what to do. Kennedy had inherited a deteriorating situation in Southeast Asia; his actions ensured that the United States would remain there a long time. Historians can never know for sure what Kennedy might have done in Vietnam had he not been assassinated, and there is much controversy on this matter. Robert Dallek, a distinguished biographer of Kennedy, suggests that had he lived, he was prepared to withdraw U.S. forces and avoid war. Your textbook author, a specialist on recent U.S. diplomatic and military history, who has written several books and many articles about the American war in Vietnam, believes that if Kennedy had lived and been reelected in 1964, he would probably have reacted much as Lyndon Johnson did in 1965 and committed the United States to full-scale war in Vietnam.

Kennedy's foreign policy approach fitted that of an orthodox Cold Warrior. Undeniably, Kennedy had the intelligence and the insight to see that the world was changing, that Third World independence movements were redrawing the map of the world. He also understood that the old bipolar world was being replaced by a more polycentric one. He understood that the U.S.–Soviet rivalry had to be replaced by *détente.* But the main thrust of his foreign policies was to escalate the arms race, sustain a tense relationship with the Soviet Union for most of his presidency, and, at one terrifying point, push the world perilously close to nuclear disaster. He built up the U.S. presence in Vietnam, assuring the debacle that followed. In the summer of 1963, he improved relations with the Soviets, and the two powers signed a nuclear test ban treaty.

DEATH OF A PRESIDENT

President Kennedy traveled to Texas in late November 1963 to mend some political fences. With the help of Vice President Johnson, who accompanied him on that fateful rendezvous, he came to unify warring factions of Texas Democrats who had feuded over policies and patronage. Texas was a populous state with a large bloc of electoral votes that Kennedy and Johnson had carried narrowly in 1960 and hoped to win again in 1964. Kennedy arrived at the Dallas airport on the morning of November 22. Governor John Connally and his wife Nellie joined the president and his wife Jacqueline in an open-air limousine for the trip into the city. The presidential motorcade proceeded from the airport into downtown Dallas. Thousands of people lined the motorcade route, most of them smiling, waving, and cheering the president as he passed by. Kennedy responded warmly to their enthusiasm, waving, frequently flashing his million-dollar smile, and stopping the motorcade twice to shake hands with well-wishers.

At 12:30 P.M., the motorcade turned onto Elm Street and drove by the Texas Book depository building. At 12:33 P.M., three shots rang out. The president clutched his neck with both hands and slumped downward. One bullet struck a tree branch, a second had passed through his throat, and a third struck the back of his head, blowing off part of his skull. Texas Governor John Connally, sitting beside the president, also had been hit by the second bullet. The president's limousine quickly pulled out of the motorcade and raced the mortally wounded leader to nearby Parkland Hospital, where, in its emergency room, Kennedy was pronounced dead at 1:00 P.M.

Within two hours of the shooting, police captured the apparent assassin, Lee Harvey Oswald, who worked in the book depository building. Oswald was a drifter with a troubled past. He had recently moved to Dallas after spending two years working in the Soviet Union. He was married to a Russian woman whom he had met while living in the Soviet Union. He was a Marxist sympathizer and admirer of Fidel Castro. Earlier in the year, he had tried to go to Cuba, but the Cuban Embassy in Mexico City, after consultations with Soviet officials, had refused to grant Oswald a visa.

Aboard the presidential plane, still on the ground at Dallas's Love Airport, ninety-nine minutes after Kennedy's death, Lyndon B. Johnson was sworn in as the thirty-sixth president of the United States. The former president's widow, Jacqueline, stood at Johnson's side. Two days later, a Dallas nightclub owner, Jack Ruby, shot and killed Oswald at point-blank range in the basement of the Dallas police station in full view of a national television audience. Ruby's murder of Oswald eliminated the possibility of ever discerning Oswald's motives for killing the president, and whether he was part of a conspiracy.

From the moment of Kennedy's death, many people doubted that Lee Harvey Oswald had acted alone. A public opinion poll, taken within a week of the president's murder, showed that only 29 percent of Americans believed that Oswald was a lone killer. President Johnson appointed a special commission, headed by Chief Justice Earl Warren, to investigate the assassination and to report its findings to the American people. Ten months later, the commission published its conclusion: "The Commission has found no evidence that anyone assisted Oswald in planning or carrying out the assassination."

The commission's findings failed to satisfy those who felt others had to be involved in a plot to murder the president. Critics undermined the credibility of the Warren Commission's analysis of evidence and its findings, which were flawed and limited. Moreover, it sealed some of its evidence for seventy-five years, thereby arousing suspicions that they had something to hide. Key sources did not tell the commission all they knew. The CIA hid its involvement with the mob and with plots to murder Castro. Robert Kennedy, who had directed Operation Mongoose, kept its operations secret from the commission.

The FBI concealed its failure to keep a close watch on Oswald whom it knew to be dangerous. Many people have proposed conspiracy theories to account for Kennedy's death, and millions of people have found them credible. These theories have implicated both pro- and anti-Castro Cubans, Texas oilmen, segregationists, Vietnamese, rogue elements within the Pentagon, the FBI and the CIA, the Mafia, the KGB, and Lyndon Johnson. The few responsible journalists and scholars who believe that it is possible that a conspiracy was involved in the assassination of the president believe that Cubans and elements within organized crime were involved.

So insistent and numerous were the doubters and critics of the Warren Report that a select congressional investigating committee reviewed it for two-and-one-half years. It released its report in 1979. Its key finding: "The scientific evidence available to the committee indicated that it is probable that more than one person was involved in the president's murder." It asserted that there was a high probability that a second gunman had fired at Kennedy and missed. It also sealed some of its most sensitive findings for fifty years, thereby further fueling speculation that persisted about what was being hidden from the public and why. Subsequently, experts, including FBI specialists, discredited the committee's flimsy evidence supporting its second-shooter theory.

In all of the time that has passed since Kennedy's murder, no tangible evidence has been found that proves that the Warren Commission's conclusion was incorrect, despite its flawed investigation of the murder. Nor has any evidence turned up that links any particular group to the assassination. If a group of conspirators killed the president, their identities remain unknown and probably unknowable.

The persistence of the belief that a conspiracy killed Kennedy mainly represents an effort to make sense out of a horrific act. The notion that a sociopath, an utterly insignificant wretch acting alone, could bring down a great leader and wreak such havoc made the crime appear senseless and devoid of any political meaning. Novelist Norman Mailer has suggested that many Americans cling to conspiracies to explain the president's death because they cannot recognize the absurdity of historical events. The belief that a great and good man had been destroyed by powerful evil forces lurking within the dark underside of the American political system made sense in a bleak, rueful sort of way to many people. Voicing that belief in crudely reductionist terms: The man was too good, therefore the evil "theys," who really run things in this country, indeed the world, had to destroy him. Belief in a conspiracy theory also reflects a need for balance. Put an admired president of the United States at one end of the scale and that waif Oswald at the other—it does not balance. Add a conspiracy, especially one engineered by powerful persons in high places to Oswald's end of the scale—it balances.

In the years following Kennedy's death, Americans watched other leaders die at the hands of assassins—Malcolm X, Martin Luther King Jr., and Robert Kennedy. These assassinations reinforced a growing sense among Americans in the 1960s that they inhabited a violent, dangerous country where criminal conspirators thought nothing of snuffing out the lives of idealistic leaders. For many Americans, the age of innocence ended on November 22, 1963, and they have found it difficult to trust government leaders ever since.

Kennedy's untimely death instantly transformed the man into a myth. After conversations with Kennedy's widow, Theodore White wrote an essay for *Life* magazine in which he compared Kennedy's presidency with the legend of Camelot. Camelot had recently been popularized in the United States by the successful Broadway run of a musical of that same name. Camelot referred to the Arthurian legend, to the mythical kingdom of Arthur and the Knights of the Round Table. According to White, Jacqueline Kennedy told him that President Kennedy at night in his bedroom before going to sleep played the recording from *Camelot*. She insisted that his administration had been a modern-day Camelot:

> a magic moment in American history when gallant men danced with beautiful women, when great deeds were done, when artists, writers, and poets met at the White House. . . . There will never be another Camelot again.[4]

Had Kennedy been alive to read such maudlin nonsense, he most likely would have derided it, but the myth of Camelot struck a chord with millions of people who had been shaken by the assassination and needed some way of affirming his presidency. For those who believed in Camelot, Kennedy had been the democratic prince whose achievements epitomized the American dream of success. His family history had been a saga of upward mobility from humble immigrant origins to the upper reaches of wealth, power, and fame. Then, in an instant, a loser's bullets had turned spectacular achievement into tragic loss.

The historical record belies the myth. Kennedy's record of accomplishment is mixed. Much of his New Frontier agenda failed to pass in his lifetime. He was mostly a cautious leader on civil rights issues. He only belatedly sensed the moral passion that motivated civil rights activists such as Martin Luther King Jr. He got only a portion of his economic program enacted. Posthumous revelations about his extramarital affairs, drug use, a myriad of serious health problems, and other Kennedy family scandals have tarnished his moral stature and diminished his reputation.

His foreign policy achievements were more significant. The Peace Corps and the Trade Expansion Act succeeded. But the Alliance for Progress flopped, neither undercutting the appeal of Castro nor promoting democracy and economic growth in most Latin American countries. Kennedy's "crisis managing" in Cuba was a disaster at the Bay of Pigs, and he risked nuclear war

---

[4] *Life*, December 6, 1963.

FIGURE 7.4   Jacqueline Kennedy, dressed in black mourning attire, holds Caroline and John Jr.'s hands as they prepare to descend a flight of stairs during President Kennedy's funeral, Washington, D.C., November 26, 1963.   *Source:* Getty Images Inc.—Hulton Archive photos.

to pry Soviet missiles out of Cuba. The Berlin issue was defused after years of tension, but its resolution owed more to Khrushchev's Berlin Wall than to any initiatives taken by Kennedy. The test ban treaty and *détente* with the Soviets in 1963 decreased the danger of nuclear war, but Kennedy had previously ordered major increases in American military spending, particularly for strategic thermonuclear weapons, which had escalated the arms race. Kennedy also significantly expanded American involvement in Vietnam, putting the country on course for war in Southeast Asia. The space program, which he set in motion, captured the imagination of millions of Americans. Beating the Soviets to the moon restored national confidence that America retained its technological advantage in the ongoing Cold War.

Any accounting of his presidency must include intangible dimensions. Kennedy was a superb politician. His intelligence, wit, and personal charm set a high tone for his presidency. His beautiful

First Lady, Jacqueline Bouvier Kennedy, became an iconic figure as the charming hostess who redecorated the White House. She also exuded high fashion, stylish good taste, and appreciated fine art and literature. John Kennedy was devoted to the ideal of national service. He paid high tribute to science and scholarship. He sought always to bring out the best in Americans, to challenge them to seek excellence in all things, especially young people, with whom he felt a special bond. Whatever the flaws and failings of the private man, the public image that Kennedy cultivated was positive, energetic, and effective. Always there must be the rueful speculation, what if he had lived? Any fair historical judgment must take into account the brutal fact of his abruptly abbreviated career, a man in his prime cut down before he could make his full mark on history.

Brief Bibliographic Essay

A vast literature has accumulated on John Fitzgerald Kennedy, his family, and all facets of his political career. Robert Dallek, *An Unfinished Life, John F. Kennedy, 1917–1963*, is the best biography of John F. Kennedy. A highly favorable insider account of his presidency is Arthur M. Schlesinger Jr.'s *A Thousand Days*. Bruce Miroff's *Pragmatic Illusions: The Presidential Politics of John Kennedy* and Garry Wills's *The Kennedy Imprisonment* are both negative assessments of his presidency. The best account of the election of 1960 remains Theodore H. White's *The Making of the President, 1960*. Carl M. Brauer's *John F. Kennedy and the Second Reconstruction* is a favorable assessment of the president as civil rights leader. Many mostly excellent historical studies of the civil rights movement have been written. Taylor Branch, *Parting the Waters: America in the King Years, 1954–1963*, is the first volume of a monumental narrative history of the Southern civil rights movement organized around the life and actions of Reverend Martin Luther King Jr. See also Howell Raines, *My Soul is Rested: Movement Days in the Deep South Remembered*, the best oral history of the civil rights movement, which draws from a wide range of participants and perspectives. A fine, recent study of Kennedy's foreign policy is Michael R. Beschloss's

The Crisis Years: Kennedy and Khrushchev, 1960–1963. Michael Dobbs, *One Minute to Midnight: Kennedy, Khrushchev, and Castro on the Brink of Nuclear War* is an excellent recent analysis of the missile crisis that stresses the theme of historical contingency. Leaders often had to make decisions on the basis of incomplete or even erroneous information. Dobbs concludes that it was more good fortune than enlightened leadership that kept events from spinning out of control and the world plunging into nuclear catastrophe. Anyone who cares to know about Kennedy's assassination must start by reading the Report of the Warren Commission on the Assassination of John F. Kennedy. Readers who want to read a fine historical treatment of Kennedy's assassination can access Michael L. Kurtz's *Crime of the Century: The Kennedy Assassination from a Historian's Perspective*. Gerald Posner's *Case Closed: Lee Harvey Oswald and the Assassination of JFK* does an effective job of demolishing the leading conspiracy theories and providing plausible answers to many of the lingering questions about the assassination. A recent book, Bryan Burrough's *Four Days in November: The Assassination of John F. Kennedy*, brilliantly reconstructs the assassination and its aftermath.

8

Great Society and Vietnam

Lyndon Johnson deftly took charge of the nation's political life following President Kennedy's shocking assassination. He skillfully steered stalled New Frontier legislation through Congress. Following his landslide election victory in November 1964, he presided over the flowering of the Great Society, a multidimensional reform program that promised to fulfill the social vision of the New Deal and improve the quality of life for all Americans.

At the same time that Johnson asserted effective leadership as a domestic reform leader, he had to manage America's far-flung international commitments. Within the context of ongoing Cold War tensions with the major Communist powers, Johnson inherited a series of difficult world situations: The NATO alliance showed signs of strain, pressures for social and political change were rising in many Latin American nations, and the Middle East remained a powder keg that could blow at any time. Most of all, Johnson inherited a growing U.S. involvement in the Vietnam War. Vietnam eventually undermined his credibility, strangled his beloved Great Society, and forced him from office.

JOHNSON TAKES CHARGE

As he assumed office at a tense moment in American history, Johnson's immediate task had been to preside over an orderly transition of power that ensured continuity in government. During his first speech given five days after Kennedy's assassination, Johnson made it clear that stalled New Frontier legislation would be the top priority on his domestic agenda.

As Lyndon Johnson took control of the reins of power during the first six months of 1964, the Republicans sought a candidate to run against him. Within Republican ranks, conservatives, unhappy with their party's tendency to nominate nonideological centrists for the presidency, were determined to nominate one of their own. Representing diverse groups mostly from the south and west, these aggressive conservatives supported the candidacy of Arizona Senator Barry Goldwater. His political philosophy blended traditional conservatism with New Right ideological discontent

FIGURE 8.1 Less than two hours after President Kennedy's death, a somber Lyndon Johnson was sworn into office aboard *Air Force One*, still parked on the ground at the Dallas Airport. He is flanked by Kennedy's widow Jacqueline and his wife Lady Bird. *Source:* AP/Wide World Photo.

with the restraints imposed by the welfare state and the Cold War. Goldwater's supporters were able to defeat an all-out effort to derail his candidacy waged by moderate Eastern Republicans.

Goldwater ran the most impolitic campaign in modern American history. He turned his 1964 electoral campaign into an ideological crusade. He staked out positions on leading issues that alienated all but his New Right supporters. He told an audience of elderly people in Florida that he favored making Social Security voluntary. In Charleston, West Virginia, located at the edge of Appalachia, one of the poorest regions in the nation, he announced that the impending war on poverty was unnecessary. He journeyed to the South to tell folks that the Tennessee Valley Authority, which was highly popular in the area, should be sold off to private utility companies. He told Midwestern farmers that he opposed high-price supports. A few pundits wondered if Goldwater really wanted to be president.

What really got Goldwater in trouble was his bellicose statements on foreign policy. He said that commanding generals in the field should be allowed to make decisions whether to use nuclear weapons, and he said that he would authorize the use of tactical nuclear weapons in Vietnam.

The Democrats spent a lot of their campaign funds on making negative television ads, which often featured clips of Goldwater making one or more of his controversial statements. One ad characterized Goldwater as a maniac whose foreign policies would destroy the world. It showed a child, a little girl, picking petals off a daisy and counting, "one, two, three. . . . " Then the child looks up startled, and the frame freezes on her eyes as she dissolves into a mushroom-shaped cloud; then the screen goes black. An explosion follows, and then the voice of President Johnson can be heard— "These are the stakes. . . . We must either love each other or we must die." The daisy spot, as it came to be known, provoked such a flood of protests, that it was pulled after only one showing. However, television news programs showed it repeatedly during the remaining weeks of the campaign. An estimated forty million Americans saw the controversial ad at least once.

Because all of the polls showed him holding a big lead over Goldwater, President Johnson did not bother to campaign until the final month. And he refused to consider debating him on television. When he did enter the fray, Johnson forged a broad electoral consensus, including much of the business community, trade unions, farmers, most middle-class voters, liberals, intellectuals, the elderly, the poor, blacks, and other minorities.

On election day, Johnson received 43.1 million votes to Goldwater's 27.2 million, and 486 electoral votes to Goldwater's 52. Johnson carried forty-four states and received 61.2 percent of the popular vote. Democrats added thirty-seven House seats and one more in the Senate. With a strongly Democratic Congress awaiting him in 1965, Johnson was poised to lead the nation. Liberalism rode at high tide.

In the aftermath of the Goldwater debacle, some analysts spoke of the impending demise of the Republican Party as a major political force. Such epitaphs were premature. It turned out that Goldwater was merely ahead of his time. Ronald Reagan, inheriting Goldwater's cause, would ride it to the White House in 1980.

Some of the election results signaled danger ahead for the Democratic Party. Five out of the six states carried by Goldwater in 1964 were Southern. Johnson barely won Florida. In many other Southern states that he carried, a majority of white voters rejected him. The Solid South was disintegrating as white voters, seeing the Democratic Party increasingly identified with the drive by African Americans for full participation in public life, abandoned their historical allegiances and voted Republican. The growth of the Republican Party in the South and Southwest proved to be one of the most important long-range trends in post–World War II American politics.

Goldwater's failed candidacy also signaled the permanent shift of African American voters from the Republicans to the Democrats. Whereas Richard Nixon had polled nearly a third of the black vote in 1960, Goldwater got only 6 percent in 1964. In the 2008 election, the Republican candidate John McCain received only 4 percent of the African American vote, the lowest ever for a candidate of the party of Abraham Lincoln.

GREAT SOCIETY

During his first six months in office, President Johnson used a successful strategy for getting Congress to enact much previously blocked New Frontier legislation. He evoked memories of the deceased Kennedy as a moral lever to pry bills out of congressional committees. He also sought to overcome conservative resistance to social reform by insisting on balanced budgets and reducing government expenditures. Johnson was both a liberal social reformer and a fiscal conservative. He obtained congressional passage of Kennedy's long-stalled tax cuts, which reduced personal and corporate income taxes about 5 percent across the board. Enactment of these tax cuts represented the first deliberate use of Keynesian fiscal policy to stimulate demand and promote investment to keep the economy prosperous and expanding, thereby generating additional tax revenues to pay for proposed reforms. Johnson's fiscal conservatism made many of his social reform measures palatable to conservatives in Congress.

Johnson also persuaded Congress to enact the most comprehensive civil rights bill in American history. The civil rights bill passed in the House in February 1964, but it ran into a Southern filibuster in the Senate that delayed its passage until June. The Civil Rights Bill of 1964 went far beyond Kennedy's original proposal. It was the most sweeping affirmation of equal rights and the strongest commitment to their enforcement ever made by the federal government. Its key provision guaranteed equal access to all public accommodations such as restaurants, bars, hotels, resorts, theaters, and casinos. Other provisions strengthened federal machinery for combating discrimination in hiring and promotions. The bill also empowered the federal government to file school desegregation suits, and it further strengthened voting rights. It also required corporations and trade unions to ensure equal employment opportunities to all applicants.

In addition to promoting tax cuts and civil rights, Kennedy was considering an antipoverty program at the time of his death. Johnson immediately adopted it as his own. In his first State of the Union address delivered in January 1964, Johnson declared "unconditional war on poverty in America." Congress, a few months later, enacted the Economic Opportunity Act, authorizing the spending of $1 billion over three years, beginning in 1965. The act created an umbrella agency called the Office of Economic Opportunity (OEO) to administer the various antipoverty programs.

Soon after his overwhelming victory, Johnson, backed by the most liberal Congress since 1936, set out to create what he called a Great Society. He organized task forces made up of his staffers, social scientists, bureaucrats, and activists to draft legislative proposals to send to Congress. Johnson and his liaison people also worked closely with Congress during all stages of the legislative process to get passage of the program. Among the most important measures enacted during 1965 was the Appalachian Regional Development Act. Appalachia, a mountainous region extending from Pennsylvania to northern Alabama, contained seventeen million people and was a vast pocket of poverty. The act provided over $1 billion in subsidies for a variety of projects stressing economic development of the region.

Congress also attacked the problem of America's decaying central cities. The Housing and Urban Development Act of 1965 provided funding for 240,000 units of low-rent housing. It also authorized spending $2.9 billion over four years for urban renewal projects. Federal rent supplements for low-income families were added in 1966. Congress also created a new Cabinet-level Department of Housing and Urban Development (HUD). President Johnson appointed Robert Weaver to head the new agency; Weaver became the first African American Cabinet member.

In addition to attacking urban problems, Congress enacted both the Medicare and the Medicaid programs in 1965. Medicare provided health care for people age sixty-five and over, while Medicaid provided health care for low-income people not eligible for Medicare. Both programs would be funded through Social Security. At the time of the passage of these programs, the United States was the only industrial democracy in the world without some form of national health insurance. Organized physicians, working through their powerful lobby the American Medical Association (AMA), had blocked all efforts to enact national health insurance since Truman had first proposed it in 1945. President Johnson overcame the opposition of the AMA and conservative legislators by limiting the insurance programs to the elderly and to the poor, and by funding them through the Social Security system. Funding Medicare and Medicaid through Social Security was another example of Johnson's fiscal conservatism that won conservative support for social reform measures.

One of the most important achievements of Great Society was the enactment of federal aid to education. The Elementary and Secondary Education Act of 1965 ended a long debate in Congress over the use of federal funds to support public schools. President Kennedy had made federal aid to public schools a top New Frontier priority and had suffered a serious defeat because of Catholic opposition to his bill, which did not fund parochial schools. By contrast, Protestant and Jewish leaders strongly opposed funding parochial schools. Kennedy could never resolve the impasse. President Johnson, believing that education was the primary way in which the federal government could promote equality of opportunity in America, overcame the religious road-block. He persuaded religious leaders to accept an aid program that provided federal funds for states based on the number of low-income students enrolled in their schools. The funds would be distributed to both private and public schools to benefit all children in need. The Elementary and Secondary Education Act was one of the cornerstones of LBJ's Great Society and the forerunner of George W. Bush's No Child Left Behind educational reform enacted by Congress in 2001. The motive driving both pieces of landmark legislation was the same: a desire to improve schools in poor neighborhoods.

Johnson rescued another stalled New Frontier reform when he secured congressional passage of the Immigration Act of 1965, the first comprehensive overhaul of U.S. immigration policy in forty years. The new law abolished the discriminatory national origins quota system implemented during the 1920s, which had restricted immigration to this country on the basis of ethnic and racial background. These ethnoracial restrictions had proved embarrassing in the context of the Cold War struggle for friends in the Third World. Under the new legislation, each country would have an annual quota of about 20,000 immigrant slots. Eligibility to fill these slots would be based upon the skills and education of the individual immigrant plus close family ties to people already here. At the time of the enactment of the immigration act, the focus of the Congress was on repealing the ancient quotas based on long-discredited racist and nativist prejudices. The framers had no inkling that the major long-term consequence of immigration reform was to work a transformation of the demography of the United States.

The family unification provisions of the new immigration law allowed a naturalized immigrant to bring to the United States not only spouses and children, but also siblings. These siblings, upon becoming citizens, could in turn bring over their spouses and children, thus creating chain migrations. These family unification provisions of the new immigration law had the unintended consequence of reviving immigration as a major social force. Since 1970, an estimated forty million immigrants have entered the United States, of which approximately twelve to eighteen million have entered illegally. The overwhelming majority of these recent immigrants have emigrated from Asian, Middle Eastern, African, Pacific Island, and Latin American countries. Population forecasters estimate that by 2050, the non-Hispanic white portion of the American population will dip below 50 percent.

Additional civil rights legislation joined the Great Society agenda in 1965. Many African Americans could not yet vote in the Deep South states, despite the enactment of three previous civil rights bills and voter registration drives by civil rights groups. Hundreds of student volunteers working in Mississippi in the summer of 1964 to register African American voters encountered stubborn, and often violent, opposition from white segregationists. In the spring of 1965, Martin Luther King Jr. prepared to lead a 50-mile march of demonstrators from Selma, Alabama, to the state capitol in Montgomery to publicize continuing denial of African American voting rights. A few days before the march was scheduled to begin, President Johnson made a nationally televised speech to a joint session of Congress calling for a voting rights bill that would close all remaining loopholes in civil rights laws. Near the end of his speech, Johnson raised his arms in the style of a country preacher and recited the words from the old black spiritual that had become the anthem of the civil rights movement: "And . . . we . . . shall . . . overcome." The demonstrators in Selma, poised to begin their march, listened to his speech through tears of joy.

As the demonstrators began their march for the right to vote, they were attacked by Alabama state troopers who gassed, clubbed, and whipped them. These vicious attacks on nonviolent prote-sters marching on behalf of a fundamental democratic right were televised nationally to a shocked nation. An angry president, viewing the attacks, federalized the Alabama National Guard and ordered it to provide protection for the marchers all the way to Montgomery. Johnson then pushed the voting rights bill through Congress. The Voting Rights Act of 1965 gave the attorney general the power to appoint federal registrars to register voters in districts where historic patterns of disfranchisement prevailed. Empowered by the new law, federal officials registered hundreds of thousands of African American and Hispanic voters in six Southern states during the next three years. The 1966 election was the first one held in this country in which most adult Southern African Americans could vote.

In addition to voting rights for African Americans, the Great Society also was committed to the cause of conservation. Congress enacted the National Wilderness Preservation Act in 1964, which incorporated all federally owned wilderness areas into a national wilderness system. It also established a program for meeting the nation's future wilderness preservation and recreation needs. Conservation and wildlife preservation laws were enacted. In early 1965, Congress passed the Highway Beautification Act, a cause pushed by First Lady Claudia "Lady Bird" Johnson. It also enacted the Water Quality Act and the Clean Air Act; these important measures provided federal funds for assisting state and local governments to set up air and water purification programs.

Two important pieces of consumer-protection legislation passed in 1966, a "Truth-in-Packaging" bill and a "Truth-in-Lending" act. The former required sellers to label accurately the contents of packages sold for household use. The latter required detailed information about the true rate of interest charged on bank loans and credit purchases. Congress added a new cabinet-level Department of Transportation in 1966 and enacted a series of highway safety laws. Consumer advocate Ralph Nader's book, *Unsafe at Any Speed*, documented the hazardous design defects in Detroit-made automobiles. Nader enhanced public awareness of these problems and helped secure passage of the new laws.

Great Society measures enacted between 1964 and 1966 represented the most far-reaching assault ever mounted on a vast array of social problems by the federal government. Most of the social problems that the Great Society addressed had been around for years, but they were challenged during the mid-1960s because of a confluence of circumstances that gave reformers opportunities normally unavailable within the American political system. The nation was prosperous, and there existed a widespread sense that Americans could afford the costs of social reform. Large liberal majorities prevailed in both houses of Congress, breaking the bipartisan conservative bloc's control. Most of all, Johnson's concern for the welfare of ordinary Americans and his extraordinary political skills made Great Society a reality.

The expanding economy provided billions of dollars of additional tax revenues to fund the new programs without incurring budget deficits or igniting inflation. Medicare and Medicaid improved the quality of health care available to the elderly and the poor. Students at all educational levels benefited from federal programs, and African Americans in the South finally had the vote. During the 1960s, the number of poor people in American declined significantly, although most experts attribute this impressive achievement more to a robust economy that generated millions of new jobs than to the antipoverty programs that proliferated during that era.

Most poor people in the United States in the 1960s, as in any industrial economy, needed much more than education, job training, or the assistance of well-intentioned, idealistic young people working in the domestic peace corps. Millions of Americans were too old, too sick, or disabled to benefit much from such efforts. Single mothers with small children needed much more, including subsidized day care. African Americans, Hispanics, and many other minorities encountered nearly universal discrimination in housing and work. Unemployment and underemployment afflicted millions of workers. Farm and migrant workers worked long hours for poverty-level wages. The hastily enacted liberal war on poverty had no solutions for these complex, deeply rooted structural problems that entrapped 35 million poor Americans in the mid-1960s.

The war on poverty was oversold and underfunded, and very little of the limited funding ever got to the poor themselves. Most of the OEO dollars covered the salaries and expenses of adminitrators and contractors who provided services for the poor. The war on poverty generated unrealistic expectations among poor African Americans and fierce resentments among working-class whites who perceived antipoverty programs as favoring strident protesters over hardworking, law-abiding people. The resultant disillusionment, anger, and cynicism contributed mightily to the growing backlash against liberal bureaucrats spending taxpayers' money on people who the backlashers believed did not deserve it.

After 1966, Congress, concerned about the expanding war in Southeast Asia, as well as rising crime rates and inflation, was reluctant to appropriate more funds for reform. Johnson, who wanted to achieve his place in history as the president who fulfilled the social vision of the New Deal, had escalated the war in Vietnam and thereby strangled his beloved Great Society. The fight for civil rights, the struggle to save the cities, the efforts to improve the public schools, and to clean up the environment—all were starved for the sake of the escalating war. The man who most wanted to extend the New Deal presided over its collapse and prepared the way for a profound shift to the Right in American politics.

THE WARREN COURT

Led by its energetic Chief Justice Earl Warren, the activist liberal majority that controlled the Supreme Court during the 1960s rendered a series of landmark decisions that struck down the last remnants of the segregation system. The Court also protected the right of dissent and expanded the freedom of the press, regulated obscene materials, and limited the expression of religion in public schools. It further altered criminal legal procedures, expanded the right to privacy, and made the American political system more inclusive.

In *Engel v. Vitale* (1962), the Court banned prayer in public schools. In a later decision, the Court banned Bible readings from public school classrooms. The Court also nullified an Arkansas law that mandated the teaching of "creation science" as an alternative to Darwinian evolutionary theory. The cumulative effect over the years of these decisions was to remove religious observances from public schools. *Engel* and other cases did more than anything else over time to arouse the religious Right to involve itself in politics.

In two controversial five-to-four decisions, the Supreme Court also enhanced the procedural rights of citizens accused of crimes. In the first case, *Gideon v. Wainwright* (1963), the Court ruled that Clarence Gideon, a career criminal, had never gotten a fair trial because he had never had an attorney to defend him in court. The Court, in effect, ruled that the right to a fair trial included the right to be represented in court by a lawyer. If the defendant could not afford an attorney, the state, at taxpayers' expense, had to furnish one.

In the second case, *Miranda v. Arizona* (1966), the Court enhanced citizens' Fifth and Sixth Amendment rights against self-incrimination and affirmed the right of citizens to have a lawyer present during questioning. According to the new rules implemented in *Miranda v. Arizona*, police were required to inform a suspect of his or her rights at the time of arrest: the suspect's right to remain silent; that anything the suspect said could and would be used in a court of law to convict him or her; the right to have an attorney represent him or her in court; and in the event that he or she could not afford a lawyer, that the state would provide him or her one free of charge.

In 1965, the Warren Court struck down a Connecticut law that forbade the sale or use of contraceptives. In *Griswald v. Connecticut*, Associate Justice William O. Douglas, writing for the majority, found the Connecticut law to be an unwarranted invasion of privacy. Nowhere in the Bill of Rights is there delineated a specific right to privacy; Douglas apparently inferred a right of privacy. Years later, this inferred right of privacy would be applied by Associate Justice Harry Blackmun to establish a woman's right to have an abortion.

In *Baker v. Carr* (1962), the Court declared that it could determine whether state legislative districts had been fairly drawn. The principle that the courts used during the 1960s to determine fairness was "one person, one vote," derived from the equal protection clause of the Fourteenth Amendment. During the 1960s, as a consequence of *Baker v. Carr*, several states, in which rural voters were overrepresented in state legislatures at the expense of urban residents, had to redraw the boundaries of their legislative districts to make them equal in population.

The cumulative effects of these Supreme Court decisions were to enhance the rights of individuals, curtail the arbitrary powers of government, and make the political system more democratic. The least democratic branch of the federal government, and the only one beyond the reach of the voting majority, had done much to strengthen American democracy and validate the growing pluralism of the political culture.

Conservatives were enraged by what they considered judicial usurpations of the lawmaking process. Law enforcement officials complained that Court decisions made their jobs more difficult, allowed obviously guilty people to avoid punishment, and appeared to place the law on the side of criminals rather than on their law-abiding victims. Religious people often were offended by the Court's proscriptions of religious observances in the public schools. As the conservative revolt gathered momentum in this country during the 1970s, one of its salient issues was curtailing the judicial activism of the Supreme Court.

CONTINUING THE COLD WAR

Johnson's early ventures in world affairs met with mixed results. In Europe, Johnson could not prevent relations with NATO allies from deteriorating. His chief difficulties came with Charles de Gaulle, who wanted France and western Europe to rid themselves of U.S. domination. The French leader spurned Johnson's offer to create a multilateral nuclear force and directed France to accelerate development of its own nuclear forces. In early 1966, the French withdrew their forces from NATO and ordered the United States to remove all of its military installations and personnel from France. France's dramatic actions signaled that de Gaulle believed that the Cold War in Europe was waning. European countries no longer feared Soviet aggression; hence they no longer felt dependent on U.S. support.

As de Gaulle challenged American influence in Europe, tensions in the Middle East caused Johnson persistent problems. He perceived Egyptian leader Gamal Abdul Nasser's efforts to promote Arab nationalism to be the chief threat to American Middle Eastern interests. The Soviet Union, backing Nasser, was gaining influence in the region. Then came another Arab–Israeli war. It occurred in June 1967, following border clashes between the Israelis and Syrians in the Golan Heights area. Nasser, backing Syria, mobilized his forces and blockaded Israel's Red Sea port of Elath. Egypt also worked out an agreement with Jordan that placed its forces under Egyptian command.

Arab leaders appeared united in their determination to demolish the Jewish state. Their military forces comprised 900 combat aircraft, five thousand tanks, and half a million soldiers. The outnumbered Israelis possessed about 250 aircraft, one thousand tanks, and 275,000 soldiers. The Israelis, concluding that an Arab attack was imminent, launched a preemptive strike on June 5. Israeli forces quickly destroyed the Egyptian air force, decimated Jordan's army, and defeated Syrian forces. Israeli tanks routed the Egyptian army. Israel won the war in six days. The key to Israel's remarkable victory was that it quickly established decisive air superiority.

When a UN-proposed cease-fire went into effect, Israel occupied the Sinai and that part of Jordan west of River Jordan (the West Bank). Israeli forces also occupied Gaza, East Jerusalem, and Syrian territory in the Golan Heights. Egyptian military power was shattered, Nasser was humiliated, and Soviet interests suffered a setback. Israel, now the major power in the region, kept all occupied territories, determined to use them to enhance its territory and guarantee its security. Israel now controlled a land area nearly four and a half times its prewar size. Israeli imperialism intensified already-powerful Arab anti-Zionist animosities.

The most important outcome of the war from Israel's perspective was that no responsible Arab leader would ever again seriously contemplate the military destruction of the Jewish state. Israel, now secure strategically, entered fully into the Middle Eastern World. Anti-Americanism increased among Arabs because Arab leaders perceived the United States to be the main backer of Israel and responsible for its smashing victory. And in the wake of the Israeli victory, U.S.–Israeli relations improved, and thousands of Jews emigrated from the United States to Israel, further inflaming Arab anti-American feelings. The aftershocks of the Six Days' War have echoed all the way to the present and the seething enmity between the Israelis and the Palestinians.

Aware of the dangers inherent in the U.S.–USSR competition for influence and strategic advantage in the Middle East and elsewhere in the Third World, President Johnson invited Soviet premier Alexei Kosygin to the United States for another summit conference. The two leaders made limited progress toward controlling the spiraling thermonuclear arms race. Johnson and Kosygin agreed that negotiations would begin soon on limiting the number of strategic bombers that each side possessed. They also announced plans to hold regular summit meetings to discuss arms control and other issues of paramount importance to both. But there would be no more summits. Johnson had planned to go to Moscow in the fall of 1968, but the Soviet Union sent its tanks into Czechoslovakia on August 20, 1968, to crush efforts by the Czechs to establish a social democratic government. Johnson canceled the impending meeting.

Johnson also had to face crises in the Caribbean, where he made preventing further Castro-like insurgencies his top priority. His first crisis came in Panama, which had long been a U.S. protectorate. Violent conflicts erupted between Panamanians and American citizens living in the Canal Zone in January 1964. The violence began when Panamanian students demanded that their national flag be flown alongside the American flag at a high school located in the Canal Zone. U.S. authorities rejected the students' demand. U.S. soldiers killed twenty-one Panamanians, and three Americans died in riots. The OAS mediated the dispute. U.S. and Panamanian negotiators then produced a series of agreements, allowing Panamanian participation in the management of the Panama Canal and granting Panama a share of canal revenues.

A more serious crisis erupted in the Dominican Republic, which also had a long history of U.S. domination. A right-wing dictator, Rafael Trujillo, was overthrown in 1961 by a military coup, ushering in years of political instability in that impoverished island country. President Kennedy, delighted to see Trujillo go, sought free elections. The elections brought Juan Bosch to power in 1962. Bosch, a social Democrat, was overthrown by another military coup seven months later. In early 1965, a coalition of liberals, radicals, and young army officers launched a revolution to restore Bosch to power.

President Johnson, fearful that pro-Castro elements might come to power and turn the country into another Cuba, sent U.S. troops to suppress the insurgency. U.S. Marines and Army infantrymen prevented Bosch's return to power. Administration spokesmen announced that U.S.

intervention had prevented a Communist takeover of the Dominican Republic. An occupation force was set up to maintain order. Elections were held in 1966, and Joaquin Balaguer defeated Bosch.

Balaguer established a government that protected U.S. interests, and Johnson withdrew the U.S. forces. But the Bosch movement was an independent, nationalistic movement, not a Communist conspiracy. U.S. intervention violated the OAS charter and canceled the U.S. pledge not to intervene militarily in the internal affairs of other Western Hemisphere countries. U.S. public opinion supported Johnson's military intervention. Liberals and foreign critics attacked his actions, but he ignored them. The campaign was limited in duration, and few American lives were lost. Johnson achieved his objectives, and his success silenced his critics.

GOING TO WAR IN VIETNAM

The roots of U.S. intervention in Southeast Asia could be traced back to Truman's presidency, but it was not until the Kennedy years that the United States became inextricably involved in a war in Vietnam. At the time President Johnson replaced Kennedy, the political situation in South Vietnam was deteriorating. A succession of inept military governments had followed Diem, none of which governed or fought effectively. National Liberation Front forces, the VietCong, supported by supplies and troops from North Vietnam, extended their control in southern Vietnam.

LBJ, just as Truman, Eisenhower, and Kennedy had before him, embraced the Cold War ideology. His primary foreign policy objectives were to contain the two Communist powers, the Soviet Union and the People's Republic of China, and to prevent revolutionary change in Third World countries. He increased the number of American advisers in South Vietnam and the level of economic aid. He also approved a series of covert operations against North Vietnam, including commando raids along the North Vietnamese coast and infiltration of CIA operatives into the North.

On August 1, 1964, while engaged in electronic espionage off the coast of North Vietnam, the destroyer USS *Maddox* was attacked by North Vietnamese torpedo boats. The *Maddox* repulsed the attackers and resumed its spy operations, joined by another destroyer, the *Turner Joy*. On the night of August 4, both ships reported that they were under attack. No one on board either ship sighted any attackers; their initial reports were based on radar and sonar contacts.

Even though evidence of a second attack was not certain, Johnson authorized retaliatory air strikes against North Vietnamese naval bases. He also asked Congress to approve a resolution, authorizing him to take "all necessary measures to repel any armed attack against the forces of the United States and to prevent further aggression." In presenting their case for the resolution, administration officials misled the Congress. Congressmen and senators were not told that the *Maddox* was on a spy mission when it was attacked, nor that the second attack may not have occurred. Secretary of Defense McNamara characterized both incidents as unprovoked acts of aggression against U.S. ships on routine patrol in international waters. The House passed the resolution unanimously, and the Senate enacted it by a vote of 88 to 2. Even though administration officials assured members of Congress that they were not planning a wider war, enactment of the Gulf of Tonkin resolution offered President Johnson a blank check to wage war against the North Vietnamese if he chose to use it.

As 1965 began, the South Vietnamese government was on the verge of defeat. To try to sustain the Saigon regime, Johnson authorized a gradually expanding bombing campaign, called Operation Rolling Thunder, against North Vietnam. There was a direct connection between the air war against North Vietnam and Johnson's decision to send U.S. combat forces to South Vietnam.

Within two weeks, General William Westmoreland, the U.S. commander in Vietnam, requested Marine combat units to defend a large U.S. Air Force base at Danang because he could not rely on South Vietnamese security forces. Johnson quickly approved his request. On March 8, two Marine battalions in full battle gear waded ashore at beaches south of Danang.

In July 1965, Johnson and his top-level advisers made a series of fateful decisions that began seven years of war in Southeast Asia. They approved General Westmoreland's requests for saturation bombing in southern Vietnam and for expanding the air war against North Vietnam. They also authorized sending an additional 100,000 combat troops to South Vietnam. Most important, President Johnson gave General Westmoreland a free hand to assume the major burden of fighting in the South.

When he committed the United States to war in Southeast Asia, Johnson did not tell the American people what he had done, and he refused to seek a formal declaration of war against North Vietnam. He claimed that the Gulf of Tonkin resolution granted him the authority to wage war. Johnson felt confident that the United States could win the war in a few years and that he could persuade Congress and most Americans to support it.

THE AMERICAN WAY OF WAR

The United States relied heavily on air power to win the war. Air Force and Navy pilots had two primary missions—to check infiltration of men, equipment, and supplies coming south from North Vietnam along the "Ho Chi Minh Trail," and to punish the North Vietnamese from the air until they abandoned the insurgency in the South and came to the bargaining table on U.S. terms. Bombing failed to achieve either objective, even though the United States waged the largest aerial war in history.

U.S. ground combat operations also escalated drastically between July 1965 and the end of 1967, when the United States had deployed nearly 500,000 troops. General Westmoreland used a strategy of attrition against the enemy. He believed that "search and destroy" operations would eradicate the enemy fighters and force them to the negotiating table. U.S. troops would use their superior mobility and firepower to counter the enemy's guerrilla warfare tactics. Since all of South Vietnam became a combat zone, U.S. soldiers found themselves fighting an unconventional war without fronts or territorial objectives. The only measure of progress toward victory in a war of attrition was the number of enemy supplies captured or destroyed, the number of enemy weapons and ammunition captured or destroyed, and most of all, the number of enemy soldiers captured, wounded, or killed.

The American takeover of the war in early 1965 had prevented certain South Vietnamese defeat. But the United States could only achieve a stalemate, not a victory. The attrition strategy was based on the assumption that U.S. forces could inflict irreplaceable losses on the enemy while keeping their own casualties low. Even though the Americans inflicted heavy casualties, both the VietCong and the North Vietnamese replaced their losses and matched each American escalation with one of their own during the period 1965–1967.

In 1967, the South Vietnamese government, headed by General Nguyen Van Thieu, attempted to build popular support among the rural population. It focused on pacification and rural development. Government cadres moved into villages, providing medical supplies and social services. They sought to promote a national rebirth, while U.S. forces tried to defeat the Communists militarily. These pacification efforts sometimes succeeded, but they more often failed. The inability of the South Vietnamese military government to solve their country's massive social problems was a major reason for the eventual failure of the U.S. effort in Vietnam.

FIGURE 8.2   The helicopter war: The Vietnam War was the first in which helicopters were used extensively to airlift men into combat. Here, riflemen of the 25th Infantry Division prepare to board a squadron of "Hueys" (Bell UH-1Ds) for an assault on Communist positions.   *Source:* U.S. Army Photo.

The steady escalation of the war between 1965 and 1967 generated both international and domestic pressures for a negotiated settlement. But the continuing stalemate on the battlefields ensured that neither side wanted negotiations. For political reasons, both sides had to appear responsive to peace initiatives, but neither side would make the concessions necessary to get serious negotiations started. Hanoi's strategy was to get maximum propaganda value out of peace initiatives, while matching the U.S. escalations until the Americans tired of the war and pulled out.

Hanoi maintained that the U.S. military presence in South Vietnam violated the 1954 Geneva Accords and that the bombing of North Vietnam was criminal aggression. The North Vietnamese also insisted that the government in Saigon would have to be replaced by a coalition government dominated by the NLF. The United States refused to withdraw its forces until a political solution could be reached in the South that excluded the VietCong. It also refused to stop the bombing, which Washington insisted was necessary to keep the Communists from overrunning the South. So the war went on, and numerous peace initiatives from various sources failed in 1966 and 1967.

WAR AT HOME

While the expanding military stalemate in Vietnam continued, within the United States, supporters and opponents of the war engaged in debates of rising intensity. On one side were the Hawks, mostly conservative Republicans and Democrats, strongly supportive of the war, who wanted to increase the U.S. war effort. On the other side were the Doves, challenging both the effectiveness and the morality of the war. The Doves represented a more diverse group: old-line pacifists, student radicals, civil rights leaders, some college professors, and liberal politicians. The most prominent Dove was Senator J. William Fulbright. Initially a supporter, Fulbright had turned against the war by 1966.

Opposition to the war took many forms. Senator Fulbright held hearings on the conduct of the war before his Senate Foreign Relations Committee, providing a forum for war critics and helping to legitimate opposition to the war. The Doves staged many protest demonstrations during 1967, the first year of extensive antiwar activity. On October 21, about 50,000 opponents of war demonstrated in front of the Pentagon. Many young men resisted or evaded the draft. Thousands fled America and its war for Canada or Sweden.

Most Americans in 1967 were neither Hawks nor Doves. Nearly all citizens had supported the initial escalations that Americanized the Vietnam War. But after two years of rising costs and casualties, popular frustration with the Vietnam War had mounted. Polls taken in August 1967 showed that a majority of Americans believed sending U.S. combat troops to Vietnam had been a mistake. But opponents of Johnson's war policy in 1967 formed no consensus on Vietnam. They were divided over whether to escalate the war drastically and win it, or to negotiate an American withdrawal.

THE TET-68 OFFENSIVE

Johnson, trying to curtail criticism of his war policy, brought General Westmoreland to Washington. Westmoreland stated that pacification was going so well that the VietCong could no longer mount a major offensive anywhere in South Vietnam. Popular support for the war increased as the year ended.

On January 30, 1968, choosing the Lunar New Year, known as "Tet" (the most important Vietnamese holiday), as a time to strike in order to catch their opponents by surprise, about 80,000 NLF and North Vietnamese troops simultaneously attacked provincial capitals, district towns, and major U.S. military bases all over the country. At most attack sites, the VietCong were beaten back within a few hours or few days and sustained heavy losses. Within a month, they had lost all of the cities they had originally taken.

Communist strategists had designed the Tet Offensive to give their forces a smashing victory over the Americans, to demoralize the Army of the Republic of Vietnam (ARVN) forces, and to bring the urban population of South Vietnam over to their side. The Communists hoped that their assaults would provoke popular uprisings against the South Vietnamese government, forcing the Americans to leave and hastening the end of the war. Although Tet caught the South Vietnamese and Americans by surprise, they had responded quickly to counteract it. Tet turned out to be a major military defeat for the Communists; they failed to achieve most of their goals and suffered heavy losses.

However, within the United States the Tet Offensive had a tremendous impact. It turned out to be a crucial psychological and thus political victory for the Communists. The Tet Offensive changed the way the media, particularly television news, covered the Vietnam War. Previously, television had usually presented a well-ordered vision of the war: on-the-scene reports of combat operations that usually were reported as U.S. victories, along with periodic analytical reports of the war's progress and of pacification programs. With Tet, viewers for the first time saw the results of a major Communist offensive striking all over South Vietnam. A rush of violent and confusing images flooded the screen. The chaos in Vietnam, vividly displayed on television, appeared to contradict all of the official reports of the past three years, which had conveyed the idea of steady progress toward military victory.

Although General Westmoreland spoke confidently about having anticipated and suppressed the Tet offensive, while inflicting heavy losses on the enemy, he soon requested an additional 206,000 troops to be able to follow up and win the war. The Chairman of the Joint Chiefs of Staff,

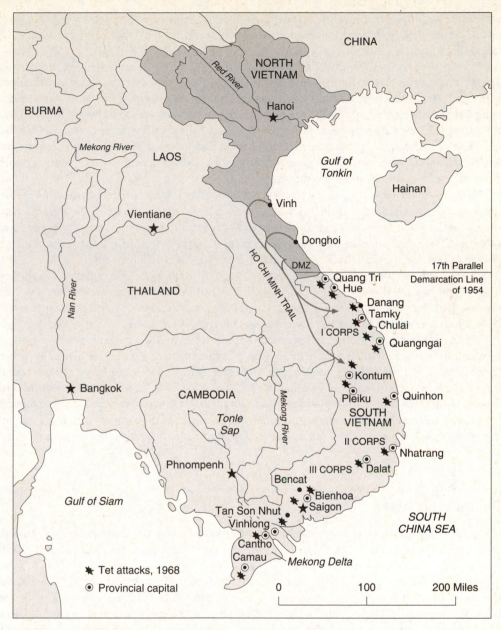

FIGURE 8.3 The Tet-68 Offensive. *Source:* U.S. Army Map.

General Earle Wheeler, told the president that the Americans could lose the war unless the requested reinforcements were sent. Johnson, confused by events and conflicting military opinions, asked his new Secretary of Defense, Clark Clifford, to conduct a thorough review of the troop request.

   Clifford conducted the first full review of the U.S. war effort in Vietnam. He demanded precise answers to fundamental questions: What were the ultimate objectives of the United States in Vietnam? How would additional forces contribute to attaining these goals? What would be the impact of a major escalation of the war on the public and the economy? How would General Westmoreland deploy these troops, and what results could be expected from this additional manpower?

The answers he got from officials in the Pentagon discouraged him. Meeting these troop requests would necessitate calling up reserves, increasing draft calls, and raising taxes. Casualties would rise, and domestic opposition would intensify. Civilian analysts in the Pentagon recommended that the United States start phasing back its military involvement and work for a negotiated settlement. They also proposed turning over more of the fighting to the South Vietnamese forces. Clifford subsequently recommended to Johnson that he reject Westmoreland's request for additional troops, assign the ARVN a greater fighting role, and seek a negotiated settlement rather than continue his futile efforts to win the war.

Congressional opposition to the war also escalated after Tet. An obscure Minnesota senator, Eugene McCarthy, challenged Lyndon Johnson as an antiwar candidate. In the New Hampshire primary, held on March 12, 1968, McCarthy received 42 percent of the vote, almost as many votes as Johnson. Four days after the New Hampshire primary, a more formidable antiwar candidate, Robert Kennedy, announced that he too would seek the Democratic nomination.

At the White House, Johnson convened a panel of distinguished civilian and military advisers who had previously endorsed his war policy. But in March these "wise men" told the president that the Vietnam War could not be won, "save at unacceptable risk" to national interests. Johnson accepted Clifford's recommendations to scale back the war.

Johnson understood that he no longer had the support needed to sustain his policy of gradual escalation. In a speech given on March 31, 1968, he told the American people that he would reduce the bombing of North Vietnam in an effort to get negotiations underway. As he neared the end of his speech, he stunned the nation by stating, "I shall not seek, nor will I accept, the nomination of my party for another term as your president." To restore unity to America, he would remove himself from politics and seek peace. Johnson's presidency was a casualty of the Vietnam War. His speech in which he announced that he would not seek reelection, amounted to a resignation of the presidency.

Brief Bibliographic Essay

Robert Dallek, *Lyndon B. Johnson*, is a condensation of his two-volume biography. It portrays Johnson as a complex and flamboyant personality deeply troubled by the failure of his Vietnam War policy and the growing polarization and fragmentation within the nation. John A. Andrew III, *Lyndon Johnson and the Great Society*, offers an assessment of the Great Society with special emphasis on the major issues of civil rights and the war on poverty. See Taylor Branch, *Pillars of Fire, America in the King Years, 1963–1965*, the second of his three-volume history of the modern struggle for civil rights. Bernard Schwartz, in *Super Chief: Earl Warren and His Supreme Court*, offers a good study of the many landmark decisions of the Warren Court and of the man who led it. Johnson's foreign policy is studied by Philip L. Geyelin in *Lyndon B. Johnson and the World*. Michael B. Oren has recently written a remarkably good book, *Six Days of War: June 1967 and the Making of the Modern Middle East*, which places the Six Days' War into its Middle Eastern and global contexts. A good general military and diplomatic history of U.S. involvement in Vietnam is George Donelson Moss, *Vietnam: An American Ordeal*, 6/e. George C. Herring's *America's Longest War: The United States and Vietnam, 1950–1975*, 4/e, is a concise diplomatic history of the war. Larry Berman's *Planning a Tragedy* is an acute study of the Johnson administration's decision to go to war in Vietnam.

9

Rebellion and Reaction

The 1960s had begun with President Kennedy's appeal for national renewal. He had urged young people to channel their energy and idealism into community service at home and the Peace Corps abroad. Thousands followed his lead. But after his assassination, the national scenario that unfolded for the rest of the decade featured sit-ins, marches, riots, bombings, the burning of cities, and more assassinations. Expectations of peace, prosperity, and justice for all vanished in the face of political polarization, social fragmentation, cultural crisis, and the Vietnam War.

A comparatively few young Americans, mostly from middle- and upper-middle-class backgrounds, were temporarily radicalized by their experiences; vastly more Americans turned conservative or simply abandoned politics. The liberal consensus that had been forged during the 1930s, 1940s, and 1950s as a consequence of fighting the Great Depression, World War II, and the early years of the Cold War disintegrated during the late 1960s and early 1970s. In its wake, a revitalized Republican Party, drawing from diverse sources, gathered strength during the 1970s and returned to power in 1980 with the election of Ronald Reagan.

During the early and mid-1960s, the economy was strong, the federal budget was balanced, inflation was low, and the nation was at peace. Most Americans were better off materially than they had ever been, and optimistic about the future. Social tranquility prevailed. Prospects had never looked better for the children of affluence. By 1968, inflation riddled the economy, the people were divided over a controversial war, and race riots tore apart major cities. Political assassinations agonized everyone; students protested on college campuses and in the streets. Other radical insurgents protested historical exclusions and injustices, and demanded their fair share of the American Dream. Drugs and violent crime became major concerns. With politics polarized and the backlash in full fury, the 1968 presidential election occurred amidst the worst backdrop of violence and disorder since the Civil War.

STUDENT RADICALS

The insurgencies that characterized the middle and late 1960s began on the campuses of some of America's leading universities, the prestigious Ivy League schools, and the great public universities such as the Berkeley campus of the University of California and the University of Michigan campus at Ann Arbor. A new generation of politically committed young people had already become involved in the civil rights movement and had also tried to organize poor people at the community level. After 1965, many of these youthful insurgents, most of them from middle-class and upper-middle-class families, became involved in protesting the Vietnam War.

In 1960, a group of young activists organized Students for a Democratic Society (SDS). In 1962, one of its leaders, Tom Hayden, wrote a manifesto for the new organization, the Port Huron Statement. Hayden criticized the apolitical apathy of college students and attacked the military-industrial complex as a threat to democracy. He called for an end to poverty in America and for the creation of "a democracy of individual participation," in which all members subject to the authority of a government institution would participate in its decision-making processes.

The first student uprising occurred on the Berkeley campus of the University of California in the fall of 1964. A group of students, many of them civil rights activists who had spent the previous summer registering voters in Mississippi, protested university efforts to prevent their using a campus area for rallying support for off-campus political activities. Student leaders Mario Savio and Jack Weinberg, both veterans of the Mississippi "Freedom Summer," formed the Free Speech Movement (FSM) to lead the resistance. When university officials attempted to discipline leaders of the FSM, about 600 students and nonstudents occupied Sproul Hall, the university administration building. After university efforts to persuade the protesters to leave failed, Governor Edmund G. "Pat" Brown ordered state police to remove and arrest them. The forced removal of the demonstrators provoked a student strike, which was supported by a large majority of the faculty. After two months of turmoil on campus, university officials rescinded the order and permitted "free speech" on campus. Student radicals, with faculty support, had won; university officials were forced to back down.

The rebellion that began at Berkeley soon spread to other campuses around the country. Insurgents attacked university complicity with racial injustice and the Vietnam War. They also attacked the universities themselves. They rebelled against receiving "assembly-line educations." Protesters demanded the right to sit on governing boards with the power to veto faculty appointments. Curricula and methods of instruction came under fire. Students objected to taking "irrelevant" courses, mostly required science and language classes. They called for fewer required courses, more electives, and fewer tests and grades. Other campus protests arose over issues concerning the personal lives of students. Protesters demanded the elimination of college parietal rules, which set curfews, imposed dress codes, and regulated visiting hours for university housing.

By the mid-1960s, the stalemated Vietnam War had become the main student protest issue. Since the military draft was the prime way the war could reach young people, opposition to the draft brought thousands of new recruits into protest politics. The SDS organized a Stop the Draft Week for October 16 to 21, 1967. It staged sit-ins at army induction centers, held meetings for draft card burnings, opposed campus Reserve Officer Training Corps (ROTC) programs, demonstrated against corporations known to be prime Defense Department contractors, and harassed military recruiters. Thousands of protesters besieged the Oakland, California, Army Induction Center; hundreds sat in the street blocking buses hauling in draftees. Between 1965 and 1968, the SDS led or joined hundreds of demonstrations at over 100 colleges and universities involving an estimated 50,000 students.

The SDS also joined a violent student uprising, which occurred at Columbia University during the first six months of 1968. The issues that sparked the conflict were two potent catalysts of student militancy—civil rights and Vietnam. Antiwar radicals and civil rights activists joined forces to attack one of the nation's most prestigious universities. The SDS sought an end to university ties with a military research institute on campus. The Black Student Union opposed university plans to construct a gymnasium on land adjacent to Harlem. Both groups occupied campus buildings to force the university to sever its ties with the military and to abandon the gym project. When negotiations between administration officials and students failed, police stormed the buildings to remove the protesters, who had barricaded doors and windows. Hundreds of students were injured, and about 700 were arrested. Following the arrests, the SDS helped organize a campus strike that forced the university to close early that spring.

American student protests in 1968 were part of a larger web of student and worker militant actions around the world. While students barricaded buildings at Columbia, ten million French workers went on strike, and students battled police in the streets of Paris. Mass demonstrations occurred in São Paulo, Brazil; the most violent street fighting in decades occurred in Italy. In London, 25,000 people protested the Vietnam War. Thousands protested the staging of the Olympic Games in Mexico City. Police sharpshooters shot and killed hundreds of the protesters. Radical political movements of every kind convulsed the planet during one of the most transformative years of the twentieth century.

FIGURE 9.1   Columbia 1968: Young people occupy an area of Hamilton Hall on the Morningside Heights campus in New York City.   *Source:* AP/Wide World Photos.

At its 1969 annual meeting, the SDS disintegrated. Its left wing, calling itself the "Weathermen," went off on its own. In October, hundreds of Weathermen staged "the days of rage" in Chicago, which they intended to be the opening campaign of a new American revolution. Rampaging through a few neighborhoods, they broke windows in buildings and smashed automobile windshields. Police arrested and jailed most of them. About 100 Weathermen went underground, forming terrorist bands that carried out sporadic bombings of public buildings and corporate headquarters during the early 1970s.

The New Left radicalized only a very small portion of the millions of young people attending college during the 1960s. Most students attended class, pursued their social lives, worked part-time, and sought conventional goals. They never participated in radical protests on or off campus. Student rebels were mostly clustered on the campuses of major metropolitan universities.

Because they were a highly visible, articulate group that received extensive media coverage, especially television news coverage, the public's perception was that student radicalism was much more prevalent than what demographic data confirmed. Most of the nation's 2,300 community colleges, state universities, private liberal arts colleges, and campuses with religious affiliations, which educated the vast majority of the nation's collegians, remained quiet, orderly, businesslike places during the 1960s. The young radicals of the 1960s were mostly the children of college-educated, liberal, affluent, and often influential parents. They formed a radical elite who rebelled against some of the institutions and practices of the affluent society.

THE GREENING OF AMERICA

Far more young people who felt alienated and frustrated by the affluent liberal society of the 1960s fled from it rather than radically confront it. These "hippies" took a path previously traveled by Bohemians during the Roaring Twenties and the Beats during the 1950s. The most prominent Beat poet, Allen Ginsberg, joined the 1960s' counterculture. The hippies embraced a new youth culture that ran counter to much that was cherished by middle-class Americans—affluence, economic growth, and high technology. The discipline of parents, schools, and jobs was abandoned for a free-flowing existence expressed by the hippie motto: "Do your own thing."

Hippies grew long hair and donned jeans, tank tops, and sandals. These refugees from the "uptight, straight" world of parents, schools, and nine-to-five jobs flocked to havens in the Haight-Ashbury section of San Francisco, the Sunset Strip in Hollywood, New York City's East Village, and elsewhere. They joined hundreds of communes that cropped up in both urban neighborhoods and rural retreats. The appeal of the commune movement lay in a romantic urge to return to the land: to adopt a simpler life, to regain physical and mental health, and perhaps to seek spiritual renewal.

The counterculture repudiated science, systematic knowledge, and rationalism. It embraced a notion of organic, mystical consciousness in which the Self merged seamlessly with Community and Nature. Infinite "being" supplanted the linear boundaries of time and space. Feeling and intuition replaced thought and knowing. Hippies explored ancient Asian and African mystical religions. Saffron-robed skinheads on San Francisco street corners chanted the "Hare Krishna." Others found the Age of Aquarius in astrology. Some hippies turned to witchcraft and demonology. Nature was valued as being superior to society and technology. A wide array of synthetic consumer products was rejected as artificial—"plastic." Hippies prized being natural, using nature's products, and eating natural foods. The hippie ideal was personal authenticity: to live a life free of conflict, exploitation, and alienation—a life in harmony with nature, family, community, and one's true self.

Hippies also repudiated the restrictive sexual practices of "Puritan" America. Although sexual behavior in this country had become more liberal, hippies moved far beyond middle-class proprieties and inhibitions. The freer sexuality of the hippie lifestyle became one of its main attractions and also provoked the wrath of elders. Casual sex was often tied to countercultural music, as flocks of teenage "groupies" sought out rock musicians. English groups, especially the Beatles and the Rolling Stones, expressed the central themes and ideals of the hippie worldview. Bob Dylan was the main American countercultural bard. He composed and sang "The Times They Are A-Changing" and "Blowin' in the Wind." In San Francisco, "acid rock" appeared. Promoter Bill Graham staged concerts at the Fillmore West, featuring the psychedelic sounds of San Francisco's homegrown bands, the Grateful Dead and the Jefferson Airplane. A young white blues singer from Port Arthur, Texas, Janis Joplin, became the queen of San Francisco's psychedelic music scene. Drugs and music formed the vital center of the counterculture. "Tune in, turn on, and drop out" urged the high priest of LSD, Timothy Leary, a former Harvard psychologist who had been fired for conducting psychedelic drug experiments on his students.

Drugs reached into the countercultural literary scene, continuing a beat generation tradition. Ken Kesey wrote part of his best-selling first novel, *One Flew Over the Cuckoo's Nest*, under the influence of LSD. With money from the book's sales, Kesey purchased a bus and named it "Further." He painted it in psychedelic Day-Glo colors, wired it for stereo, and he and his friends, who called themselves the Merry Pranksters, toured up and down the West Coast. Everywhere they went, they conducted "acid tests," wild parties featuring LSD-spiked Kool-Aid, loud rock music, and light shows.

Marijuana use was far more widespread than LSD. "Pot" became the common currency of the counterculture and spread into mainstream society. Marijuana turned up at high school and college parties during the 1960s. Hippies experimented with other drugs as well, including mescaline and methedrine. Countercultural drug use provoked a pathetic debate over whether smoking marijuana was less harmful than smoking cigarettes or drinking alcoholic beverages. All of these substances could be harmful if used excessively, but that fact was beside the point because the debate really was about values and lifestyles.

FIGURE 9.2 The Beatles. (L-R): John Lennon, Paul McCartney, George Harrison, and Ringo Starr. *Source:* St. Louis Mercantile Library. Used with permission.

One of the major events in the life of the counterculture occurred in the summer of 1967 in San Francisco's Haight-Ashbury district—"the summer of love." Hippies sought a cultural counterpart to SDS's proclaimed summer of protest against the Vietnam War. Just as radical politics was transforming American political life, the summer of love would transform society by creating a community of young dropouts uninhibitedly enjoying the pleasures of the flesh.

The reality of what occurred was mostly dismal. Thousands of youngsters showed up; most of them runaways from troubled homes, utterly unprepared to support themselves. Often they were reduced to panhandling, drug dealing, and prostitution to survive. Sexual promiscuity and rampant drug use led to epidemics of venereal disease and drug overdoses. Far from fleeing the social problems of the larger society, the runaways brought them with them. The writer Joan Didion, who visited the Haight-Ashbury district during the summer of 1967, in an essay, "Slouching Toward Bethlehem," famously depicted the squalor and aimlessness of hippie existence. Didion found the summer of love to be

> the desperate attempt of a handful of pathetically unequipped children to create a community in a social vacuum. . . . They are less in rebellion against society than ignorant of it.[1]

The hippie triad of "drugs, sex, and rock music" came together at rock festivals, the most important ritual of the countercultural community. The most famous of these "happenings" occurred at Woodstock in August 1969. At a site in New York's Hudson River valley, between 300,000 and 400,000 young people gathered to hear music, enjoy drugs, and engage in casual sex.

Charles Reich wrote in *The Greening of America* of a new consciousness that would renew America, forming the basis of another American revolution, one without tears or violence. The new order would just happen. But the counterculture's expected new utopia never arrived. Instead it turned sour and disintegrated. Hard drugs replaced marijuana. Violence, most of it connected with illegal drug traffic, destroyed much of what had been attractive in the hippie culture.

Greed and selfishness also pervaded the counterculture, contradicting its presumptions of innocence. Another rock festival, promoted by the Rolling Stones held at the Altamont Raceway in Northern California, was marred by violence when the Hell's Angels, an outlaw motorcycle gang, hired by promoters to provide security, savagely beat people and even killed a person.

The counterculture lasted for about half a decade; then much of it simply evaporated, quickly becoming only an exotic memory. It had sprung to life because of some special circumstances prevailing during the 1960s. The postwar baby boom had created a large population cluster of young people between the ages of fourteen and twenty-five. Such a huge youth population created, for a moment, a consciousness of a separate culture. Permissive child-rearing practices also contributed to the formation of the counterculture. These children of abundance confronted a complex world of protracted education; large-scale corporate and government bureaucracies; an intricate, powerful technology; severe social conflicts and inequities; and most of all the military draft and a controversial war in Vietnam. Young people recoiled in fear and loathing over a world that they had never made. Some of them became "flower children," urging others to "make love, not war."

But only a minority of young people joined the counterculture. Most went about the difficult enterprise of growing up and entering the adult world without visible alienation or protest.

---

[1] Joan Didion, *Slouching Toward Bethlehem* (New York: Washington Square Press, 1968), p. 127.

The greatest gap in the 1960s social fabric was not a generation gap between children and parents, but between different segments of the youth population. The more significant gap was intragenerational, not intergenerational. Value conflicts between middle-class and working-class young people were profound and occasionally violent. Upper-middle-class campus radicals scoffed at bourgeois sensibilities and burned their draft cards. Young workers, for whom middle-class respectability remained a cherished ambition, defended their way of life and patriotically supported the Vietnam War. Long-haired hippies and antiwar demonstrators infuriated working-class youth. One of the most violent riots of the era occurred in New York City when hard-hat construction workers attacked a crowd of antiwar demonstrators.

Although short lived and engaging only a fraction of young people during the 1960s, the counterculture left its mark. It called attention to the negative ecological and human consequences of technology, and they forced some people to confront the disparities between their professed ideals and the lives they lived. But the most enduring impact of the counterculture came in lifestyle realms—in diet, dress, decorative art, music, and sexual practices. People became more concerned with developing their inner selves, with achieving their "human potential."

THE FIRE THIS TIME

The civil rights movement crested in 1965 when Martin Luther King Jr. led the Selma march and Congress passed the Voting Rights Act. Five days after President Johnson signed that historic measure, the Watts section of Los Angeles went up in flames. It ushered in the first of several successive "long, hot summers." The Watts riot, a weeklong orgy of burning and looting, claimed thirty-four lives, injured 1,100 people, and destroyed $40 million worth of property.

Watts was not physically an inner city, since families did not live in crowded, dilapidated tenements; they lived in single, detached houses with lawns located along palm-shaded boulevards. Three African Americans sat on the Los Angeles City Council; Watts was represented by a black Congressman and two black state assemblymen. Economically, African Americans living in Watts were better off than blacks in any other large American city.

Watts revealed a depth of antiwhite bitterness and alienation that few civil rights workers of either race even knew existed. The enactment of liberal civil rights bills had only raised exaggerated expectations and intensified the rage of many Watts residents. It was obvious that the rioting had enjoyed wide support within the black community. When Reverend King walked the streets preaching nonviolence, the people mostly ignored him.

A special commission investigating the Watts upheaval warned that if the breach between the races was not healed, the riot might be a curtain-raiser for future racial blowups. The commission's warning proved prophetic. Between 1965 and 1968, hundreds of inner cities exploded into major riots.

The worst violence occurred in Newark and Detroit within the same week of July 1967. In Newark, 26 people died, and 1,200 were injured. In Detroit, 43 people died, and another 2,000 were hurt. Fires burned out the center of the nation's fifth largest city. For two weeks that summer, Detroit was a war zone with tanks rolling through the streets and the sound of machine-gun fire piercing the air.

Detroit's riot was the most alarming, not only because of the loss of life and the extensive destruction of property, but also because it occurred in a city governed by a coalition that included extensive African American participation. Great Society reformers had lavished extensive antipoverty and urban renewal programs on the Motor City. One-fourth of all workers employed in the automobile industry, Detroit's major business, were black; the UAW was a progressive, integrated union. About 45 percent of Detroit's African American families owned their own homes.

Analysts of the Detroit riot drew a portrait of the typical rioter—a young adult black male, a high school graduate, employed, often an autoworker and a union member, a veteran, married, and with an annual income slightly below the national median for his age group. These data suggest that the typical Detroit rioters were neither juveniles out on a spree nor despairing members of a black underclass. The rioting did not occur in the poorest neighborhoods but in black working-class neighborhoods containing a high percentage of owner-occupied homes and intact families. African American rage and violence in Detroit were apparently provoked more by provocative police tactics than by deprivation and despair.

Nearly all major race riots started from minor episodes, often from incidents growing out of white police arresting African Americans. Watts blew up when a crowd gathered to protest the arrest of a drunken motorist. Newark exploded after police arrested an African American taxicab driver, John Smith, for following a police car too closely. Smith protested and was beaten by the arresting officers; news of the beating provoked the riot. Detroit erupted when police raided an after-hours bar hosting a party for two returning Vietnam veterans.

A pattern prevailed in the major urban riots. Most rioting occurred within inner city confines; most of the destruction was inflicted upon inner city homes and businesses; and most of the violence occurred between rioters and law enforcement personnel. Over 80 percent of the fatalities were rioters, shot either by the police or soldiers.

The racial antagonisms that exploded into riots during the late-1960s had deep urban roots, particularly in residential discrimination. Confrontations between blacks seeking housing and working-class whites, who were determined to keep them out, had exacerbated race relations and complicated politics in many Northern cities since the years of World War II. These antagonisms had reached a breaking point by the mid-1960s, infuriating blacks and frightening whites. By the time the most destructive riots occurred in 1966–1968, Americans, most of whom did not live in the cities where battle lines were drawn and riots erupted, had become genuinely alarmed at the ever-rising levels of unrest, disorder, and violence. Demographic trends fed the rising violence in Northern cities, including the coming of age of baby boomers and the peaking of the major south-to-north migrations. By the mid-1960s, the inner cities were home to a large population of young black men.

Studies of all major riots also suggested that the underlying causes of the uprisings were chronic slum conditions, aggravated by rough police tactics and hot, humid weather. Frustration with the slow pace of black economic progress, despite years of civil rights agitation, Great Society reforms, and the war on poverty, also fueled the rioting. The National Advisory Commission on Civil Disorders called attention to a crucial reality about black inner cities: "White institutions created it, white institutions maintain it, and white society condones it."

BLACK POWER

Urban riots were the most destructive display of black militancy. The slogan "black power" made its appearance in 1966 when James Meredith attempted to march from Memphis, Tennessee, to Jackson, Mississippi, to inspire African Americans of his native state to assert their rights. He got only ten miles into Mississippi when a sniper using a 16-gauge shotgun wounded him. Dr. King and other civil rights leaders quickly arrived to complete his march. Two of the marchers, young leaders of the Student Non-Violent Coordinating Committee (SNCC), began chanting "black power." Soon, most of the marchers were chanting the same slogan.

Initially, "black power" was a cry of outrage and defiance. It later became political doctrine, although meaning different things to different people. For SNCC leader Stokely Carmichael, "black power" meant that African Americans should take control of the civil rights movement and develop their own institutions and instruments of power. Implicit in these actions were the rejection of integration, scorning white allies, and the approval of self-defensive violence.

Black power advocates soon cropped up in Oakland, California. Huey Newton and Bobby Seale called their organization the Black Panther Party for Self-Defense. They founded it after San Francisco police had killed an unarmed sixteen-year-old black youngster. The Panthers set up free health clinics, ran educational programs, and offered free breakfasts for schoolchildren. They also cultivated a paramilitary image. They armed themselves, formed patrols, and preached a blend of black nationalism and Marxian socialism. They proved skillful at getting media attention, and their movement spread rapidly in 1966 and 1967. By 1968, at their peak, they had perhaps 5,000–6,000 members mostly in 12–15 chapters located in cities with large black populations.

The Black Panthers had a penchant for violence and gunplay. In the late 1960s, approximately twenty Panthers died in conflicts with police, the FBI, each other, and various militant rivals. By the end of the 1960s, the organization was in disarray. Its leaders were dead, in jail, or had fled the country. But a Panther mystique lived on. They were praised by some white liberals who had held fund-raisers on their behalf. A famous poster of Newton sitting in a rattan chair with a spear in one hand and a rifle in the other adorned the dorm rooms of many a black and white radical student in the late 1960s and early 1970s.

At the extremes, "black power" became an expression of African American separatism. Separatist doctrine traced its roots to a long tradition of black nationalism in this country. Black Muslims articulated the most important expression of 1960s black nationalism. Founded during the 1930s in Detroit by Elijah Poole, who called himself the Prophet, Elijah Muhammad, it remained a small, obscure religious sect with about 100,000 members until the 1960s. Black Muslims had recruited many of their followers from the bottom ranks of black society—street hustlers, drug addicts, and ex-cons. Their most famous recruit was world heavyweight boxing champion Cassius Clay, who changed his name to Muhammad Ali following his conversion to the Black Muslim sect in 1965.

The sect's most articulate spokesman was Malcolm Little, an ex-con who took the name of Malcolm X. During the early 1960s, he proffered a nationalistic alternative to civil rights. He jeered at Dr. King's tactics of nonviolent Christian love; he both angered and frightened whites with his tirades against integration with "white devils." In 1964, he was expelled from the Black Muslim organization after a dispute with Elijah Muhammad.

He made a pilgrimage to Mecca in 1964, and this experience enabled him to escape from the antiwhite racial nationalism espoused by the Black Muslims. He moved to New York and founded his own movement. When he was murdered during the spring of 1965, his political ideas were still evolving. His assassination had been ordered by Elijah Muhammad, or by members of his inner circle. Malcolm X's book, written with Alex Haley, *The Autobiography of Malcolm X*, became a posthumous best seller.

"Black power" also expressed African American pride; it became a celebration of African American culture, of "blackness itself." African American students in high schools and colleges demanded that courses be added to established curricula in African American history, literature, and languages. Black hair and dress styles appeared. "Black power" encouraged young blacks to seek success and remain "black," to avoid emulating white role models. The popular soul singer James Brown sang, "Say it loud, I'm black and I'm proud."

During the late 1960s, as the civil rights movement became radicalized and fragmented, King, who remained committed to the tactic of nonviolence and to the goal of an integrated, color-blind society, remained the foremost black leader. But he found that his methods did not work in the North. He tried and failed to desegregate Chicago. Tactics that had been effective against the *de jure* segregation of Southern towns could not overcome the *de facto* segregation of Northern cities. King also became increasingly involved in protesting the Vietnam War because it drained away funds for civil rights and Great Society reforms. His attacks on the war alienated President Johnson and cost him the support of the NAACP.

The civil rights movement, politically successful in the South but an economic failure in the North, was faltering by 1967. In the spring of 1968, trying to regain momentum, King prepared to lead a poor people's march on Washington. He also took time to go to Memphis to support a garbage workers' strike. Early evening on April 4, while standing on a Memphis motel balcony, King was shot and killed by James Earl Ray, a white ex-con and drifter. News of King's murder provoked 168 race riots in cities and towns across the land. Rioting occurred in the nation's capital. Buildings burned within a few blocks of the White House, and soldiers mounted machine guns on the Capitol steps to protect the building from assaults by American citizens.

BROWN AND RED POWER

Other minorities, spurred by the example of African American insurgents, rebelled during the 1960s. Hispanic militants made their presence felt. Latinos living within the United States were diverse. They shared a common heritage based on the Spanish language and culture, but their families had come from Mexico, Puerto Rico, Cuba, Nicaragua, El Salvador, and a dozen other nations. It was impossible to form a pan-Hispanic organization or to articulate goals that all Latinos shared. Puerto Rican students in New York demanded that courses in Puerto Rican studies be added to high school and college curricula. Mexican American militants also waged campaigns for recognition and self-assertion. Brown power militants began calling themselves "Chicanos," turning a term of opprobrium into a badge of pride and an assertion of ethnic identity that did not depend on a relationship with the "Anglo" world.

The most prominent Chicano militant of the 1960s was labor leader Cesar Chavez. A migrant farmworker-turned labor organizer, Chavez founded the National Farm Workers Association (NFWA) in 1963. The NFWA joined with other farmworker unions to form the United Farm Workers Organizing Committee (UFWOC), affiliated with the AFL-CIO. Chavez organized lettuce workers and grape pickers, using techniques developed by civil rights organizers, including marches, rallies, songs, and symbols that stressed the Chicano cultural heritage. Chavez led successful strikes in California's San Joaquin Valley in the 1960s. Uniting workers as never before, the UFW joined a strike of grape pickers in the vicinity of Delano, California, which Chavez called *La Huelga* (the strike). His movement obtained crucial assistance from urban, liberal, middle-class support groups that raised funds for the strikers and staged consumer boycotts, making table grapes picked by "scab" (nonunion) labor forbidden fruit.

Native American militants demanded respect for their cultural traditions and called attention to their economic needs, particularly repayment for ancestral lands that had been illegally taken from them by Europeans and their descendants. Red power militant Vine Deloria Jr. wrote *Custer Died for Your Sins*, emphasizing the historical injustices European settlers in the New World had committed against Native Americans. A group of attorneys, including Native American

FIGURE 9.3 Cesar Chavez (checked shirt, right) leads striking grape pickers. Most of the pickers working the grape fields of California in the 1960s and 1970s were of Mexican descent. *Source:* National Archives and Records Administration.

lawyers, formed the Native American Rights Fund to seek the return of tribal lands illegally taken from Indians and to obtain compensation for other properties confiscated by whites.

GAY-LESBIAN LIBERATION

Another expression of the 1960s' insurgent spirit was the open avowal of homosexuality by formerly closeted gays and lesbians. If people could mobilize for political action around the issues of race, ethnicity, and gender, so too could they fight for their sexual identities and preferences. A dramatic event ignited the gay liberation movement: On June 29, 1969, police raided the Stonewall Inn, a gay bar located in Greenwich Village. Instead of meekly submitting to arrest, patrons defiantly hurled bottles at the police. They sent a message: There was a new militancy and pride growing among members of the gay community; they were no longer willing to passively accept police harassment and society's condemnations.

Gay and lesbian ideologues developed theories that defined homosexuality as a legitimate sexual preference; they insisted that it was not abnormal, it was not sick, and it was not perverse. Gay and lesbian theorists attacked the psychoanalytic establishment for diagnosing homosexuality as a form of mental illness.

Within gay-lesbian communities, a debate occurred over whether homosexuality was innate or a consequence of socialization. Essentialists argued that individuals were born gay or lesbian; others argued that gay and lesbian identities were socially constructed. Although gays and lesbians could not resolve the debate over nature versus nurture, the gay liberation movement enabled millions of homosexuals to come out of the closet and to make their claim for acceptance into the larger society. Militant homosexuals marched in gay liberation parades chanting, "Say it loud, gay is proud." Gay and lesbian activists organized for political action, seeking an end to legislative and job discrimination against homosexuals and a diminution of massive homophobic prejudices and violent assaults.

THE REBIRTH OF FEMINISM

The social and cultural ground was being prepared during the 1950s for a rebirth of feminism. By 1960, it had become the norm for middle-class white married women to perform paid work outside of the home. By 1962, married women accounted for nearly two-thirds of the female workforce. At the same time that they were entering the paid workforce in ever-greater numbers, more and more women were going to college and earning degrees. In 1961, women received over 40 percent of all baccalaureate degrees awarded.

Women took mostly "women's jobs" such as nursing, clerical work, teaching, and domestic service, jobs that paid less than men's and offered few prospects for promotion. In 1960, the median compensation for women working in full-time, year-round employment was 61 percent of men's earnings. Traditional assumptions about the proper societal roles for men and women remained deeply ingrained. They were continuously reinforced by all of the mass circulation women's magazines, all of which were controlled by men. There was no organized feminist alternative to challenge male hegemony. The wife who worked was perceived to be helping her family achieve a middle-class lifestyle, not pursuing a career of her own. As the 1960s began, there existed an ideological lag; feminine consciousness lagged behind social reality. Even though cultural norms remained unquestioned, there was increasing evidence that many college-educated, middle-class women were unfulfilled by lives that increasingly diverged from prescribed roles.

Because women, as women, did not share a common social experience, they tended to view their problems as being individual rather than socially derived. It was left to the founder of the modern women's movement, Betty Friedan, author of the best-selling *Feminine Mystique* (1963), to show middle-class suburban housewives that what they had previously understood to be their individual problems were in fact women's problems. They were caused not by personal inadequacies but by deeply rooted attitudes that would have to be changed before women could achieve equality and fulfillment. Friedan, giving voice to the discontents of middle-class college-educated women, called the suburban, split-level home "a comfortable concentration camp." She called attention to the "problem which has no name": feelings of emptiness, of being incomplete, of wondering, "Who am I?" She asked, "What is the cause of the identity problems which bothers so many women who have ostensibly fulfilled the American dream?" She urged women to listen to that still-small voice within that demands "something more than my husband and my children and my home."[2]

Friedan's book defined and created the modern women's movement, but in so doing, her focus on passive and frustrated suburban housewives obscured other women's realities during the 1950s. Millions of working and middle-class women, of various ethnoracial backgrounds, worked outside the home, often struggling to improve working conditions. Women were active in civic reform movements, trade unions, peace movements, and the civil rights struggle.

It was the civil rights struggle of the early 1960s that catalyzed a sense of grievance among women. Women often joined civil rights demonstrations. The civil rights movement also provided a model for political activity. Women made connections between black demands for freedom, equality, and dignity and their own lives; they saw possibilities for acting for themselves, of mobilizing for group political action. Women perceived that the same society that oppressed blacks also oppressed women; both groups had been assigned separate and unequal spheres and told to stay in their respective places. Any efforts at self-assertion or challenges to the status quo were considered deviant. Women reasoned that if it was wrong to deny an opportunity to one group because of skin color, it was wrong to deny it to another group because of gender.

Great Society also helped the cause of women's rights. When the bill that eventually became the Civil Rights Act of 1964 was being drafted in committee, Congressperson Martha Wright Griffiths, a powerful representative from Michigan serving on the House Ways and Means Committee, led the drive to bar discrimination on the basis of sex as well as race, religion, or national origin.

---

[2] Betty Friedan, *The Feminine Mystique* (New York: Dell, 1963), *passim*.

Initially, the Equal Opportunity Employment Commission (EEOC), which had responsibility for enforcing Title VII of the Civil Rights Act of 1964, did not enforce the provision against sex discrimination. In response to the EEOC's failure to enforce Title VII on behalf of women workers, Betty Friedan and other women activists formed the National Organization for Women (NOW) in 1966 to pressure the commission to take sex discrimination in hiring seriously. Other groups soon mobilized, and the women rights movement was reborn.

These women's groups sought to mobilize public opinion and obtain litigation on behalf of their cause. They sought change from within the existing structure. In part, the new feminism was a species of liberal reform. It called for equal pay for equal work and demanded that women have equal access to all professional schools and occupations. To allow women to compete equally in the job market with men, feminists demanded publicly funded child care centers for women with preschool-aged children, and they sought legislation ending all forms of gender discrimination.

There was also a radical dimension to the emerging feminism of the 1960s that grew out of the experiences of young women in SDS and SNCC. These radical young women coined the term "sexism." Mary King and Casey Hayden, both civil rights activists within SNCC, had come to resent the arrogance of male activists who expected women to work hard, take risks, and leave policy making to the men. When women raised these issues at an SNCC convention, the male leaders responded by laughing at them. The SNCC chairman, Stokely Carmichael, quipped, "The position of women in our movement is prone."

These radical women gradually evolved a language to express their grievances. They defined the problem as "sexism," or "male chauvinism." Having diagnosed the illness, they proposed a cure—"women's liberation." While liberal feminist reformers in NOW fought for equal pay for equal work, radical feminists like King and Hayden demanded control over their own bodies. They called for wider distribution of birth control literature, tougher enforcement of rape laws, the sharing of housework and child-rearing duties with husbands, and the right to abortion on demand. They met in small groups for intense "consciousness-raising" sessions. These sessions also allowed women to understand that their personal problems were connected to the larger realms of social power, of "sexual politics." Feminist writer Robin Morgan contributed the defining slogan of the women's liberation movement: "The personal is political."

The reborn feminist movement encountered a formidable array of obstacles from the beginning. Many women as well as men rejected feminist demands. A 1970 Gallup poll showed that 70 percent of American women believed that they were treated fairly by men. Other polls revealed that a majority of housewives stated they were content with their lives. Many resented being told by liberal feminists that raising families was boring. Other women questioned the emphasis that NOW spokespersons placed on the satisfactions of working outside the home. Most working women derived little satisfaction from the jobs open to them, which were mainly low paying and sex segregated. If family budgets permitted it, they often returned to their homes.

Feminist leader Gloria Steinem acknowledged that she spoke for only a minority of women, but attributed that reality to cultural conditioning. She asserted that women had been brainwashed to accept their oppression; they required "consciousness-raising" sessions to ignite a sense of grievance. Many men worried about the loss of male prerogatives that had long been "givens" in the culture. Fundamentalist Christians were incensed because feminist demands violated Biblically ordained roles for women.

The most serious obstacle faced by feminists trying to build a movement based on women's common problems and concerns was the diversity of the women the movement was trying to organize. Women were differentiated on the basis of race, ethnicity, class, age, education, occupation, and sexuality. Feminists quickly discovered that they had sharp differences among themselves on

FIGURE 9.4 Women protesters outside the Atlantic City, N.J., Convention Hall, where Miss America will be crowned that evening. *Source:* AP/Wide World Photos.

many matters. There were disagreements over priorities, long- and short-term goals, and methods and tactics. Was the most pressing problem economic—an economic system that oppressed women? Or was it cultural—male chauvinism? Because of the diversity prevailing among women activists, the reborn feminist movement of the 1960s spawned a proliferation of organizations, tactics, ideologies, and goals.

BACKLASH

By 1967, a new rights consciousness pervaded American society. Those groups who perceived themselves as oppressed, disadvantaged, and denied their full measure of freedom, equality, opportunity, and dignity rose in rebellion. These militants were no longer willing to play the game by the old rules. Never in the history of the republic had so many groups mounted such a radical assault on traditional values, mores, and institutions.

The radical insurgencies of the late 1960s provoked a backlash, a furious response from the middle-class majority of Americans determined to uphold traditional American ways. The news media, particularly television, which pumped images of rioting blacks and protesting students into millions of living rooms on the nightly news, intensified the backlash. The backlash, which polarized Americans, was rooted in profound divisions of race and class.

A mix of forces drove the backlashers. In part it was simply residual antiblack racism. Many Northern white ethnics and Southern white working-class people had been taught to hate and fear black people and consider them inferior. They did not want to associate with them, they did not want their children attending school with them, and they surely did not want to have to compete with them in the workplace. They especially resented the antipoverty programs that appeared to reward black rioters, while law-abiding whites got nothing except higher tax bills.

Economic insecurities also drove the backlash. By the late 1960s, many Americans were feeling the effects of inflation, heavy indebtedness, and declining real income. Black demands for employment, rising taxes, and expensive governmental programs appeared to be direct threats to the economic well-being of increasingly hard-pressed middle-class Americans.

Most of all, it was a sense of cultural crisis that activated the backlash response. The demands of the militants, magnified by extensive media coverage and commentary, represented an attack on the traditional American way of life and its most cherished values and institutions: patriotism, the work ethic, family, and religion. The largest number of backlashers came from the ranks of white people who were followers of prominent evangelists such as Billy Graham and Oral Roberts. Devout Catholics also often joined the ranks of the backlashers.

They felt uneasy about many aspects of America's modern secular pluralistic culture. They disliked the teaching of Darwinian theories of evolution in public schools. They resented the experts and social engineers who drafted the complex Great Society legislation, which extended the reach of the federal government and allowed it to intrude more and more into their lives. They were upset by militant blacks, feminists, hippies, antiwar demonstrators, and the Warren Court, which coddled criminals and banished religion from the classroom.

By the mid-1960s, these folks were beginning to involve themselves in politics, especially in the South, Southwest, and Southern California. Ronald Reagan, who was elected governor of California in 1966, was the first prominent antiliberal political leader to actively politicize their concerns. These politicized evangelicals of the mid-1960s expanded into a new and powerful force in American politics in the 1970s, the Religious Right.

The rise of the backlash was another important indicator of the conservative drift that was underway in American political culture. By the late 1960s, many working-class white families had come to distrust what they had held in high regard since the 1930s, centralized government power. During the 1930s, New Dealers had used the power of the federal government to establish a lifeline for millions of Americans who were left impoverished and bewildered by the Great Depression.

By the 1960s, decades of ever-expanding prosperity had created a huge middle class that included millions of working-class families who opposed higher taxes and many of the social programs they funded. These middle-class Americans also embraced traditional values and were unhappy when liberal Democratic leaders did not denounce immorality and social disorder. It also appeared to them that liberals were much too attentive to the needs of poor people, minorities, and radical students and were neglecting the needs of hard-working patriotic people like themselves. The backlash was the most obvious sign of the growing antigovernment mood, but it was only part of a larger revolt, a much deeper disillusionment with liberal government and the experts who championed it.

THE ELECTION OF 1968

The radical insurgencies loose in the land, coupled with the intense backlash that they provoked, guaranteed that the 1968 election would occur against a backdrop of the worst conflict and violence within American society since the Civil War. The Democratic Party was splintered by divisions seething within the deeply troubled nation. The antiwar candidacies of Senators Eugene McCarthy and Robert Kennedy gained momentum in the spring primaries. Party regulars backed Vice President Hubert Humphrey, a Cold War liberal supporting Johnson's Vietnam policy. It was a wide open race, with public opinion polls giving Kennedy an edge over Humphrey and McCarthy.

Although Robert Kennedy focused his presidential bid on opposing Johnson's Vietnam War policy, he understood that the liberal consensus of social reform at home and containing Communism abroad had sundered. Kennedy groped for an alternative social vision that might appeal across a broad spectrum of constituencies now at war with one another and restore the majority Democratic coalition that could take him to the White House. He visited Native Americans on reservations, and he broke bread with Cesar Chavez in California. Robert Kennedy was the only established white politician with any credibility among black people following the assassination of Martin Luther King Jr. Kennedy also reached out to white, working-class backlashers. He sought a new community, more inclusive and more involved in the process of self-government.

For the most part, he tried to revitalize and reshape liberalism, but he also picked up the growing conservatism of many Americans and sounded some of its themes. He criticized welfare programs because they created a class of dependents who existed on government handouts. He proposed job programs and community development programs involving local people and the private sector.

In the California primary, Kennedy and McCarthy waged a decisive showdown battle. Kennedy, cashing in on his remarkable ability to attract black, Hispanic, and white working-class voters, narrowly defeated McCarthy. But on victory night, he was fatally wounded in Los Angeles. His assassin was Sirhan Sirhan, a deranged Arab nationalist who apparently hated Kennedy for his strong support of Israel. Once again, a senseless act of violence had struck down another popular leader. Once more the nation paused, hurt and saddened, to pay their final respects to a fallen political star.

Robert Kennedy's murder removed any chance that antiwar forces could win at the Democratic Party's Chicago convention. The convention was a bitter affair. Humphrey won an easy first-ballot nomination. Convention delegates, after a lengthy, angry debate, adopted a pro-administration plank on the Vietnam War. The rest of the platform focused on domestic issues and reflected traditional liberal stands: consumer protection, increasing farmers' incomes, and supporting trade unions. Humphrey chose Senator Edmund Muskie of Maine, a respected party leader, as his running mate.

As the Democratic delegates gathered in Chicago to nominate a presidential candidate, some 10,000 to 12,000 antiwar radicals gathered in the Windy City to protest the war. Most came to support the efforts of antiwar Democratic politicians. More militant groups came to disrupt the convention and to provoke confrontations with the police. The demonstrators came up against Mayor Richard Daley, the convention host, who had vowed that there would be no disruptions. Ironically, Daley was a supporter of the late Robert Kennedy and had become a strong opponent of the Vietnam War because it had claimed the lives of so many young working-class men. His forces cordoned off the convention site, and Daley deployed his police in the parks of Chicago, where protesters had gathered. He also had thousands of National Guardsmen and federal troops available if he felt they were needed. The total number of available police, guardsmen, and federal troops outnumbered the protesters.

The night that Hubert Humphrey was nominated, violence reigned in the streets of Chicago. Protesters, attempting to march on the convention, were blocked by police. They taunted them, shouted obscenities at them, and threw rocks and bottles at them. As some of the demonstrators attempted to break through police cordons, the police attacked in force. In a frenzy of violence, some of the police, chanting "Kill! Kill!" indiscriminately clubbed and gassed demonstrators, newsmen, and bystanders. Television cameramen brought the violence into millions of living rooms. Many liberal Democrats were everlastingly horrified by the actions of the Chicago police.

FIGURE 9.5   The Battle of Chicago. Police battle demonstrators outside of the Democratic Convention on the night that Hubert Humphrey was nominated.   *Source:* CORBIS-NY.

But millions of other Democrats in white-collar suburbs and blue-collar neighborhoods cheered the police, seeing in the radical politics and countercultural lifestyles of the youthful protesters an intolerable threat to order and traditional values. The different reactions to the televised violence reflected the profound divisions seething within the American society and culture created by the Vietnam War, race riots, and domestic insurgencies. Hubert Humphrey emerged from the political ruins as the candidate of a profoundly divided party.

The divisive Democratic Convention and the violence in the streets of Chicago played into the hands of the Republicans, who had previously held an orderly convention in Miami. They had nominated Richard Nixon, who had made a remarkable comeback. Nixon had retired from politics following a disastrous defeat in the 1962 California gubernatorial election, but he had worked hard for Republican candidates in 1964 and 1966, building support among party regulars. He had won a series of primary victories and gathered hundreds of delegates from nonprimary states. He came to Miami the front-runner and easily repelled his only remaining serious challenger, California governor Ronald Reagan, who was making the first of his several runs at the presidency. Nixon chose Spiro T. Agnew, the governor of Maryland, who had a reputation for talking tough on law and order issues, to be his running mate. The Republican platform called for an all-out war on crime, reform of the welfare laws, an end to inflation, and a buildup of defense forces. On the crucial Vietnam War issue, the Republicans promised to end the American War through purposeful negotiations but not to accept "camouflaged surrender."

Behind the Republican platform rhetoric and the choice of Agnew for vice president lay a shrewd political strategy. Nixon perceived that Southerners had become a power within his party. He also understood that Americans had become more conservative since 1964, when Johnson had scored his landslide victory over the hapless Goldwater. Nixon cut his ties with declining Northeastern liberal Republicans to forge an alliance with conservative Southerners led by Strom Thurmond.

Nixon promised Thurmond that he would never abandon the South Vietnamese government and that he would slow the pace of school desegregation. He also promised to crack down hard on demonstrators who broke the law. Nixon's "Southern strategy" stopped Ronald Reagan's bid for the presidency, which had counted on winning the votes of Southern delegates. The only reason the Southern strategy did not give Nixon the entire South was because a popular third-party candidate who had a Southern base entered the campaign.

George Wallace, governor of Alabama and leader of the American Independence Party (AIP), mounted a presidential campaign with popular appeal in all sections of the nation. Wallace, formerly a Southern populist Democrat, had become increasingly unhappy with the Democratic national policies. He left the party, formed the AIP, and chose General Curtis Lemay, formerly the chief of the Strategic Air Command, as his vice presidential running mate.

Wallace articulated the frustrations and resentments of his followers, who were upset by radical disruptions in the land and by the liberal politicians and intellectuals who appeared to sanction them. Wallacites could be found in the greatest numbers within the ranks of Northern blue-collar workers and Southern lower-middle-class whites. Many of these people had also lost faith in the leadership offered by the two major political parties. Wallace told his followers that there was not "a dime's worth of difference" between the Democrats and Republicans.

His main issue was playing to white antipathy toward civil rights and antipoverty programs. He was the first prominent political leader to center his campaign on the backlash. Wallace possessed a remarkable talent for voicing the fears and resentments of working-class whites, especially young men. He chiefly attacked liberal intellectuals, black militants, antiwar protesters, and hippies. Although his message was never a purely racist one, most of his appeal derived from white anxieties about integration and black progress. Opposition to race-related federal initiatives was always at the heart of Wallace's message to his supporters. But he learned to soften his language; he replaced the racist venom spewed by extremists with a set of coded phrases such as "law and order" and "welfare chiselers" that ignited raw racial anger without making his supporters feel as if they were racists.

Wallace championed free enterprise capitalism and traditional moral values. He also took a more hawkish stance on the Vietnam War than either Humphrey or Nixon. Polls showed that Wallace was a political force to be reckoned with. At the beginning of the presidential campaign, polls gave him 21 percent of the vote, almost as many as supported Humphrey. Had he held that 21 percent to November, he would have denied any candidate an electoral college majority and thrown the election into the House of Representatives. That was his strategy and goal—to play the role of "spoiler" and to force Nixon and Humphrey to bargain for his support to win the presidency.

Meanwhile, Nixon mounted the most expensive, sophisticated presidential campaign in American political history. His acceptance speech had sounded his principal theme, a promise to heed the voice of "the great, quiet forgotten majority—the non-shouters and the non-demonstrators." He called for unity and a lowering of voices. He pledged "peace with honor" in Vietnam. His appeal reached millions of voters yearning for an end to years of discord. It was a smooth, professional campaign. Nixon campaigned at a deliberate, dignified pace. He projected an image of maturity and inner tranquility; commentators spoke of a "new Nixon" who had replaced the fiery Red-baiter of the 1950s. His campaign featured slick television commercials and short speeches filled with patriotic generalities. Admen packaged and tailored Nixon's ads to particular constituencies. He offered his candidacy as a receptacle into which frustrated, fearful, and angry voters could dump all of their antagonisms and insecurities.

While Nixon played the role of unifier and harmonizer, his vice presidential running mate Spiro Agnew took the offensive. His task was to battle Wallace for the backlash vote. Agnew attacked the media for promoting radicalism, and he took a hard law-and-order line. Journalists dubbed Agnew "Nixon's Nixon." Polls taken in early October showed Nixon well ahead of both Humphrey and Wallace.

Humphrey's campaign floundered along, disorganized, short of both money and campaign workers. McCarthy initially refused to support Humphrey, who was hurt badly by his identification with an unpopular administration and its unpopular war. Reflecting the growing conservatism of the electorate and the power of the backlash, millions of nominally Democratic voters were turning to Nixon and Wallace.

But in October, Humphrey's campaign suddenly came to life. He distanced himself from Johnson's war policy by calling for a bombing halt. Union leaders campaigned hard for Humphrey, and many antiwar activists drifted back into his fold, preferring a flawed liberal to either the hated Nixon or the populist demagogue Wallace. McCarthy finally endorsed Humphrey on October 29. Johnson helped his chances by halting all bombing of North Vietnam and talking as though the war were about to end. Humphrey sliced into Nixon's lead. Wallace's support eroded. On election eve, pollsters said that the election was too close to call.

But Humphrey's late surge fell just short. Nixon held on for a narrow victory. He received 31.7 million votes to Humphrey's 31.2 million and Wallace's 9.9 million. Nixon received 43.4 percent of the popular vote to Humphrey's 42.7 percent and Wallace's 13.4 percent. Nixon carried thirty-two states with 301 electoral votes. Humphrey carried thirteen states with 191 electoral votes, and Wallace carried five Southern states with 46 electoral votes.

There were clear indicators that the Democratic political future was troubled. The 1968 election marked an enormous turnabout from 1964. The huge majority of sixteen million votes that Johnson had rolled up only four years ago had completely evaporated. Between them Nixon and Wallace had received 57 percent of the vote. Nixon would be a minority president with the Democrats controlling both houses of Congress. Having offered little in the way of specific programs or policies, Nixon had no mandate whatsoever except maybe to dismantle or at least curtail Great Society.

On the surface, the electorate appeared to speak in many voices, reflecting the acute political divisions within the country. The old Democratic coalition had fractured, split by civil rights issues and divisions over the Vietnam War. Humphrey retained urban and union voters, although in reduced strength, and he got most of the African American vote. But his appeal was confined largely to the Northeastern industrial states. The rest of the country voted for Nixon, except for five Deep South states that went for Wallace.

The 1968 election revealed that the Democratic Solid South had vanished. Humphrey received only 31 percent of the Deep South vote, mostly from newly enfranchised African Americans. About 90 percent of Southern whites voted either for Nixon or Wallace. Racial antagonisms were significant vote determiners in 1968, the year of the backlash. The large "silent majority" of American voters, as political analyst Richard Scammon observed, constituted "the unyoung, the unblack, and the unpoor."

SUMMING UP THE SIXTIES

Forces that had been building for years climaxed in 1968 in full-blown social and cultural crises. The Cold War consensus was fractured beyond repair. The forces of reform liberalism achieved their greatest victories with Johnson's smashing electoral victory in 1964 and the subsequent enactment of Great Society. But at its moment of triumph, Great Society unraveled. The liberal reform coalition fragmented mainly over the Vietnam War and black power militancy. Congress, faced with the mounting costs of the war, rising crime and disorder at home, and growing opposition to liberal reforms, was loath to expand the boundaries of the welfare state. Great Society weakly expired in 1966–1967.

Beneath the surface of polarized politics, a profound cultural crisis gripped the increasingly fragmented society in 1967 and 1968. A relatively small number of articulate radicals not only rejected established political processes, but they also attacked traditional American institutions, mores, and values. The far more numerous backlashers vociferously and sometimes violently defended those same political processes and traditional values. The large majority of Americans got caught in the middle of this cultural warfare waged by extremists during the election of 1968.

Most insurgencies did not survive the 1960s. The most important one that endured has been the women's movement. The New Left fragmented in 1969, and a small faction functioned as a terrorist underground for a few more years. The counterculture simply evaporated, much of it coopted by the mainstream culture. The civil rights movement also fragmented. Some of its most militant leaders fled into exile or were killed. Some leaders such as Jesse Jackson moved into the political mainstream and became powers within the Democratic Party. Environmentalism, a cause that would become much more important in the 1970s and 1980s, derived in part from the 1960s' upheavals. Former hippies became environmentalist advocates, as did some former antiwar activists.

The year 1968 can also be read as a turning point in American politics. It marked the end of a period dominated by the forces of liberal reformism and the start of a conservative resurgence. The stalemated war in Vietnam that was inflating the economy and undermining U.S. power in the world also discredited liberalism, as did what many perceived to be the expansion of governmental power associated with Great Society reforms. Public opinion polls taken from the mid-1960s on revealed that smaller and smaller percentages of American voters trusted their elected officials or believed in the ability of government to get things right. The turnout of eligible voters for presidential elections, having reached a postwar high in 1960, thereafter dropped consistently in subsequent contests. The fall-off in voting and interest in politics generally was disproportionally higher among poor people, working-class, and lower-middle-class voters, most of whom had previously voted Democratic. Their abandonment of politics contributed to the decline of the major political parties, especially the Democratic Party, and the ability of organized interest groups to play greater roles in governing the country.

The spreading perception that liberalism was a prescription for dysfunctional policies at home and abroad fueled a rising conservatism. Conservative forces would steadily gather strength during the 1970s and would come to power in 1980 with the election of Ronald Reagan. The upheavals of the late 1960s left liberalism discredited and in decline. The decline of liberalism opened the political door for the growing legions of conservatives who had first surfaced as fervent supporters of Barry Goldwater in 1964 and who then turned to either Nixon or Wallace four years later. The year 1968 proved to be pivotal in the political history of the United States. The social and cultural antagonisms that polarized politics and fragmented the society could not be contained or resolved. They would dominate American politics in the decades ahead.

Brief Bibliographic Essay

Scholars have found the protest movements of the 1960s and their impact on American society and culture fascinating subjects to study. Clayborn Carson's *In Struggle: SNCC and the Black Awakening of the 1960s* shows how black power militancy grew out of the experiences of civil rights activists working in the South during the early 1960s. See also William H. Chafe's *Civilities and Civil Rights: Greensboro, North Carolina, and the Black Struggle for Freedom.* The best biography we have of Dr. Martin Luther King Jr. is Stephen Oates's *Let the Trumpet Sound: The Life of Martin Luther King Jr.* A reading of *The Autobiography of Malcolm X* (cowritten with Alex Haley) will provide an understanding of the sources of black nationalism during the 1960s. See also Rebecca E. Klatch, *A Generation Divided: The New Left, the New Right, and the 1960s.* A new survey of the turmoil characterizing the 1960s is Mark Hamilton Lytle's *America's Uncivil Wars: The Sixties Era from Elvis to the Fall of Richard Nixon.* A recent collection of essays edited by Peter Braunstein and Michael William Doyle, *Imagine Nation: The American Counterculture of the 1960s and 70s*, shows that the counterculture was never a social movement. It was an unstable amalgam of attitudes, gestures, "lifestyles," and hedonisms. Julian Messner's *The Superstars of Rock: Their Lives and Their Music* contains insight into the pop music of the 1960s. Barbara Deckard, in *The Women's Movement*, offers a fine account of Second Wave feminism. Alfredo Mirande's *The Chicano Experience* documents militancy in the Mexican–American world. Vine Deloria Jr.'s *Custer Died for Your Sins* records centuries of white mistreatment of Native Americans. Richard Krickus, *Pursuing the American Dream: White Ethnics and the New Populism*, is a study of blue-collar culture and its resentment of liberal welfarism, student radicals, hippies, and black militants. Lisa McGirr's *Suburban Warriors: The Origins of the New American Right* is a rich study of the origins of the new American Right among middle-class families living in Southern California. Lewis Gould's *1968: The Election that Changed America* is a fine recent analysis of that significant election.

10

Pragmatic Centrism

Richard M. Nixon was elected president by a narrow margin amidst the worst domestic violence and disorder in nearly 100 years. He made his top priorities restoring national unity and quickly phasing out the U.S. war in Vietnam. He failed to do either, in part because some of his policies exacerbated domestic discord and because he expanded the controversial war.

Reelected by a landslide margin in November 1972, President Nixon was never able to exercise the full powers of the presidency because of the enveloping Watergate scandals. Ultimately the president and his men were overwhelmed by media investigations, federal grand jury probes, special prosecutors, congressional investigations, the Supreme Court, and public opinion. He was forced to resign the presidency to avoid impeachment, conviction, and removal from office.

A CLOSET LIBERAL?

Nixon came to office determined to restore the consensus politics that had prevailed in this country during the 1950s and early 1960s before being shattered by the Vietnam War, the civil rights struggle, and other domestic insurgencies. To achieve his goal, he moved in different policy directions simultaneously. His general thrust was toward the center, but he also struck out in conservative directions in pursuit of his Southern strategy, and he proposed far-reaching reforms to co-opt liberal causes. But he failed to restore the lost consensus during his first term because he could not end the U.S. war in Vietnam. His pursuit of his Southern strategy perpetuated the social and cultural divisions he hoped to end.

Like Kennedy, Nixon always considered domestic affairs secondary to foreign policy concerns. He once told an associate that he thought the country could run its domestic affairs without a president. His own lack of interest, the fact that 57 percent of the voters in 1968 preferred another candidate to him for president, and Democratic control of Congress, all diminished his influence over domestic affairs.

Democrats in control of Congress pursued a more liberal course than he would have preferred, but he often went along with them, in part because he did not care much about domestic matters, in part because he recognized the political gains to be made from supporting popular social legislation, and in part because he was something of a closet liberal himself. Richard Nixon was the most liberal Republican president in modern times.

He signed an impressive number of important Congressional legislative enactments that catered to the strong sense of entitlement and rights consciousness percolating in the culture. The list included extending the Voting Rights Act of 1965 for five more years, increased funding to find a "cure for cancer," increased spending for food stamps, increased Social Security benefits, and increased federal aid to education. Congress also enacted a Supplementary Security Income (SSI), which replaced existing federal-state assistance programs to aid the elderly poor, blind, and other disabled persons with a national program. Payments under SSI were much larger than they had been under previous programs and were indexed against inflation. Another reason Nixon signed the SSI legislation and enhanced Social Security payments is that he was maneuvering to win the support of the elderly in the 1972 election. Older people, through the American Association of Retired People (AARP), an effective, rights-conscious lobby, had become major players in Washington. Because of Congressional action, which Nixon abetted, the poverty rate dropped to its lowest point in American history, 11.1 percent.

Congress also proposed the Twenty-sixth Amendment, which was ratified in 1971, enfranchising eighteen-year olds. The new amendment added twelve million potential voters to the rolls.

Nixon proposed policies reflecting the growing conservatism of voters who were opposed to solving social problems by expanding the powers of the federal government and spending more money on them. A major target was the welfare system. He proposed a work-incentive program to replace the costly Aid to Families with Dependent Children. Called the Family Assistance Plan, it guaranteed a family of four with no other income $1,600 per year plus food stamps and Medicaid. It further required that all heads of households on welfare, except for single mothers with preschool-aged children, register for job training. Congress passed only the job-training feature, requiring heads of households to register for job training.

Nixon's other innovative proposal, revenue sharing, was part of what he called the "New Federalism," designed to reduce the power of the federal government and to strengthen state and local agencies. Congress enacted a revenue-sharing program to begin in 1972, when $30 billion in federal funds would be split over five years, two-thirds to local governments and one-third to the states.

NIXONOMICS

Nixon spent much of the time that he devoted to domestic affairs trying to manage an increasingly erratic American economy. The economic difficulties stemmed mainly from the Vietnam War and former president Johnson's fiscal irresponsibility. Johnson had drastically increased spending for the war in the midst of a booming economy, without raising taxes. Prices rose 5 percent in 1968, the highest inflation rate since the Korean War. Nixon initially applied the monetarist theories of economist Milton Friedman, who claimed that prices could be lowered by reducing the money supply. The stock market suffered its worst crash since 1929, unemployment doubled, and prices continued to rise. Monetarism generated both inflation and recession, creating "stagflation."

Appalled by its results, Nixon abandoned monetarism for a new economic approach, "jawboning," which amounted to pressuring both business and trade unions to keep down prices and wages. Jawboning produced only continuing stagflation. Nixon then decided that economic decline was a greater evil than inflation. Reverting to Keynesian practices, he deliberately unbalanced the budget to stimulate demand and increase employment. Stagflation stubbornly persisted as unemployment and inflation both remained high. The U.S. economy also ran its first trade deficit since 1893.

Still searching for an effective policy, Nixon once again revamped his economic policies. On August 15, 1971, he froze wages, prices, and rents for ninety days; asked Congress for tax cuts to promote business expansion; devalued the dollar; and clamped a 10 percent tax on imports. At the end of ninety days, he replaced the freeze with more flexible guidelines, allowing annual price increases of 2.5 percent and wage increases of up to 5.5 percent. These drastic measures worked for a short term. The trade deficit vanished, and inflation was halved. The economy snapped out of recession, and the GDP rose sharply. The improved performance of the economy contributed to his landslide reelection victory in November 1972. By early 1973, pressures from business and labor had undermined the controls, and the inflation rate soared.

THE SOUTHERN STRATEGY

Despite Nixon's appeals for unity and peace, discords inherited from the Johnson years continued and, at times, intensified. Between September 1969 and May 1970, at least 250 bombings linked to terrorist groups erupted across the nation. Targets included ROTC buildings, draft boards, induction centers, and other federal buildings. Bombs also exploded at the New York headquarters of IBM and Socony Mobil.

Nixon's most divisive actions occurred when he implemented his Southern strategy. It aimed to outflank Wallace and secure the votes of Southern whites, Northern ethnics, and suburbanites. He also sought to attract voters from the Sunbelt, the most dynamic region of the country. The Southern strategy involved stressing "law and order," phasing out most antipoverty programs, and slowing the rate of school desegregation in the South.

Nixon's efforts to slow the pace of school desegregation involved his administration in a controversy over busing to achieve school integration. The Justice Department filed suits prohibiting transporting children to desegregate public schools. The busing issue had risen in 1971 when the Supreme Court had ordered the Charlotte-Mecklenburg school system in North Carolina to use busing to achieve school integration after its efforts at voluntary desegregation had failed. Soon many other Southern school districts were under court orders to bus children to achieve school integration. It worked, and within a few years many Southern public schools were largely desegregated. Far more public schools were racially integrated during Nixon's presidency than under Kennedy and Johnson.

Court-ordered busing spread to Northern cities, where resistance was fierce and occasionally violent. The worst incidents occurred in Boston in 1974, when a federal judge ordered busing to integrate its public school system. Over half of the public schools in Boston had student bodies that were 90 percent black. White pupils boycotted South Boston High School rather than accept integration. Buses hauling in African American students were stoned, and several youngsters were injured.

In one important case, the Supreme Court's ruling bolstered the Nixon administration's efforts to slow the pace of school integration. In *Milliken v. Bradley* (1974), the Burger Court rendered suburbs safe from busing. The *Milliken* decision, reflecting the backlash, was pivotal in the modern history of race relations. Excluding the suburbs from school integration busing programs accelerated white flight from central cities to suburbs now perceived as safe from integration. The decision undermined liberal hopes of overcoming *de facto* segregation of schools. White flight also eroded central-city tax bases as a "white noose" tightened around Detroit, Cleveland, and other cities in decline.

Nixon's Southern strategy also influenced his choices to fill Supreme Court vacancies, four of which opened up during his first term. He tried to appoint a Deep South conservative, but the Senate rejected both of his choices. His four appointees, including the new Chief Justice Warren Burger, who replaced the retired Earl Warren in 1969, were all strict constructionist conservatives. But the more conservative "Nixon Court" did not overturn any of the controversial decisions of its activist predecessor. It upheld busing and the publication of the *Pentagon Papers*. It struck down death penalty laws and limited Justice Department's efforts at electronic surveillance.

However, it issued some rulings that weakened efforts to use busing as a means to integrate schools, including the aforementioned *Milliken* decision. Other rulings appeared to strengthen the hands of law enforcement personnel and undermine criminal rights. The Court also sustained laws banning pornography, where those statutes reflected "community standards." Overall, the Nixon court proved to be an unpredictable, politically independent agency, whose decisions often angered conservatives and administration officials.

Nixon deployed Vice President Agnew to implement part of the Southern strategy. Agnew campaigned extensively during the 1970 midterm elections on behalf of Republican congressional candidates. During the elections, he tried to link his Democratic opponents to campus upheavals, race riots, bombings, rising crime rates, drug use, and pornography. Agnew's verbal onslaughts had little noticeable impact on the elections. Republicans gained two Senate seats, but lost nine seats in the House. The Democrats remained entrenched in Congress.

As part of its law-and-order campaign, the Justice Department prosecuted antiwar activists. The most important trial occurred in Chicago in 1971, involving a group of radicals known as the "Chicago Seven." The trial turned into a farce because of the disruptive antics of the defendants and the extreme bias against them of the judge, Julius Hoffmann. Six of the seven activists were convicted of various charges stemming from their roles in organizing demonstrations at the 1968 Democratic Convention in Chicago. All of the convictions were subsequently overturned on appeal because of Judge Hoffmann's procedural errors and bias.

Along with its efforts to prosecute antiwar activists, the Nixon administration also took a hard line on crime and drug use. During his 1968 presidential campaign, Nixon had blamed the rise in street crime and drug use on "liberal permissiveness" and had promised a crackdown on both if elected. In 1969 and 1970, Nixon proposed tough anticrime legal reforms. The Democrat-controlled Congress responded by enacting a series of anticrime laws. The main effect of the new laws was to increase penalties for federal crimes. In 1972, the Nixon administration declared war on drugs, particularly on heroin. The president created a new agency called the Office for Drug Abuse and Law Enforcement (ODALE) to spearhead the assault on heroin dealers. A few celebrities joined the war on drugs, including Sammy Davis Jr. and Elvis Presley. Neither crime rates nor drug use showed appreciable drops during Nixon's presidency, but his strenuous efforts on behalf of these issues paid political dividends. Nixon campaigned for reelection in 1972 as a champion of law and order and as a leader concerned with diminishing the contagion of violence and drug use in America.

In one important civil rights area, the Burger Court moved far beyond its more liberal predecessor; that area involved discrimination based on gender. Frequently using the provisions of the Civil Rights Act of 1964 that prohibited gender-based segregation, the Court struck down many laws that had in various ways made women subordinate to men. In *Phillips v. Martin*

Marietta (1971), the Burger Court nullified corporate hiring practices that discriminated against women with small children. In an important 1973 decision, *Frontero v. Richardson*, the Court ruled that the U.S. armed forces had to provide the same fringe benefits and pensions for female veterans as they did for males.

In 1973, the Supreme Court went far beyond questions of equal pay and employment rights for women. In *Roe v. Wade*, the justices struck down all state laws restricting abortions. Feminist attorneys had challenged a Texas law that made any abortion a felony, on behalf of a poor single woman, Norma McCorvey, who could not afford to raise the impending child properly. Associate Justice Harry Blackmun, who wrote the majority decision, anchored the right of a woman to have an abortion in a right to privacy, which, while not explicitly stated in the Constitution, according to Blackmun's reading of that document, could be inferred. The decision granted women an absolute right to obtain an abortion during the first trimester of pregnancy, because medical experts all agreed that the fetus was not viable during that phase of pregnancy. During the second trimester, when fetus viability was possible, states could regulate abortions. During the third trimester, according to *Roe v. Wade*, states could prohibit abortions.

Roe v. Wade was the most controversial Supreme Court decision since the Warren Court's famed 1954 *Brown* decision that had outlawed segregation in public schools. *Roe v. Wade* immediately provoked an angry outcry from Catholics, the Religious Right, prominent conservative politicians, and many others. For the next thirty-plus years, the waters of public life would be frequently roiled by controversy over *Roe v. Wade*. The issue proved impossible to compromise politically, because it involved two absolutist moral views that flatly contradicted each other. As conservative political forces steadily built up their strength during the 1970s, repealing or at least restricting *Roe v. Wade* became one of their most powerful rallying points.

Although it was certainly true that an integral part of Nixon's Southern strategy was to try to slow the pace of school integration in order to court white Southern voters, some of the Nixon administration actions helped black people and other minority groups make significant progress in many important arenas during the 1970s. Nixon strongly believed that African Americans and other groups ought to be given a chance to compete fairly. Nixon supported Secretary of Labor George Schultz, who established what came to be known as the Philadelphia plan. It required all construction unions within Philadelphia to set up programs and timetables for hiring black apprentices. The plan was later incorporated into government regulations applied to all federal hiring and contracting. The national application of the Philadelphia Plan also had the effect of transforming the meaning of "affirmative action." When President Johnson had issued an executive order calling on employers to pursue affirmative action, it had been to counter discrimination against individuals. Henceforth, under the new regime, hiring would be color blind and meritocratic; it would apply to protected groups, and it would be done without regard to race, religion, sex, or national origins. President Nixon also expanded set-aside programs for minority-owned companies and aided historically black colleges.

ACTIVISTS AND REFORMERS

The women's movement gained momentum as more women opted for many new career choices. The number of women in medical schools, law schools, and graduate business programs doubled between 1970 and 1974. Representative Edith Green introduced legislation, Title IX of the Education Act of 1972, to achieve gender equity in college sports. It cleared Congress and was signed into law by President Nixon. New magazines devoted to women's issues emerged. The most successful of these publications was *Ms.*, edited by Gloria Steinem. *Ms.* focused on the emotional and political needs of women, explored the frustrations of working women, and gave liberated women a forum of their own.

Changing cultural mores and values benefited women. Probably the most important cultural change to emerge from the 1960s was the hastening of the sexual revolution. Magazines and movies more openly depicted sex. Increasing numbers of Americans, particularly younger Americans, and most of all, younger women from affluent families, sensed that they had a wider range of options than previous generations. They felt no need to sacrifice themselves for the sake of a job, a family, or a spouse as their mothers had done. They sought growth and fulfillment, and they did not want to wait.

Political opposition to feminism in the 1970s came from a conservative antifeminist leader, Phyllis Schlafly, head of the Eagle Forum. Schlafly led an effort to defeat the Equal Rights Amendment (ERA). She insisted that its passage would not help women and would take away rights that they already had, such as the right to be supported by a husband, the right to be exempted from conscription, and the right to special job protections. Schlafly succeeded when the ERA fell three votes short of the thirty-eight needed for ratification.

Native American activists occupied Alcatraz Island in San Francisco Bay in November 1969. The protesters wanted to highlight their demand that the Bureau of Indian Affairs respond more effectively to a myriad of Native American social problems. In 1973, members of the American Indian Movement (AIM) occupied the South Dakota town of Wounded Knee, the site of an 1890 massacre of Lakota Sioux Indians by U.S. soldiers. AIM activists wanted to call attention to the misery of the poverty-stricken Native American inhabitants of Wounded Knee and to the hundreds of Indian treaties broken by the federal government. In negotiations that followed, government officials agreed to examine conditions among the Indians and their treaty rights. The Second Battle of Wounded Knee signaled that a new era of Indian activism had arrived.

FIGURE 10.1 Native Americans standing guard at Wounded Knee. *Source:* Corbis/Bettmann.

Hispanic organizations also were active in the early 1970s. Young Chicanos formed a militant organization that called itself the Brown Berets. The Brown Berets were active in the Midwest and Southwest. Some Chicano activists also joined the antiwar movement. Spokesmen called attention to Chicano casualty rates in Vietnam that were proportionally higher than those of the Anglo population. Aware of the political activity of some Mexican Americans, President Nixon set out to win their support, offering them political appointments and programs. The effort paid off; in the 1972 election, Nixon received 31 percent of the Mexican American vote, which helped him carry California and Texas. In 1974, the Supreme Court responded to another Chicano concern when it ruled that public schools had to meet the learning requirements of youngsters with limited English language skills. That decision led to the federal funding of bilingual education programs.

ENVIRONMENTALISM AND CONSUMERISM

Environmentalism was another movement that emerged during the 1960s and grew rapidly during the early 1970s. The origins of the modern ecology movement lay in a book written by Rachel Carson called *Silent Spring* (1962). When there was almost no concern about ecological issues, Carson wrote about environmental damage caused by chemical pesticides, particularly DDT. Her writings spawned a cause that grew into a movement. The Great Society contained an important environmentalist component. By 1970, a broad-based, diverse environmentalist movement was active on a variety of fronts and drew from many sources.

During the Nixon presidency, Congress responded to growing environmental concerns. Legislators enacted the Water Quality Improvement Act in 1970, tightening existing safeguards against threats to water quality. The National Air Quality Standards Act required automakers to reduce exhaust emission pollutants significantly by 1975 and required the federal government to establish air quality standards. The Resource Recovery Act provided $453 million for resource recovery and recycling systems. Congress also created the Occupational Safety and Health Administration (OSHA) and enacted an Endangered Species Act.

In 1971, Congress created the Environmental Protection Agency (EPA), which combined many separate federal agencies concerned with pesticides, nuclear radiation, auto exhaust emissions, air and water quality, and waste disposal under a single cabinet-level department. Nixon appointed William Ruckelshaus to head the new agency. Under Ruckelshaus's aggressive leadership, the EPA quickly initiated action on several fronts. It provoked a reaction from Detroit automakers, who insisted that EPA emission and safety standards were too expensive and beyond their technological capabilities. Nixon's Secretary of the Interior Walter Hickel, a conservative, self-made oil millionaire, also turned out to be an energetic environmentalist who protected the public domain.

Nixon had little interest in environmental problems; he said they were boring, but he knew better than to oppose popular reforms. However, Nixon vetoed a mammoth $24.7 billion measure to clean up America's polluted rivers and lakes. He claimed that it was much too costly, but Congress enacted the law over his veto. Environmentalism was a political issue that cut across party, class, and ideological lines. Almost everyone endorsed in principle the need for clean air and water and the protection of natural resources, scenic landscapes, and wilderness areas. But not everyone was willing to pay the high costs of environmental safeguards. At times, environmentalists clashed with vested economic interests.

Related to the ecology movement and sometimes overlapping with it, a strong consumer movement developed during the early 1970s that concerned itself with protecting consumers from unsafe, shoddy products and with making the business community more responsive to consumers' interests. An anticorporate gadfly, Ralph Nader, whose attacks on the auto industry during the mid-1960s had led to the enactment of federal safety laws, headed the consumer movement of the 1970s. Operating out of a small office in the nation's capital, Nader organized task forces of volunteers called "Nader's Raiders," who examined many industries and governmental agencies and followed up these investigations with critical reports and proposals for reform.

Nader's Raiders attacked governmental regulatory agencies for being more protective of the businesses that they were supposed to regulate than of the consumers who used the products made by these businesses. These latter-day Muckrakers also attacked the multibillion-dollar processed food industry, accusing it of serving American consumers a "chemical feast" of harmful food additives. They also attacked agribusiness for its use of chemical fertilizers and pesticides that harmed the environment and put toxic substances into the nation's food supply. Because of the growing consumer movement, millions of Americans became much more concerned about product safety and quality, and more assertive of their rights as consumers.

THE 1972 ELECTION

The Democratic Party was still in disarray from the upheavals of 1968, and its members remained deeply divided over emotional issues such as the Vietnam War and busing to achieve racially integrated schools. Nevertheless, many Democrats sought their party's nomination at the outset of the 1972 campaign. They included Senators Edmund Muskie, Hubert Humphrey, and George McGovern, who was an outspoken critic of the Vietnam War. After these contenders came two formidable possibilities, Senator Edward "Ted" Kennedy and George Wallace. Kennedy's appeal had been badly tarnished by his behavior following an auto accident in which a young woman had died; but he still retained the vote-getting magic of the Kennedy name. George Wallace, back in the Democratic Party, also remained a major player.

Muskie flamed out early, in part the victim of Watergate "dirty tricks," as the nation would discover a year later. A would-be assassin eliminated Wallace by wounding him severely and forcing him out of the campaign in May. With Muskie and Wallace eliminated, McGovern moved strongly ahead. He won a series of primary victories, including California, where he beat Humphrey, and he rolled on to a first-ballot nomination at the Democratic Party convention in Miami.

New rules that a Commission on Party Structure (which McGovern had chaired) had implemented in the years following the contentious Chicago Convention in 1968 set aside greatly increased percentages of delegate seats for women, blacks, and young antiwar activists. These insurgent practitioners of a "new politics" took control of the convention and forged McGovern's victory. His supporters drafted a platform calling for an "immediate and total withdrawal of all American forces in Southeast Asia." It also supported busing to achieve school integration, full employment, tax reform, and various social reforms.

Meeting in Miami after the Democrats, the Republicans unanimously chose Nixon and Agnew to run again. The Republican platform staked out a clear strategy. It called for a "new American majority to repudiate McGovern's program." It also called for full employment, and tax reform. It opposed busing. On the crucial Vietnam War issue, Republicans insisted that the United States could not honorably withdraw from Vietnam until all of the U.S. prisoners of war had been returned.

McGovern's campaign suffered serious damage at the outset when the public learned that his vice presidential running mate, Senator Thomas Eagleton, had undergone psychiatric care in the past. At first, McGovern stood behind Eagleton, but after a week's adverse publicity, he panicked and forced Eagleton off the ticket. McGovern then began a search for a replacement and suffered six embarrassing turndowns before finally persuading Sargent Shriver, former director of the Peace Corps and the War on Poverty, to accept. McGovern's inept, expediential handling of the Eagleton affair managed to alienate both young idealists and party regulars.

The presidential campaign turned out to be boring and one-sided. McGovern never had a chance, and most Americans quickly lost interest in the contest. The Democrats remained divided. Most Wallace supporters and about half of Humphrey's followers voted for Nixon. Organized labor, the strongest power bloc within the party, refused to endorse McGovern, and millions of unionized workers voted for Nixon.

Nixon possessed formidable political assets that made him practically unbeatable. The president had achieved impressive diplomatic victories, capped by *detente* with the Soviets and the opening to China. The American war in Vietnam was winding down, and most U.S. troops had been withdrawn. At home, the economy was reasonably strong, and the society had calmed to some extent. Nixon had signed many popular pieces of social and environmental legislation. He also stood foursquare against all of those features of American life that drove the backlash and had given liberalism a bad name during the late 1960s and early 1970s—busing to achieve racially integrated schools, the coddling of criminals and welfare chiselers, antiwar activists, drug use, and sexual permissiveness. He also employed, it was later revealed, an undercover army of political hirelings, using their arsenal of "dirty tricks" to sabotage the Democratic campaign.

There was a potential chink in Nixon's political armor—corruption. McGovern called Nixon's administration "the most morally corrupt in history." He cited several seamy deals where corporations and trade associations had given the GOP large campaign donations in exchange for political favors. The most blatant case of corruption involved a break-in at Democratic Party national headquarters at Watergate Towers in Washington on June 17, 1972. Five men had been caught trying to photograph and steal documents and install electronic bugging equipment. Two others, G. Gordon Liddy and E. Howard Hunt, who had directed the operation, were also arrested. It appeared that members of the Republican campaign organization and even members of the president's staff had engaged in espionage against their opponents. But news of the burglary produced little public concern at the time, and the prominent mass media exhibited little sustained interest in the bizarre event after a day or two of sensational headlines. Republicans denied all of McGovern's charges and dismissed the Watergate break-in. McGovern failed to generate much voter interest in Watergate or the corruption issue. Within less than a year it would turn out that McGovern had touched only the tip of the corruption iceberg.

In November Nixon scored his predicted landslide victory, carrying forty-nine of fifty states and rolling up an electoral vote of 521 to 17. He swept the South and even got a majority of the urban vote. The "Silent Majority," whom the president had courted—middle- and lower-middle-class whites, blue-collar voters, Sunbelt inhabitants, and Westerners—all voted for him. The 1972 election was the first in which eighteen- to twenty-one-year-olds could vote. McGovern spent much of his time campaigning for their vote, considering the youth vote his secret weapon. Only one-third of these young people voted, and half of them opted for Nixon.

Despite Nixon's sweep, Democrats retained control of Congress, even gaining two seats in the Senate while losing twelve seats in the House. Such ticket-splitting suggested that millions of voters had cast their ballots for Nixon because they could not abide McGovern. Clearly the political climate had become more conservative by 1972; however, except for the South, the results gave no indication that political realignment was occurring, or that a new Republican majority was emerging. American voters mainly repudiated a candidate whom they saw as lacking in leadership qualities and being way too liberal, and they chose to keep the incumbent, whom they perceived as a capable leader with many significant accomplishments.

WATERGATE

President Nixon began his second term in January 1973, convinced that his landslide victory was a mandate for moving in more conservative directions. His new budget cut spending for welfare and education. He removed all remaining controls from the economy and impounded billions of dollars appropriated by Congress to control water pollution. Nixon also began reorganizing the federal government to make the bureaucracies more efficient and more responsive to his authority. His attitude toward the Democratic Congress was belligerent and contemptuous. He believed that the large majority of American citizens supported him and his agenda. Richard Nixon was riding high that spring of 1973. Then his administration began to self-destruct.

Watergate, latent since the break-in, suddenly erupted with a rash of disclosures and confessions that made it one of the most serious political scandals in American history. Watergate activities fell into two categories—those occurring before the June 17, 1972, break-in, and those following. The break-in turned out to be only one event in an extensive dirty-tricks campaign developed by the Committee to Re-elect the President (CREEP) and White House staffers to prevent news leaks, to spy on radicals, and to ensure Nixon's reelection. Investigators eventually unearthed an astonishing web of criminal activities and abuses of power that had begun early in Nixon's presidency. These activities included illegal wiretaps placed on government bureaucrats and journalists suspected of leaking embarrassing information about administration policies to the press, using the IRS to harass political opponents, and raising millions of dollars in illegal campaign funds.

The Watergate burglars had been caught red-handed. CREEP officials and White House staffers who sent them in could have confessed and resigned. Such actions would have embarrassed the Nixon administration, but the president would still have been reelected easily. Instead White House officials opted to try to cover up their and CREEP's involvement. The cover-up began immediately after White House officials learned that the burglars had been caught. White House aides moved to destroy all evidentiary links between the burglary, themselves, and CREEP, and to concoct denials and alibis. An FBI investigation of the break-in and testimony before a federal grand jury were carefully limited so that they could not uncover any tracks leading to CREEP or the White House.

President Nixon was directly involved in the cover-up activities from the start. He put White House counsel John Dean in charge; at times, Nixon himself directed the cover-up activities. From the moment the cover-up efforts began, a process was set in motion that would create a constitutional crisis, provide some of the most bizarre political theater in American history, and ultimately destroy Nixon's presidency.

The cover-up orchestrated by Nixon, Dean, and other top White House aides succeeded for a time. In September 1972, the federal grand jury indicted only the seven men involved in the burglary. The cover-up also held through the November election and was still holding as the trial of the seven burglars opened in March 1973.

But too many connections among the burglars, CREEP, and White House survived. Two young reporters from the *Washington Post*, Carl Bernstein and Bob Woodward, were able to trace some of the illegal campaign funds to CREEP. The Senate created a Select Committee on Presidential Campaign Activities, soon to be known as the Watergate Committee, chaired by Senator Sam J. Ervin, to investigate the burglary and other dirty tricks that may have influenced the outcome of the 1972 election. Federal prosecutors, continuing the federal grand jury probe, continuously investigated the burglary, other dirty tricks, violations of campaign spending laws, and the cover-up. The Watergate trial judge, John J. Sirica, who did not believe the burglars when they told him that they alone had planned the break-in, pressured them to tell the truth.

The cover-up began to come unglued when one of the convicted burglars, James McCord, hoping to avoid a long prison term, wrote a letter to Judge Sirica implicating CREEP and prominent White House officials in the planning of the Watergate burglary. After McCord cracked, the whole cover-up edifice crumbled. Accused officials promptly implicated others in the hope of getting immunity from prosecution or a lighter sentence.

Nixon, scrambling to protect himself, fired several senior advisers implicated in the cover-up—L. Patrick Gray III, acting director of the FBI, John Erlichman, H. R. "Bob" Haldeman, and John Mitchell, the director of CREEP. Nixon also fired John Dean for telling the Watergate Committee staffers that the president had been involved in the cover-up from the beginning.

President Nixon maintained publicly that he had only learned about the cover-up from Dean in March 1973, and since then he had done everything he could to cooperate with investigators and get out the truth about Watergate. Nixon tried to discredit Dean by suggesting that he had directed the cover-up without the president's knowledge. To reinforce the image of a president concerned with getting to the bottom of the scandal, Nixon agreed to appoint a special prosecutor, Harvard law professor Archibald Cox, to continue the Justice Department's investigation of the Watergate cover-up.

On May 17, 1973, public interest in the scandal increased dramatically when the Senate Watergate Committee began holding televised hearings. The committee started with low-level hirelings who did the dirty work. Gradually they worked their way up the chain-of-command in CREEP and in the Nixon White House. On the way up, millions of American citizens who watched the proceedings daily got a riveting tour through the dark underside of American politics. They learned about shredding documents, blackmail, bribery, forgery, and "laundered money." They also learned about the misuse of government agencies, including the FBI and the IRS. And they learned about illegal fund-raising techniques that often amounted to blackmail. The televised hearings made a folk hero out of the committee's chairman, seventy-nine-year-old

FIGURE 10.2 In May 1973, the Senate Watergate Committee began holding televised hearings. For months, millions of Americans were treated to exposures of corrupt political practices that pervaded the Nixon presidency. *Source:* Corbis/Bettmann.

Sam Ervin. Ervin's folksy manner and good humor cloaked a keen intellect and a fierce moral outrage at the steady parade of criminals and corrupt politicians who appeared before his committee.

By mid-June, the key question had become whether President Nixon had been involved in the Watergate cover-up. On June 25, John Dean appeared before the committee. For two days he read a lengthy 250-page statement describing the cover-up: Nixon knew all about it and had played a central role in it from the outset. Despite efforts by the White House to discredit Dean's testimony, the fired counselor came across as credible to members of the committee and to the large television audience.

But Dean's testimony was legally inconclusive. It depended entirely on his ability to recall the events and conversations that he described before the committee. He had no corroborative evidence to substantiate his testimony. Only Dean had implicated President Nixon in the cover-up activities. The president had denied all of Dean's accusations and fired him. Dean himself was deeply involved in the cover-up. All of the Nixon loyalists who had appeared before the committee had insisted on the president's innocence, and they all accused John Dean of masterminding the cover-up. They also accused him of trying to pin the blame on an innocent president in order to save his own skin.

DECLINE AND FALL

On July 16 came a sensational discovery. The committee learned that President Nixon had recorded White House conversations and phone calls on a secret tape-recording system installed in the Oval Office. If the disputed conversations between Dean and Nixon were on tape, it would be possible to find out which one of them was telling the truth and if the president had been involved in the cover-up. From that date on, the Watergate drama focused on the tapes and the prosecution's efforts to obtain them from the president, who was determined not to surrender them.

Immediately both the Watergate Committee and the Special Prosecutor subpoenaed the tapes of the Nixon–Dean conversations. Nixon rejected both subpoenas. Both investigators then asked Judge Sirica to force Nixon to honor their subpoenas. Nixon's attorneys defended his right to refuse to surrender the tapes on the grounds of "executive privilege." Judge Sirica rejected the argument and ordered Nixon to release the tapes. Nixon's attorneys appealed his ruling. The appeals court upheld the ruling, saying that "The president is not above the law's commands."

While the battle for control of the tapes was raging, another White House scandal surfaced, unrelated to Watergate, involving Vice President Agnew. Justice Department investigators learned that Agnew, when governor of Maryland during the 1960s, had taken bribes from construction companies in return for favorable rulings on their bids. He had continued to receive payments while serving as vice president. Agnew was charged with bribery, extortion, conspiracy, and income tax evasion. Knowing that the federal prosecutors had hard evidence against him, Agnew accepted a deal. He pled *nolo contendere* to a single count of tax evasion. He resigned, was fined $10,000, and given three years' unsupervised probation.

President Nixon chose House minority leader Gerald R. Ford of Michigan to succeed the fallen vice president. Ford was a conservative, a Nixon loyalist, and popular with his colleagues. There were no political or personal scandals in his life. This last factor was crucial, because many Senators who voted to confirm Ford knew that if the tapes substantiated Dean's charges, Nixon was not only selecting a vice president, he was choosing his successor.

Meanwhile, Archibald Cox and the Watergate Committee were pressing the Nixon administration for tapes of key conversations with his top aides pertaining to the Watergate cover-up. The release of these tapes posed a mortal danger to the president, which he knew better than anyone. Nixon decided on a bold move to avoid surrendering them: Unless a compromise was arranged, permitting the president to keep custody of the tapes, Nixon would dismiss Cox and prepare his own summaries of the tapes for Judge Sirica. Efforts to forge a compromise failed. On Saturday evening, October 20, Nixon ordered Attorney General Elliot Richardson to fire Cox. The attorney general refused and resigned. Nixon then directed Deputy Attorney General William Ruckelshaus to fire Cox. Ruckelshaus also refused, and Nixon fired him. Finally, the third-ranking officer at the Justice Department, Robert Bork, dismissed Cox. Nixon also abolished the Special Prosecutor's office and ordered the FBI to seal all of the office files.

Journalists dubbed these resignations and the firing of Cox the "Saturday Night Massacre." The firings provoked a dramatic outpouring of public protest. Over one million letters, telegrams, and phone calls poured into Senate and Congressional offices, nearly all of them denouncing the Saturday Night Massacre. Eight resolutions of impeachment were introduced into the House of Representatives. Nixon's approval rating dropped sharply, and polls revealed that most Americans suspected that the president was trying to hide his involvement in criminal activities. In addition to his Watergate actions, Nixon was accused of charging the government for making improvements to his real estate holdings in Florida and California, which were primarily for his personal use. The IRS also investigated Nixon for tax evasion.

Nixon tried hard to repair the largely self-inflicted damage with a public relations campaign. He agreed to release the original tapes ordered by Judge Sirica. He replaced Cox with another Special Prosecutor, Leon Jaworski, a Houston corporation lawyer. He released a detailed financial statement to dispel doubts about his personal finances. Before an audience of newspaper publishers, he insisted that he was "not a crook." His efforts failed. Except for hard-core loyalists, the public, the media, and Congress remained skeptical of Nixon's efforts at reassurance. Whatever credibility he retained was further undermined when White House officials admitted that two of the nine subpoenaed tapes, covering important conversations with Dean, did not exist. Even worse, an eighteen-and-one-half-minute segment of a crucial conversation between Nixon and Haldeman, held three days after the break-in, had been erased. A panel of experts determined that the missing eighteen-and-one-half minute segment had been deliberately erased.

In the wake of his failed public relations campaign, Nixon grew defiant. He refused Jaworski's requests for more tapes. On March 1, 1974, the grand jury indicted several key players in the cover-up, including Erlichman, Haldeman, and Mitchell. It labeled Nixon "an unindicted co-conspirator." At about the same time the grand jury issued its indictments, the House Judiciary Committee began impeachment proceedings against the president. When its staff sought tapes and documents from the White House, Nixon refused its requests as well. Both Jaworski and the House Judiciary Committee then issued subpoenas to obtain the desired evidence.

Nixon was caught in a serious bind. He knew that refusal to comply with subpoenas would not work; the courts would not sustain his efforts. He also knew that conversations on several of the requested tapes would ruin him if released. He tried to escape the trap. He decided to release edited transcripts of the requested tapes. In a speech to the American people, dubbed "Checkers II," he made a final effort to retrieve his failing political reputation. He told his vast audience of his intent to release the transcripts. "These materials will tell all," he said. The next day, the transcripts were published in full.

Response to Nixon's ploy was again emphatically negative. House Judiciary Committee members, comparing the edited versions with tapes already released, discovered many discrepancies. They refused to accept the edited versions and told the president that as far as they were concerned, he had refused to comply with the committee's subpoena for the tapes. The contents of the edited tapes were even more damning to the president's cause because of the impression they conveyed of Nixon's conduct of the presidency: crude, vulgar language; the voicing of racial and ethnic stereotypes; and a complete lack of scruples or morality.

Both the House Judiciary Committee and Jaworski continued their demands for more tapes from the White House. Nixon refused all of their requests. Jaworski subpoenaed sixty-four additional tapes. Nixon tried to quash the subpoena, but Judge Sirica upheld it and ordered Nixon to release the tapes.

When the White House announced that it would appeal the ruling, Jaworski asked the Supreme Court to decide the matter. It agreed to do so. The question before the Court was clear: Who had the final authority to decide whether a president had to obey a subpoena, the subpoenaed president himself or the courts? The Court heard arguments by both sides. Nixon's attorneys argued that the president had the right to decide; the only way the law could be applied to the president was through the impeachment process. Jaworski countered with the argument that if the president decides what the Constitution means, "if he is wrong, who is there to tell him so?"

In the case of *United States of America v. Richard M. Nixon*, the Supreme Court ruled unanimously that Nixon had to surrender the subpoenaed tapes to Judge Sirica. On the same day the Court announced its verdict, the House Judiciary Committee began voting on articles of impeachment against the president. Within a week, it voted to send three articles of impeachment to the full House. Article I accused the president of obstructing justice for his involvement in the cover-up of the Watergate break-in. Article II accused the president of abusing power by his involvement in the cover-up of the Watergate break-in. Article III accused the president of unconstitutionally refusing to honor the Committee's subpoenas.

If the full House of Representatives adopted at least one of the three approved articles, Richard Nixon would become the second president in U.S. history to be impeached. Nixon would then be tried in the Senate, who would sit as a jury of 100 members. The Senators would decide whether Nixon would be removed from office for "high crimes and misdemeanors" or be allowed to continue serving as president.

The evidence that completed the destruction of Nixon's presidency was a tape released on August 5, 1974, of a conversation between Nixon and Haldeman, held on July 23, 1972, six weeks after the Watergate burglars had been caught: Nixon can be heard ordering Haldeman to tell the CIA to fabricate a national security operation to keep the FBI from pursuing its investigation of the burglary. Here was the "smoking gun," proof of a criminal act—conspiring to obstruct justice. The taped conversation also proved that Nixon had been lying about his Watergate involvement. He had known of the cover-up and had been involved in it from the beginning.

On August 7, Republican Congressional leaders called on Nixon at the White House. They told the president that he faced certain impeachment, conviction, and removal from office. That night he decided to resign. On the evening of August 8, President Nixon spoke to the American people for the last time. He was not apologetic. He admitted to making "errors in judgment." He did not admit to breaking any laws or to any wrongdoing. He claimed that he was resigning only because he had lost his political base and could no longer govern effectively. At noon the next day, Gerald R. Ford took the oath of office as the thirty-eighth president of the United States. He began his short acceptance speech by saying, "Our long national nightmare is over."

Americans, divided along class, racial, and ideological lines, reacted differently to the Watergate scandals. For millions of Americans who had voted for Nixon in 1972 in good faith, Watergate was a series of painful disillusionments. For young people especially, Watergate was traumatic. Even to the bitter end, Nixon retained many defenders; they insisted that the only

FIGURE 10.3 President Nixon resigns. *Source:* CORBIS.

mistake Nixon made was to not burn the tapes. It was the tapes that ruined him because they provided his enemies in the liberal political and media establishments with the opportunity to destroy him. Then there were the Nixon haters. They rejoiced in their long-time political adversary's humiliation and fall from power. For them, his disgrace was poetic justice.

Analysts searched for the major causes of the Watergate scandals. Some found them within the personality and approach to politics of Richard M. Nixon. Relentlessly ambitious, intensely partisan, insecure, and perhaps even paranoid, Nixon was willing to use or countenance ruthless, even criminal, means to advance his career, achieve his policy goals, and defeat his enemies. Others located Watergate in the institution of the presidency itself, in the rise of an "imperial presidency" since the 1940s. The presidency dominated the federal government, particularly in the realms of national security and foreign policy. All modern presidents wielded awesome powers, above the restraints of the Constitution and the claims of morality.

George McGovern correctly labeled Nixon's administration the most corrupt in U.S. history. But the corruption of the Nixon White House, Agnew excepted, was not the common-place corruption of thieves, bribers, grafters, and influence peddlers that infested past presidencies. It was a more dangerous kind of corruption that threatened to replace a government based on constitutional law with the rule of a powerful leader heading a staff of loyalists, whose highest calling was to do his bidding and vanquish his enemies. These enemies would be contained by any means necessary, including wiretapping, surveillance, burglary, blackmail, political sabotage, and intimidation.

But arbitrary power was thwarted and a constitutional crisis was resolved. Eventually due process ran its course. Three hundred seventy-eight officials, including three former Cabinet members and several top-level White House aides, either pleaded guilty or were convicted of Watergate-related offenses. Thirty-one went to prison. It is probable that only President Ford's pardon kept Nixon from prison. Assisted by some good fortune, the system of checks and balances established by the founding fathers eventually worked. The Supreme Court firmly established the principle that no one, including the president, is above the law. Congress, spearheaded by the Senate Watergate Committee and the House Judiciary Committee, overrode efforts at executive usurpation.

Watergate left a mixed legacy. Paradoxically, it revealed both the terrible vulnerability and the underlying strength and resiliency of the American political system. The abuses of power by the president and the president's men were finally checked. But it took an agonizingly long time for the mainstream media to get involved, for the public to become aroused, and for Congress to take action. Suppose the tapes had not been discovered? Or suppose that Nixon had ordered them destroyed?

Watergate's outcome provided no guarantee that the system would be able to contain a subsequent president's abuse of power. Watergate, along with the Vietnam War, made Americans skeptical, even cynical, about politics and politicians. Watergate created a distrust of government and politicians that occasionally receded, but never went away.

Compared with the Vietnam War, the Watergate crisis was a much lesser ordeal for most Americans. It had no direct impact on the lives of ordinary Americans, and it had only a minor effect on the day-to-day functioning of the federal government. Nixon and his defenders repeatedly charged that his opponents who were obsessing over Watergate issues were undermining his foreign policies. There is some truth to these charges, for both Congressional Democrats and Soviet leaders, perceiving Nixon's declining control over events, were less supportive of *detente*.

The central issue raised by Watergate, how to make the federal government, especially the president, more accountable to the American people, was not resolved. Congress enacted the Federal Elections Campaign Act (FECA), a law to regulate campaign financing, and a Freedom of Information Act in 1974, but neither of these measures proved effective because presidents and other politicians figured out ways to evade them. Controversial actions taken by subsequent presidents in times of crisis, particularly Ronald Reagan's performance during the *Iran-Contra* scandal, which seriously damaged U.S. interests in the Middle East, and several measures implemented by George W. Bush in the ongoing War on Terror, which exceeded constitutional boundaries and curtailed civil liberties, have caused some observers to regard the wrongdoings of Watergate retrospectively as relatively trivial.

Brief Bibliographic Essay

A large historical literature on Richard Nixon's life and political career has accumulated since he was swept from office, especially biographical studies of this controversial public figure. The most thorough of these works is Stephen E. Ambrose's three-volume biography: Volume 1 is entitled *Nixon: The Education of a Politician, 1913–1962*, Volume 2 is entitled *Nixon: The Triumph of a Politician, 1962–1972*, and Volume 3 is entitled *Nixon: Ruin and Recovery*. A recent popular biography, Anthony Summers, *The Arrogance of Power*, calls attention to Nixon's erratic behavior and mental instability occurring throughout his political career. The best recent book on Nixon and his turbulent times is Rick Perlstein, *Nixonland: The Rise of a President and the Fracturing of America*. Perlstein notes that the political and cultural divides that opened during the Nixon era still afflict Americans in the twenty-first century. The former president is himself the author of several books, the best of which is his autobiography, *RN: The Memoirs of Richard Nixon*, one of the finest presidential memoirs ever done. The best historical study of the Watergate crisis is Stanley I. Kutler's *The Wars of*

Watergate. Kutler sees Watergate as a reflection of the essence of Nixon's political career and presidency. Kutler has also edited *Abuse of Power: The New Nixon Tapes.* These tapes fill in some of the remaining gaps in the Watergate story and provide more evidence of criminal behavior of the president and the president's men. The title of Carl Berstein's and Bob Woodward's famed book is *All the President's Men.* Kevin B. Phillips's *The Emerging Republican Majority* is an important theoretical tract that influenced Richard Nixon's domestic political strategies. Allen J. Matusow's *Nixon's Economy: Booms, Busts, Dollars, and Votes* is a recent study of Nixonomics. Dean J. Kotlowski's *Nixon's Civil Rights: Politics, Principle, and Policy* argues that, despite the Southern strategy, Nixon generally pursued progressive civil rights policies. Melvin Urofsky's *The Continuity of Change: The Supreme Court and Individual Liberties, 1953–1986* contains a good section on the Burger Court.

CHAPTER

11

Calming the Cold War

Aware that America's Vietnam entanglement was dividing the nation, sapping its strength, and diverting it from full pursuit of its global rivalry with the Soviet Union, the new president made phasing out the Vietnam War his top foreign policy priority. Aware also that the world was rapidly changing in the early 1970s, Nixon, aided by his most prominent foreign policy adviser, Henry Kissinger, tried to forge a more realistic foreign policy. They sought three major goals: to bring America's foreign policy commitments in line with the nation's ability to meet them more effectively, to ensure that the United States continued to play the central role in world affairs, and to erect a structure of peace that would last a generation.

During Nixon's presidency, significant changes occurred in all facets of American diplomacy, including a dramatic opening to China, the relaxation of tensions with the Soviet Union, and the eventual phaseout of the Vietnam War. Nixon proved to be a bold, innovative diplomatist who achieved the respect of other world leaders. However, many of his and Kissinger's foreign policy achievements turned out to be short lived. Relations between the Soviet Union and the United States deteriorated as his presidency was ending. The Cold War heated up.

DETENTE

Nixon, who had built his political reputation as a hard-line Cold Warrior, assisted by Henry Kissinger, launched a new era of *detente* with the Soviet Union, built on a relaxation of tensions and realistic diplomacy. The development of new relations with the Soviets reversed the direction American foreign policy had taken since 1945. A glimmer of *detente* had surfaced in 1963 in the aftermath of the Cuban Missile Crisis with the signing of the Nuclear Test Ban Treaty. However, relations between the United States and the Soviet Union were strained at the time of Nixon's accession to office, and ongoing efforts at arms control negotiations were unproductive.

Since the beginning of the Cold War, U.S. foreign policy had been premised on the necessity of responding to threats to American interests posed by expansionist Communist states. Both

Nixon and Kissinger knew that the model of a world dominated by a bipolar struggle between Communism and the Free World was obsolete. Power now flowed along a pentagonal axis representing the United States, western Europe, the Soviet empire, China, and Japan.

Nixon and Kissinger also understood that U.S. power had suffered relative decline since the late 1950s. America no longer dominated its major allies. They also understood that the unity of the Communist world had been fatally sundered. In early 1969, the most serious international conflict pitted the two major Communist states, the Soviet Union and the People's Republic of China, against each other. Kissinger and Nixon perceived that, in the case of the quarreling Communist giants, questions of conflicting national interests overrode their ideological kinship. Nixon and Kissinger set out to use this rift between the two Communist powers to improve U.S. relations with both, and to enhance American power in the world.

Nixon and Kissinger had many reasons for seeking *detente* with the Soviets. They hoped to persuade the Soviets to help them achieve a satisfactory peace in Indochina by linking Soviet willingness to persuade the North Vietnamese to accept U.S. terms with improved relations between the two superpowers. They also expected *detente* to enable the United States to maintain influence over its NATO allies, who had recently shown a tendency to make deals of their own with the Soviets and with the eastern bloc countries. Another powerful motive for *detente* was the desire of U.S. industrial and financial interests to move into Soviet and eastern European markets. Powerful U.S. agricultural interests saw the Soviets as major customers for their wheat and other commodities. Most important, Nixon and Kissinger had to be concerned by the ever-present danger of nuclear war arising from the spiraling arms race.

In 1969, Nixon signed a Nuclear Non-Proliferation Treaty with the Soviets. At Nixon's initiative, U.S. and Soviet delegates began strategic arms limitation talks (SALT) in April 1970 at Helsinki and Vienna. Nixon wanted nuclear weapons agreements with the Soviets to be the key to *detente* and to an expanding network of agreements with the Soviets. As he pushed for SALT to begin, Nixon expanded America's nuclear arsenal, believing that the United States must always negotiate from a position of strength with the Soviets. At the time, both nations possessed roughly equal nuclear arsenals, and both were refining and expanding their nuclear weapons systems. Nixon wanted to add two new weapons systems to the U.S. arsenal, an antiballistics missile (ABM), which would protect U.S. missiles from a possible first strike, and a multiple, independently targeted reentry vehicle (MIRV), which would make it possible for multiple nuclear warheads to be fired from a single missile in flight at several targets simultaneously. The Soviets also had begun work on ABMs and MIRVs.

Nixon also began a phased reduction of U.S. conventional military forces. These military cutbacks coincided with a general scaling back of U.S. global commitments. In August 1969, the president proclaimed the Nixon Doctrine. According to this new doctrine, America would no longer provide direct military protection in the Far East. Nations must henceforth assume greater responsibility for their strategic security. The United States could furnish economic and technical assistance, and logistic support, but not troops. There would be no more Vietnams or Koreas. The new doctrine also signaled that a new dynamic U.S. policy of negotiation and maneuver was supplanting the essentially static policy based on military containment of Communism.

While SALT negotiators representing both sides grappled with the intricate technical questions involved in controlling the asymmetric nuclear weapons systems of the United States and the Soviet Union, other negotiators concluded a series of important economic agreements. In November 1971, representatives of both governments signed agreements whereby the United

States would sell the Soviets $136 million worth of wheat and $125 million worth of oil drilling equipment. Arrangements were also concluded on a joint venture, the building of a large truck factory within the Soviet Union. These and many other smaller deals led to a threefold increase in U.S.–Soviet trade over the next three years.

In March 1972, Nixon sent Kissinger to Moscow to make preparations for a summit meeting between the U.S. president and Leonid Brezhnev, general secretary of the Soviet Communist Party. Nixon later journeyed to Moscow where he and Brezhnev met for a series of talks. Three major agreements signed by both leaders in May 1972 came from these talks. The first agreement limited each country to two ABM sites and also set a ceiling on the number of ABMs per site. The second agreement, an interim one called SALT I, froze the number of strategic missiles in both arsenals at the 1972 levels for five years, but it put no limit on MIRVs, which both sides continued to build.

Neither the ABM treaty nor SALT I ended the thermonuclear arms race, but the arms agreement did bring a measure of stability and control welcomed by both powers. The third agreement, "Basic Principles of U.S.-Soviet Relations," committed both sides to accept strategic equality as the basic premise for future arms control negotiations. Americans no longer sought nuclear superiority over the Soviets; they had accepted sufficiency. Congress subsequently approved all three agreements by large bipartisan majorities. These breakthrough agreements fundamentally altered U.S.–Soviet relations and constituted the bedrock of the new superpower relationship founded on *detente.*

Other significant diplomatic agreements between the United States and the Soviet Union were concluded. The Berlin question, a recurring flash point in the Cold War, was resolved. Both sides signed the Berlin Agreement of 1971, which clearly defined the political status of Berlin and created mechanisms for the peaceful resolution of any conflicts that might arise. The next year, the two German states normalized relations, and America recognized East Germany as a legitimate state.

All of these agreements forged during the most productive era in U.S.–USSR relations since World War II did not end the rivalry between the superpowers. But *detente* had created the opportunity for realistic agreements between the two countries, which stabilized the arms race, reduced the risk of nuclear war, and resolved several long-standing problems that had divided them. Competition and rivalry between the superpowers would continue, especially in the Third World, but "peaceful coexistence" had become a reality.

The Nixon and Kissinger policy of *detente* with the Soviet Union came under attack from Democratic Cold Warriors who controlled Congress. Senator Henry "Scoop" Jackson, from the state of Washington, emerged as the leader of the Democratic opposition to *detente.* Jackson attacked SALT I as giving the Soviets a dangerous advantage over the United States, because it allowed them to keep more land-based ICBMs. Jackson ignored the fact that the United States relied for strategic deterrence on a triad of land-based missiles, submarine-launched missiles, and strategic bombers. The Soviets, lacking equivalent submarine and bomber forces, required additional ICBMs to offset the American advantage.

Jackson also criticized the Nixon administration for its tolerance of Soviet human rights violations, particularly Moscow's refusal to let Soviet Jews emigrate. Jackson's criticism was valid, although the Soviets liberalized their emigration policy and permitted 30,000 Jews to leave the country during 1973, the largest number ever. Jackson helped push the Jackson–Vanik Amendment through Congress, which denied the Soviet Union "most favored nation" trading status with the United States, until they stopped human rights abuses and allowed unlimited emigration.

THE CHINA OPENING

Nixon's most dramatic foreign policy achievement was the famed opening to China. For over twenty years, America and China had had no commercial, diplomatic, or cultural relations, and the United States had prevented China from joining the United Nations. Americans were forbidden to travel to China. The United States also maintained a trade boycott and loan ban against China, and it attempted to prevent other nations from trading with the Chinese.

When Nixon took office in 1969, China was emerging from years of upheaval caused by Mao Zedong's "Cultural Revolution." Chinese leaders, worried about threats to China's security posed by conflicts with the Soviets, sought contacts in the West. Mao was hopeful that friendly relations could be developed with the United States, a country he had long admired.

Nixon, sensing possibilities for rapprochement with the People's Republic, responded positively. Trade and travel restrictions between the two countries were eased. In April 1971, the Chinese invited an American table tennis team to visit China to play against Chinese athletes. This "ping-pong gambit" preceded the major breakthrough that came in July when Henry Kissinger secretly visited China. Nixon then stunned the American people when he announced on July 15 that Kissinger had made arrangements for him to visit China in early 1972.

Nixon sought to improve relations with China for several reasons. Most of America's European allies had long since normalized relations with China, and he knew that the U.S. policy of nonrecognition no longer worked. Nixon also knew pressures were mounting within the United Nations to evict Taiwan and seat China in its stead. Further, Nixon also expected to play the "China card" to incline the Soviets to conclude arms control and other agreements with the Americans. Improved relations with China were also part of Nixon and Kissinger's strategy for removing the United States from its Vietnam entanglement. They hoped that Chinese leaders would be helpful in persuading Hanoi to negotiate a settlement of the war that Washington could accept. Normal relations with China would also help America reassert its power in Southeast Asia and develop a wider network of interests in that economically and strategically important region. Nixon knew that his impeccable anti-Communist credentials protected him from right-wing attacks about his being soft on Communism. He also expected that media coverage of the China trip would boost his political stock at home during an election year.

The announcement that Nixon was going to China was greeted with tremendous enthusiasm by almost all Americans, regardless of their political leanings. Kissinger returned to China in November 1971 to finalize the arrangements. While he was in Beijing, the United Nations expelled Taiwan and awarded its seat on the Security Council to China. Some critical voices, mostly on the Republican Right, were raised in protest over Washington's quick abandonment of its longtime ally and friend.

President Nixon arrived in China on February 22, 1972, accompanied by advisers and a host of U.S. journalists. Back in America, millions of fascinated viewers watched spectacular live television coverage of Nixon's arrival at the Beijing airport, his journey into the Forbidden City, and many other highlights of his five-day visit. Nixon and his entourage were the first Americans to go to China officially in over twenty years. The video images beamed back to America through a communications satellite were the first live U.S. television coverage ever shot in China. Nixon met with Premier Zhou En-lai several times for hours of discussion. Nixon and Kissinger also had a lengthy meeting with Mao Zedong. The U.S. delegation was the guest of honor at a lavish banquet hosted by the Chinese leaders inside of the Great Hall of the People.

FIGURE 11.1 Richard Nixon's most significant diplomatic achievement was the opening to China, achieved when he journeyed to that great country in 1972. Here he meets Mao Zedong at his apartment. *Source:* National Archives and Records Administration.

At the conclusion of the historic visit, Nixon and Zhou En-lai issued a joint statement, the Shanghai Communique, which defined the terms of the new U.S.–Chinese relationship. Each country agreed to open a legation in the other's capital. America removed its restrictions on trade and travel to China, and it acknowledged that Taiwan was part of China.

There was no agreement on the Vietnam War. Both China and the United States reaffirmed support for their respective sides in that ongoing war. But the joint communique itself, the fact that it was being promulgated jointly by former adversaries, signaled that the United States was moving beyond the Vietnam War toward a larger role in Southeast Asia. Within a year of Nixon's visit, American travelers flocked to China. Trade between the two nations increased dramatically. Both countries exchanged diplomatic missions. The China opening was the high point of Nixon's presidency and the most significant diplomatic achievement of any modern American president.

VIETNAM: A WAR TO END A WAR

The most urgent problem confronting Nixon was extricating America from Vietnam. He tried new approaches to end the war, but his policies suffered from the same flaw as Johnson's. Nixon sought to maintain an independent non-Communist South Vietnamese state, which the North Vietnamese and the NLF refused to accept—the war went on.

Even though Hanoi had consistently rejected any settlement that would leave a non-Communist government in the South, Nixon and Kissinger believed that they could compel Hanoi to accept one. They planned to use the improved relationship between the United States and the USSR by linking increased trade and arms agreements with the Soviets to their willingness to pressure Hanoi into accepting U.S. terms in Vietnam.

Nixon also escalated the war by removing the limits Johnson had placed on the use of military force in Southeast Asia. In the spring of 1969, Nixon ordered a bombing campaign to begin against VietCong and North Vietnamese sanctuaries in Cambodia. Because Cambodia was a neutral nation, the bombing was illegal. It was kept secret from Congress and from the American people.

In addition, Nixon, through Soviet intermediaries, offered the North Vietnamese more realistic peace terms. He proposed withdrawing both American and North Vietnamese troops from the South and reinstituting the demilitarized zone as the boundary between North and South Vietnam. At the same time, to please American public opinion that had turned against the war, Nixon announced a phased withdrawal of U.S. combat troops from Vietnam.

But Hanoi was neither intimidated by threats nor lured by concessions into changing its terms. The Paris talks remained deadlocked. Hanoi continued to demand the unilateral withdrawal of all U.S. forces from South Vietnam and the installation of a coalition government in the South, excluding General Thieu. Nor did the Soviets cooperate. The linkage strategy proved to be a failure.

Nixon faced a dilemma; unable to extract the slightest concession from Hanoi, he had to choose between a major escalation of the war or a humiliating withdrawal. Unwilling to make concessions and unable to use greater force because he did not want to arouse domestic opponents of the war and because of concerns about its effectiveness, Nixon offered what Secretary of Defense Melvin Laird called "Vietnamization." The United States would continue gradually to withdraw its troops while building up South Vietnamese forces. The South Vietnamese forces would become strong enough to prevent a Communist takeover following the U.S. pullout.

At the time Nixon announced his Vietnamization plan, it had already been in place for a year. He had inherited it from Johnson and given it a new label. While U.S. forces battled the North Vietnamese and the VietCong, American advisers built up the South Vietnamese armed forces. Pacification and rural development programs accelerated. In March 1970, President Nixon announced that 150,000 U.S. combat troops would be withdrawn that year.

In neighboring Cambodia, neutralist leader Prince Sihanouk was suddenly overthrown by his pro-American prime minister, Lon Nol. Nixon, fearing that the North Vietnamese might take over Cambodia following the coup, and responding to a U.S. Army request to attack North Vietnamese sanctuaries in that country, ordered U.S. troops into an area of Cambodia about 50 miles northwest of Saigon. The Cambodian incursion produced mixed results. It relieved pressure on Saigon and bought more time for Vietnamization. But it also widened the war and provoked Hanoi into a full-scale support of Cambodian insurgents fighting Lon Nol's forces. America now had two fragile client states in Southeast Asia to defend against insurgents backed by North Vietnam and China. The Vietnam War had become an Indochina War.

Nixon did not anticipate the furious domestic reaction to the Cambodian invasion. College campuses across the land exploded at the news of an unexpected widening of a war that he had promised to phase out. At Kent State University tragedy occurred when Ohio National Guardsmen opened fire into a crowd of student protesters, killing four of them and wounding nine others. Following these shootings, hundreds of student strikes forced many colleges to shut down. More than 100,000 demonstrators gathered in Washington to protest the Cambodian invasion and the "Kent State Massacre."

The Senate repealed the Gulf of Tonkin resolution and voted to cut off all funds for Cambodia. But the fund cutoff failed to clear the House. Both the North Vietnamese and the VietCong broke off negotiations in protest, confident that domestic political pressure would eventually force U.S. withdrawal from both Cambodia and South Vietnam.

To appease Dovish critics at home, the president accelerated the timetable for troop withdrawals in 1971. He expanded the air war by ordering more bombing missions into Cambodia and along the Laotian panhandle. He also authorized an ARVN raid into Laos to disrupt enemy supply routes, but the raid failed to achieve most of its objectives.

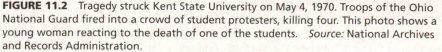

FIGURE 11.2   Tragedy struck Kent State University on May 4, 1970. Troops of the Ohio National Guard fired into a crowd of student protesters, killing four. This photo shows a young woman reacting to the death of one of the students.   *Source:* National Archives and Records Administration.

During the spring and summer of 1971, two events shocked the war-weary nation. First came the court martial of Lieutenant Willam Calley. It was followed by the publication of the Pentagon Papers.

On March 29, a military court convicted Lieutenant William Calley of multiple murders and sentenced him to life imprisonment for ordering his infantry platoon to kill hundreds of Vietnamese civilians at a hamlet called My Lai. Calley's men had massacred the villagers at close range with pistols, grenades, and automatic rifle fire.

Calley's attorneys claimed that he only followed orders. U.S. Army attorneys insisted that Calley had misunderstood his orders. Many Americans felt sympathy for Calley and his men; a public opinion poll showed that a majority of Americans blamed the media for reporting the incident, which had exposed the Army's efforts to cover up the affair. Responding to the angry outcry over Calley's conviction, President Nixon reduced Calley's sentence. Some Americans wondered how many other My Lai–type massacres had gone undetected. Others found cold comfort in the fact that VietCong had murdered thousands of civilians. There also was the troubling inconsistency of convicting one young junior officer for mass murder in a war where long-range artillery fire and aerial bombing had killed thousands of villagers.

No sooner had the uproar over Calley's conviction subsided than the *New York Times* began publishing excerpts from *The Pentagon Papers*, secret documents pertaining to the Vietnam War, which had been stolen from files of the RAND Corporation by a former employee, Daniel Ellsberg. The papers revealed that American leaders had deliberately escalated the war, had ignored peace offers, and had often lied to the public about their actions. These revelations increased war weariness and further undermined the credibility of government officials.

An increasingly frustrated president fought back against the mounting opposition to his war policy. He ordered that wiretaps be placed on National Security Council staffers and journalists suspected of leaking secret information to the media. He ordered illegal surveillance of antiwar groups by the CIA. Nixon administration lawyers tried to prevent the *Times* from publishing *The Pentagon Papers.* They secured a court injunction against their publication on the grounds that their release compromised national security. An appellate judge quashed the injunction, and the Supreme Court sustained his ruling.

Blocked by the U.S. Supreme Court, the president approved the creation of a special White House undercover unit, the "Plumbers," to prevent leaks from within the government and to discredit Ellsberg. Under extreme pressure, Nixon felt beset by enemies in the Congress, the media, the bureaucracies, and the streets, all of whom, he believed, were working to undermine his authority to govern. Nixon's paranoid attitudes, which drove him to order his men to commit illegal acts, were one of the prime causes of the Watergate scandals.

A survey of public opinion taken during the summer of 1971 revealed that two-thirds of Americans supported the withdrawal of all U.S. troops from Vietnam by the end of the year, even if that meant a Communist takeover in the South. Twice the Senate passed resolutions setting a deadline for withdrawal of all troops as soon as North Vietnam released U.S. prisoners of war (POWs).

Nixon responded to these signs of increasing war weariness by making new, secret peace proposals to Hanoi: In exchange for the release of American prisoners, the United States would withdraw all of its troops within six months and would no longer insist that Hanoi withdraw its troops. These new U.S. concessions started the first serious negotiations since talks had begun in 1968, but deadlock continued because Washington insisted that Thieu remain in power in the South, whereas Hanoi insisted that his removal was a precondition of any settlement.

The war entered its final phase in 1972. North Vietnam launched its largest offensive of the war. Simultaneously, VietCong guerrillas resumed their attacks in rural areas to disrupt pacification efforts. The United States retaliated with massive B-52 bombing raids against targets in the Hanoi-Haiphong area. Tactical bombers pounded the North Vietnamese invaders and their supply lines. The North Vietnamese and VietCong continued to press their attacks. Nixon then ordered a naval blockade of North Vietnam and the mining of Haiphong Harbor, and escalated the bombing campaigns. In addition to his military responses, Nixon also approached the Soviets again about persuading Hanoi to accept a diplomatic settlement of the war.

Nixon's decisive response to the North Vietnamese assault received strong support at home. By summer, the North Vietnamese offensive had stalled. South Vietnam managed to survive the assaults because of the strong response by the United States. Both the Soviets and the Chinese, while loudly condemning the U.S. response publicly, privately exerted pressure on Hanoi to end its war with the United States. *Detente* with the two Communist powers at last bore fruit and helped Nixon bring the U.S. war in Southeast Asia to an end.

The North Vietnamese had expected their spring offensive, combined with the approaching American election, to force Nixon to accept their terms and remove Thieu. But the president's powerful response had neutralized their assault and inflicted heavy losses. Soviet and Chinese pressures on Hanoi pushed the North Vietnamese toward a diplomatic settlement. George McGovern, the inept Democratic challenger, posed no threat to Nixon. A combination of military losses, economic strains, and diplomatic isolation forced Hanoi to seek a settlement with the United States, as long as it did not conflict with their long-range goal of achieving a unified Vietnam under Communist control.

Secret negotiations resumed in Paris. Hanoi dropped its demand that Thieu must go before any settlement could be reached. By October 11, 1972, Kissinger and the North Vietnamese emissary, Le Duc Tho, had forged an agreement: Within sixty days after a cease-fire, America would remove all of its remaining troops, and North Vietnam would release the U.S. POWs. The Thieu government would remain in power, pending a political settlement in the South. North Vietnamese troops would remain in the South, and the National Liberation Front, now known as the People's Revolutionary Government (PRG), would be recognized as the legitimate government in areas under NLF control.

But General Thieu refused to accept the agreement, and Nixon supported him. The North Vietnamese, believing themselves betrayed, angrily broke off negotiations. The October agreement was placed on hold, and the war went on. Nixon, reelected by a landslide, tried to secure peace terms that were more favorable to the South Vietnamese government. He ordered air attacks on North Vietnamese targets in the vicinity of Hanoi and Haiphong. The so-called "Christmas bombing" lasted from December 18 to 29. At the same time he turned the U.S. Air Force loose on the North, Nixon significantly increased U.S. aid to South Vietnam. He also told Thieu to accept U.S. peace terms or the United States would settle without him.

The Christmas bombing provoked worldwide criticism and a storm of protest at home. Congress moved to cut off all funding for the war. With time running out on his options, Nixon told the North Vietnamese that if they agreed to resume negotiations, he would halt the bombing. The North Vietnamese accepted his offer, and the talks resumed. Kissinger and Tho reached an agreement signed by all parties on January 27, 1973. The January agreement was similar in all major provisions to the suspended agreement of October 11. This time Nixon imposed the agreement on Thieu, who signed reluctantly.

Although Nixon insisted that the peace agreement had brought "peace with honor" to Indochina, the January accords represented a disguised defeat for the United States, which permitted the Americans to extricate themselves from a war that they no longer believed in, at the same time retrieving their POWs. It also permitted North Vietnamese forces to remain in the South, and it granted the PRG political legitimacy. It allowed the Thieu regime to survive in the South for a time. The major question over which the war had been fought for nearly a decade, who would govern in the South, was deferred, to be resolved by political means in the future. But the political provisions of the treaty proved unworkable in practice, so the question of who would govern in the South would finally be settled by force of arms.

MIDDLE EASTERN DILEMMAS

As they sought to extract the United States from the Indochina War, Nixon and Kissinger had to cope with another crisis in the Middle East. Since the 1967 Six Days' War, a state of simmering hostility between Arabs and the Jewish state had prevailed; no progress toward resolving their serious differences had been made. Israel refused to surrender any of the Arab territories that it had seized during the Six Days' War—East Jerusalem, the West Bank, the Golan Heights, and the Sinai. The Arabs, for their part, refused even to meet with Israeli representatives or to accord the Jewish state the right to exist.

In the fall of 1970, Gamal Abdul Nasser, the Arab Nationalist leader, suddenly died, to be replaced by Anwar Sadat. The new leader found the tense state of relations between his country and Israel intolerable; he plotted with his ally Syria to stage another attack on Israel. The ground was prepared for another bloody Middle Eastern war.

On October 6, 1973, the fourth Arab–Israeli war began. Choosing Yom Kippur, the holiest day of the year for Jews, the Egyptians and Syrians launched surprise attacks on Israeli positions in the Sinai and along the Golan Heights. Syrian forces regained territory in the Golan Heights region and threatened to slice Israel in two. Caught off guard by the surprise Arab attacks, Israeli Prime Minister Golda Meir appealed to Washington to send the Israelis more planes, tanks, and ammunition. The United States responded promptly with an airlift of war matériel to their beleaguered ally.

Washington's decision to resupply the Israelis provoked Saudi Arabia to impose an oil embargo against the United States as reprisal for its support of Israel. The oil embargo desta-bilized world oil markets. It also created the first of a series of "energy crises" in the United States that had devastating impacts and far-reaching consequences. The stock market dropped sharply and stagflation worsened.

Amply resupplied by their American patrons, the Israelis launched counterattacks in the Sinai and Golan Heights regions. They drove the Syrians from the Golan Heights. In the Sinai, Israeli tanks halted the Egyptian offensive and drove them back toward the Suez Canal. Sadat turned to his ally, the Soviet Union, for help, a move that alarmed Washington because it appeared to threaten *detente*.

On October 20, Nixon dispatched Kissinger, now Secretary of State as well as National Security Adviser, to Moscow to meet with Brezhnev. The U.S. envoy told the Soviet leader not to send forces to the Middle East. Kissinger also rejected a Soviet proposal that the United States and the Soviet Union jointly impose a cease-fire. Meanwhile, Israeli armor crossed the Suez, enveloped large numbers of Egyptian troops, and placed troops on Egyptian soil. The Soviets grew more nervous as Sadat's situation deteriorated.

The anxious Soviets warned the Israelis not to continue their war or else risk Soviet military reprisals. On October 25, Nixon responded to the Soviet threat to Israel by ordering U.S. forces around the world to go on full military alert. The next day, the president announced that intelligence sources had evidence that the Soviets were preparing to airlift combat forces to the Middle East. The tensest moment in U.S.–Soviet relations since the Cuban Missile Crisis was at hand.

The crisis passed. The Soviets quickly made it clear that they would not send troops to the Middle East. A United Nations peacekeeping force that excluded both U.S. and Soviet troops was dispatched to the region. Kissinger, shuttling back and forth between Cairo and Jerusalem, persuaded the Egyptians and Israelis to accept a cease-fire that left the Israelis in control of more territory than when the Yom Kippur War had begun, but it permitted the Sadat regime to survive. The cease-fire was the first of a series of Middle Eastern agreements facilitated by Kissinger's "shuttle diplomacy." Subsequently, the Suez Canal was reopened, and the Arabs lifted their oil embargo. Egypt and Syria resumed diplomatic relations with the United States.

Paralleling their shuttle diplomacy vis-à-vis the seemingly intractable Arab–Israeli conflict, Nixon and Kissinger sought to strengthen U.S. relations with Iran. Washington wanted to involve Iran in U.S. efforts to contain Soviet expansionism into the Middle East. More important, Nixon and Kissinger intended to use Iran as a stabilizing force within that turbulent region to enable the United States to distance itself from the chronic Arab–Israeli disputes. Washington tapped Iran to become the major U.S. ally in the Persian Gulf region.

The United States began importing more oil from Iran, and Iran quickly became the preeminent military power in the region and the leading purchaser of U.S. arms. With help from Washington, relations improved between Saudi Arabia and Iran, who historically had been rivals. The rapprochement between the Saudis and Iranians strengthened the Organization of Oil Exporting Countries (OPEC), an emerging consortium of leading oil exporters that challenged the power of the Western oil companies, which had hitherto controlled the world's oil markets. Washington's opening to Iran sacrificed the interests of the major oil companies to the larger goals of Nixon and Kissinger's Middle East diplomacy. These goals included keeping the Soviets out, stabilizing the region, ensuring Israel's security, maintaining good relations with moderate Arab regimes, and neutralizing the effects of the Arab–Israeli conflict. Nixon and Kissinger's grand design for the Middle East would come apart in 1978 when the Shah of Iran was overthrown by anti-Western Islamic fundamentalists.

Further to the east, the United States became embroiled in a regional dispute between India and Pakistan. The cause of the conflict was Pakistani efforts to suppress a Nationalist rebellion in its East Bengal territory. India intervened in the civil war on behalf of the Bengali rebels. Nixon and Kissinger decided to support Pakistan to prevent the Indians from going to war against the Pakistanis. The Soviets backed the Indians and the rebels; the Chinese, fearful of a Soviet–Indian alliance, supported the Pakistanis, making the Americans and the Chinese, in effect, allies. The United States suffered a diplomatic setback when the Bengalis, assisted by the Indians and Soviets, won their independence from Pakistan and became the new state of Bangladesh.

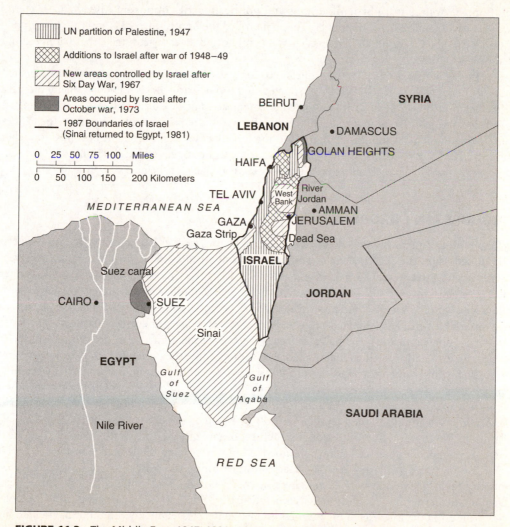

FIGURE 11.3   The Middle East, 1947–1981.   *Source:* U.S. State Department.

CHAOS IN CHILE

Nixon and Kissinger's foreign policy focused on the nations of the northern tier; they were relatively unconcerned about the affairs of most Pacific Island, African, and Latin American countries located in the Southern Hemisphere of the planet. One significant exception to this general pattern of neglect of much of the Third World was Chile. In 1970, Chile's national congress elected a Marxist, Salvador Allende Gossens, as Chile's president, even though he had received only a third of the popular vote.

Upon his election to office, Allende quickly moved to nationalize U.S.-owned enterprises in Chile, including two copper mining companies and telephone companies. He also established friendly relations with China, the Soviet Union, and Cuba. Responding to Allende's socialist agenda, Washington declared economic war on Chile. U.S. banks no longer loaned Chile money. Washington also prevented international agencies such as the International Monetary Fund and the World Bank from providing Chile with financial assistance. All military assistance programs to Chile's armed forces were suspended. The American Institute for Free Labor channeled millions of dollars to right-wing unions and political parties opposing Allende. CIA agents worked to destabilize Chilean politics. They bankrolled the opposition press and the main opposition party, the Christian Democrats. They also supported a Teamsters strike that paralyzed the nation's economy.

By the summer of 1973, the Chilean economy was in ruins and the newly impoverished middle classes were in revolt. With CIA support, a group of army officers, led by General Augusto Pinochet, overthrew Allende, who was killed or committed suicide during the *coup d'etat*. Pinochet instituted a reign of terror that resulted in the deaths of hundreds of Allende supporters, the torture and imprisonment of thousands more, and the forced exile of additional thousands. Pinochet restored the U.S. properties to their former owners. The United States quickly lifted all restrictions on economic and military assistance to Chile. Pinochet ruled Chile for the next sixteen years.

TROUBLES IN EUROPE

When Nixon came to the presidency, a number of factors were creating serious strains between the United States and the three major powers of western Europe—Great Britain, France, and West Germany. All three were asserting greater autonomy from the United States. Nixon and Kissinger perceived the danger in this west European trend to their carefully crafted strategy of *detente* with the Soviet Union. *Detente* could never realize its full potential unless the NATO nations as well as the eastern bloc nations remained subservient to their respective superpower patrons.

In response to the growing assertiveness of the Western European nations, Washington sought a new relation with its major allies. At the same time, they intended to hold the evolving new relationship somewhat short of full autonomy for Great Britain, France, and West Germany. They hoped to find ways to use western Europe's new power and wealth globally but at the same time to keep the major Western nations from asserting their independence from American world leadership. Washington failed to achieve most of its goals in western Europe during Nixon's tenure. NATO retained its traditional structure, organization, and strategic goals, but West Germany, France, and Great Britain continued to draw away from the United States.

By 1970, a prosperous West Germany was beginning to reassert its traditional national identity. Social Democrat Willy Brandt became chancellor, the leader of a coalition of the Social Democratic Party (SDP) and the Free Democratic Party (FDP), a liberal party committed to policies promoting the interests of big business and free enterprise. Quickly Brandt implemented his *Ostpolitik*, the most serious challenge to U.S. hegemony in western Europe since the end of World

War II. *Ostpolitik* entailed opening up the markets of eastern Europe and the Soviet Union to West German high-tech exports. It also entailed investments, loans, and joint ventures with these nations.

The British and French also began a series of collaborations that ran counter to U.S. interests. The French, under the leadership of Georges Pompidou, dropped their long-standing opposition to British membership in the European Economic Community (EEC), also known as the Common Market. The French apparently were alarmed by the growing economic power of the Germans and sought closer ties with the British to offset it. The British, for their part, now appeared ready to join the EEC. Reduced tariffs would enable them to sell their exports on the lucrative continental market, and a recent devaluation of the pound sterling made their goods more competitive. In September 1971, the British parliament voted by a large majority to join the EEC.

The most spectacular achievement of the new Anglo-French togetherness was to form a consortium to construct a new supersonic airplane capable of flying across the Atlantic Ocean at twice the speed of sound. It was designed to compete with a planned American supersonic aircraft called the supersonic transport (SST). The new French–British plane, called the Concorde, had British engines and a French airframe. It flew its maiden transatlantic flight in 1976. Meanwhile, the Democratic-controlled Congress had killed the SST project, despite intense pressure from the Nixon White House to go ahead with it. Congressional leaders viewed it as too expensive and too noisy.

THE EMERGENCE OF JAPAN

By the early 1970s, Japan was the most important nation in the American Far Eastern economic and strategic system. From Washington's perspective, Japan posed some serious problems. Like the prosperous nations of western Europe, Japan exhibited some of the same tendencies to take a foreign policy tack more independent of Washington. The Japanese also contributed a minuscule fraction of their gross domestic product to their own national defense. They continued to rely on the American nuclear umbrella for their strategic security. Washington had been annoyed that the Japanese had not supported the U.S. effort in Vietnam with any enthusiasm, even though one of the reasons the United States had intervened in the Indochina War was to protect Japanese economic and strategic interests in that region. The Japanese in turn were annoyed at the United States for Nixon's peaceful overtures to China. Further, the Japanese, with their rebuilt modern economy, were increasingly selling cars, television sets, and cameras in American markets during the early 1970s, hurting U.S. domestic industries in these crucial high-tech fields.

Washington hoped to rein in the high-flying Japanese and make them pay more of the costs of their own defense. Washington also wanted to slow the penetration of American markets by Japanese exporters. In 1971, Nixon erected a 10 percent surcharge on all imports from Japan, which was aimed primarily at Japanese automakers.

REALIST DIPLOMACY IN PERSPECTIVE

Nixon's greatest success came with transforming U.S. relations with the major Communist powers, the Soviet Union and the People's Republic of China. Nixon and Kissinger were less successful in Indochina. It took considerably longer than they had expected to phase out the U.S. Indochina War. The 1973 Paris Accords that they managed to arrange after four more years of warfare failed to save South Vietnam from a Communist takeover two years later. But in the aftermath of the failed

Vietnam enterprise, America made important gains in its East Asian and Southeast Asian relations. Outside of Indochina, no more dominoes fell to Communist "wars of national liberation." Since 1975, most of the nations of Southeast and East Asia, such as Thailand, Malaysia, and South Korea, have become more stable, strong, and prosperous, enjoying friendly ties and strong commercial relations with the United States.

The foreign policy analyst Franz Schurman has written about the development of a world economic system during the 1970s, by which he means the emergence of an international economic system within which the national economies of most countries are inextricably interlinked in numerous ways. Trade has been integrated, a global monetary system has arisen, and capital markets have become interdependent. Political links have likewise arisen through networks of political leaders, civil servants, and senior military officials. The creation of a world economy suggested, among other things, that the traditional distinction between foreign policy and domestic affairs have been breaking down. During the Nixon administration, foreign and domestic policy, especially economic policy, became inseparable. Nixon's frequent efforts to try to fix the U.S. economy involved changing U.S. foreign economic policies that were influencing trade, tariff rates, and exchange rates.

Nixon's foreign policy, by reducing the threat of war with the major Communist powers and by bringing them, at least to a limited extent, into the evolving world economic system, which is essentially a world capitalist system, ensured the further development of an interdependent global economy. His grand design also ensured that the United States would continue to occupy the central place in that world system, because the prosperous Western European nations accepted America's central role, perceiving that their own future prosperity was inextricably linked to the United States. In broad historical perspective, Nixonian diplomacy is best understood as capping the end of a thirty-year era that began with Truman in 1945 rather than viewed as a guide to future U.S. foreign relations of the 1980s and 1990s.

But there were many failures in Nixonian diplomacy during the early 1970s. The Iranian revolution, in time, destroyed all of his plans for the Middle East. His neglect of the poor nations of the Southern Hemisphere in Africa and Latin America ensured political instability in those important parts of the world during the 1980s. The Nixon Doctrine, which was supposed to be a post-Vietnam politico-military strategy for dealing with insurgencies in the Third World, failed to work effectively. Most of all, Nixon's grand goal, a generation of peace, proved unattainable. Much of his foreign policy demonstrated a short-term brilliance, but it lacked staying power. By the late 1970s, *detente* was discredited, and Jimmy Carter revived the Cold War. If one of the purposes of Nixon's foreign policy was ultimately conservative and counterrevolutionary, that is, as an effort to stem the Marxist revolutionary tide in the Third World, it must also be counted as mostly a failure. Communism did ultimately fail, but its failure did not derive from any diplomatic, strategic, or economic maneuvers by Nixon and Kissinger.

Brief Bibliographic Essay

Most helpful in understanding Nixon's conduct of foreign policy are the relevant chapters in the second volume of Stephen E. Ambrose's three-volume biography entitled *Nixon: The Triumph of a Politician, 1962–1972*. After his forced retirement from the presidency, Mr. Nixon wrote several books about world affairs. The best of these books was his first, his memoirs, entitled *RN: The Memoirs of Richard Nixon*, which contains extensive treatments of his foreign policies. A critical view of Nixon and Kissinger's foreign policies can be found in Tad Szulc's *The Illusion of Peace: Foreign Policy in the Nixon Years*. Franz Schurman, in *The Foreign Politics of Richard Nixon*, offers an original analysis of the politics of Nixon and Kissinger's diplomacy. Robert Dallek, *Nixon and Kissinger: Partners in Power*, is a recent excellent joint biography of the two leaders who dominated the world stage for five critical years. Margaret MacMillan, *Nixon and Mao: The Week that Changed the World* is a recent and very readable account of one of the most dramatic occurrences in modern world history. Jeffrey Kimball's *Nixon's Vietnam War*, has established itself as the definitive account. For Nixon's Middle Eastern diplomacy, see the relevant portions of Daniel Yergin's *The Prize*. Henry Kissinger has written two important books, *The White House Years* and *Years of Upheaval*, about U.S. foreign policy on their watch.

CHAPTER

12

Era of Limits

During the 1970s there was a historic shift in the trajectory of the American economy. The longest boom cycle in American history, which had ignited during World War II and had continued, with occasional recessions, for thirty years, halted during the early 1970s. The seemingly perpetual prosperity, caused by a high-growth rate, federal spending, innovative technology, and (most of all) credit-fueled consumerism, stalled. It was replaced by "stagflation," an inflationary recession, which eroded purchasing power and lowered living standards for millions of American families.

A long-term structural shift contributed powerfully to stagflation. The American economy during the 1970s accelerated its movement away from its historic manufacturing base toward a "postindustrial" society increasingly dependent on the rapidly expanding service sector. In a service economy, technological advances are small, gains in productivity are modest, and wages and salaries are generally much lower than that for workers in traditional manufacturing industries.

Vietnam and Watergate ushered in a time of troubles for Americans. They experienced ineffective presidential leadership, partisan squabbling, continuing social divisions, severe economic dislocations, energy crises, and international disorders. All of these problems were compounded by a massive loss of faith in politics and government, especially among young people. They believed that government was incapable of solving their many complex, often interrelated, problems.

Economic decline and perceived failures of political leadership all contributed to the most important political trend of the 1970s, the continuing drift to the Right of substantial segments of the American electorate. The ground had been prepared for the Republican resurgence during the late 1960s and early 1970s. The election of 1980 brought Ronald Reagan to the White House and Republicans regained control of the Senate for the first time since 1952.

ECONOMIC DECLINE

During the thirty-year boom cycle lasting from the early 1940s to the early 1970s, most American families had enjoyed unprecedented prosperity. Real per capita family income doubled, and the GDP more than doubled during those three decades of strong economic growth. The steadily expanding economy and rising living standards over a long period of time convinced most Americans that prosperity was perpetual. But during the early 1970s, stagflation replaced perpetual growth and created a set of economic circumstances that eroded the prosperity that middle-class Americans had taken for granted for decades.

During the early 1970s, the declining U.S. economy was also showing the effects of strong foreign competition. The industrial economies of West Germany and Japan, rebuilt using the latest technologies after having been destroyed during World War II, were more productive than the older U.S. industries. U.S. shares of many world markets declined. Within America, many industries lost large shares of the domestic market to their foreign competitors. In 1970, about 10 percent of new cars sold in America were imported; by 1980, that figure had reached 30 percent.

Inflation, deficits, and loss of both domestic and export markets combined to create a serious balance of payments problem by 1972, which threatened to undermine the value of the dollar. When the Nixon administration in response devalued the dollar by severing it from gold, his action unleashed an orgy of gold speculation in the world that drove the price from $35 an ounce to over $800 an ounce and added to the inflationary burden of American consumers.

The struggles of millions of American families for economic survival during the 1970s were exacerbated by structural trends that weakened the economic foundations of American middle-class society. As the economy became increasingly based on high-tech service and information-oriented industries, the number of jobs that provided middle-class incomes declined. A service economy employs millions of clerical workers, salesclerks, waiters, bartenders, cashiers, and messengers. Wages for these jobs are comparatively low. While millions of new service-sector jobs were created during the 1970s, the number of higher-paying manufacturing jobs decreased.

During the 1970s, millions of factory jobs disappeared because of declining productivity and cutbacks in capital spending, and because production work became increasingly automated. Trade unions lost hundreds of thousands of members to automation and to declines caused by foreign competition in manufacturing industries. These displaced workers usually could not find alternative employment that offered comparable pay and fringe benefits. Their options were early retirement, if they could afford it, or accepting jobs in the rapidly expanding service sectors of the economy. But most of these service jobs were low paying, with minimal opportunities for advancement or a career. In any case, most of these new service-sector jobs went to women, minorities, and youngsters. The fastest-growing sector of the service economy in the 1970s, which carried into the 1980s, was the fast-food industry. McDonald's became the nation's largest employer. During the 1970s, the fast-food industry added workers faster than manufacturing lost them. On average, these "Mcjobs" paid one-third as much and came with far fewer benefits.

Real income declined 15 percent from the early 1970s to 1980. Simultaneously, inflation drove housing and new car prices upward. The median price of new homes doubled during the decade.

The 1970s appeared to reverse the social and economic trends of the 1940s, 1950s, and 1960s. These reversals led to a loss of faith in economic progress; during the 1970s, millions of families faced what they had come to believe could never recur—economic retrogression, the first since the early 1930s.

For generations, Americans had been sustained by their belief in economic individualism: Talent, initiative, and hard work generated upward mobility and economic security, enabling men (and women) to provide for their families and ensure that their children would have a better life than what they had. But during the era of limits, faith in the work ethic was eroded. Millions of Americans could not find steady employment in the 1970s. Millions who worked found not affluence but subsistence. For millions of young people, the struggle was not to reach the top, but to not to fall any lower. Millions of middle-class youngsters could not realistically expect to earn as much, own as much, and be as successful as their parents. At a time when racist and sexist barriers to advancement were crumbling and the American dream was opening to all Americans for the first time, economic obstacles were growing stronger.

The inflation rate soared beyond 10 percent in 1974, spurred by wage hikes, increased consumer demand, and budget deficits. The Ford administration attacked inflation by slowing down the economy with tight money policies. Tight money brought the worst downturn since the Great Depression of the 1930s. U.S. multinational corporations relocated their manufacturing facilities overseas to take advantage of lower costs, tax breaks, and cheap labor. Unemployment climbed to 7 percent by year's end and reached 9 percent in 1975.

ENERGY CRISES

In October 1973, the Organization of Petroleum Exporting Countries (OPEC) embargoed oil shipments to the United States. The oil cutoff was initiated by Saudi Arabia and other Arab members of OPEC to protest U.S. support of Israel in its recent war with Egypt and Syria and to force a settlement of the war favoring the Arabs. Americans experienced shortages of heating oil and power "brownouts." Impatient motorists formed long lines at the gas pumps.

The energy crisis had been building for years; the OPEC embargo triggered it. American postwar growth and prosperity had been founded on cheap energy. U.S. domestic oil production began declining in 1969, while demand continued to rise. By 1970, America, with only 6 percent of the world's population, used over one-third of the world's energy. To meet the ever-increasing demand for oil, U.S. oil companies bought more and more imported oil. Daily consumption of imported oil rose from 12 percent in 1968 to 36 percent by 1973. An increasing proportion of imported oil came from OPEC nations, and two-thirds of OPEC oil came from the Middle East.

FIGURE 12.1 Energy Crisis USA. Motorists line up to get gas at a service station in Los Angeles. *Source:* National Archives and Records Administration.

The OPEC embargo was short lived. Arab countries removed it after a few months, and oil shortages quickly vanished. But gasoline prices rose from 30¢ to 70¢ a gallon during that period, and they stayed there. In 1970, the average price of a barrel of crude oil was $2.53; it was averaging $31.00 a barrel in 1980. Much higher energy prices became a permanent fact of U.S. economic life. Higher oil prices sent an inflationary jolt coursing through all facets of the American economy because oil had seeped into the fabric of American life. Oil heated homes; it was synthesized into fibers and plastics; farmers used it for fertilizer, pesticides, and fuel; and it was crucial to all forms of transportation. Rising energy prices struck hardest at the older industrial centers of the Northeast and the Great Lakes region, because they had to import most of their energy. Cutbacks in federal spending fell hardest on cities in these regions, given their shrinking tax bases, declining industries, and expensive social services.

Before he was forced to resign, Nixon had battled the energy crisis. He created the Federal Energy Office to formulate a national energy policy and to promote conservation. He proposed a plan called "Project Independence" to make America energy-independent by 1980. The plan called for increasing domestic oil production by tapping Alaskan oil fields and accelerating offshore drilling; producing more natural gas, coal, and nuclear energy; extracting oil from shale deposits; and developing renewable energy sources. Project Independence made little progress. With the lifting of the embargo and the return of normal supplies of oil, most people rapidly forgot about the energy crisis, although motorists complained about the high price of gasoline.

Ford tried to continue Nixon's energy program, but he encountered opposition from various interest groups. Environmentalists opposed many of its features. Antinuclear groups opposed building additional nuclear power plants. Ford tried to deregulate domestic oil and natural gas prices, only to be blocked by the Democratic majority in Congress, who believed that deregulation would hurt low-income families and aggravate inflation. Congress enacted legislation in 1975, giving the president standby authority to ration gasoline, to create a strategic petroleum reserve, and to set mandatory fuel economy standards for new cars. Three years later, the United States imported 40 percent of its daily oil requirements, more than the quantity it imported when OPEC embargoed oil.

CARS AND COMPUTERS

Despite stagflation and energy crises, Americans during the 1970s continued their longtime love affair with the automobile. Registrations reached 90 million in 1970 and 118 million in 1980. Americans accounted for about one-third of all of the cars owned in the world in 1975. Millions of Americans purchased automobiles manufactured in Europe and Japan during the 1970s. High-performance sports cars, small trucks, and vans became more popular. Consumers became more value conscious and safety conscious. Manufacturers responded by offering their customers a far greater choice of vehicles than had been previously available. The application of new technologies meant that the 1970s' automobiles were more aerodynamically designed, more fuel efficient, safer, and much easier to handle than the cars of the 1950s and 1960s had been. Automobiles of the 1970s were also much more expensive and, especially the American-made cars, much more prone to breakdown and costly repairs.

Automobiles continued to be the primary means of intercity travel in the United States during the 1970s, although commercial airlines did increase their share of the travelers' market, from about 5 percent to 10 percent. Despite sizable increases in their business, most domestic airlines found themselves in serious financial difficulties during the late 1970s. Most of these difficulties derived from the deregulation of the airline industry, implemented during the Carter presidency. Several well-known airlines went out of business, including Eastern and Braniff.

In the short term, passengers obviously benefited from the far greater variety of flights offered at lower prices generated by a new era of cutthroat competition. In the long run, weaker competitors were driven to bankruptcy and either forced to shut down or be absorbed by the stronger airlines. Serious questions of reliability and safety also arose.

The most dramatic technological innovations of the 1970s were all connected to the computer revolution. America was computerized during the 1970s. There were approximately 6,000 computers in use in this country in 1972; by 1980, there were millions. The agent of revolution was the microcomputer. The use of microcomputers vastly enhanced the abilities of individuals working in a wide variety of fields to calculate and retrieve information. Individuals using computers could also build statistical models and process words. The key invention that brought forth the microcomputer was the microprocessor, or computer chip, perfected by Ted Hoff in 1972. Hoff was a young engineer on the staff at Intel Corporation when he designed the world's first microprocessor, which started the revolution in electronic technology. The computer revolution made possible the information revolution of the 1970s and 1980s, which transformed the way Americans lived and worked.

The first personal computers were marketed in the mid-1970s. In California's "Silicon Valley," a suburban area located about 40 miles south of San Francisco, dozens of small computer companies found themselves on the cutting edge of technological revolution. In 1976, two young men, Steven Wozniak, a computer genius, and Steve Jobs, an entrepreneurial visionary, opened a small business in a garage they had rented for $50 a month. Wozniak designed and Jobs sold small, inexpensive personal computers. They called their fledgling company Apple. Sales were slow at first; no one appeared to be interested in a small, relatively inexpensive personal computer. However, sales picked up and by the mid-1980s Apple had become a multibillion-dollar business.

A FORD NOT A LINCOLN

The new president was as different as possible from the charmless and conflicted loner whom he succeeded. Gerald Ford possessed a warm and gregarious personality. A nation that was weary of war and political scandal appreciated his personal charm, modesty, and integrity when he reminded his fellow citizens, "I am a Ford, not a Lincoln."

Sensing the malaise of the nation in the wake of the Vietnam War and Watergate, Ford made "binding up the nation's wounds" and restoring national confidence his top priorities. He endeavored to send a message of continuity and stability to the nation, while also trying to separate his administration from the Watergate scandals. As he struggled to take the reins of power, President Ford's most difficult decision was granting a pardon for former president Richard Nixon. If he did not pardon him, Ford feared that Watergate would haunt the nation for years as the possibility of Nixon's ongoing trial loomed.

Although many historians who initially strongly criticized the decision came to revise their views in later years, Ford paid a steep price at the time. The Nixon pardon ruined the new president's chances for receiving bipartisan support for his policies from the Democratic-controlled Congress. Despite his denials, many Americans suspected that Ford and Nixon had made a deal—Nixon had chosen Ford to replace Agnew, with the understanding that if Nixon resigned or was removed from office, Ford would pardon him. Further, it seemed patently unfair to send underlings to jail for their parts in Watergate while the leader whose directives they followed went free. Polls consistently showed that most Americans believed that if Nixon had broken the law, he should have to face trial like any other citizen. Ford's pardon of Nixon perpetuated the suspicions and resentments of Watergate that the new leader was trying to dispel, tied his presidency to that of his despised predecessor's, hurt Republicans in the 1974 elections, and may have cost him the 1976 presidential election.

Ford generated further controversy when he established an amnesty program for the thousands of young men who had violated draft laws or deserted from the military during the Vietnam era. According to its terms, if they agreed to perform public service for one to two years, their prison terms would be waived or reduced. Hawks condemned the plan as being too lenient; Doves denounced it as punitive. Another of Ford's efforts to bind up national wounds had the opposite effect of reopening them.

Partisan conflicts between the Republican president and the Democratic-controlled Congress hampered government effectiveness during Ford's tenure. He vetoed sixty-six bills enacted by Congress, including federal aid for education, a health care measure, a housing measure, and a bill to control strip mining. During Ford's presidency, Congress extended the Voting Rights Act of 1965 and increased Social Security benefits.

The 1974 midterm elections took place amidst an atmosphere of continuing political controversy and public mistrust, much of which had been inadvertently perpetuated by Ford's own actions. The Democrats gained forty-three seats in the House and four seats in the Senate, increasing their margins to 291 to 144 in the House and to 61 to 38 in the Senate. More voters than ever before called themselves "Independents," and only 38 percent of those eligible to vote went to the polls.

Shortly after the midterm elections had taken place, a Senate committee led by Senator Frank Church of Idaho investigating CIA operations discovered that over the years it had been involved in numerous assassinations or attempted murders of foreign leaders, including Fidel Castro. A commission headed by Vice President Nelson Rockefeller found that the CIA had routinely kept citizens under surveillance and had conducted drug experiments on unwitting victims. The CIA had also engaged in illegal domestic espionage and compiled files on dissenters. The Church Committee discovered that the National Security Agency (NSA) had intercepted the phone calls and telegrams of Americans. Other investigations revealed that the FBI also had engaged in a variety of lawless actions, including wiretapping, spying, burglary, blackmail, and sabotage. Former FBI director J. Edgar Hoover had conducted a personal vendetta against civil rights leader Martin Luther King Jr. FBI agents spied on King and his associates, read his mail, tapped his phones, bugged his hotel rooms, and blackmailed him.

These discoveries of official lawlessness, occurring during Kennedy's, Johnson's, and Nixon's presidencies, confirmed that the CIA, the NSA, and the FBI, in their obsessive pursuit of internal security, had repeatedly violated the constitutional rights of American citizens. In response, President Ford issued new directives providing for greater congressional oversight of CIA activities and for restricting the CIA's covert operations. The Justice Department issued new guidelines for the FBI. In 1978, Congress enacted the Foreign Intelligence Surveillance Act (FISA), which required approval of a special court for eavesdropping on American soil. Over thirty years later, in the spring of 2006, a strikingly similar drama unfolded as another Senate committee held hearings on domestic eavesdropping by the NSA without warrants in violation of FISA.

EXTENDING *DETENTE*

Henry Kissinger, whom Ford had inherited from former president Nixon, doubled as secretary of state and head of the National Security Council. Kissinger had a major part in implementing U.S. Middle Eastern policy following a fourth Arab–Israeli war that began on October 6, 1973 (see Chapter 11). Kissinger persuaded the Egyptians and Israelis to accept a cease-fire. The cease-fire was the first of a series of Middle Eastern agreements facilitated by Kissinger's "shuttle diplomacy." Kissinger capped his Middle Eastern efforts in 1975 by arranging an important new Sinai agreement between Egypt and Israel. According to its terms, UN peacekeeping forces would remain, and an early warning system would be set up in the Sinai to prevent future surprise attacks by either side. These Sinai accords made possible the subsequent achievement of the Camp David agreements during Jimmy Carter's presidency.

Ford and Kissinger tried but failed to improve relations with China and the Soviet Union. Ford visited China in 1975, but U.S. support of Taiwan prevented him from forging closer ties with Beijing. Efforts to extend detente and to forge a second SALT agreement with the Soviets failed.

Another effort to extend *detente* brought together Ford and Soviet leader Leonid Brezhnev with European leaders at Helsinki in August 1975. Both sides agreed to recognize the political boundaries dividing eastern and western Europe since the end of World War II. For the first time, the United States recognized the legitimacy of East Germany. For his part, Brezhnev agreed to ease restrictions of the right of Soviet Jews to emigrate.

VIETNAM: THE END

The Vietnam War ended in April 1975, when North Vietnamese forces overran the South and captured Saigon, two years after all U.S. forces had been withdrawn. President Ford tried to help the dying South Vietnamese regime, but Congress refused to enact his request for additional aid.

During the final years of the U.S. involvement in Southeast Asia, Congress sought a greater role in the conduct of foreign policy and also sought to reduce the power of the president to make war. The War Powers Act, passed over President Nixon's veto in 1973, ordered the president to consult with Congress before sending U.S. forces into war. This enactment was largely symbolic. Ford believed it was unconstitutional and ignored it.

The fall of Saigon in 1975 opened the door to the Republican Right. Conservatives chafed against an ascendant press, the War Powers Act, and post-Watergate reforms that curtailed the executive branch's prerogatives and tilted power back toward Congress. Donald Rumsfeld replaced Alexander Haig as President Ford's chief of staff and then went on to become secretary of Defense. Richard "Dick" Cheney, Rumsfeld's assistant, replaced him as chief of staff. As these two young hawks gained influence within the Ford administration, they worked to undercut the power of Henry Kissinger and to challenge his policies of *detente* and arms control with the Soviet Union.

THE ELECTION OF 1976

As the 1976 election approached, Ford appeared to be politically vulnerable. Having achieved the office of the president only through the grace of Nixon's appointment, Ford had proven to be an ineffective caretaker during his two years of office. He faced a powerful challenge from within Republican ranks by Ronald Reagan, the leader of a growing conservative movement.

The surprise of the 1976 Democratic race proved to be the sudden emergence of James Earl Carter Jr., who called himself "Jimmy." Carter was a political unknown outside his native Georgia where he had served one term as governor. He won a series of primary victories in both the North and the South. When the Democratic convention opened in New York, Carter had more than enough votes to ensure a first-ballot nomination. He chose a Midwestern liberal for his running mate, Senator Walter Mondale, from Minnesota. They ran on a platform attacking Ford's "government by veto" and Kissinger's "manipulative" foreign policy.

Carter's capture of the Democratic Party nomination in 1976 was one of the most remarkable achievements in modern American political history. His victory could only have happened within the context of post-Vietnam, post-Watergate massive disillusionment with politics as usual in this country.

Ford, meanwhile, was locked in a fierce struggle for the Republican nomination with Ronald Reagan, leader of the resurgent Republican Right. Ford adopted a Centrist stance, projecting an image of a moderate leader healing the nation's wounds, promoting economic recovery, and keeping the nation at peace. He beat Reagan decisively in the early primaries. When the Sunbelt primaries came up in the spring, Reagan ran off a string of victories, surging ahead of Ford in the delegate count. Ford rallied with victories in several Northern industrial states. Reagan countered with a big win in California.

When the Republican convention assembled in Kansas City, the two candidates were so close that the winner would be the one who captured a majority of the few uncommitted delegates. Ford managed to win a close first-ballot nomination, but the Reaganites forced Ford to move to the Right in order to survive, and they influenced the drafting of a conservative platform. For his vice presidential running mate, Ford selected a conservative, Kansas senator Robert Dole, to replace Rockefeller, who chose not to run again.

Although Reagan endorsed Ford, many of his supporters did not. Ford led a divided party into battle against a Democratic Party united behind the candidacy of Jimmy Carter.

When the campaign began, polls showed Carter leading the incumbent by twenty percentage points. The campaign itself turned out to be rather dull and unenlightening. Neither man made much impact on a wary electorate. Neither candidate stood out in a series of three televised debates. Ford ran on his record, which was unimpressive. Carter conducted a vaguely liberal, populistic, and moralistic campaign. He promised to tame Washington's bureaucracy, and he pledged to craft a government that was "as good and honest as are the American people." Ford and Dole campaigned energetically throughout October and steadily whittled down Carter's lead.

Carter managed to score a narrow victory, receiving forty-one million votes to Ford's thirty-nine million. His winning margin in the electoral vote was 297 to 241. Carter carried the South, several border states, and some Northern industrial states. He lost most of the Midwest and carried no state west of the Mississippi River. Black votes provided his margin of victory in the South. He also did well among traditional Democratic voters—labor, urban, Jewish, liberals, and intellectuals. Carter's party ran much better than he did. Democrats retained their large majorities in both houses of Congress.

Carter's victory suggested that a bare majority of voters were willing to entrust the reins of government to an inexperienced outsider from a Southern village. Given a choice between "fear of the known and fear of the unknown," the citizenry opted for a fresh, new face who promised to tell the truth.

Carter's winning the Democratic nomination before the convention signaled an important new political reality; most states were now holding presidential primaries. The primary process opened up the nominating process to the mass of voters and reduced the importance of political parties. It also lengthened the campaigns, greatly increased their costs, and enhanced the role of television. Ford and Carter both accepted $22 million of federal funds to finance their fall campaigns, and both renounced private fund-raising. They were the first presidential candidates to use new federal spending laws that were enacted following the Watergate disclosures of fund-raising abuses.

MR. CARTER GOES TO WASHINGTON

Carter came to office knowing that millions of Americans were still deeply suspicious of the political system. He strove from the outset to "de-imperialize" the White House and to restore popular faith in national politics. He also brought many previously excluded groups into the higher levels of the federal government. Out of his 1,195 full-time federal appointments, 12 percent were women, 12 percent were black, and 4 percent Hispanic.

But Carter's top priority became slashing the size and cost of the government. The growing conservatism of large segments of the American electorate was the most significant political trend of the 1970s. More and more Americans repudiated 1960s-style liberalism, which they associated with foreign policy failures, inflationary domestic policies, oversized government, high taxes, and a generalized permissiveness and moral decay. A 1978 poll revealed that conservatives outnumbered liberals by a ratio of more than two to one.

When Carter took office, the inflation rate stood at 6 percent and the unemployment rate at 8 percent. Carter had gotten political mileage during his campaign against Ford by attacking the incumbent's failure to solve these serious economic problems, labeling the combined total of inflation and unemployment rates the "misery index." He called the "misery index" of fourteen intolerable and promised to reduce it drastically.

Carter first tried stimulating the economy to reduce unemployment by implementing traditional Keynesian "pump priming" programs: growing the economy by pumping federal money into it via public works projects. Congress enacted a $6 billion local public works bill, an $8 billion public service jobs bill, tax cuts, and an increase in the minimum wage. Unemployment declined to 6 percent in two years.

However, these stimulatory measures designed to grow the economy and drop the unemployment rate simultaneously drove up the inflation rate to 10 percent in 1978. It zoomed to 12 percent in 1979 and 13 percent in 1980.

Confronted with hyperinflation, Carter radically shifted his economic focus. He adopted fiscal restraints similar to Ford's. In October 1979, Carter signaled the end of the Keynesian era when he appointed Paul Volcker to head the Federal Reserve. Volcker immediately imposed severe monetary restrictions on the economy that drove interest rates to historic highs. Economic growth slowed to a recessionary crawl, unemployment soared upward, and deindustrialization in the rust belt accelerated.

Declining productivity signaled another kind of economic rot that beset Americans. Productivity had increased an average of 3 percent per year between 1945 and 1965. During the 1970s, productivity rose at an annual rate of only 1 percent. Up to 1968, the American economy had been the most productive in the world; by 1980, it had slipped to the twentieth place.

Energy problems compounded America's economic difficulties. Despite the 1973 energy crisis, Americans imported a steadily increasing proportion of their daily requirements throughout the 1970s. Domestic oil production continued to decline. In April 1977, Carter developed a comprehensive energy plan that he called "the moral equivalent of war" (MEOW). Congress rejected the plan, and MEOW quickly faded from view, but not before comedians had a field day with Carter's acronym.

In 1979, a second oil crisis hit the deteriorating U.S. economy when the new Islamic revolutionary government of Iran cut off its oil exports. Gasoline shortages again forced angry motorists to line up at the pumps. Carter responded to this second crisis by implementing a phased deregulation of domestic oil prices to spur production. Oil deregulation immediately raised gasoline prices by 50 percent (from 70¢ to over $1 a gallon) and increased oil company profits, some of which the government siphoned off as excise taxes.

President Carter, baffled by the failures of Americans to solve their serious economic and energy problems, invited an eclectic group of 130 establishment leaders to Camp David for six days of meetings to determine what was wrong with the nation. From these intensive discussions, the president concluded that the nation was facing "a crisis of the spirit." On Sunday evening, July 15, 1979, Carter told Americans that they faced a crisis of confidence that posed a fundamental threat to American democracy—they had lost faith in themselves and their institutions; they had lost faith in the future.

Critics of the Carter administration suggested that the major problem facing the nation was failed presidential leadership. Carter never firmly grasped the reins of government and never established effective liaison with Congress. He failed to develop a consistent approach to public policy. He was a compulsive micromanager who mastered the technical details of problems, but could never project a broad national vision or a sense of direction. He never communicated effectively with the press or with the American people.

At the time he made his "malaise" speech, his approval rating in the polls stood at 26 percent, lower than Richard Nixon's on the eve of his forced resignation of the presidency. Liberal journalist Tom Wicker called Carter's administration the greatest presidential failure since Herbert Hoover's performance during the Great Depression. The decline of the Democrats as the national majority party and the abandonment of New Deal liberalism as the national creed accelerated during Carter's years in office.

A NEW FOREIGN POLICY APPROACH

Carter announced at the outset of his administration that he would make human rights the distinctive theme of his foreign policy. Carter's emphasis on human rights expressed both his streak of Wilsonian idealism and his desire to move beyond the realm of Nixon–Kissinger realism. He wanted to reclaim the ideological high ground in the ongoing Cold War competition with the Soviet Union.

Carter's most significant diplomatic achievement occurred in the Middle East, where he played a major role in achieving peace between Egypt and Israel. He built upon a foundation laid by Kissinger's shuttle diplomacy and the extraordinary actions taken by Egyptian leader Anwar Sadat. Sadat, perceiving that the Egyptians could never dislodge the Israelis from the Sinai by force, offered them peace in exchange for the return of Egyptian lands. Sadat electrified the world when he went to Jerusalem in the fall of 1977. He told Israelis that any permanent agreement between Egypt and Israel must include Israeli withdrawal from the West Bank and the Golan Heights, a homeland for Palestinian Arabs, and recognition of the Palestine Liberation Organization (PLO) as their government.

Israeli prime minister Menachem Begin was willing to strike a bargain with Egypt on the Sinai, but he balked at the Palestinian issues. Negotiations between the two countries reached an impasse after six months. Carter then invited both leaders to Camp David for conferences. After two weeks of intense negotiations in which Carter was fully engaged, they achieved a framework of peace for the Middle East. Egypt agreed to a separate peace with Israel, and the Israelis agreed to return the Sinai region to Egypt. The Palestinian issues were left vague, their political status to be

FIGURE 12.2 The signing of the Camp David Accords. President Carter looks on as Israeli prime minister Menachem Begin (to Carter's left) and Egyptian president Anwar Sadat (to Carter's right) sign the historic pact on March 26, 1979.   *Source:* National Archives and Records Administration.

worked out in subsequent negotiations. Sadat and Begin signed the historic peace agreement, which ended more than thirty years of war between their countries, on March 26, 1979, in Washington.

President Carter had hoped that the Camp David Accords would launch a new era of peace in the Middle East, but insurmountable obstacles persisted. No other Arab nation followed Egypt's lead. Negotiations on the Palestine question went nowhere. The Palestine issue was further complicated by the outbreak of civil war in Lebanon between Muslim and Christian factions over PLO camps located in southern Lebanon.

In April 1978, Carter persuaded the Senate to ratify two treaties turning the Panama Canal over to Panama by 2000. These treaties permitted the gradual phasing out of the last vestiges of U.S. colonialism in Central America. The United States reserved the right to intervene to keep the canal open and also retained priority of passage in the event of a foreign crisis.

Elsewhere in Latin America, Carter changed U.S. policies. He withdrew support for a Rightist dictatorship in Chile that Ford and Kissinger had backed. In February 1978, he cut off military and economic aid to the Nicaraguan dictator Anastasio Somoza. Deprived of aid, Somoza was soon overthrown by revolutionaries who called themselves *Sandinistas*. The United States promptly extended a $75 million aid package to the new government. In El Salvador, Marxist guerrillas, assisted by the *Sandinistas*, began a civil war against their government. The Rightist government fought back brutally. The United States suspended aid to the Salvadoran government following the murder of three American nuns by government troops.

In the Far East, Carter completed the process Nixon had begun with his historic opening to China in 1972. The two nations established normal relations with an exchange of ambassadors in 1979. Carter wanted to use good relations with China as a lever to pry cooperation out of the Soviet Union. U.S. businessmen eagerly anticipated tapping into China's consumer economy of one billion people. U.S.–China trade expanded rapidly.

U.S. relations with sub-Saharan Africa improved during Carter's tenure. He appointed Andrew Young, a former civil rights activist, as the U.S. ambassador to the United Nations. President Carter made a successful trip to Liberia and Nigeria in 1978. Good relations with Nigeria were especially important, as it was the richest, most populous African nation and the second largest foreign supplier of oil to the United States.

THE DECLINE OF *DETENTE*

Detente had already begun to decline under Ford and Kissinger, and it continued to decline during Carter's presidency. Carter's diplomatic efforts toward the Soviet Union were hindered by his inexperience. Carter sent what he intended to be a friendly signal to the Soviets: He announced his intention to withdraw U.S. troops from Korea. Far from responding in kind, the Soviets took Carter's gesture as a sign of weakness. They responded to this conciliatory act by becoming more aggressive. They extended their influence in Africa, using Cuban soldiers as proxies, and they increased their military forces stationed in Cuba. Carter had hoped to achieve quick ratification of SALT II, but he angered the Soviet leaders by proposing additional cuts in the two nations' strategic arsenals, which delayed negotiation of the new agreements. His granting of full diplomatic recognition to China further annoyed the Soviets.

SALT II also encountered strong opposition within the Senate. The chief senatorial critic was Henry "Scoop" Jackson, who insisted that the proposed agreement allowed the Soviets to retain strategic superiority in several weapon categories. Conservative critics of SALT II were uncomfortable with the fact that the treaty acknowledged that the Soviets had achieved nuclear parity with the United States, a reality that they interpreted as symbolizing the relative decline of U.S. strategic power. Some liberal senators were unhappy with SALT II because it did not eliminate key weapons systems such as the huge Soviet land-based ICBMs and the new U.S. cruise missiles.

Carter himself lost faith in SALT II and did not press the Senate for ratification. Instead, he persuaded NATO allies to agree to install new Pershing II missiles in western Europe to counter the SS-20 intermediate-range missiles that the Soviets were installing in eastern Europe. Installing these weapons in Europe represented a major escalation of the nuclear arms race.

While the Senate was debating SALT II, in December 1979, 85,000 Soviet troops invaded Afghanistan to suppress a Muslim rebellion against a faltering Marxist regime. Alarmed, President Carter called the Soviet invasion "the most serious threat to world peace since the Second World War." Carter canceled grain shipments to the USSR, suspended high technology sales to the Soviets, and ordered U.S. athletes to boycott the Olympics that were to be held in Moscow the following summer. He also increased military spending and removed restrictions on CIA covert operations. He withdrew SALT II from Senate consideration and proclaimed the Carter Doctrine for Southwest Asia. Calling the Persian Gulf a vital U.S. interest, he declared that the United States would repel "by any means necessary" an attack in that region by outside forces. The man who began his presidency espousing kind words for the Soviets killed *detente* and resuscitated the Cold War.

DEBACLE IN IRAN

It was in the Persian Gulf region that the United States suffered a foreign policy disaster that humiliated President Carter and contributed to his political downfall. Iran was America's major ally in the Persian Gulf area. It played a key role in containing the Soviet Union. It was a major supplier of top-grade oil, and Iranians annually purchased billions of dollars worth of U.S. arms.

The shah of Iran allowed the CIA to station electronic surveillance equipment along Iran's border with the Soviet Union. Iran was a vital U.S. interest, much more important than Vietnam had ever been.

Iran in the late 1970s seethed with anti-shah and anti-American fervor. Only the shah and his ruling elite were genuinely pro-American. Carter, in contradiction of his human rights policy, traveled to Iran in late 1977 to pay tribute to the shah. At a state banquet held in his honor, President Carter toasted the shah for "the admiration and love your people give to you." He called Iran "an island of stability in one of the most troubled areas of the world." The clueless CIA station chief in Teheran issued a report in 1978, stating that Iran was not even near a revolutionary situation.

The assault on the shah was led by clergy who were intent on establishing an Islamic republic. Their leader was Ayatollah Ruholla Khomeini. The Iranian army, forbidden by the shah to fire upon the rioters for fear it would ruin the chances of his son succeeding him, was demoralized. During his last days in power, the desperate shah told the American ambassador that he could not order his troops to suppress the revolutionaries except on orders from Washington. Those orders President Carter refused to give. On January 16, 1979, the shah fled his country. One of the most bizarre events of modern times had occurred; a virtually unarmed people led by clergymen had overthrown one of the world's most powerful rulers.

U.S. leaders, thinking in customary Cold War terms, did not know how to deal with Khomeini, a man who denounced both the United States and the Soviet Union with equal vehemence. Fearing Soviet intrusion into Iran and the loss of a crucial source of Western oil, Carter tried to establish normal relations with the new Iranian government, which proved to be impossible. Khomeini, who called the United States the "Great Satan," refused all American overtures.

Meanwhile, President Carter allowed the shah, who was suffering from terminal cancer, to enter the United States for medical treatment. On November 4, 1979, a well-organized core group of about sixty Iranian university students scaled the walls of the embassy compound and seized the embassy building. They bound and gagged about sixty Americans, including the embassy's top foreign service and CIA officers, military liaisons, and a detachment of Marine guards. The invaders demanded that the United States immediately return the shah "to face revolutionary justice." Carter refused the demand. He froze all Iranian assets in the United States, suspended arms sales, and clamped a boycott on all U.S. trade with Iran. The subsequent standoff became one of the paradigmatic international crises of modern times. The Iran hostage crisis is now recognized as America's first encounter with militant Islamists. There would be many more.

The hostage crisis dominated U.S. foreign policy for the next fourteen months. It also dominated American television screens. Each night, when the most popular television news program, the CBS Evening News with Walter Cronkite, would sign off, the viewing public would be reminded of just how many days of captivity the hostages had endured. The popular late-night television news show *Nightline* originated as a series of special reports on the hostage crisis. For months, U.S. officials negotiated futilely for release of the hostages with a series of Iranian governments.

Carter eventually severed diplomatic relations with Iran and authorized a secret military operation to attempt a rescue. On the night of April 24, 1980, at a staging area in the Iranian desert, owing to freak dust storms, several helicopters had to set down or turn back, and the entire operation had to be aborted. During the withdrawal, one helicopter collided with a C-130 transport, exploded into flames and left eight American Marines and airman dead. For days afterwards, the news media bombarded Americans with striking visual images of the wreckage and charred American corpses. The failed rescue attempt also symbolized the impotence of the United States and its inability to protect its citizens against terrorism.

FIGURE 12.3   Carter's most serious setback and the nation's greatest humiliation occurred in 1979 when Iranian militants occupied the U.S. embassy in Iran and took Americans hostage. Here their captors put blindfolded hostages on display soon after taking them prisoner.
Source: Bettmann Archive

Prospects for resolving the hostage crisis improved in late 1980. The ailing shah died in July. On September 22, Iraq suddenly invaded Iran and provoked a war between the two nations. Khomeini reacted by authorizing serious negotiations with the Americans. In October, Carter offered to release frozen Iranian assets and to resume normal relations with Iran in exchange for release of the hostages. Khomeini was responsive to Carter's offer. He needed money for the war with Iraq, and the shah's death had removed any reason for keeping the hostages. Iran agreed to release them in exchange for the return of $8 billion of Iranian assets. In a final humiliation for Carter, the hostages were all released on January 20, 1981—Inauguration Day for Ronald Reagan, the man who had defeated him, made the announcement to the American people that the hostages were freed and coming home.

THE CONSERVATIVE ASCENDANCY

In the early 1970s, conservatives of various stripes voiced their vehement opposition to many liberal policies. People in both the North and the South attacked what they called "forced busing" to integrate the public schools. They also denounced affirmative action programs that guaranteed minorities, particularly African Americans, equal opportunity in their quest for schooling and employment. Antifeminist conservatives opposed the Equal Rights Amendment and helped defeat it. They also opposed efforts to protect the rights of gays and lesbians. Most conservatives opposed all gun control measures and favored the restoration of capital punishment.

Conservatives were outraged when the Supreme Court issued its controversial *Roe v. Wade* (1973), which granted women the right to an abortion on demand during the first trimester of a pregnancy. Conservatives also attacked other Supreme Court rulings made during the 1970s that outlawed prayer in the public schools and appeared to strengthen the rights of criminals at the expense of law enforcement personnel. Most conservatives attacked welfare programs and other forms of social spending. Traditional business conservatives championed free-enterprise capitalism; they criticized government regulation of economic activity, called for tax cuts, and attacked trade unions.

New Right conservatives, whose chief national leaders were Barry Goldwater and Ronald Reagan, insisted that America must maintain an arsenal of thermonuclear and conventional weapons to contain the aggressive tendencies of the Soviet Union and its clients. These conservatives fretted over the decline of U.S. power and prestige in the world, symbolized by the Vietnam debacle and the Iranian hostage crisis.

Evangelical Christians formed one of the most powerful elements within the rapidly growing conservative political movement. They stressed the cruciality of religion, tradition, and family values. They supported the "right to life" movement, denounced *Roe v. Wade*, and condemned abortion. They opposed most feminist demands and the Equal Rights Amendment. They initiated a war on pornography and insisted that homosexuality was a sin. Evangelicals sought to reintroduce school prayer, and they campaigned to have "creation science" offered as an alternative to the theory of evolution in public schools. They attacked what they called "secular humanism," the view that all truths were relative, all moral values were situational, and all ethical judgments were necessarily tentative. They were especially incensed when the Internal Revenue Service (IRS) appeared to be considering removing the tax exemption for some private religious schools that had been established in the South in the wake of the integration of southern public schools.

Reverend Jerry Falwell, an evangelical leader, became a prominent conservative political activist. In July 1979, he formed the Moral Majority. Combining old-time religion with the latest computer technology, his organization targeted potential contributors and kept score-cards on how politicians voted on key issues such as the ERA, school prayer, and funding for abortions. For the 1980 election, Falwell's Moral Majority activists developed a "hit list" of liberal senators and congressmen; then mailed out more than one billion pieces of campaign literature to selected voters.

The varied groups that called themselves conservative, led by Ronald Reagan, gradually brought about a remarkable transformation in the way the American people viewed conservatism. Since the New Deal era of the 1930s, the term "conservative" had been a political epithet; conservativism connoted elitism, greed, anti-intellectualism, and most of all, an irrational clinging to traditional ways in the face of novel, unprecedented challenges. But during the 1970s, with the Democratic Party and especially its liberal wing under siege as the icons of discredited and dysfunctional policies, conservatives stepped forward as reformers. Millions of their fellow conservatives were recent recruits from the ranks of disaffected Democrats who responded positively to Reagan's dynamic candidacy.

THE ELECTION OF 1980

As the 1980 election approached, Carter was clearly in deep political trouble. Inflation was out of control, and there was also the daily embarrassment of the hostages held in Iran. Carter also had to fight off a primary challenge from Senator Edward "Ted" Kennedy. But Kennedy's old-fashioned liberal philosophy was out of sync with the times, and Carter easily deflected his challenge.

Many candidates entered the race for the Republican nomination, but from the outset, Ronald Reagan was the clear choice of most of the party faithful. Reaganites controlled the Republican convention and pushed through a conservative platform, calling for deep tax cuts,

cuts in social spending, large increases in defense spending, a balanced budget, constitutional amendments banning abortions and restoring prayer in public schools, and opposition to the Equal Rights Amendment. Reagan chose George H. W. Bush for the vice presidential slot after failing to get former President Ford for the position. A third party candidate joined the race, John Anderson, a socially moderate Republican congressman from Illinois, running as an Independent.

Reagan was favored to win when the presidential campaign began in August. But he made several erroneous statements concerning important issues, which conveyed the impression that he might be dangerously out of touch with the times. Within a month, Carter had caught up. Sensing an advantage, Carter attacked Reagan personally. He accused him of racism and war-mongering, and he raised the question of his age. At 69, Reagan was the oldest major party candidate ever to seek the presidency. Liberal opponents waxed eloquently about Reagan's alleged lack of intellectual capacity and ignorance of many important issues. But as the campaign progressed, it became obvious that Reagan was a formidable opponent. Despite his age, he remained a handsome, energetic, and eloquent candidate. He sloughed off all the personal attacks and soon regained the momentum.

The Moral Majority threw all of its considerable political resources into campaigning for Ronald Reagan. However, Reagan, confident that the Evangelicals and other social conservatives were with him, concentrated his fire on Carter's handling of the economy at a time of historically high "stagflation." He also attacked Carter's handling of foreign policy at a time when the world was especially unstable and when the hostages were in Iranian hands. Most of all he projected his vision of America as an exceptional nation. He reminded Americans that their country had a unique mission to accomplish—the overthrow of Communism with its threats to the freedom and dignity of humanity.

The candidates staged one televised debate, held during the final week of the campaign. The candidates were evenly matched through the early rounds of questioning. Then, Reagan scored impressively when he responded to Carter's attacks on his record on Medicare. Using his actor's skills, pretending to be saddened by Carter's assaults, Reagan shook his head, saying, "There you go again." In the manner of a parent correcting an erring child, he then firmly set the record straight.

In terms of content, the debate was a draw. On the cosmetic issues of appearance and personality, Reagan won decisively. In 90 minutes, Reagan had erased the view that Carter had been projecting about Reagan throughout the campaign—the image of Reagan as a combination scrooge and mad bomber. During the debate, Reagan came across as a firm, genial leader who would never push the nuclear button in panic or anger. He sealed Carter's political fate when he closed the debate by asking the huge television audience a series of rhetorical questions: Are you better off than you were four years ago? Is America as respected throughout the world as it was four years ago? Are we as strong as we were four years ago?

Reagan received 44 million votes to Carter's 35 million and Anderson's 5.7 million. Reagan swept the election with 489 electoral votes to Carter's 49, with zero for Anderson. The Republicans gained thirty-three seats in the House, which remained under Democratic control. The most surprising outcome of the 1980 election was the Republican reconquest of the Senate for the first time since 1954. Republicans gained twelve senatorial seats, giving them fifty-three, the largest Republican total since 1928. The Moral Majority played a major role in bringing about the Republican takeover of the Senate and significantly reducing the Democratic majority in the House of Representatives.

To a large majority of voters, the conservative Republican combination of family values, supply-side economics, and a hard-line, anti-Soviet foreign policy looked quite like a much-needed program to revitalize America. Reagan's diverse coalition decimated the old liberal coalition that had prevailed from the 1930s through the 1960s. Reagan carried blue-collar voters, middle-income voters, the Catholic vote, the ethnic vote, and the Southern vote. He carried all the populous Northern industrial states. He brought an important new class of voters into the Republican fold— "Reagan Democrats." Millions of voters who did not share Reagan's conservative philosophy voted for the man because they liked his upbeat message and they could no longer abide the likes of Jimmy Carter in the White House.

The vote revealed two cleavages among voters. African Americans voted 90 percent for Carter; whites voted 56 percent for Reagan. For the first time in the sixty years since women had achieved the vote, a gender gap appeared in the electoral results. Whereas 56 percent of men voted for Reagan and only 36 percent for Carter, 47 percent of women voted for Reagan and 45 percent for Carter. Reagan's opposition to abortion and the ERA, plus his aggressive foreign policy proposals, alienated women voters. Many working women, struggling to cope with precarious economic circumstances, feared that Reagan might call for Congress to eliminate governmental programs upon which they and their families depended.

The 1980 election represented a significant turning point and is comparable in some ways to the election of 1932. During that fateful campaign, the American people, weary of a feckless incumbent unable to solve serious economic problems, tossed out the dour Herbert Hoover and chose the bouyant Franklin Roosevelt to deliver them from the darkness. Carter was the first incumbent president since Hoover to lose in a bid for reelection. Many citizens also liked Reagan's promises of deep tax cuts and slashing government spending, promises Roosevelt also made in 1932.

A TIME OF TROUBLES

In the aftermath of the upheavals of the late 1960s, the disastrous outcome of the Vietnam War, the Watergate scandals, and the revelations of wrongdoing by the CIA and FBI, millions of Americans lost faith in politicians and in political institutions. Gerald Ford and Jimmy Carter confronted challenges, conditions, and problems beyond their capacities to control or master. Ford never had a realistic chance to lead; he was an unelected president chosen to serve out the unfinished term of the disgraced Nixon. Carter, elected on a wave of public disenchantment with politics as usual, appeared initially to represent the aspirations of millions of ordinary citizens who wanted to make a clean, fresh start in politics. But the inexperienced Carter could never transcend his outsider status and take hold of the levers of power. Within a few years, his bumbling, directionless presidency demonstrated that good intentions were insufficient for governing a modern complex society experiencing a series of challenging problems.

Soaring inflation coupled with high unemployment, "stagflation," did not yield to Ford's and Carter's efforts to manage them. Purchasing power and living standards for millions of families were eroded. Productivity declined. Major manufacturing industries lost large market shares to efficient foreign competitors. Energy crises exacerbated economic woes and added an element of uncertainty to an already clouded future.

The United States appeared to be a declining entity in the world. An aggressive Soviet Union was gaining ground in the Cold War. Prosperous western European nations increasingly asserted their independence from American initiatives, and the Japanese had become formidable commercial rivals. The Iranian hostage crisis was a daily reminder of American fecklessness in world affairs.

By the time of the 1980 election, pundits were writing that the United States had become an ungovernable nation of dysfunctional institutions and demoralized citizens. They feared that the presidency had grown too large and too complex for any one person to control. They feared that America no longer worked; its economy was in decline, its society fragmented, its population increasingly polarized, and its political system controlled by leaders who lacked both vision and practical solutions to pressing problems. Americans turned to a former actor and television personality who promised to revitalize the American economy, reassert American primacy in the world, and restore the American Dream.

Brief Bibliographic Essay

A recent excellent interpretation of the seventies is Bruce J. Schulman, *The Seventies: The Great Shift in American Culture, Society, and Politics.* James T. Patterson, *Restless Giant: The United States from Watergate to Bush V. Gore* has several informative chapters covering the years of the Ford and Carter presidencies. A good study of the energy crises of the 1970s is Richard Victor's *Energy Policy in America Since 1945.* A fine recent study, edited by Michael A. Bernstein and David E. Adler, *Understanding American Economic Decline* examines the causes of the economic downturn that began in the early 1970s. A good study of the impact of computer technology on American society and culture is Tracy Kidder's *The Soul of a New Machine.* John Osborne, *White House Watch: The Ford Years,* is a good account of the Ford presidency. Stanley Hoffmann's *Primacy and World Order* is a critical assessment of the Ford administration's foreign policy. A negative study of the Carter presidency is Clark Mollenkoff, *The President Who Failed: Carter Out of Control.* David Farber, *Taken Hostage: The Iran Hostage Crisis and America's First Encounter with Radical Islam,* considers the hostage crisis within the context of the larger war on terrorism. Donald T. Critchlow, *The Conservative Ascendancy: How the GOP Right Made Political History,* tells the whole story of the Right's takeover of the Republican Party and their rise to power when Reagan won the 1980 election. Critchlow takes seriously the ideas that motivated the Right—anti-Communism, concerns about domestic spying, libertarianism, opposition to the vast expansion of the national government, and defending the Judeo-Christian tradition—and treats them as legitimate positions. A recent book, Andrew E. Bush, *Reagan's Victory: The Presidential Election of 1980 and the Rise of the Right,* is much the best account of this pivotal election.

CHAPTER

13

Social and Cultural Transformations

The decade of the 1970s was characterized by a series of significant social and cultural transformations that confirmed both the pluralism and volatility of American life. These changes often reflected and paralleled underlying technological, economic, and demographic developments that rapidly altered the contours of American society and changed the ways most Americans lived and worked. New attitudes toward sex, fashion, music, art, and lifestyles changed the nature of many important American institutions. Cultural historians see in these 1970s trends the origins of our contemporary faddish, consumer-driven, media-dominated, and celebrity-centric popular culture.

Many members of two important groups, African Americans and women, maintaining the momentum generated by the movements of the 1960s, made dramatic gains during the 1970s in education and income. But at the same time that thousands of women and African Americans were taking advantage of new opportunities to achieve middle-class status, many other women and blacks remained locked into low-paying, low-status jobs, or slipped even further into the ranks of welfare dependency and poverty.

A DEMOGRAPHIC PROFILE

There were 205 million Americans in 1970 and 227 million by 1980. Regionally, Southern and Western states accounted for 90 percent of that population increase. Many Northeastern and Midwestern states showed little or no growth, and several lost population. Population trends that had first appeared soon after World War II continued. The Sunbelt, stretching from South Carolina to Southern California, contained the dynamic centers of the nation's technological innovation, economic growth, and population increase.

Two additional demographic shifts with profound social implications occurred during the 1970s—the birthrate fell sharply, and human longevity increased significantly. Twentieth-century birthrates peaked in 1947, at 26.6 live births per thousand, and tumbled to 18.1 per thousand in 1975.

Low birthrates meant that adults were not bearing enough children to replace themselves, and that only expanded immigration prevented long-term U.S. population decline. Increasing longevity derived from advances in medicine and nutrition. But the most important causes of rising longevity were reductions in the infant mortality rate and the childhood death rate. By 1975, median longevity in America had reached 73.1 years. The fastest-growing age group consisted of people age seventy-five and older. The median age of the U.S. population reached thirty years on April 1, 1980, making America one of the older societies in the world.

The traditional American household comprising a nuclear family of four declined sharply during the 1970s. Nearly half of the households added in the 1970s consisted of persons living alone or with nonrelatives. Declining birthrates, declining marriage rates, high divorce rates, households occupied by unmarried couples, households occupied by single-parent families, and the existence of millions of men and women living alone all suggested that household arrangements in America increasingly reflected the sociological diversity that has become America's most salient characteristic.

By the late 1970s, one of the most rapidly growing population segments comprised the thirty-somethings, the advance wave of baby boomers. This group received much media attention, particularly the better-educated "yuppies." Yuppies were upwardly mobile, affluent young Americans. Having few or no children, yuppie couples often held two high-paying jobs. Businesses and advertisers catered to their large disposable incomes and lifestyle preferences based on buying expensive homes, cars, and clothes; dining in upscale restaurants; and taking costly vacations.

But yuppies did not represent the boomer norm. Of the seventy-eight million baby boomers, only 5 percent had incomes of $40,000 or more in the late 1970s. The median income for baby boomers in 1977 was $16,000, below the national average. Too many boomers were chasing too few educational and economic opportunities. Opportunities for baby boomers also were curtailed by the energy crisis and the high inflation of the late 1970s and early 1980s. Furthermore, the annual growth rate of the American economy averaged a sluggish 1.6 percent per annum during the 1970s, and long-term unemployment rates were the highest since the 1930s. Baby boomers as a whole were less upwardly mobile than their parents, the first such group in America since the generation that came of age during the Great Depression of the 1930s.

NEW IMMIGRANTS

Because the Immigration Act of 1965 abolished the discriminatory national origins system dating back to the 1920s, there occurred both a huge increase in immigration and a significant shift in the sources of immigrants. Once again, large-scale immigration to the United States became a vital part of the American experience. Most of the millions of immigrants who came to the United States in the 1970s and 1980s were Asians and Latin Americans. Mexico furnished the largest number of immigrants. Along with Mexicans came Cubans, Puerto Ricans, and Central Americans, particularly people from El Salvador and Nicaragua. Some of these new arrivals were fleeing religious and political oppression, but most of them came for the same reasons that have always attracted newcomers to America—opportunities for a better job and a better life for their families.

The United States, true to its ancient heritage, remained one of the few countries in the world to freely welcome these millions of newcomers from foreign lands. But many native-born Americans were alarmed by the flood of poor immigrants arriving annually, especially the "illegals" who came mostly from Mexico through a porous membrane called the United States–Mexico border. They feared that these people would take jobs from native-born workers; lower wages and living standards; overload the medical, welfare, and school systems; and become a permanent underclass of poor people amidst an affluent society.

Their fears were exaggerated and based upon dubious assumptions and misperceptions. Studies have shown that most immigrants take jobs at pay levels that most native-born Americans scorn, and they pay more in taxes than they ever collect in government services. Many of these immigrants also strive to become law-abiding, hard working, and productive citizens.

Another problem posed by elements in the Hispanic American population, fueled by large-scale immigration from Mexico and other Hispanic countries, is the ancient question of assimilation. Hispanics often have formed their own communities, or "barrios," where they can get along quite well without having to speak or write English. Some Hispanics have also insisted that their children be taught in bilingual schools, and the Supreme Court has authorized bilingual instruction in public schools.

Spokesmen for the native-born population have argued that the existence of large, Spanish-speaking populations clustered in Southern California, southern Florida, the Southwest, and sections of New York and Chicago pose a threat to national unity and to the political cohesiveness of the American system. Hispanic spokesmen insist on their rights to have their children educated as they see fit. They also insist on retaining their language and cultural identity as a distinct ethnic group within a pluralistic society.

After Hispanics, Asians have furnished the largest supply of newcomers. They have come mainly from Hong Kong, Taiwan, mainland China, Vietnam, Korea, India, and the Philippines. Between 1970 and 1980, the Filipino population within the United States more than doubled, from 343,060 to 774,652. Two-thirds of the additional Filipino population were new immigrants. By 1980, Filipino Americans were the second largest Asian American group after Chinese Americans.

Their numbers boosted by large-scale immigration, the Asian American population has doubled in the past decade, from two million people to more than four million. Asians are among the most upwardly mobile population groups within American society. Seventy-five percent of Asian Americans have graduated from high school. One-third of Asian American adults have four or more years of college, twice the rate for Americans of European descent. In the economic sphere, data from the 1980 census show that the Asian American median annual income was more than $2,000 above the national median annual income.

Success has not come easily for Asian Americans. Historically, they have been the victims of exclusion, prejudice, discrimination in various forms, and violent assaults. Not all Asians have achieved success in America. Many recent Asian immigrants remain mired in poverty, alienated from the mainstream of American life, and tempted by vice and crime. Many struggle to fathom a mysterious language and culture that is neither open nor friendly to them. Incidents of violence against Asian immigrants abound. Many recent arrivals from Vietnam, Cambodia, and Laos, refugees from oppression in their homelands, have encountered only grief and failure in this country.

AFRICAN AMERICANS: A DUAL SOCIETY

For millions of African American families, the decade of the 1970s was one of significant progress. Institutionalized racism and other obstacles to black achievement weakened. Affirmative action programs, spawned by the civil rights movements of the 1960s, paid off for middle-class African Americans in the 1970s and carried into the 1980s. The greatest progress for African Americans came in education. By 1980, more than one million black people had enrolled in colleges, and thousands attended the finest universities and professional schools in the country. Thousands of young African American men and women became doctors, lawyers, college professors, government bureaucrats, and business executives. The size of the African American middle class increased rapidly, and black per capita income rose appreciably. African American couples married, had children, and bought homes in the suburbs, their lifestyles being much like that of their white counterparts in similar circumstances. Many young black professionals, reared and educated in the North, flocked to the Sunbelt cities to live and work. Many black Americans found that urban life in Atlanta, Houston, and New Orleans offered more opportunities for ambitious careerists than the supposedly more liberal Northern cities. African American political participation in Southern states also far outstripped that in the North.

Despite significant gains for many, millions of African Americans lost ground during the 1970s. Affirmative action admissions programs were challenged by the *Bakke* case. Allen Bakke, a white applicant to the University of California at Davis Medical School, sued the university when his application was rejected. He showed that his qualifications were superior to several minority candidates who were admitted as "disadvantaged students" under a special quota reserved for them. The state supreme court ruled in his favor, as did the U.S. Supreme Court in a 1978 5 to 4 decision. The Supreme Court held that Bakke's rights to equal protection under the Fourteenth Amendment had been violated, and it nullified the school's affirmative action program based on racial quotas. But by a similar 5 to 4 decision, the Court upheld the right of the university to use race as "one element" in its effort to recruit medical students. Meanwhile, Davis had admitted Bakke to its medical school, and he went on to become a physician. The university also continued an affirmative action admissions program without explicit quotas for minority group students. The Supreme Court appeared to be saying that limited affirmative action policies could continue if they did not rely on numbers or if they did not try to do too much too fast.

The plight of poor inner-city blacks worsened during the 1970s. Unemployment among African Americans remained high, about twice the national average, averaging 14 percent to 15 percent. Unemployment among African American teenagers skyrocketed to the 40-to-50 percent range by 1980. Black median family income was $12,800 in 1980, only about half that of whites. Ironically, African American income was proportionately higher in 1950, when racial segregation was still intact; antiblack racism was nearly universal; and before the modern civil rights movement, civil rights legislation, and affirmative action programs had appeared.

Among poor inner-city African Americans, statistics revealed a frightening pattern of intertwined social pathologies—rising drug usage, delinquency, vice, and crime; rising school dropout rates and unemployment rates; and rising numbers of illegitimate births and households headed by a single female who had never married. A permanent underclass was being forged within black America, without having the possibility of integrating into the American mainstream.

According to the sociologist William Julius Wilson, one of the nation's most eminent scholars, the fundamental cause of the social misery and disorganization afflicting the black inner city was economic. Factories and businesses providing good jobs at good wages had disappeared from most of the black inner cities of America. Most prosperous black working-class and middle-class families had long since exited once-thriving neighborhood communities. Without the prospect of good jobs and positive role models to set good examples, many of the inner-city dwellers were deprived of opportunities to seek productive and fulfilling lives. Wilson believed that without the economic and moral anchor of respectable employment, there was little chance of solving the nearly intractable social problems of the black inner cities.

By the mid-1970s, African Americans had forged a dual society—on the one hand, a thriving middle class that had achieved a place for itself roughly equal to white Americans, and, on the other hand, an underclass rotting on the mean streets of inner cities.

WOMEN: CHANGING ATTITUDES AND ROLES

Of all of the movements born during the upheavals of the 1960s, the one that retained its momentum and had the greatest impact on society during the 1970s was the women's movement. Feminists challenged men and women to refashion their identities, to abandon traditional notions of masculinity and femininity. Women exhorted their "sisters" to demand an end to second-class citizenship, class discrimination, and sexual exploitation. Other activists encouraged women to no longer confine themselves to domesticity, rather to seek fulfillment in new roles and statuses beyond those of mother, wife, and homemaker.

Because the women's movement during the 1970s was so diverse and decentralized, it suffered from serious internal conflicts. Lesbian and straight women often discovered that they did not share the same goals and priorities. Radical feminists called for fundamental changes in the social and political structures; liberal reformers sought to achieve their goals by working within the system. Feminist intellectuals often engaged in ideological controversies that divided women into hostile camps. More serious conflicts of interest often divided women along the fault lines of class and race. Middle-class white women found, for example, that they had little in common with black working women, nor did they share the same perceptions, beliefs, and values.

The women's movement also encountered much opposition and resistance from groups within the larger society. Women antifeminists like Phyllis Schlafly and Anita Bryant successfully campaigned against the Equal Rights Amendment. They also attacked the gay rights movement and fought to repeal the right of women to have an abortion on demand. Antifeminists won an important victory in 1980, when the Supreme Court upheld the constitutionality of a congressional law prohibiting federal funding of abortions for poor women. Antifeminists also charged the women's movement with being responsible for the spiraling divorce rate and the breakdown of family life in America.

Many men felt threatened by the women's movement. They perceived that their power and privileges were under assault, that many women expressed hostility toward men *qua* men. Some men responded negatively to the women's movement and abandoned their traditional roles as financial providers and authority figures for their families. Many women who had devoted their lives to being good mothers, wives, and homemakers felt that feminists judged them as victims and failures.

Despite its internal conflicts and despite encountering powerful and widespread opposition, the women's movement of the 1970s helped bring about major social and cultural changes. Attitudes toward gender roles changed dramatically during the 1970s. When a Gallup Poll in 1962 asked women if they believed they were discriminated against, two-thirds said no. In 1974, two-thirds of women responded yes to the same question, and they also indicated that they favored efforts to improve their status.

The women's movement had its greatest influence on young college-educated women during the 1970s, many of whom were movement activists. Surveys showed that a majority of women graduating from college during the 1970s believed that a career was as important to a fulfilling life as a good marriage. These women believed that women and men were born with the same talents and potentials. These same women also stated that they expected equality in their sexual relations. Surveys revealed that three-fourths of college women had engaged in premarital sex, and that college women were more active sexually than college men.

Such attitudinal changes reflected the accelerated pace of women's entry into the workplaces of America during the 1970s. Since 1945, the rate of employment for women had risen steadily. By 1970, over half of women with children over age six worked full-time or part-time outside of the home. But during the 1970s, a major change occurred in women's employment patterns. The proportion of younger women with children who worked increased dramatically. By 1980, more than half of the mothers with children under age six found themselves in the labor force. For many women, the notion of work had been redefined during the 1970s. Work for women had become a life vocation. Women expected to work for most of their lives, with a few years off for childbearing and child rearing. They expected to have careers of their own. This new concept of work as career for young women of the 1970s contrasted dramatically with their mothers' concept. For the older generation of women, work came after child rearing; it was defined primarily as helping the family enjoy a more affluent lifestyle, not as an opportunity to have a career.

Female enrollment in colleges, graduate schools, and professional schools expanded rapidly during the 1970s. The proportion of women entering law school increased fivefold. Some entering classes at medical schools were 30 percent to 40 percent women. Women earned 25 percent of all doctoral degrees awarded during the 1970s. Women also entered the corporate world in ever-increasing numbers. Roles for some women television stars changed during the 1970s. The *Mary Tyler Moore Show* depicted an ambitious television studio executive, economically independent, who remained single. Other shows featured women as tough, aggressive, and violent as in *Charlie's Angels* and the *Bionic Woman*. Working-class women continued to join unions, enter the skilled trades, and increase their numbers in previously all-male occupations. Both federal and state laws were enacted that helped women obtain credit, start their own businesses, and buy homes. Other women made their way in politics. Several were elected state governors and U.S. Senators. At the

FIGURE 13.1 Office staff talking at desk. *Source:* Photo Researchers, Inc. Photo by Richard Hutchings.

same time women flooded into professional fields hitherto exclusively or overwhelmingly male; the proportion of women entering the traditionally feminine fields of nursing, library work, and elementary school teaching declined sharply.

Despite their many impressive successes, women continued to encounter barriers in their struggle to overcome historical disadvantages and to achieve genuine equality in contemporary American society. "No-fault divorces," initially hailed as a great victory for women, proved to be a two-edged sword, because equality before the law did not bring equality in the marketplace. Compounding their economic difficulties, many divorced women, who had obtained custody of their children, found that their former husbands defaulted on child support payments. The courts were often lax in forcing ex-husbands to pay.

Sophisticated postfeminist analysts faulted the liberal leaders of the women's movement for being too concerned with achieving legal and political equality and thereby neglecting structural economic forces that women faced in a society where male economic domination remained a continuing reality. They also criticized feminists who were obsessed with getting middle-class women into previously all-male professions and occupations, while neglecting the interests of the more numerous working-class women mired in low-paying, sex-segregated occupations.

Economic realities limited opportunities for women during the 1970s. For every glittering career success scored by ambitious, capable, upwardly mobile women, many more women worked in low-paying jobs, which offered few opportunities for promotion or substantial pay increases. Occupational segregation, in which women remained concentrated in low-paying positions while men earned much higher incomes for their work, remained a persistent problem for women during the 1970s. Most of the new jobs created in the service sectors of the economy were taken by women, and these jobs invariably paid less than manufacturing or professional jobs. In the mid-1970s, women earned only 60¢ for every dollar earned by men. The 60¢ represented an improvement over previous decades, but it fell far short of economic parity with men.

Women also were the victims of the "superwoman syndrome." Early feminist leaders proffered an idealized image of the woman who could have it all—career, home, husband, and family—a life of perfect equality and complete fulfillment. In practice, having it all often meant doing it all: Women worked full time all day outside of the home, just like men, then they came home to continue working—doing all or most of the cleaning, cooking, and caring for their children—while men watched *Monday Night Football* with their neighbors, drank beer, listened to music, and played with the family dog.

During the 1970s, the divorce rate rocketed upward. By 1980, more than 40 percent of marriages ended in divorce. The median length of a first marriage fell to seven years. The median length of a second marriage fell to four years. The number of households headed by a single parent, almost always a female, climbed rapidly during the 1970s. The large majority of women entering the workforce during the 1970s did so because they had to support themselves or because they headed a single-parent household. They were not college-educated professionals choosing a career; they were working women who had to find work to survive economically within the American system. Inflationary pressures during the 1970s also drove many women into the workforce to ensure that their families could still enjoy a middle-class lifestyle no longer affordable on a single income. Many women slipped into the ranks of the working poor during the 1970s as a result of being divorced and saddled with child-rearing duties. The feminization of poverty and the fact that millions of children were growing up poor were two ominous socioeconomic realities directly affecting the status of women during the 1970s.

PUBLIC SCHOOLS IN DECLINE

In 1975, an estimated ten million students were enrolled full-time or part-time in the nation's 2,500 institutions of higher learning. Americans continued to spend far more on post–high school education than any other people, and America possessed 100 of the world's finest universities. American scholars led the world in many disciplines, especially the sciences. Each year, several U.S. scientists usually won Nobel Prizes in physics, chemistry, medical research, and economics. America's great universities were the vital centers of the nation's flourishing intellectual life.

In contrast to the turbulent 1960s, college campuses were mostly tranquil places in the 1970s. Students, reverting to historical norms, were much more interested in preparing for well-paying careers than they were in protesting public issues or trying to make society better. Yet some students could still respond to issues of conscience. Thousands of students joined protests against the nuclear arms race and called for universities to divest themselves of securities issued by companies doing business with the repressive apartheid regime in South Africa. Others continued to express concern about ecological and social issues.

For most students, it was business as usual—attending classes, playing sports, perhaps working part-time, and enjoying an active social life. College students of the 1970s were much less attracted to the humanities and social sciences than they had been a generation earlier. Students of the 1970s flocked to majors in math, economics, finance, business, engineering, and computer science. Many students, including the brightest ones, demonstrated deficiencies in verbal skills and a general decline in cultural literacy. A generation of technocratic "wannabes" had no time to pursue the traditional goal of a broad liberal arts education.

While colleges flourished, in many cities, American public schools deteriorated. Scholastic aptitude scores declined during the 1970s, and the high school dropout rate increased. About one in three eighteen-year-olds was declared functionally illiterate in 1980. At a time when competition for jobs and all of the accouterments of the American-style good life were intensifying, and when employers were demanding brighter and better educated employees, the public school system increasingly failed to meet individual and national needs. In May 1983, the National Commission on Excellence in Education reported that

> if an unfriendly foreign power had attempted to impose on America the mediocre educational performance that exists today, we might well have viewed it as an act of war.[1]

Many culprits were blamed for the dismal performance of the public schools during the 1970s. Television has been cited for keeping youngsters from reading books and for fostering boredom in the classroom. Indifferent parents, who neither set a good example nor encouraged their children to do well in school, were part of the problem. Popular entertainers and professional athletes whose riches and fame derived from talent rather than study in schools were accused of setting bad examples and leading youngsters astray. In addition, the best and brightest college graduates rarely went into elementary and secondary teaching. Entry-level salaries were low, and

---

[1] Quote is taken from *Report of the National Commission on Excellence in Education*, May 1963, p. 1.

teaching commanded little prestige as a profession. Americans once believed that education could solve all social problems; by the 1970s, to many social critics, the schools had become a social problem. One study found that 10 percent of teachers were incompetent; they could neither teach nor keep order in the classroom. Another 20 percent were considered only marginally qualified to teach youngsters in any subject.

THE MOST RELIGIOUS NATION IN THE WESTERN WORLD

The United States in the 1970s remained the most religious nation in the Western world. Nearly all Americans espoused a belief in God, and 60 percent of the population claimed membership in a church in 1976. Members of the more liberal Protestant churches and Reformed Jews became more accepting of divorce, homosexuality, birth control, and women clergy. The ministers and rabbis of these groups often urged their congregants to work for a more humane and just social order. American Catholics in the 1970s and 1980s were concerned with the continuing consequences of Vatican II, the church council that had met in the early 1960s to bring the church more into accord with modern life. After Vatican II, the liturgy was given in English, and the laity sang hymns during services. Priests were allowed more latitude in their interpretations of the Bible, and they sought ecumenical dialogues with Protestant ministers and rabbis. Catholics recognized the legitimacy of non-Catholic and non-Christian faiths and condemned anti-Semitism.

Church leaders spoke out on issues. In 1983, American Catholic bishops condemned nuclear war and urged the superpowers to disarm. In 1985, the bishops criticized the American capitalist economy for not meeting the needs of the millions of disadvantaged Americans. Many educated, liberal, middle-class Catholics welcomed the changes induced by Vatican II. But many traditionalists felt betrayed and were disturbed by these changes. They continued to adhere to the church's traditional teachings on sex; birth control; abortion; homosexuality; and a celibate, male priesthood.

Evangelical Christians formed one of the most powerful elements within the ranks of the growing conservative movement of the late-1970s and early-1980s. These fervent souls emphasized the personal responsibility of each individual believer. A sinner could be redeemed only by being "born again," that is, by confessing his or her sins, accepting Jesus Christ as a personal savior, and thereafter living a righteous life. Books by evangelical authors became best-sellers. "Christian Yellow Pages" appeared in many large cities. Millions of schoolchildren attended Christian elementary, middle, and high schools, where subjects were taught from an evangelical perspective. In Christian nightclubs, patrons could order fruit juice cocktails and listen to gospel singers. As the 1970s ended, over 1,500 radio stations were owned by evangelical Christians.

Television quickly became the prime conduit for spreading the evangelical message and promoting its conservative social and political agenda. Pat Robertson started the 700 Club, aired over his Christian Broadcasting network. One of the regulars on his show, Jim Bakker, spun off to create his own program, the PTL (Praise the Lord) Club, starring his wife Tammy Faye Bakker, formerly a country-and-western singer. Bakker's show combined sermons, faith healing, inspirational stories, and musical entertainment, often featuring his wife joining the choir or doing a solo number. The PTL Club quickly became the most widely viewed television program on the planet. By 1980, Bakker's organization was taking in $25 million a year in contributions.

THE "ME" DECADE

While some idealistic Americans carried the activist reform spirit of the 1960s into the 1970s, many more turned inward. They wanted to change themselves, not the external world of politics and society. They incorporated many of the elements from the hippie countercultural rebellion into their lifestyles—drug use, permissive sexuality, and above all, the "consciousness revolution." Participants included mostly young, middle-class professionals who prized affluence and professional attainment but who defined success primarily in psychological rather than material terms. It was important to them to fulfill their "human potential" as they accumulated wealth.

The cutting edge of the consciousness revolution could be found in California, home of the new lifestyles based on developing one's inner resources. Facilities like the Esalen Institute at Big Sur offered weekend encounter sessions for seekers wanting to "get in touch with themselves." Another entrepreneur of the human potential movement offered Erhard Seminars Training (est), built around marathon encounter sessions in which participants were encouraged to confront their most powerful inner feelings. Journalist Tom Wolfe labeled these the "Me" generation, and he compared their movement to a religious revival. According to Wolfe, the whole effort was aimed at remaking "one's very self," to strip away the artificial elements of personality that had been added by society "in order to find the Real Me."

As millions of Americans joined the consciousness revolution to seek salvation in narcissistic self-absorption, others sought refuge from the stresses of secular society by joining religious cults. Some of these religious orders embraced Eastern mystical religious practices such as Transcendental Meditation (TM) or Zen Buddhism. One cult, led by Indian holy man Bhagwan Rajneesh Maharishi Yogi, established a flourishing colony near Antelope, Oregon. Thousands of people, attracted by the Bhagwan's message of spiritual rebirth combined with permissive sexuality, lived and worked in apparently joyous harmony for a time. But the cult disintegrated in 1986 because of internal dissension among its leaders. Rajneesh was deported for violations of immigration laws and he returned to India.

The most prominent of the religious cults was the Unification Church, founded by Korean businessman and preacher Sun Myung Moon, who relocated to the United States. Moon, trained as a Presbyterian minister, developed his own brand of religion. He claimed to be the son of God and to receive divine revelations. His movement was controversial. His disciples were accused of kidnapping and brainwashing some of their young recruits. Reverend Moon also ran afoul of the law and was convicted on several counts of income tax evasion. Another cult came to a horrible end in November 1978, when its megalomaniacal leader, Jim Jones, led the cult members from California to Guyana and later convinced more than 700 members to engage in a ghastly ritual mass suicide by drinking poisoned Kool Aid.

CULTURAL TRANSFORMATIONS

The 1970s were an era of comparative civic and social tranquility. In the words of historian John Wiltz, in America during the 1970s, "the national society became more mellow." No more fiery urban riots or militant campus protests convulsed the nation. Gone was the strident rhetoric of youthful radicals denouncing government policies at home and abroad, and challenging traditional American values, mores, and institutions.

Several factors accounted for the calming down of American during the 1970s. The end of the Vietnam War removed the single most powerful source of dissidence. The decline of the economy, stagflation, and energy crises shifted the attention from political and cultural conflicts to more fundamental economic and financial dysfunctions. The successes, or at least the partial victories, of many of the 1960s movements led some of their participants to cease their activism in the 1970s with a sense of having accomplished their missions. Some radicals, suffering from moral and political exhaustion, abandoned their futile efforts to refashion American politics and society, retreating into a sullen personalism and quietism. Some joined the "Me Generation," redirecting their reformist energies away from the world and toward their own personalities. Others, reaching adulthood, made an accommodation with the system that they had previously spurned. Hippies and campus radicals abandoned their countercultural ways, discarded their tie-dyed tank-tops and sandals, shaved their beards, trimmed their hair, donned three-piece suits, and became yuppies. Scholarly types completed their graduate school studies and joined the faculties of colleges and universities.

Retreating into private realms, Americans embraced a variety of activities. Others joined (or rejoined) the suburban mall-spending culture. Some aesthetic types abandoned the artistic search for sincerity and authenticity enshrined by the 1960s counterculture for the campy and self-referential art created by Andy Warhol and his disciples. Beneath the calmer surface of the 1970s flowed some dark, nervous, and edgy currents.

Disco dancing, which had begun in the underground gay, black, and Latino nightclubs, became enormously popular. Couples, often fueled by cocaine, danced the night away beneath pulsating lights in one of the hundreds of nightclubs that sprung up across America in the mid-1970s. Discos were places where marginalized groups such as racial minorities and gay men could interact with white middle-class yuppies. The most famous disco was New York's Studio 54. An attractive African American soul singer, Donna Summer, became the "Queen of Discoland"; her records sold millions of copies during the years of the disco craze. A powerful film, *Saturday Night Fever*, starring John Travolta, with its electrifying dance sequences, popularized disco dancing; it also captured some of the emptiness and hopelessness of the 1970s.

During the 1970s, millions of Americans became more diet conscious than ever before. People reduced their salt and cholesterol intake. Others stopped drinking alcoholic beverages and caffeinated drinks. Closely related to dieting and part of the new health consciousness, millions of people embraced the so-called fitness revolution. They became avid weight lifters as well as weight watchers. They swam, jogged, and rode bicycles; they joined health clubs, played racquetball, and performed aerobic exercises. In another indicator of growing health consciousness during the 1970s, millions of people abandoned smoking cigarettes. By the end of the 1970s, approximately 30 percent of the adult population smoked, the lowest percentage since the 1920s.

If Americans were smoking fewer cigarettes during the 1970s, they were drinking more alcoholic beverages, especially beer. The per capita alcoholic consumption increased from 22 gallons in 1970 to 27 gallons in 1980. Televised sporting events invariably featured numerous beer commercials associating good times with their products. Directing their ads mainly toward single young men, breweries strove to link beer drinking with male fantasies about sexy young women.

During the late 1970s, alcohol abuse among teenagers and college students became a serious national issue. Studies found that thousands of high school students were alcoholics. In 1975, out of the approximately 45,000 Americans killed in traffic accidents, more than half died in accidents in which at least one of the drivers had been drinking. Fatal auto accidents were one of the leading killers of young people between the ages of fifteen and twenty-five. Another survey found that at least ten million Americans were alcohol abusers.

Americans used other drugs besides alcohol in increasing amounts during the 1970s. The use of marijuana ("pot"), which had become a potent symbol of the youth revolt during the turbulent

FIGURE 13.2   An aerobics class.   *Source:* Mimi Forsyth.

1960s, expanded in the 1970s. Pot farming became a major underground industry in many parts of the country; one study discovered that pot farming was California's leading cash crop. Surveys showed that nearly half of the nation's college students during the 1970s used marijuana. Because most experts believed that the effects of the drug were comparatively mild if used in moderation, the federal government and most states reduced the legal penalties for possession of small amounts of pot from felonies to misdemeanors. A far more serious drug problem arose in the early 1970s when there occurred a surge in heroin addiction. The nation discovered that it had nearly a million heroin addicts on its hands by 1975.

Americans during the 1970s discovered the microwave oven, and they consumed a record number of frozen dinners annually. American families also dined out much more often than ever before, especially at fast-food places. The major cause of the 1970s eating-out phenomenon was the fact that more than 50 percent of married women with children now worked full-time outside the home. The new dining-out patterns attested to a major cultural transformation: The great American dinner was being redefined for families with children. Dinner was no longer a significant private familial activity; it had increasingly become a public activity.

BLOCKBUSTERS ON THE BIG SCREEN

Hollywood turned out many fine films, some of which set box-office records. In 1972, the brilliant young director, Francis Ford Coppola, made *The Godfather*, starring Al Pacino, Marlon Brando, and Diane Keaton. Based on a novel by Mario Puzo, the film was an epic about a powerful Mafia family making a place for itself in America through criminal activities. Then in 1973 there came the occult classic, *The Exorcist*, starring a talented child actress, Linda Blair. Based on a novel by William Blatty, the film dealt in dramatic fashion with demonic possession and the valiant efforts of a Roman Catholic priest to exorcise the devil from the body of the child. The techno-thriller *Jaws* was released in 1975, produced by a brilliant young filmmaker, Steven Spielberg. It was a terrifying account of a great white killer shark attacking swimmers. The star of the film turned out to be Jaws himself, the technological monster that terrorized a New England town: It was shown devouring swimmers in gruesome detail. *Jaws* had the largest box office gross of any film ever made.

Jaws' record take at the box office was broken in 1977 by *Star Wars*, the first of a brilliant series of science-fiction films by George Lucas, another major filmmaking talent that burst on the Hollywood scene in the 1970s. Set in the distant past, *Star Wars* was essentially a child's fantasy, a fairy tale about high-tech adventures in space, starring Mark Hamill as Luke Skywalker, Harrison Ford as Hans Solo, and Carrie Fisher as Princess Leia. They were supported by a charming cast of bizarre-looking but gentle aliens and humanlike machines called androids. The plot was a simple morality tale, of the good guys triumphing over the bad guys, who control the evil Galactic Empire. Lucas reasserted the pleasures of straightforward, unironic storytelling, along with acces-sible, two-dimensional characters whose adventures ended happily. Much of the appeal of *Star Wars* lay in the fact that it had no message, no sex, and only the mildest of violence. It could be enjoyed by "kids" of all ages. It relied on a dazzling array of special effects and technological wizardry to mesmerize its audience. One critic called it a Wild West adventure in outer space. Another analyst, pondering the deeper meanings of *Star Wars*, suggested that it pointed the way toward a new American mythology in the wake of the disillusionment with Watergate and the Vietnam War, which destroyed the American frontier myth. *Star Wars* represented a creative effort to reclaim lost American innocence.

TELEVISION: THE NEW CULTURAL PLURALISM

Surveys revealed that Americans watched more television shows than ever before during the 1970s. New technologies significantly enhanced the range and capabilities of the electronic medium. Communication satellites in geosynchronous orbits hundreds of miles in space enabled television news to provide live, instantaneous coverage of events from anywhere on the planet. With the arrival of cable television, viewers were liberated from having to rely on the three major networks that controlled prime-time programing. The most important new television technology of the 1970s was the introduction in 1975 of the videocassette recorder, or VCR. Early versions of VCRs were difficult to use and rather expensive; they were slow to catch on. Sales of VCRs boomed in the 1980s and wrought another revolution in the nation's television- and movie-viewing habits.

During the 1970s, prime-time television shows reflected the growing cultural pluralism of the American people. Game shows remained popular, especially *Let's Make a Deal*, and producer Chuck Barris's increasingly raunchy remakes of his 1960s hits, *The Dating Game* and *The Newlyweds*. Variety shows such as *The Mike Douglas Show* and *The Merv Griffin Show* also contin-ued to be popular. *The Tonight Show Starring Johnnie Carson* reigned as the unchallenged king of late-night television.

A carryover from the sixties, *Rowan and Martin's Laugh-In*, often topped the rating charts. Hosted by straight man Dan Rowan and his goofy sidekick Dick Martin, the show featured a *melange* of skits, jokes, and musical numbers carried out by a talented cast of regulars and special guest stars. Much of the appeal of *Laugh-In* came from its good-humored irreverence; it skewered prominent figures who often appeared on the show to join in the fun. Richard Nixon made a famous appearance on *Laugh-In* during his 1968 election campaign. *Laugh-In* ushered in a generation of unconventional and iconoclastic shows, notably *Saturday Night Live*.

The Mary Tyler Moore Show, which premiered on CBs in 1970, represented a breakthrough of sorts for women's liberation. The show revolved around Moore's character, Mary Richards, a divorced thirty-something, who works as an associate producer of the evening news watched by a large metropolitan audience. Richards has a demanding job, which puts her in charge of a stable of all-male news anchors. She functioned as a positive role model for young women at a time when a generation of baby boomers were making their way into management positions in various industries. Much of the popularity of the show depended on the characters having to deal with challenging work and life situations within an essentially comic context. The show's enduring popularity also derived from the acting skills of Moore, who played her role with consummate wit and grace.

African American actors and performers appeared with increasing frequency throughout the 1970s in prime-time TV programs. However, most of their appearances were limited to either comic or subservient roles with predominantly black casts, which perpetuated negative stereotypes of black people and black culture among the overwhelmingly white audiences. *Julia* was the first weekly TV series that depicted an African American central character in a nonstereotyped role. The show starred Diahann Carroll, who played a nurse, a widowed single mother, whose husband, a fighter pilot, had been shot down in Vietnam. *Julia* ran on NBC from 1968 until 1971. Even though it represented a breakout for black actors, *Julia* remained a light-hearted sitcom, and, to keep it safe, all of Julia's romantic interests were played by black actors.

Cop shows were among the most popular TV programs during the 1970s, supplanting the ubiquitous Westerns, which had dominated prime-time television programing during the 1950s and had carried into the 1960s with such shows as *Gunsmoke* and *Bonanza*. One of the iconic cop shows of the 1970s was *Starsky and Hutch*. It starred Paul Michael Glaser as David Starsky and David Soul as Ken "Hutch" Hutchinson, two streetwise undercover cops. Both men were often in trouble with the police chief for their unorthodox, vigilante-like methods of crime-solving.

The show was popular for years because of the male-bonding of its stars, a strong supporting cast, and its clever writing. Mainly, the show was popular because of its violence, and the brutal ways criminals, the "bad guys," were taken out. The star of the show was often a red two-door 1974 Ford Gran Torino with a large white stripe that resembled the Nike swoosh logo. The dramatic high point of many a *Starsky and Hutch* episode was a spectacular car chase usually ending with the villains (drug traffickers and arms smugglers) dying in a flaming crash as they tried to escape justice. The show eventually came under attack for its excessive violence, which caused producers to curtail the violence, which in turn curtailed the audience, and *Starksy and Hutch* went off the air.

M*A*S*H (Mobile Army Surgical Hospital), based upon a movie of that title, was an immensely popular prime-time television show during the 1970s, which carried into the 1980s. Although its setting is the Korean War of the early 1950s, *M*A*S*H* was understood by most viewers as an ongoing commentary upon the American Vietnam War, which was entering its final phase when the show debuted. Much of *M*A*S*H*'s popularity derived from the dialog and actions of its central characters. "Hawkeye" Pierce, played by Alan Alda, was a skilled and caring surgeon, who saved the lives of horribly wounded soldiers all the while deploring the war and chafing under military discipline, which he considered arbitrary and ridiculous. His foil was head nurse, Margaret "Hot Lips" Hoolihan, a dedicated, by-the-book career army officer, played by Loretta Swit. For over a decade, *M*A*S*H* entertainingly conveyed a deeply pacifistic message: War solves no problems and destroys lives.

PROFESSIONAL SPORTS AS BIG BUSINESS

Because so many sporting events were televised during the 1970s, commercial spectator sports became a more important part of popular culture than ever before. Major professional spectator sports flourished, especially the National Football League (NFL), the National Basketball Association (NBA), and Major League Baseball.

Due in large part to television, professional football became the most popular national sport. During the 1970s, The Dallas Cowboys, under the direction of their passionless technocratic coach Tom Landry, earned the title of "America's team." Pro football is a fast-paced, complex, fiercely competitive, violent game played by tough, smart, and highly skilled athletes. Some analysts have linked its powerful hold on fans to the fact that pro football was a microcosm of the hi-tech corporate economy that America had become in the 1970s. Pro football can be compared to the Internet economy—endlessly innovative and disruptive. Football coaches routinely revolutionize the game with new strategies and formations. One year the St. Louis Rams' offense featuring multiple deep passing formations carried them to a Super Bowl victory. The next year, the Baltimore Raven's defensive formations, featuring zone blitzes, carried them to the championship. Pro football was the iconic 1970s sport with its endless variations and transformations.

College sports, particularly football and basketball, grew rapidly in popularity largely because of television. The growth of these major college sports was tinged with scandals. Some schools recruited athletes who were not equipped to succeed academically. Unless they were among the very few elite athletes who went on to successful careers as professional athletes, most left school after their athletic eligibility was expended without degrees and without the prospect of professional careers of any kind.

Other scandals that plagued college football and basketball programs included illegal payments to "amateur" athletes by alumni boosters, drug use, and other criminal behavior among some athletes. The National Collegiate Athletic Association (NCAA) exercised a rather ineffectual policing function over intercollegiate athletics. From time to time, they would investigate collegiate athletic programs, find illegalities, and impose penalties. One had a sense that the NCAA had sporadically discovered the tip of a scandalous iceberg.

Amidst the commercialism and scandals of collegiate sports, there was one positive innovation. Women athletes demanded parity with men at the nation's colleges and universities. Although most schools fell far short of achieving gender equality in their sports programs, scholarship support for female athletes significantly increased. Several college women's sports flourished, including basketball, volleyball, swimming, and softball; these breakthroughs for women athletes represented another victory for the powerful women's movement of the 1970s.

Brief Bibliographic Essay

Historians are acquiring a broader appreciation of the 1970s, an era that until now has not fared well in scholarly hands. One of these new studies is the aforementioned Bruce J. Schulman, *The Seventies: The Great Shift in American Culture, Society, and Politics.* Another recent survey of the 1970s is Edward D. Berkowitz, *Something Happened: A Political and Cultural Overview of the Seventies.* The implications of recent demographic shifts are discussed in Joseph J. Spengler's *Population and America's Future.* For studies of African Americans in the 1970s, read Ken Auletta's *The Underclass* and William Julius Wilson's *The Declining Significance of Race.* David M. Reimore's *Still the*

Golden Door: The Third World Comes to America highlights the most significant cultural transformation of the 1970s, one that revitalized the defining theme of America as a nation of immigrants: the historic shift of the main sources of immigrants from Europe to Asia and Latin America. There is an extensive and generally excellent literature on women during the 1970s. Much the best history of the modern women's movement and its impact on American society and culture is Ruth Rosen, *The World Split Open: How the Modern Women's Movement Changed America.* Mary Ann Mason's *The Equality Trap*, offers a perceptive study of the limitations of liberal feminism and its failure to cope with the economic plight of divorced working women. Christopher Lasch's *The Culture of Narcissism: American Life in the Age of Diminishing Expectations* catches many of the anxieties and discontents of the American people during the era of limits. Gillian Peele, in *Revival and Reaction: The Right in Contemporary America*, offers a study of religious and political conservatism. Education trends are analyzed in Sanford W. Reitman's *Education, Society, and Change.* Movie buffs will want to read Robert Bookbinder's *The Films of the 1970s.* Students of popular culture may want to read John-Manuel Andriote's *Hot Stuff: A Brief History of Disco.*

14

America Revived

In modern times, only Franklin Roosevelt has had a greater personal influence on American politics than Ronald Reagan. The new president had begun political life as a passionate New Deal liberal and later became a trade union leader. By the time he entered the White House in 1981, Reagan had repudiated liberal welfarism; he sought to reshape government policies along conservative lines.

He moved quickly to jump-start the economy and bring inflation down, thereby ending years of "stagflation" that had undermined the living standards of millions of American families. His economic policies, dubbed "Reaganomics," were based on supply-side economic theory that broke sharply with Keynesian policies, which had dominated since the New Deal era. The Reagan administration also moved to deregulate important sectors of the economy in order to promote economic growth.

Americans continued to drift to the Right during the 1980s. Support for environmentalist and feminist causes diminished. A backlash against affirmative action slowed black progress. Baby boomers, now entering their twenties and thirties, focused on work, family life, and being good consumers. The commitments of the sixties and the anxieties of the seventies had vanished.

REAGANOMICS

Reagan grounded his program for economic recovery in "supply-side" economic theory. Rejecting Keynesian theory, which relied on government spending and tax cuts to boost consumer demand, supply-siders favored cutting both federal spending and taxes at the same time. They believed that the private sector, freed from shackles imposed by government regulation and high taxes, would increase its investment in productive enterprises, thereby generating economic growth and creating millions of new, well-paying jobs. Economic growth would also cut inflation and generate increased tax revenues, despite the lower tax rates. Government expenditures would be trimmed by shrinking government benefits. Spending cuts, coupled with the projected economic expansion, would bring in a balanced budget.

The president appointed James A. Baker as his chief of staff. Baker urged Reagan to move quickly on his two key issues—tax cuts and the military buildup. David Stockman, who had been a member of the Leftist Students for a Democratic Society while enrolled at Michigan State University, became director of the Office of Management and Budget. By 1981, Stockman had evolved into a supply-side zealot; he carried to Congress Reagan's program of cutting spending and reducing taxes. While Stockman overhauled the federal budgetary process, Paul Volcker, a Carter holdover and chairman of the Federal Reserve Board, kept tight reins on the money supply by raising interest rates to historic highs. Volcker's "tight money" strategy was not in accordance with supply-side theory, but Reagan strongly backed Volcker's efforts to break the inflationary spiral even though they both understood that high interest rates were driving the economy deeper into recession.

Stockman made cutting federal spending the Reagan administration's top priority. He slashed $41 billion in means-tested social spending for food stamps, public service jobs, student loans, school lunches, and welfare payments. Social Security was exempted, and Reagan also left what he called a "safety net for the truly needy."

At the same time he was cutting back social spending, Reagan increased military spending sharply. Reagan made a dramatic personal appearance before a joint session of Congress to plead for his tax cutting and spending programs only a few weeks after being seriously wounded during an attempt on his life. His performance, carried live on all major television networks, sent his poll ratings soaring to new heights. Many Democrats who opposed his budget and could not abide Reagan's conservative political philosophy were on their feet, applauding the gallant old actor. They were also reluctant to oppose a leader working hard to translate a popular mandate into effective policies.

The new president persuaded many Sunbelt Democratic congressmen to accept his budget and deep tax cuts. These "boll weevils," led by Representative Phil Gramm of Texas, were crucial in getting his program through the Democratic-controlled House. Reagan built up a strong bipartisan coalition in the House and won a commanding 253 to 176 victory. His winning margin in the Senate was even more impressive, 78 to 20. Many liberal Democrats were skeptical that supply-side economics could work, but they lacked an alternative program that commanded public support.

The Economic Recovery Tax Act of 1981 was the most significant legislation of the Reagan era. Based on a proposal by Senator William Roth and Congressman Jack Kemp, the across-the-board tax cuts reduced basic personal income tax rates by 25 percent over three years. It reduced the top marginal rate on individuals from 70 percent to 50 percent. It also indexed tax brackets, which kept tax rates constant when incomes rose solely because of inflation. Congress wrote additional tax concessions into an omnibus bill. Capital gains, inheritance tax, and gift taxes were reduced. Business tax write-offs were enhanced. The Reagan tax cuts, with congressional sanction, were the most generous tax reductions in the nation's history.

Reagan also sought to reduce federal regulation of the economy. He appointed men and women to regulatory agencies who shared his views that markets, not governmental agencies, ought to direct the national economy. He appointed Anne Gorsuch Burford, who opposed air quality and toxic waste regulations, to head the Environmental Protection Agency (EPA). During her tenure, the EPA budget was slashed, and all of its enforcement efforts were weakened.

Reagan's most controversial appointment was James Watt, to head the Department of the Interior. Watt had directed an antienvironmentalist legal action group before his appointment to the Interior Department. He supported strip-mining and favored opening up public lands to private developers, including offshore oil-drilling sites. Reagan tried to eliminate the Department of Energy; failing to do that, he settled for severe cuts in its budget and operations.

He also tried to dismantle the Department of Education, which he failed to achieve. But he persuaded Congress to cut federal spending for elementary and secondary education. Many of the responsibilities, and the costs of regulatory activity, were shifted to the states. Drew Lewis, Reagan's secretary of transportation, removed many of the regulations to reduce pollution and increase driver safety that had been imposed on the U.S. auto industry during the 1970s.

Lewis opposed an illegal strike by the Professional Air Traffic Controllers' Organization (PATCO). President Reagan fired the 11,500 striking controllers, decertified the union, and directed Lewis to train and hire thousands of new air controllers to replace them. The destruction of the air traffic controller's union was the most devastating defeat for organized labor in modern times. It demoralized a labor movement already reeling from the decline of American manufacturing and the loss of political clout. Thereafter the number of strikes per year plummeted to all-time lows, and some of the largest of these failed. The destruction of PATCO contributed to the

FIGURE 14.1 Sandra Day O'Connor. *Source:* National Geographic Society, Courtesy of the Collection of the Supreme Court of the United States.

long-term decline of the American labor movement. The person who did more damage to the modern American labor movement than any other president is the only chief executive to ever carry a union card and to have been a trade union leader.

By the end of the summer of 1981, "Reaganomics" was in place. Reagan had seized the political initiative, redefined the public agenda, and got most of his program implemented. *Time* magazine observed, "No President since FDR had done so much of such magnitude so quickly to change the economic direction of the country." Reaganomics amounted to a conservative assault on the liberal welfare state that had been erected during the previous fifty years.

Aware that few African Americans had voted Republican, the Reagan administration was unresponsive to black concerns. Federal support for civil rights weakened. Reagan opposed affirmative action hiring programs. His attorney general, Edwin Meese, opposed busing to achieve school desegregation. The number of African American officials appointed to major government positions declined. Both the staff and budget of the Civil Rights Division of the Justice Department were cut.

Reagan's record for appointments of women was better than his record for African Americans. He appointed a few highly visible women to top government positions. He fulfilled a campaign pledge and made a major symbolic gesture to women when he appointed Sandra Day O'Connor to the Supreme Court, the first women jurist ever chosen. He appointed Jeane Kirkpatrick as the U.S. ambassador to the United Nations. Several women served in his cabinet.

RECESSION AND RECOVERY

After a year, it was evident that Reaganomics had not brought about an economic revival but instead brought forth a severe recession. Unemployment exceeded 9 percent, the highest rate since 1941. Business bankruptcies rose to depression levels. Steep interest rates priced homes and cars beyond the reach of millions of families and plunged those two major industries into depression. The nation was mired in its worst slump since the Great Depression. Manufacturing output declined, and the construction industry slumped. In Detroit, unemployment reached 20 percent. Bewildered and angry workers, many of them "Reagan Democrats," lined up to receive their unemployment checks. A class of "new poor," not seen since the 1930s, appeared on the streets: homeless, unemployed workers and their families.

Supply-side economics did not work as advertised, and the promised increased tax revenues from economic growth never materialized. Instead, a combination of deep tax cuts, steep hikes in military spending, and drastic economic shrinkage drove the federal budget deficit to over $100 billion, the highest ever. The one bright spot in an otherwise dark economic picture was declining inflation. It dropped from 13 percent in 1980 to 9 percent in 1981, and fell to 5 percent in 1982.

The short-term failure of Reaganomics derived from two fiscal realities: the failure of the tax cuts to stimulate increased business investment and continuing high interest rates that put a crimp in both business spending and consumer purchases. The recession worsened throughout 1982. Toward the end of the year, unemployment reached 10 percent; over eleven million Americans were out of work.

The 1982 midterm elections took place amidst the worst economic conditions this country had seen in over forty years. The election amounted to a referendum on Reaganomics. The Democrats picked up twenty-five House seats, but the Republicans retained control of the Senate. When the new Congress convened in January 1983, Reagan lost his bipartisan majority coalition that had pushed through Reaganomics. House speaker Thomas "Tip" O'Neill, the leader of the opposition to Reaganomics, persuaded the president to accept budget compromises in 1983. Cuts in social spending were lessened, and increases in military spending were reduced. Reagan was not a rigid ideologue; he understood that various social programs had powerful advocates, and he also knew that he lacked the power to phase out or even sharply curtail social welfare programs. The most he could accomplish was to slow their rate of growth.

The economy recovered strongly in 1983, and the surge continued in 1984. The GDP rose by 6.8 percent in 1984, the largest one-year gain since the Korean War. Unemployment and interest rates declined. Housing starts and new car sales picked up. The rate of inflation dropped to 4 percent for both years, the lowest since the early 1970s. Personal income rose; consumer and business confidence soared. Abundant world oil supplies were an important cause of the drop in the rate of inflation. By the end of 1984, OPEC was in disarray, and world oil prices were plummeting. The price of a gallon of gas at the pump dropped from $1.40 to $1.00, and stayed there for the rest of the decade. The economic expansion that began in 1983 continued into the early 1990s. Economic growth generated 18 million new jobs and tripled the price of stocks by 1990.

Despite the strong rebound in 1983, serious problems continued to plague the American economy. Tax cuts combined with large increases in military spending to generate record federal deficits. The tax cuts, along with America's thin social safety net, aggravated growing economic inequality, which was sharper within the United States than any other industrialized nation. The nation's international trade deficit reached a record $108 billion in 1984. The main causes of the soaring international debt were the nation's continuing thirst for foreign oil and imported manufactures, such as autos, VCRs, cameras, and stereos. During Reagan's first term, the national debt doubled. Amidst the economic revival, over 7.5 million Americans remained out of work. The Census Bureau reported that the nation's poverty rate reached 15.2 percent in 1983, the highest since 1965. There were 35 million poor people in America, six million more than when Reagan assumed office.

THE 1984 ELECTION

Since taking office in January, 1981, Reagan had been repeatedly savaged by liberal pundits. Historian John Wiltz called Reagan "the least cerebral" of modern presidents. Critics portrayed him as a kind of ceremonial president: While he looked and acted the part, an inner circle of advisers made policy and ran the country. In contrast to Nixon and Carter, who were grim workaholics, Reagan appeared to view the presidency as a part-time job; he spent more than a year of his time as president either at his ranch located in the foothills above Santa Barbara, California, or on weekend retreats at Camp David.

Reagan also employed an erratic management style; he cared passionately about a few issues, but appeared oblivious to much else. He tended to disengage himself from the details of his day-to-day administration, and he allowed his advisers to implement his policies and programs without giving them much direction. He often appeared dependent on his wife Nancy for advice and guidance. Reagan sometimes confused events that had transpired in the celluloid world of Hollywood films with political reality. He often was given to misstatements. During his presidency, Reagan's staffers became adept at putting the proper "spin" on his more ludicrous remarks.

Reagan's detractors, who ridiculed his intellectual and administrative shortcomings, also underrated Reagan's remarkable political talents. Liberal intellectuals might scoff at the old actor's simplistic ideas, but Reagan understood that average American citizens could not care less whether the president of the United States possessed a powerful mind or had mastered all of the details of a program. They wanted a leader, not a policy wonk, in office. Reagan also had a clear vision of the direction in which he wanted to move the country. He was stubbornly determined to reverse the fifty-year trend whereby the federal government assumed increasing responsibility for underwriting the economic security and general welfare of the population. He was also determined to restore U.S. military primacy in the world and to contain Soviet expansionism, as Americans had done in the 1940s and 1950s before the Vietnam debacle sapped their will.

In response to a succession of lackluster and failed presidencies extending from Lyndon Johnson to Jimmy Carter, it had become part of the conventional political wisdom to assert that the presidency had grown too large, that contemporary problems had become too complex, for any mortal to master. Reagan's performance in office disproved such notions. He set out to strengthen the office of the presidency, to prove that he could do the job and do it well. He refurbished executive authority. He reasserted influence over Congress. He centralized the budget-making process and brought the bureaucracies to heel.

Using his extraordinary political and oratorical skills, Reagan largely succeeded in moving Congress and the American people in accordance with his conservative vision. He retained the trust and affection of a large majority of his fellow citizens for most of his presidency. The social service state was pared down, and the social contract was attenuated. The economy, after enduring a bitter recession in 1982, rebounded strongly. Inflation was brought under control, and long-term stable growth for the rest of the decade of the 1980s ensured national prosperity. Reagan strengthened the armed forces, and Americans were treated with a new respect in the world by both friends and foes. Most Americans became more optimistic about both their present conditions and the future of the nation. Reagan's stirring speeches helped lift the malaise that had fastened itself on the nation during the era of limits.

But there was a dark side to the Reagan record of success and growing popularity. While yuppies prospered, the number of poor Americans increased. Ronald Reagan presided over a major redistribution of national income. Median family income for African Americans and for people of Hispanic origin declined during Reagan's presidency. Over half of the new jobs created during the 1980s were low-wage entry-level jobs that could not sustain a family. The Reagan administration had scant interest in civil rights or ecological concerns. Drugs poured into the country, and crime rates soared. Reagan was excruciatingly slow to respond to the AIDS epidemic that ravaged the gay community during the 1980s.

Preparing for the 1984 election, political action committees (PACs) supporting Reagan's reelection amassed over $7 million compared with less than $1 million raised by groups favoring his Democratic opponent, Walter Mondale, who had been Carter's vice president. Reagan's campaign managers made effective use of slick television commercials that emphasized the restoration of the national economy and national pride, while avoiding specific issues. His commercials stressed the themes of redemption, family values, and patriotism. His chief speechwriter, Peggy Noonan, wrote the best line of his campaign: "America is back: It's morning again." Reagan was also helped significantly by what liberal Democratic Congresswoman Pat Schroeder called the "Teflon presidency": The public and most of the established media did not hold Reagan accountable for his failures or for wrongdoing by members of his administration. Reagan, during his first term, enjoyed the most favorable press of any modern president.

Mondale never found an issue that enabled him to cut into the president's huge lead. Public opinion polls showed that voters disapproved of many of Reagan's specific policies, but they were voting for him because they liked and trusted the man. Mondale also hurt whatever chance he might have had to win by announcing bluntly to American voters at the outset of his campaign that he intended to raise taxes if he won.

In defeat, the Democrats made history twice. First, Jesse Jackson, the first major African American candidate for president, conducted a spirited primary campaign, getting 18 percent of

FIGURE 14.2   The Democratic Party made history in 1984 when delegates chose Geraldine Ferraro as its first female vice presidential candidate.   *Source:* AP/Wide World Photos.

the vote and winning 373 delegates to the Democratic Convention. Second, Mondale's running mate, Representative Geraldine Ferraro, became the first woman vice presidential candidate on a major party ticket. But she was on the defensive during much of her campaign because of her violations of campaign spending laws and because of some of her husband's questionable business practices. Jackson's political base never reached much beyond the African American community.

Reagan received 525 electoral votes, the largest total in history. Mondale carried only his home state of Minnesota and the District of Columbia. Reagan got 52.7 million votes to 36.5 million for Mondale. The Republicans gained thirteen seats in the House and won 17 of 33 senatorial elections, retaining a 54 to 46 majority. Reagan's reelection victory crossed all regional and most demographic lines. The Democrats appeared to have no remaining regional base of support. In the once Solid South, every state went for Reagan by decisive majorities. In the West and Southwest, Reagan won easily. The Northeast, once the stronghold of both moderate Republicans and liberal Democrats, also voted for Reagan. He swept the industrial states of the Great Lakes and the Midwestern farm belt, despite continuing economic problems in both of those regions.

All age groups voted for him. He did especially well among young, first-time voters. Baby boomers voted 2 to 1 for Reagan. Half of union members voted for Reagan, even though Mondale's chief backers were the AFL-CIO leadership. Class and ethnic differences were visible in the voting returns. Middle-class and wealthy voters overwhelmingly supported Reagan. Less affluent voters generally supported Mondale. Ninety percent of blacks voted for Mondale, as did 60 percent of Hispanics. Election results showed Hispanics to be an emerging political force in California, Texas, and Florida.

The 1984 election results demonstrated that the Republican Party had made dramatic gains since the Watergate scandals of 1973–1974. Reagan's triumphant reelection also moved some Democrats toward the Right. Centrist and conservative Democrats created the Democratic Leadership Council (DLC). These "New Democrats" set out to broaden the party's appeal. They encountered much opposition from liberal Democrats, including Jesse Jackson. Battles between these two factions ensured that the Democrats would remain a divided party for years to come.

Reagan's smashing reelection revealed the growing conservatism of mainstream American voters and exposed the developing disconnect between liberal Democrats and ordinary Americans. The baby boom generation, now in their twenties and thirties, some of whom had embraced radical political causes and countercultural lifestyles during the 1960s, had gotten jobs, had married, had children, and bought homes in the suburbs. Having resources to lose, they were becoming more conservative on economic issues, and some baby boomers embraced conservative social and cultural issues.

Reagan's performance in office restored the majesty of the presidency. The return of good times had restored many Americans' faith in their system of political economy. Reagan's relentless optimism, his vision of America as a great and exceptional nation, had an infectious appeal to his fellow believers. Reagan biographer Lou Cannon observed, "Reagan succeeded in reviving national confidence at a time when there was a great need for inspiration. This was his great contribution as president."

SECOND EFFORTS

Reagan made tax reform his top legislative priority for his second term. The federal tax system had become exceedingly complex over the years as Congress had factored in a great many exemptions and loopholes favoring corporations and wealthy individual taxpayers.

Bipartisan support for tax revision gradually emerged in Congress, led by Democratic congressman Daniel Rostenkowski and Republican senator Robert Packwood. In the summer of 1986, Congress passed the Tax Reform Act, which brought the first fundamental overhaul of the modern federal income tax system since its inception during World War II. The act simplified the tax code by eliminating many tax shelters and deductions. It reduced multiple tax brackets on individuals to just three, at rates of 15 percent, 28 percent, and 33 percent. It removed 6 million low-income Americans from the federal tax rolls and lowered the tax burden for a majority of taxpayers. The new law shifted some of the tax burden to the business community by closing loopholes and eliminating write-offs and exemptions.

Reagan shared another major achievement when his administration supported a landmark immigration bill passed by Congress in October 1986. The bill revamped the 1965 act, offering legal status to millions of aliens living illegally in the United States. It also required employers to ask for identification, verifying the citizenship of job applicants, and it levied fines on employers who hired illegal aliens. The continuing flood of illegal immigrants coming to the United States, mainly from Mexico, would gradually undermine the effectiveness of the 1986 law. With its long southern border with Mexico out of control as millions of illegal immigrants continued to enter the country, Washington, in the summer of 2006, would face another immigration crisis.

Another pressing problem to which Reagan was slow to respond was acquired immune deficiency syndrome (AIDS). An AIDS epidemic swept the country during the mid-1980s, and each year killed thousands, mostly gay males. By the mid-eighties, researchers had identified the infectious agents—human immunodeficiency viruses (HIV)—but they had no medications to alleviate the syndrome, let alone cure it. A diagnosis of AIDS was a virtual death sentence. For years, the administration refused to publicly acknowledge AIDS, and it was, at least in the eyes of those most concerned about fighting the disease, painfully slow to support increased AIDS research and study.

Many religious conservatives who supported the Reagan presidency insisted that AIDS was a divinely ordained "gay plague" to punish homosexuals for deviant behavior that violated Biblical injunctions. Religious conservatives also opposed the use of condoms and sex education programs to combat the disease. Administration officials mainly called for the mandatory testing of categories of people thought to be at risk, or those who held positions of public responsibility. Meanwhile, the disease continued to wreak devastation. AIDS became a worldwide epidemic in the mid-1980s, and it struck with a special fury among the people of several Central and East African nations.

Reagan had come to Washington in 1981, committed to waging a war on drugs and bringing the international drug trade under control. Drug traffic in marijuana, cocaine, and heroin flourished in the mid-1980s. America was the world's major consumer of illicit drugs. The immense costs of America's gargantuan drug habit included thousands of deaths annually, health problems for millions, huge increases in urban crime, corruption in the criminal justice system, and loss of productivity.

Efforts to enforce drug laws and U.S.-financed efforts to eradicate drug crops at their sources in Asia and Latin America continued to be ineffective. One of the major reasons for the failure of the Reagan administration's war against drugs, popularized by First Lady Nancy Reagan, was its inability to slow the great American appetite for drugs. All efforts to curtail the supply side of the drug problem were doomed to fail until a measure of control could be imposed on the demand side. After years of activity and having spent $3 billion, Reagan announced early in 1988 that the war against drugs had been won. His claim was preposterous. According to contemporary surveys, 25 million Americans regularly used marijuana, six million regularly used cocaine, particularly "crack," and another million were heroin addicts.

THE "GO-GO" ECONOMY

The economy continued to perform strongly through Reagan's second term. Inflation remained under control, and oil supplies were plentiful. Growth rates averaged 3 percent to 4 percent per annum; many corporations enjoyed record sales and profits, and continually expanded their production. The stock market continued to push through record highs as the great bull market of the 1980s roared on. Consumer spending and consumer confidence remained high.

Despite the economy's strong performance, individual and corporate indebtedness increased rapidly. The takeover mania that had gripped Wall Street during the 1980s continued. Most of these corporate buyouts were severely "leveraged"; that is, they were financed by consortia of bankers and brokerage houses that often sold huge portfolios of "junk bonds" (high-yield, high-risk securities issued by companies with low-credit ratings) to raise the vast sums of capital needed to buy out shareholders at above market prices. Leveraged buyouts (LBOs) usually did not make the economy more productive or competitive; in fact, they often left companies weaker and in serious debt, with no funds for research or the development of new products. Toward the end of Reagan's presidency, investigations exposed some of the financial wizards who had brokered corporate takeover deals as criminals who had violated laws against insider trading. The two biggest names were high-fliers Ivan Boesky and Michael Milken, both of whom served years in jail and paid millions of dollars in fines.

Budget deficits continued to grow, exceeding $200 billion in 1986. During Reagan's presidency, the national debt tripled—from $1 trillion to $3 trillion. Paying the annual interest due on the national debt became the third largest item in the federal budget, after Social Security and defense. The national debt became so large during Reagan's presidency that servicing it absorbed much of the net savings accrued by individuals and businesses each year. Pressures on interest rates were eased, because foreign investors, particularly the Germans, Japanese, and Saudi Arabians, bought up about 20 percent of the U.S. debt each year. Even so, the federal government had to take so much money from the private capital markets to fund the debt each year that the money available for investment in research, product development, new technologies, and increased productive capacity was significantly curtailed. There was a link between the huge federal indebtedness and declining American competitiveness in the world's marketplaces.

In December 1985, Congress enacted the Gramm–Rudman Act, a measure that required automatic annual reductions in the budget deficit if the president and Congress failed to agree on cuts. The following year, the Supreme Court nullified the law, and the deficit for 1986 came in at a record $226 billion. Congress then enacted a modified version of Gramm–Rudman, but the White House and congressional legislators agreed to accounting procedures that effectively gutted the law. Several large spending programs were declared "off-budget" and not included when figuring the deficit in order to evade Gramm–Rudman limits. It took a record one-day crash of the stock market on October 19, 1987, and fears of an impending recession, to force Reagan and Congress to reduce the budget deficit.

Trade deficits also had expanded rapidly between 1980 and 1985, as imports increased 41 percent while exports decreased slightly. Every week during the Reagan presidency, American consumers spent about $1 billion more buying imported goods than foreigners spent buying American-made products. To offset that imbalance in international trading, huge amounts of American securities, real estate, and factories were purchased by foreign investors who had to recycle their surplus dollars. By the end of Reagan's presidency, U.S. assets in foreign lands totaled less than the U.S. assets owned by foreigners. Until the early 1970s, America had been the world's leading creditor nation. By the end of the Reagan presidency, it had become the world's leading debtor.

Other economic trends alarmed Americans. Increasing numbers of U.S. manufacturing concerns moved their operations overseas to get away from unionized workers and high taxes, and they took thousands of good jobs with them. At the same time, foreign investors continued buying up U.S. assets. By the end of Reagan's presidency, foreign corporations owned American banks, investment houses, fast-food restaurants, motion picture studios, landmark skyscrapers, thousands of acres of farmland, publishing firms, and supermarket chains.

While foreigners continued to buy up U.S. properties, other foreign competitors steadily increased their share of American domestic markets for autos, electronic products, cameras, clothes, and shoes. Many of these developments reflected a new reality, that the economic lives of nations were increasingly intertwined. By the mid-1980s, the American economy was intricately plugged in to a global economic system. Henceforth, more and more of the economic and financial activities of Americans would be influenced by decisions made in corporate boardrooms in Tokyo, Riyadh, and Bonn.

Another sign of trouble in America that surfaced in the late 1980s—disaster in the savings and loan industry—was entirely homegrown. The savings and loan debacle was an unintended consequence of bipartisan good intentions. Deregulation was a policy idea that was first implemented during the Carter years, in the airline and trucking industries. The Reaganauts embraced deregulation in the name of greater productivity plus economy in government. Under the influence of supply-side economic theory, federal agencies relaxed or abolished regulations affecting the operations of a wide range of American industries. One of these was savings and loan banks (S&Ls). Historically, S&Ls loaned money to individuals to buy homes in local areas where the banks were located. Home mortgages tended to be low-risk, low-profit investments. Savings and loan banks were noted for being safe, sound, and a little dull.

At the urging of the Reagan administration, Congress deregulated the savings and loan industry in 1982. Consequently, S&Ls could offer a much wider range of loans; they could invest depositors' funds in commercial real estate, in undeveloped land, in just about any kind of high-risk project imaginable. They also could loan funds for national and even international projects. Even if these high-risk operations went bust and the banks collapsed, the existence of the Federal Savings and Loan Insurance Corporation (FSLIC) meant that the bankers would not incur personal liabilities and that the depositors would get back their money from the insurance fund.

In many parts of the nation, especially in the Southwest and West, the new era of deregulation attracted a generation of incompetent and crooked buccaneers into the banking industry. They proceeded to invest billions of dollars of depositors' funds in a bewildering variety of dubious projects, knowing that they might reap huge profits from their high-risk undertakings but took no risk of incurring personal responsibility for any losses because of the existence of the FSLIC. Deregulation of the savings and loan industry eventually reaped a financial disaster that left taxpayers saddled with a tab that ran into hundreds of billions of dollars.

Although the economic expansion of the "go-go" years of the 1980s was real, it also could be selective and spotty. It excluded large numbers of Americans. The chief regional beneficiaries of the Reagan boom years were the Northeast and California. Both regions were on the cutting edge of the computer revolution, and both had extensive military and aerospace industries. In these areas, good jobs at good salaries abounded; real estate prices for both residential and commercial properties soared upward.

But in the states of the upper Midwest, the site of the traditional smokestack industries, economic conditions deteriorated. Agricultural and energy-producing states also slumped during the 1980s. While the Northeast and the West Coast boomed, much of the rest of the country was mired in a decade-long stagnation and recession. Real wages, adjusted for inflation, continued to stagnate in many parts of the country during the 1980s. Real take-home pay for factory workers declined slightly from 1975 to 1987.

Revenue-sharing with state and local governments, enacted by Richard Nixon in 1972, was cut during the Reagan administration. Infrastructure repairs to roads and bridges were neglected. Cities, strapped for funds by shrinking tax bases and increasingly needy populations, were especially hard-hit by these losses of federal funds. Social services deteriorated.

During the 1980s, income differentials between upper-income and lower-income families widened. The number of poor women and children increased. One of the main reasons poverty was increasingly feminized was because of a sharp increase in the number of unwed mothers; the rate of children living with a never-married mother increased threefold during the 1980s. By the end of the 1980s, one-fourth of the children born in the United States were born to a never-married mother. The Reagan administration made matters worse for them by cutting funds for the Special Supplementary Nutrition Program for Women, Infants, and Children (WIC), which provided both prenatal and postnatal care to low-income women.

During the 1980s, the poverty rate in America regressed to approximately where it had been in the mid-1960s, to about 15 percent. But poverty in America had changed by the mid-1980s. Whereas the elderly had comprised a majority of the poor people of America in the mid-1960s, by the mid-1980s, most of the poor consisted of single mothers, children, and young men with low educational and job skills. A sizeable proportion of the 1980s poor worked full- or part-time at minimum-wage levels. Millions of the new jobs created during the 1980s were full-time or part-time service-sector jobs that paid only minimum wages.

Homeless people constituted a growing proportion of the 1980s poor population. The homeless, the poorest of the poor, came from many backgrounds: the unemployed, the mentally ill, the drug and alcohol abusers, people with serious medical problems (including AIDS victims), racial minorities, runaways, dysfunctional Vietnam veterans, and women fleeing abusive husbands. Many of the homeless struggled to survive, living on the streets of large cities and begging for food and money.

If prospering yuppies represented the glittering successes of the Reagan era, the homeless represented the abject failures. Nobody knew exactly how many homeless there were in America in the 1980s. Estimates ranged from a low of 200,000 up to more than a million. President Reagan, while expressing his personal sympathy for the plight of the homeless, proposed no new federal programs to alleviate their suffering or to get them off of the streets. The assistance that existed for the pathetic armies of the homeless came mostly from local governments, private charities, churches, and compassionate individuals. Most Americans, embracing individualistic values, apparently oblivious to the medical, cultural, and socioeconomic causes of destitution, in Barbara Ehrenreich's words, "relieved their consciences by vilifying the destitute."

Washington's lack of interest in the plight of homeless people, AIDS victims, and the poor generally, even for the problems besetting millions of hard-working middle-class families, characterized an era that celebrated crass materialism. Although personally kind and of humble origins, President Reagan saluted the culture of greed when he announced that he wanted America always to remain a country where anyone could get rich. First Lady Nancy Reagan set the tone for the 1980s, wearing gowns designed by the world's most exclusive couturiers, as she hosted glittering White House galas attended by Hollywood celebrities and wealthy corporate executives. Actress Jane Fonda, who had traveled to Hanoi to protest the Vietnam War in 1972, became an entrepreneur in the 1980s. Fonda made millions promoting physical fitness and selling exercise videos. In 1987, Donald Trump, a billionaire real estate magnate, wrote a book, *Trump: The Art of the Deal*, that became a best-seller. Trump emerged as an icon of the era of greed.

Social and cultural critics vigorously attacked the dominant values of the New Gilded Age and its foremost practitioners. They attacked the rampant individualism and the obsessive focus

FIGURE 14.3   Street people who live on the top of the steam vents of the Philadelphia sidewalks get comfortable for the night.   *Source:* AP/Wide World Photos. Photo by Putsy Kennedy.

on wealth-getting. They called for people to embrace a more communitarian ethic and to show a greater regard for the well-being of all Americans. In 1987, Oliver Stone, the son of a stockbroker, directed *Wall Street*, a movie in which Gordon Gecko, a ruthless speculator who specialized in hostile takeovers that made him fabulously wealthy, played by Michael Douglas, proclaims "Greed is Good!" Novelist Tom Wolfe's *The Bonfire of the Vanities* portrayed New York City as a violent concrete jungle riven by class and racial divides that separated rich from poor and blacks from whites. The focus of Wolfe's satire was on small groups of bond traders and corporate lawyers who proclaimed themselves "masters of the universe."

RESHAPING THE SUPREME COURT

In the field of civil liberties, Reagan, like most conservatives, believed that the court system favored the rights of accused criminals over law-abiding citizens, who were often victims of violent crimes. During the 1980s, both the Congress and the states, responding to widespread popular concerns, took a stronger law-and-order line. Longer, mandatory sentences were imposed for many crimes. Many states reinstituted the death penalty for heinous crimes. By the end of the 1980s, over a million Americans were incarcerated, the highest rate of incarceration for any country in the world. Each year during the 1980s, many more new prisons than new schools were constructed.

Over the course of his presidency, Reagan appointed over 400 federal judges; these jurists constituted about 60 percent of all sitting federal judges in 1989. The president also appointed a chief justice and three associate justices to the Supreme Court. The administration searched for strict constructionists whose constitutional views could also incorporate right-wing social agendas, including opposition to affirmative action programs, abortion, and pornography. Reaganite judges were also expected to support efforts to restore prayer in the public schools and to favor the death penalty.

In 1981, Reagan had appointed Sandra Day O'Connor, and in 1986 he selected Antonin Scalia to be associate justices of the Supreme Court. Both O'Connor and Scalia were conservatives. Reagan had also replaced retiring chief justice Warren Burger with Associate Justice William Rehnquist, the most conservative member of the Court. Reagan's efforts to add a third justice to the High Court proved difficult. His first choice, Appellate Judge Robert Bork, was rejected by the Senate because of his extreme views concerning First Amendment rights. Reagan eventually appointed another judicial conservative, Anthony Kennedy, who was unanimously confirmed by the Senate in February 1988.

Gradually, the Reagan appointees on the Supreme Court shifted the tenor of its decisions in a conservative direction. It chipped away at some of the rights of the accused established in previous decisions. The Reagan Court also put some restraints on government affirmative action policies. In *City of Richmond v. J. A. Croson Company* (1989), the Court nullified a government set-aside program that reserved a proportion of government contracts for minority groups.

THE SLEAZE FACTOR

In December 1987, former White House adviser Michael Deaver, who operated a political consulting service, was convicted on three counts of perjury for denying that he improperly used his White House connections to help clients. In February 1988, Attorney General Edwin Meese became the latest in a long line of Reagan administration officials to be accused of having a conflict of interest and of conducting himself improperly. The charges against Meese stemmed from his alleged financial relations with a small company that received a defense contract. He came under further attack for his alleged awareness of a proposal to bribe Israeli officials to guarantee that they would not attack a planned oil pipeline construction project in the Middle East. Further problems for Meese developed at the Justice Department when several top officials resigned in April 1988 because they believed that Meese's mounting problems prevented him from exerting strong leadership of the department. Despite his troubles and declining credibility, Meese continued to enjoy the support of President Reagan, who gave his longtime friend and adviser a strong vote of confidence.

In addition to these revelations of wrongdoing and improprieties at high levels in the White House came the disclosure in 1988 through the memoirs of Donald Regan, who had formerly been Reagan's secretary of the treasury and then chief of staff, that the president, following the attempt on his life, had permitted his wife Nancy, who had consultations with an astrologer, to influence his scheduling. By the end of Reagan's presidency, allegations of illegal and unethical activities tarnished the reputations of more than 100 of Reagan's current and former White House officials.

Reagan administration officials were not the only politicians to be plagued by scandal in 1987 and 1988. The leading contender for the Democratic presidential nomination, Gary Hart, had to abandon his campaign for seven months when a newspaper reporter disclosed that Hart had spent a weekend with an attractive model. When Hart belatedly reentered the race in 1988, he found that he had lost all of his organization and most of his popular support, and he had to abandon his candidacy. Another Democratic presidential hopeful, Senator Joseph Biden of Delaware, had to withdraw when reporters learned that he had frequently plagiarized the speeches of other politicians and had padded his academic record.

Brief Bibliographic Essay

A recent book, *The Age of Reagan: A History 1974–2008*, by Sean Wilentz, is the best study yet done on how the modern conservative movement came to power and has dominated national politics for most of the past three decades. Wilentz shows why Ronald Reagan has been the single most important political figure of the conservative era. Lee Edwards, *The Conservative Revolution: The Movement That Remade America*, traces the rise of modern conservatism from its origins in Cold War anti-Communism. Another recent book, *Transforming America*, by Robert M. Collins, is a balanced survey of the Reagan presidency. John Ehrman, *The Eighties: America in the Age of Reagan*, is the best account of domestic politics during the Eighties. The most informed account of the Reagan presidency is Lou Cannon's *President Reagan: The Role of a Lifetime*. President Reagan has written a solid memoir, *An American Life*. Garry Wills, *Reagan's America: Innocents at Home*, is an interpretive account. P. C. Roberts' *The Supply-Side Revolution* defends Reaganomics. T. B. Edsall's *The New Politics of Inequality* attacks the president's economic policies.

CHAPTER

15

Reviving the Cold War

Reagan's conduct of U.S. foreign policy was shaped by his core belief that the United States was an exceptional nation with a mission—to outlast and ultimately destroy Communism and to spread democracy throughout the world. He unshackled the CIA, using it to counter terrorist threats and Soviet intervention into Afghanistan. He supported U.S. interventionism in the Caribbean basin and Central America in order to prevent the Soviet Union from acquiring additional influence in the Western Hemisphere.

During his second term, he pursued a more pragmatic policy toward the Soviet Union and its reformist leader Mikhail Gorbachev. The two presidents held a series of summit conferences and eventually produced a treaty, which required both sides to eliminate a whole class of nuclear missiles. The agreement significantly reduced tensions between the two superpowers. Reagan's presidency ended before the collapse of the Soviet Empire in eastern Europe, followed soon after by the dissolution of the Soviet Union itself, which suddenly ended the Cold War.

Also during Reagan's second term, the Iran-Contra scandals threatened for a time to ruin his presidency; however, improving relations with the Soviet Union restored his popularity. He left office in January 1989 as one of the most popular presidents of the modern era.

THE OLD COLD WARRIOR

For the new president, the traditional verities of the Cold War still prevailed: America and its allies were locked in a life-or-death struggle for survival with a ruthless, expansionist Soviet empire. Reagan repudiated previous efforts at *detente* and announced his intention to challenge the Soviets around the globe. He launched a rapid buildup of military power. He also announced what came to be known as the "Reagan Doctrine"—that the United States would help anti-Communist resistance movements wherever they cropped up in the world. Reagan was the first president to take the offensive both ideologically and strategically against Communism since Harry Truman proclaimed his doctrine of Containment in 1947.

Reagan intended to use the CIA as an instrument of American foreign policy, especially its covert paramilitary operations. He freed U.S. arms sales from the restrictions imposed by the Carter administration and scrapped Carter's human rights policies. Reagan viewed the Cold War between the United States and the Soviet Union as fundamentally a moral conflict. He denounced the Soviet Union in a speech before the United Nations in 1982, charging that Soviet agents were working everywhere in the world, "violating human rights and unnerving the world with violence." Addressing the British Parliament, he insisted that "communist tyranny could not stop the march of freedom" and the Soviet Union would end up on "the ash heap of history." He told a gathering of evangelical Christians in Orlando, Florida, in May 1983, that the Soviet Union was "an evil empire."

Secretary of Defense Caspar Weinberger proposed a $1.2 trillion defense buildup, which Reagan strongly supported. It called for doubling U.S. military spending over five years, from $171 billion in 1981 to over $360 billion in 1986. Weinberger insisted that during Carter's presidency the Soviets had achieved strategic superiority over the United States. A "window of vulnerability" existed for American land-based missiles that could tempt the Soviets to try a "first-strike" nuclear attack. Weinberger ordered building a new strategic bomber, a new strategic missile, and an expanded Navy. Reagan and other top officials spoke of being able "to prevail" in the event of a nuclear war with the Soviets. Such rhetoric, yoked to the increases in military spending, frightened millions of Europeans and Americans, who feared that Reagan was preparing for a nuclear war with the Soviets.

Reagan initially found it difficult to assert pressure on Communist states. In late 1981, the Soviet Union forced Poland to impose martial law in order to crush a trade union movement that was pushing Poland toward democratic socialism. Reagan, outraged, found his options limited. He could not risk nuclear war with the Soviet Union. He could not persuade NATO allies to impose economic blockades on the USSR or Poland.

Reagan had more success in stymieing Soviet efforts to crush Afghanistan's *mujahadin* rebels during the early 1980s. The CIA shipped arms to Pakistan, which were then smuggled into Afghanistan. The Soviets soon found themselves bogged down in a Vietnam-like quagmire. The Soviets also tried to interdict the movement of arms and supplies from Pakistan and threatened the Pakistanis if they did not desist, all to no avail. The *mujahadin*, despite absorbing heavy casualties, maintained a determined resistance to Soviet efforts to pacify them. The application of the Reagan Doctrine in Afghanistan succeeded.

Reagan succeeded in implementing Carter's 1979 initiative to place 572 intermediate-range cruise and Pershing II missiles in western Europe, which could strike targets in the western regions of the Soviet Union. These missiles would counter Soviet SS-20 missiles already deployed and aimed at NATO countries. This initiative provoked an angry response from the Soviets, who tried to stop it. It also aroused opposition from political leaders and peace groups in Europe, and from a "nuclear freeze" movement in the United States. In the spring of 1982, nearly a million nuclear freeze supporters gathered in Central Park, the largest political rally in U.S. history.

To offset European and domestic opposition to his plan, Reagan offered two new arms control initiatives. The first, called the "zero option," offered to cancel the proposed deployment of cruise and Pershing missiles in exchange for Soviet removal of their SS-20 missiles. The second, at a new series of arms talks between American and Soviet negotiators in Geneva, called START, proposed that both sides scrap one-third of their nuclear warheads and permit land-based missiles to have no more than half of the remaining warheads. The Soviets did not take these proposals seriously and quickly rejected both. They had no incentive to remove missiles already in place in exchange for cancellation of weapons not yet deployed. They rejected the second offer because 70 percent of their warheads were on land-based missiles, compared with about one-third for the United States. However, these U.S. arms control proposals reassured nervous Europeans and slowed the nuclear freeze movement. When the new missiles began arriving in Great Britain and West Germany in 1983, the Soviets broke off the START talks.

The United States escalated the arms race in 1983, when Reagan ordered the Pentagon to develop a Strategic Defense Initiative (SDI). The SDI was an immensely complex antimissile defense system that used high-powered, space-based lasers to destroy enemy missiles in flight. The SDI was quickly dubbed "Star Wars" by its critics. Many scientists expressed skepticism that the SDI could work. If it could be built, they estimated that it would take years and cost $1 trillion. If it proved successful, the defense system also would destabilize the arms race because it would force the Soviets to build more missiles and develop an SDI of their own.

Reagan passionately supported the SDI, which personally engaged him more than any other policy of his presidency except possibly the tax cuts. He assumed that SDI could be built and that it would free the world from the deadly trap of deterrence based on mutually assured destruction (MAD). He felt a visceral horror of nuclear warfare and believed that MAD locked both sides in a suicide pact. Whatever his public image or the views of his critics, Ronald Reagan was at heart an antinuclear idealist. He wanted to break the irrational logic of MAD, which kept both sides feverishly building ever more efficient weapons of mass destruction and also kept both societies in a state of perpetual angst.

The costly and dangerous nuclear arms race between the two superpowers roared on. Both sides continued to develop new weapons systems and to refine existing ones. Although both sides observed the unratified SALT II agreement, it placed few curbs on their activities. Arms control negotiations were suspended. The death of Russian leader Leonid Brezhnev, followed by two short tenures of old and sick successors, created a succession crisis for the Soviets.

In March 1985, a dynamic new leader emerged in the Soviet Union, Mikhail Gorbachev. Future negotiations on arms control between the two superpowers again became possible. Although he had escalated the arms race, and intensified the Cold War, Reagan's efforts against the Soviets did restore a measure of American pride and self-confidence. Reagan showed that he had no fear of the Soviet Union and exuded confidence that America would eventually win the Cold War. His great insight, derived at a time when few defense experts and Sovietologists shared his views, was that the Soviet Union was both evil and weak; it could be beaten if Americans kept the faith and increased defense spending. During his second term, he helped Gorbachev along in the dismantling of the Soviet empire that prepared the ground for the sudden collapse of Communism in eastern Europe.

THE PACIFIC RIM

Asia comprised a vast region of diverse nation-states which, many experts believed, was destined to become the center of American diplomatic concerns by the dawn of the twenty-first century. The most important nations were China, home to a quarter of the planet's six billion inhabitants, and Japan, a nation that had risen from the ashes of total defeat at the end of World War II to become an economic powerhouse by the 1970s. The economies of South Korea, Taiwan, Hong Kong, Malaysia, and Singapore were also thriving in the early 1980s; their prosperity in large measure fueled, like Japan's, on the sale of manufactures to the United States and western Europe.

Washington did not have good relations with China initially, mainly because of Reagan's efforts to bolster the military forces of Taiwan, which the Chinese considered an integral part of their country. In 1984, Sino-American relations improved when Premier Zhao Ziyang of the PRC visited the United States and signed agreements pledging cooperation between China and the United States in the crucial areas of industry, science, and technology. Reagan later visited China and signed pacts, pledging renewed cultural exchanges between the two countries.

Diplomacy with Japan was the Reagan administration's top priority. Japan's rapid economic growth during the 1970s and 1980s appeared to threaten American primacy. Japanese purchase of such cultural landmarks as CBS Records, Rockefeller Center, and Columbia Pictures highlighted the problem. The Reagan administration's first diplomatic initiative was an effort to get Japan to pay a larger share of its defense costs rather than continue to sit comfortably behind the nuclear shield provided by U.S. taxpayers. The Japanese subsequently increased their defense outlays, to about 0.75 of 1 percent of GDP, much less than what the Americans wanted.

Washington was also concerned about the growing imbalance in U.S.–Japanese trade that increasingly favored the Japanese. The imbalance had reached $10 billion in 1980 and $16 billion in 1981. The largest part of the imbalance derived from the sale of Japanese cars to U.S. consumers. In 1981, Japanese automakers sold almost 2 million cars to American buyers, hurting domestic automakers, who had lost 25 percent of their market to the Japanese in a decade. U.S. negotiators persuaded the Japanese to reduce voluntarily auto shipments to America for 1982, and they also convinced the Japanese to reduce barriers to the importation of U.S. agricultural commodities. Despite these concessions, the trade imbalance continued to grow in favor of Japan for the rest of the decade.

The Communist leaders of Vietnam discovered that they were far better equipped to fight U.S. imperialism than they were to provide a prosperous economy for their people. Soviet subsidies kept the backward Vietnamese economy afloat. Each year, thousands of Vietnamese fled the country for Taiwan, Hong Kong, France, and the United States. Vietnam also maintained 200,000 troops in Kampuchea (formerly Cambodia) to support a puppet regime that the Vietnamese had installed in 1979. The Reagan administration indicated its displeasure with Vietnamese imperialism and also sought an accounting from the Hanoi government of the fate of thousands of American servicemen still missing in action (MIA) from the war. Washington made it clear to the Vietnamese leaders that there could be no improvement in official American–Vietnamese relations until Vietnam pulled its troops out of Kampuchea and settled the MIA issue to the satisfaction of the concerned families.

DISASTER IN LEBANON

In the Middle East, the Reagan administration tried to continue the peace process established by Carter by providing Israel with strategic security and giving the Palestinians a homeland on the West Bank. The larger goal of U.S. Middle Eastern policy continued to be containing Soviet influence in that strategic region. While trying to implement its policies, the United States became embroiled in a civil war going on in Lebanon. Israel continued its policy of gradual annexation of the West Bank, ignoring the national aspirations of the Palestinians. In June 1982, in an effort to destroy the PLO, Israeli forces invaded Lebanon and besieged West Beirut, where refugee camps contained thousands of Palestinians and provided a base for PLO fighters. The PLO and other Muslim factions in Lebanon turned to Syria and to Hezbollah, a terrorist organization controlled by the Ayatollah Khomeini, in order to counter the Israeli forces.

U.S. policy in Lebanon appeared contradictory. Even as it supported the Israeli invasion, the Reagan administration employed an envoy of Lebanese descent, Philip Habib, who arranged for the Israelis to lift their siege, while a UN force supervised the removal of PLO forces. Following the removal of the PLO, the Israelis reoccupied West Beirut. On September 17, 1982,

Lebanese Christian militia, working closely with Israeli forces, entered two Palestinian refugee camps and slaughtered hundreds of people in reprisal for the murder three days earlier of a Christian leader. In a well-intentioned, but clumsy and dangerous, move, President Reagan sent U.S. forces to Beirut to try to restore order.

The U.S. forces came under siege themselves as civil war raged in the streets of Beirut between Christian and Muslim militias. Syrian forces, aided by the Soviets, occupied eastern Lebanon and controlled most of the Muslim factions. Hezbollah militants also provided support and helped to train the militias. Israeli troops remained in southern Lebanon. The 1,500 U.S. Marines, isolated at the Beirut airport, without a clear-cut mission or sufficient force to maintain order, were perceived by the Muslims and their foreign supporters to be aligned with the Christian forces.

Early on the morning of October 23, 1983, a yellow Mercedes truck, loaded with explosives, slammed into the U.S. Marine compound near the Beirut airport. The powerful blast

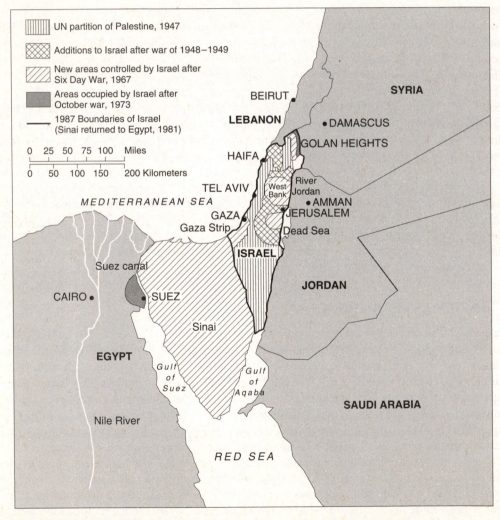

FIGURE 15.1 The Middle East, 1947–1981. *Source:* U.S. State Department.

killed 241 Marines who were sleeping inside. Reagan was forced to withdraw the remaining U.S. forces in February 1984. The civil war went on. Syria remained the major force in Lebanese affairs. Lebanon became a fertile source of kidnappings and terrorist attacks on U.S. citizens. Moderate Arab states refused to support U.S. Middle East policy, and the peace process appeared hopelessly stalled. Lebanon was a humiliating defeat for the Reagan administration, and the slaughter of the Marines constituted the worst U.S. military disaster since Vietnam.

POLICING THE WESTERN HEMISPHERE

Reagan administration officials also gave a high priority to Western Hemispheric affairs. Canada and America had long been each other's principal trading partner, and the two democratic nations shared the longest unfortified international boundary in the world. Canada was also the chief supplier of foreign oil to the United States. Even so, relations between the two countries had not been warm in recent years. Canadian nationalists had long resented U.S. domination of many sectors of their economic life, and the two countries often were at odds over trade policies, NATO affairs, fishing rights, disarmament policies, and pollution.

Relations between the two nations improved after a new conservative government, headed by Brian Mulroney, came to power in 1984. Mulroney and Reagan soon established a warm, personal relationship. Together they brought about a historic agreement: a treaty removing all barriers to trade between their two countries. The agreement went into effect in December 1988, making the Canadian–U.S. market the largest international free-trade zone in the world.

Washington made its top priority overthrowing the Sandinista government in Nicaragua. Reagan viewed the Sandinista regime as having the potential of becoming another Cuba. He feared that the Sandinistas would use Nicaraguan military bases as staging areas to export Marxist-Leninist revolution to neighboring countries. He accused the Sandinistas of aiding Marxist rebels in nearby El Salvador.

In the spring of 1982, Reagan approved the use of CIA political and paramilitary operations to interdict arms shipments from Nicaragua to El Salvador and to overthrow the Sandinista regime. Washington's chosen instrument for deposing the Sandinistas was to be a "Contra" military force recruited from various groups of anti-Sandinista Nicaraguans, including former supporters of the deposed dictator, Anastasio Somoza Debayle.

Congress, skeptical of Reagan's Central American policy, enacted the Boland Amendment in December 1982, which forbade the CIA or the Pentagon to provide any funds or training to anyone for the purpose "of overthrowing the government of Nicaragua." Reagan appealed to Congress in 1983 for funds to "hold the line against externally supported aggression" in Central America. Congress initially rejected Reagan's request for $80 million to support CIA covert operations against Nicaragua; later, it approved $24 million for those activities.

Meanwhile, the CIA continued its war on the Sandinistas. Contra forces, trained by the CIA at bases in neighboring Honduras, began operations inside Nicaragua. Other CIA-trained forces attacked various port installations at several sites. In early 1984, helicopters flown by CIA-trained operatives mined three of Nicaragua's major harbors. When Congress learned that CIA-trained forces had mined Nicaraguan harbors and damaged merchant ships, it cut off all

American aid for the Contras. The World Court later ruled that the United States had violated international law and that Nicaragua could sue America for damages.

With funding of its secret war in Nicaragua cut off by Congress, the Reagan administration made a deal with the Saudi Arabians, whereby the United States sold the Saudis 400 Stinger aircraft missiles, in return for which they agreed to provide the Contras with $10 million. The administration also persuaded Israel to aid the Contras, and wealthy Americans also chipped in money. The Iran-Contra scandal originated in these efforts at creative financing to keep Washington's proxy war in Nicaragua afloat and to circumvent the will of Congress embodied in the Boland Amendment.

In El Salvador, the war between left-wing guerrillas and a right-wing government continued. Carter had cut off U.S. aid to the government following the murder of three American nuns by government forces. The Reagan administration restored and increased U.S. assistance and sent in forty-five U.S. military advisers to help government forces. The United States backed a government headed by a moderate democrat, Jose Napoleon Duarte. Duarte defeated the candidate of the extreme Right, Roberto d'Aubisson, in a 1984 election, and he began a reform program. He also tried to curb the excesses of right-wing "death squads" that had murdered thousands of civilians since the war began. But Duarte's forces could not defeat the rebels. The civil war in El Salvador raged on.

While the Reagan administration pursued its proxy war against the Sandinistas in Nicaragua and backed the Duarte government in El Salvador, it also fought a brief miniwar for control of Grenada, a small island in the eastern Caribbean. On October 25, 1983, two days after the terrorist attack that had killed 241 U.S. Marines near the Beirut airport, 1,900 U.S. forces stormed ashore in Grenada. The main purpose of the invasion was to overthrow a Marxist regime headed by General Hudson Austin, who had recently come to power. What most concerned the Reagan administration was the construction of an airport at Point Salines that was capable of accommodating Fidel Castro's air force. The runway could also serve as a refueling station for Soviet aircraft ferrying weapons to the Sandinistas. Within four days, U.S. forces had overwhelmed the small Grenadian army and 784 Cuban construction workers who had been working on the airport. U.S. forces deposed the Austin regime and shipped the Cubans back to their island. U.S. officials installed a friendly, interim government and granted it $30 million in military and economic assistance. UN spokesmen, and, within the United States, liberal media pundits and politicians, condemned the Grenada operation. But most Americans supported Reagan's strong actions in defense of U.S. interests in the Caribbean.

While these dramatic developments were occurring in Grenada, the Reagan administration continued its support of the Contra rebels fighting to overthrow the Sandinistas. In the summer of 1985, Congress approved $100 million in support of the Contras.

A peaceful alternative to war in Nicaragua surfaced late in 1987, when President Oscar Arias Sanchez of Costa Rica, speaking for the leaders of four Central American republics meeting in Guatemala City, proposed a plan calling for an end to U.S. military backing of the Contras, the restoration of democracy in Nicaragua, and negotiations between the Sandinista government and Contra leaders leading to a cease-fire. Reagan administration officials agreed to let Arias try to implement his plan, and Nicaraguan leader Daniel Ortega Saavedra appeared willing to accept some of the proposals. In April 1988, both sides agreed to a temporary cease-fire, and Congress voted $48 million for humanitarian aid for the Contras.

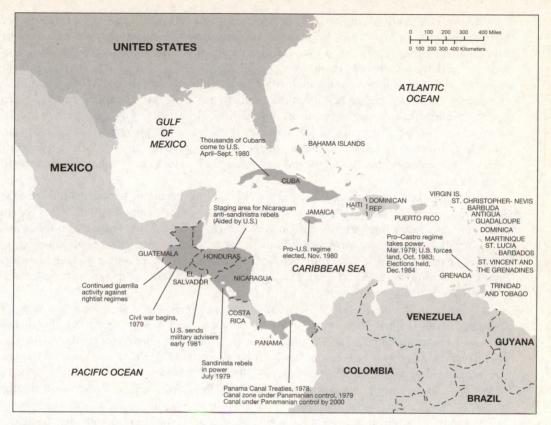

FIGURE 15.2   The United States in Central America, 1978–1990.   *Source:* Public Domain Map.

INTERNATIONAL CRISES

During his second term, President Reagan had to deal with many challenging international problems. Global financial crises threatened as Third World nations sank deeper into debt. The collective debt of Argentina, Brazil, and Mexico approached $250 billion, most of it owed to U.S. and European banks. The possibility of these countries ever repaying their debts appeared nil, and default, which could derange international financial transactions and do serious harm to major U.S. banks, remained a constant danger.

International terrorism was another mounting problem. Beginning in the 1970s, terrorist attacks had escalated during the 1980s. Between 1981 and 1986, thousands of people were kidnapped, injured, or killed by terrorists. The State Department estimated that approximately 700 major terrorist assaults occurred in the world in 1985. Many terrorists had their roots in the bitter conflicts in Lebanon between Christian and Arab factions, and in the continuing war between Israelis forces and Palestinian fighters. Arab terrorist organizations, dedicated to the destruction of Israel and to attacking its Western supporters, frequently targeted Americans. The slaughter of the American Marines in Beirut in 1983 was the worst of many Muslim terrorist attacks against Americans. In June 1985, Lebanese Muslim terrorists hijacked an American jetliner and held thirty-nine Americans hostage for seventeen days. In October 1985, four members of the Palestinian Liberation Army seized an Italian cruise ship, the *Achille Lauro*, killing a disabled elderly American. In April 1986, U.S. military installations in West Germany were bombed by Palestinian terrorists supported by Libya. In retaliation, American bombers attacked targets in and near the Libyan capital of Tripoli.

In South Africa, a racist white minority continued its rule over black, Asian, and mixed-race groups that comprised 86 percent of the population. The Reagan administration, following a policy it called "constructive engagement" toward the South African *apartheid* regime, refrained from public criticism and tried to nudge it toward democracy. The policy produced few results, and South Africa was racked by violence in the mid-1980s as government security forces violently repressed black demonstrators. Angry and frustrated blacks sometimes retaliated with terrorist attacks of their own.

Critics of "constructive engagement" believed that only economic pressure could force the South African government to dismantle *apartheid*. Fourteen states and forty-one cities passed divestiture laws restricting or prohibiting the investment in South Africa of pension funds and requiring the selling off of current holdings in South African securities. Some universities ordered partial or full divestment. In October 1986, Congress, overriding a presidential veto, imposed economic sanctions on South Africa, including a boycott of South African products and a ban on new U.S. loans and investment in that country.

The Reagan administration also had to confront a crisis in the Philippines, the former territory and longtime ally of the United States. For years, a corrupt military dictator, whom Washington had supported, Ferdinand Marcos, had been losing power. Communist rebels were gaining strength in several regions of the country. Pressure from U.S. officials forced Marcos to permit elections that had been suspended since he took office. In February 1986, he was challenged by Corazon Aquino, the widow of an assassinated political opponent of Marcos. Both sides claimed victory in an election marked by violence and fraud. U.S. officials, worried about the declining Philippine economy and the rising Communist insurgency in a strategically important country, pressured Marcos to resign. He fled Manila in March 1986, and Aquino assumed office. She worked to restore political democracy, revamp the economy, maintain friendly relations with America, and remove the Communist threat.

THE IRAQI–IRANIAN WAR

The continuing Iraqi–Iranian War reached menacing proportions in 1987. The stalemated war spilled into the Persian Gulf and threatened vital oil shipments that flowed daily from the Gulf oil fields to Europe, Japan, and the United States. Iraq attacked Iran's oil-export terminals and also struck at Iranian tankers carrying oil from the Gulf. Iran could not strike at Iraqi oil shipments directly because Iraq's oil traveled through pipelines to terminals on the Mediterranean and Black Seas, but the Iranians attacked ships hauling oil from Kuwait, an Arab emirate that was bankrolling Iraq's war against Iran.

Soviet entry into the Gulf, along with both Iraqi and Iranian threats to Gulf oil shipping, caused President Reagan to send a large fleet of U.S. Navy vessels to the region to provide naval escorts for oil convoys. In what amounted to armed intervention into the shipping war, Washington agreed to reflag and escort tankers carrying oil produced by Kuwait. In the summer of 1987, an American guided-missile frigate, stationed in the Gulf, was attacked, apparently by accident, by an Iraqi plane, resulting in the loss of thirty-eight lives. Then, on July 3, 1988, there occurred an even more ghastly accident when the destroyer USS *Vincennes* fired a missile that brought down an Iranian airliner, killing all 290 people aboard. Crewmen aboard the American destroyer apparently thought that it was an Iranian fighter closing in on their ship for an attack.

Washington feared that a victory by either Saddam Hussein's secular Iraqi regime or Khomeini's Islamic fundamentalist Iranian government would make the winner the dominant power in the Persian Gulf. To prevent either side from winning the war—a victory that could threaten the political stability of Saudi Arabia, Kuwait, and other moderate Arab regimes, and disrupt the flow of oil to the United States and its allies—America, behind an official facade of neutrality, secretly aided whichever side appeared to be losing.

In the early years of the war, Washington helped Iran, but after 1986, America aided Saddam Hussein's Iraq. In April 1988, there occurred a series of clashes between U.S. and Iranian naval units.

The Iraqi–Iranian War ended in August 1988 when Ayatollah Khomeini accepted a UN-proposed cease-fire. At the time, Iraq had gained the upper hand, and the Iranian enthusiasm for war had subsided after six years of slaughter. Saddam Hussein, weary of the long war, readily consented to the cease-fire. Mutual exhaustion had brought an end to war. During the war, the Iraqis had used poison gas against the Iranians and were feverishly working to develop nuclear weapons. Despite these ominous indicators, the Reagan administration continued to back Iraq, considering it a necessary counterforce to the Iranians. Washington's support of Saddam Hussein in the late 1980s is one of the background causes of the 1991 Persian Gulf War.

As the war between Iraq and Iran ended, the Arab–Israeli conflict took another violent turn. Palestinians living in the West Bank and Gaza took to the streets to protest the continuing Israeli occupation of the two territories. This Palestinian *intifida* ("uprising") continued intermittently through 1988 and 1989, resulting in the deaths of hundreds of Palestinians and a dozen Israeli soldiers. The Israeli government, headed by Prime Minister Yitzhak Shamir, refused to consider any resolution of the conflict that established a Palestinian state in the occupied territories. He also refused to meet with Yasir Arafat and the PLO, the only organization that represented a majority of the Palestinians. The Reagan administration backed the Shamir government's refusal to meet with PLO leaders, but supported political arrangements in the occupied territories that would give the Palestinians autonomy.

IRAN-CONTRA

Two weeks after the midterm elections in November 1986, Americans were shocked to learn that the Reagan administration had entered into secret negotiations with Iranian officials that involved selling them arms in exchange for the release of American hostages held captive in Lebanon by Muslim terrorists. Two weeks after Americans had learned of the arms-for-hostages deals with Iran, Attorney General Edwin Meese told a stunned press conference audience that his investigators had discovered that profits from the Iranian arms sales had been sent to Contra rebels fighting in Nicaragua, even though Congress had enacted legislation forbidding U.S. military aid to the rebel fighters.

President Reagan denied that he had authorized trading arms for hostages, and he insisted that he had no knowledge of any such transactions. He claimed that an operative with the National Security Council, Marine Lieutenant Colonel Oliver North, was mainly responsible for both the dealings with Iran and the Contra arms sales, and that only North's immediate superior, National Security adviser Vice Admiral John Poindexter, knew of his activities. For the first time in his presidency, Reagan's integrity and competence were seriously questioned by the citizenry. His public approval rating dropped precipitously, from 67 percent to 46 percent. For a time, the Iran-Contra scandal threatened to ruin the Reagan presidency; some commentators had visions of Watergate *redux*.

The origins of the Iran-Contra scandals went back to 1981 when President Reagan ordered CIA director William Casey to organize an anti-Sandinista force among Nicaraguan exiles living in Honduras. Over the next several years, these Contra forces waged a guerrilla war against the Sandinista forces. Congress enacted the Boland Amendment, which forbade the use of any U.S. funds for the purpose of trying to overthrow the Sandinista government. Reagan, committed to the goal of overthrowing the Sandinistas, instructed the CIA, the National Security Council, and the Pentagon to ignore the Boland Amendment. Casey, National Security adviser Robert McFarlane, and one of McFarlane's aides, Colonel North, persuaded a handful of U.S. allies, including Israel and Saudi Arabia, to provide funds for the Contras.

While President Reagan and his subordinates supported the Contras in Nicaragua, the administration also began an involvement with Iran aimed at freeing U.S. hostages being held in Lebanon by pro-Iranian Muslim terrorists. In July 1985, an Iranian arms dealer, Manucher Ghobanifar, met with McFarlane. Ghobanifar claimed to represent a moderate faction within the Iranian government that wanted to improve relations with America. He proposed to McFarlane that the United States, working through Israeli middlemen, arrange for the delivery of TOW antitank missiles to Iran that the Iranians desperately needed for their ongoing war with Iraq. In return, the moderates would work to arrange the release of some of the American hostages. A few months later, Reagan authorized the sale of 100 TOW missiles to Iran. At the time he authorized the sale of the weapons, Reagan clearly understood that the United States was trading arms for hostages. He also knew that it was against the law and contrary to U.S. policy to sell weapons to Iran because of its support of international terrorism.

But no hostages were freed after this initial transaction. Ghobanifar told McFarlane that the Iranians wanted an additional 400 missiles in exchange for the release of a single hostage. McFarlane arranged for the missiles to be sent, and on September 15, 1986, one of the American hostages, Benjamin Weir, was set free. In November, Ghobanifar was back with another deal: Send Iran 100 HAWK surface-to-air missiles and five American hostages would be freed. In December, President Reagan signed a secret document, called a "finding," which approved the proposed sale. The finding described the transaction as an arms-for-hostages deal.

Even though the several arms sales to Iran had yielded only one released hostage, John Poindexter, who replaced McFarlane as National Security adviser in December 1985, working through North, arranged for another shipment of arms to Iran. Colonel North arranged to have 3,000 TOW missiles and another 100 HAWK missiles sent in exchange for the remaining six Americans who were still held captive by terrorists in Lebanon. Both Secretary of State George Schultz and Secretary of Defense Caspar Weinberger strongly opposed the arms-for-hostages transactions because they were illegal and did not serve the national interest.

It was North who devised the plan to divert the profits from the sale of arms to the Iranians to the Contras. In February 1986, a sale of 1,000 TOW missiles to the Iranians netted a profit of about $8 million. North gave the money to retired Air Force Major General Richard Secord to buy arms for the Contras.

In March, two more Americans in Lebanon were taken hostage. After four arms shipments to the Iranians, more Americans than ever were held hostage. On July 26, Iran arranged for the release of another American hostage. Another shipment of missiles was sent to Iran, but it resulted in no further prisoners being freed. On November 2, just before the midterm elections, a final arms shipment was sent to Iran, which resulted in the release of another hostage, David Jacobsen.

On October 5, 1986, a plane hauling weapons to the Contras was shot down, and the Sandinistas captured an air crewman, who confessed to his captors that he was part of a secret U.S. program to aid the Contras. On November 1, the Lebanese magazine *Al Shiraa* ran a story about the U.S. arms-for-hostages deals with Iran, which Iranian officials quickly confirmed.

Three weeks later, Edwin Meese made his stunning announcement that money from the sale of arms to Iran had been diverted to the Contra war effort against the Sandinistas.

The fallout from the Iran-Contra scandal was far worse than Watergate. It severely damaged U.S. foreign policy. The Saudis and other moderate Arab states felt an acute sense of betrayal over the news that U.S. officials had sold antitank and antiaircraft missiles to Khomeini's government in the hope of securing the release of seven Americans being held hostage in Lebanon. At home, there was widespread condemnation for conducting a clandestine foreign policy in Central America against the expressed wishes of Congress, contrary to public opinion, and in violation of the law.

The essence of the Iran-Contra scandal involved officials within the Reagan administration selling weapons to an outlaw regime to raise money for illegal purposes. Constitutional scholars saw an important principle at stake. By circumventing the congressional ban on aid to the Contras, the architects of the Iran-Contra scandal also had circumvented Article 1 of the Constitution, which vested all control over public moneys in Congress.

Following the revelations about trading arms for hostages and aiding the Contras, there occurred several official investigations of the details. A federal court appointed an independent counsel, Lawrence Walsh, to investigate the scandals. President Reagan appointed a commission headed by former Senator John Tower to investigate the affair. Both the Senate and House appointed committees to examine the scandals. The Tower Commission's report was made public in March 1987. It portrayed Reagan as an out-of-touch president who had surrounded himself with irresponsible advisers pursuing ideologically driven policies that harmed the national interest.

Reagan responded with a speech to the American people on March 4. He acknowledged responsibility for the Iran-Contra affair, but he insisted that it was not his intent to trade arms for hostages and that he knew nothing about using some of the money obtained from Iran to buy arms for the Contras. Reagan's pseudoconfession partially restored his popularity, but the investigators kept on digging.

In the summer of 1987, the combined congressional committees began holding televised hearings. At times, the hearings evoked memories of Watergate as congressmen tried to follow the money trail, find out how the profits from arms sales to Iran were channeled to the Contras, and discover who profited from all of these illegal transactions.

Two of the witnesses appearing before the committees, General Secord and Robert McFarlane, implicated the president in their testimonies. They insisted that Reagan was repeatedly briefed about the arms sales to Iran and approved of the efforts to get the hostages released. They also implicated the late CIA Director William Casey, who may have been the mastermind behind the Iran-Contra operations and who may have worked through Colonel North and former National Security adviser Vice Admiral John Poindexter to avoid congressional oversight and public disclosure as required by law.

The two key witnesses to appear before the committees, Colonel North and Vice Admiral Poindexter, both insisted that they had kept President Reagan uninformed about the details of the Iranian negotiations and that they never told him of the government's involvement in shipping arms to the Contras. They also admitted that they had deliberately misinformed Congress and the press about their actions. Colonel North passionately defended his actions as being moral and patriotic, even though they did defy Congress and break the law.

The Congressional hearings were seriously flawed. They were hastily conducted, and investigators lacked crucial documents that would have enabled them to discover more of the

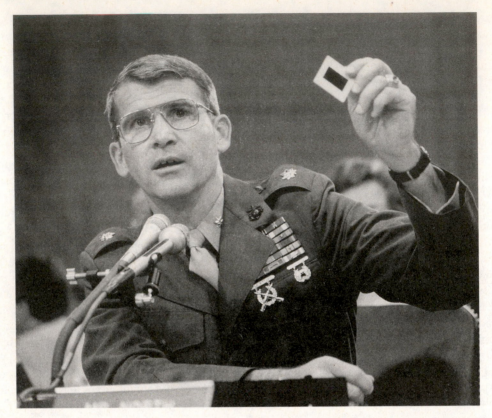

FIGURE 15.3   Lt. Col. Oliver North.   *Source:* AP/Wide World Photos. Photo by Lana Harris.

truth about the Iran-Contra scandals. Key witnesses lied or gave evasive answers. The investigating committees clearly did not have the stomach to press their investigation too close to Reagan, nor to consider the possibility of impeaching him. Walsh stated that if Congress had had all the facts in 1987 that his investigations later unearthed, it should have considered impeaching Reagan.

The committees issued a joint 450-page report on November 18, 1987, that was scathingly critical of the president. The report bluntly accused Reagan of not obeying his oath to uphold the Constitution and the laws of the land, and it said he bore "the ultimate responsibility" for the wrongdoing of his aides. The report stated that the Iran-Contra affair was "characterized by pervasive dishonesty and inordinate secrecy." It also voiced the suspicion that the president knew more about the arms sales and Contra-funding efforts than he acknowledged and challenged the credibility of Colonel North's and Vice Admiral Poindexter's testimony. Without citing specific individual actions or naming specific laws, the report asserted that "laws were broken" in the Iran-Contra affair.

Walsh continued his investigations. In March 1988, a federal grand jury indicted four of the most prominent participants in the Iran-Contra scandal, including Colonel North and Vice Admiral Poindexter. All were charged with multiple offenses, including conspiracy, fraud, theft, perjury, and covering up illegal operations. At his trial in 1990, Poindexter repudiated his testimony previously given before the congressional committees. He stated that Reagan was in charge of the Iran-Contra operations from the beginning and had ordered him, North, and others to violate the Boland Amendment.

President Reagan, now out of office, was called to testify at Poindexter's trial. In answers to 127 questions put to him by prosecutors, Reagan frequently gave confused and vague answers, and often he could not recall the names of subordinates or their activities. He reiterated that he was not involved in any wrongdoing and that he did not know what his subordinates were doing, or that they traded arms for hostages or diverted the profits to the Contras. It was a humiliating performance by Reagan. Some observers believed that he was exhibiting the early stages of Alzheimer's disease, which he later contracted. Poindexter was convicted of five felonies, including perjury. North was convicted of obstructing Congress and destroying confidential documents.

Walsh's investigations of officials involved in the Iran-Contra scandals did not have any significant impact even though he ultimately secured eleven convictions. Poindexter's and North's convictions were overturned on appeal. On Christmas Eve, 1992, President George H. W. Bush pardoned six others convicted of Iran-Contra crimes. Bush's pardons concluded this shabby episode that had stained the reputation and undermined the popularity of President Reagan.

THAWING THE COLD WAR

Reagan alarmed most of his conservative supporters when he softened his hard-line approach to the Soviet Union and authorized the resumption of arms negotiations. A dramatic moment in world history occurred when Soviet leader Mikhail Gorbachev and President Reagan met in Geneva from November 24 to November 27, 1985, the first summit conference since Carter had journeyed to Moscow in 1979. They achieved no major agreements on arms control because Reagan insisted that America would continue its development of the SDI, while Gorbachev demanded that the United States abandon the SDI before he would sign any arms control pacts.

A developing friendship between the two world leaders was the main consequence of the meetings. President Reagan toned down his anti-Communist rhetoric, saying Gorbachev was a man with whom he could do business. In the Soviet press, a new image of Reagan as a man who could be reasoned with had replaced a hostile version in which he had often been compared to Hitler.

Other summits followed the Geneva conference. At the first of these held in Reykjavik, Iceland, in October 1986, Gorbachev and Reagan almost reached major agreements on nuclear arms control. For one extraordinary moment at Reykjavik, both leaders flirted with the idea of *eliminating all American and Soviet nuclear weapons within ten years*! But a disagreement over Star Wars and the Anti-Ballistic Missile treaty caused both men to back away from any sweeping agreement on strategic nuclear weaponry. Frustrated by his failure to strike a deal with Gorbachev, President Reagan stood before the Brandenburg Gate in divided Berlin on June 12, 1987, and challenged the Soviets: "Mr. Gorbachev, open this gate! Mr. Gorbachev, tear down this wall!"

During the next year, Reagan replaced many of his hard-line anti-Communist advisers with a new breed of more pragmatic bureaucrats, who favored reaching arms control agreements with the Soviets. Frank Carlucci replaced Weinberger at Defense. Army General Colin Powell became the new head of the National Security Council. Senator Howard Baker replaced Donald Regan as the president's chief of staff. First Lady Nancy Reagan, concerned about her husband's place in

FIGURE 15.4   On December 8, 1987, President Reagan and General Secretary Mikhail Gorbachev signed the INF treaty, which eliminated an entire class of nuclear weapons. *Source:* National Archives and Records Administration.

history in the aftermath of the Iran-Contra scandal, urged him to seek a major arms control agreement with Gorbachev.

A year after Reykjavik, Gorbachev journeyed to the United States where he and Reagan signed a historic agreement in December 1987, known officially as the Intermediate-Range Nuclear Forces (INF) treaty, that eliminated an entire class of weapons, intermediate-range thermonuclear missiles, which had been located mostly in Europe. It also provided for inspectors of both nations to observe the dismantling and destruction of the intermediate-range missiles. The INF treaty was a major step toward reduction of tensions between the world's two most powerful nations.

The signing of the INF treaty and the return of *détente* with the Soviets also held out the promise of future agreements cutting strategic weaponry on both sides. Negotiators from both countries continued to work on a Strategic Arms Reduction Treaty (START).

In 1988, the Soviets also announced that they were ending a costly, futile war in Afghanistan, and their troops were withdrawn the following year. In addition to phasing out the Afghan quagmire, Gorbachev undertook a worldwide scaling back of Soviet diplomatic activity. He indicated that the Soviets might end their economic and military support of the Sandinistas. He urged the PLO to recognize Israel's right to exist. He pressured Hanoi to pull its troops out of Kampuchea. He pulled Soviet forces back from the Sino-Soviet border regions, and he urged the Soviet satellites in eastern Europe to reform their economies and become more involved with the nations of western Europe.

The sudden and quite remarkable turnabout in U.S.–Soviet relations culminated in Reagan's triumphant visit to Moscow in June 1988. He made a televised speech to the Soviet people and embraced his friend Mikhail Gorbachev at the site of Lenin's tomb. Gorbachev made another visit to America in December 1990. Reagan and Gorbachev staged a photo opportunity in front of the Statue of Liberty. Restoring *détente* with the Soviets represented President Reagan's most important diplomatic achievement.

Brief Bibliographic Essay

James T. Patterson, *Restless Giant,* has an informative chapter on Reagan's foreign policies. Sean Wilentz, *The Age of Reagan,* has a fine chapter on Reagan's conduct of the Cold War. Michael Mandelbaum's *Reagan and Gorbachev* is a good account of their personal diplomacy. Strobe Talbott's *Deadly Gambit* is a lucid analysis of the arcane complexities of arms control. Edward N. Luttwack's *Making the Military Work* is a critical study of the Reagan administration's military policies. The most thorough account of the Iran-Contra scandal that rocked the Reagan administration in 1986 and 1987 is Theodore Draper's *A Very Thin Line: The Iran-Contra Affairs.* Seth P. Tillman's *The United States and the Middle East: Interests and Obstacles* is a balanced treatment of American policy in that troubled region. Stansfield Turner's *Terrorism and Democracy* is a thoughtful study of one of the most serious and agonizing problems that U.S. presidents have had to deal with since the 1970s. Roy Gutman's *Banana Diplomacy* is a critical study of U.S. foreign policy in Nicaragua and El Salvador in the 1980s.

CHAPTER 16

Culture Wars and Social Tensions

The ideological and cultural warfare that raged during the 1990s originated in some of the conflicts that had begun in the 1960s. Culture wars intensified after 1992, following Bill Clinton's electoral triumph, which broke the Republican twelve-year hold on the White House. Deeply disappointed conservatives, particularly those on the Religious Right, believed that Clinton, the first baby-boomer president, epitomized all that had gone wrong with contemporary society and culture. They decried what they perceived to be a wide range of declines. Liberals, tolerant of many of the trends that conservatives denounced, joined by commercial interests profiting from some of them, battled back. They denounced conservatives as fanatics, bigots, and censors.

American society was also riven during these years by profound divisions. An immigration explosion, an unintended consequence of the liberal overhaul of American immigration policy during the heyday of Great Society reformism, revived immigration as a powerful social force and gave rise to demands for imposing new restrictions. An upsurge of multiculturalism, driven by the rights-conscious efforts of second-generation middle-class Asians and Hispanics, challenged the Anglocentrism of American popular culture. These challenges provoked furious responses from the defenders of the status quo. The class and racial divisions that had forever separated African Americans and white people continued in the 1990s, ensuring that black-white racial polarization perpetuated the most serious economic and social fissures of the era.

THE NEW ECONOMY

Many serious, intertwined economic problems, exacerbated by the recession that struck during the early 1990s, vexed the American people. Annual trade deficits ranged between $40 billion and $60 billion. Federal deficits continued to run up huge amounts of red ink. During the recession, about nine million workers were without jobs. Housing starts, new car sales, and business investment plummeted.

The recession had two major causes: cuts in defense spending in the aftermath of the Cold War and the collapse of commercial real estate markets in the wake of the overexpansion of the 1980s. More important, long-term structural weaknesses that had first appeared during the 1970s persisted into the 1990s. The fundamental problem was the slow rate of economic growth. From 1890 to 1970, the U.S. economy had grown at an annual rate of 3.5 percent, adjusted for inflation. Since 1973, including the boom years of the 1980s, the annual rate of growth averaged 2.2 percent.

By the mid-1990s, the U.S. economy had fully recovered from recession. From 1995 through 1999, the economy grew at an annual rate of 3.4 percent. By 1996, American industry once again led the world in productive efficiency. The stock market soared to record highs in the late 1990s, with high-tech stocks leading the way. Microsoft became the largest corporation in the world, primarily because of its virtual monopoly of Windows operating platforms. Bill Gates, the CEO of Microsoft and its largest individual stockholder, became the world's richest person. Gates personified the new economy of the 1990s, becoming an iconic figure.

There was a down side to the high-flying high-tech economy of the late 1990s. Corporate managers enjoyed high incomes, while blue-collar workers of the same companies struggled to earn a living wage and sustain their families. Many companies resorted to downsizing to increase profits or to survive in a more competitive environment. IBM laid off over half its workforce in the 1990s. Savings rates for Americans reached historic laws during the late-1990s. Millions of families reported a negative savings rate, and consumer debt rose rapidly.

During the peak years of the new economy, a ten-by-thirty-mile strip of Santa Clara County, California, located about 40 miles south of San Francisco, became the center of the microelectronics industry. In this "Silicon Valley," the consumer electronics revolution that had originated in the 1970s created a vast web of hundreds of high-tech firms that manufactured and distributed new information technologies.

Silicon Valley attracted extensive media attention, which reinforced its popular image as a place where brilliant, hard-driving entrepreneurs founded companies that churned out technological marvels and accumulated great personal fortunes. America had not seen anything like this generation of electronic buccaneers since the industrial revolution of the 1880s and 1890s.

Silicon Valley and the other regions within the United States where high-tech companies flourished plugged into the rapidly expanding global economy. U.S. companies competed fiercely with their rivals in Japan, Taiwan, and Korea. Silicon Valley also reflected the growing multiculturalism of American society; perhaps one-third of the engineers and technical personnel developing the software and hardware driving the new economy were people of Chinese or East Indian descent, many of them immigrants.

THE INFORMATION SUPER HIGHWAY

The revolution in telecommunications created the global information superhighway. The most significant electronic development was the creation of cyberspace, that abstract conceptual region occupied by people linked via global computer networks. The Net grew out of America's hysterical reaction to the Soviet launch of *Sputnik* in 1957. President Eisenhower created the Advanced Research and Design Projects Agency (ARPA) within the Department of Defense to ensure that U.S. scientists retained their lead over Soviet scientists in developing new technologies applicable to the military. ARPA scientists also turned their attention to computer networking and communications. They sought ways of linking universities, defense contractors, and military command centers in order to promote development of new weapons systems and to sustain vital communication pathways in the event of nuclear attacks.

They developed a network, called ARPANET, which went online in 1969. ARPANET linked giant computers housed at four universities—UCLA, Stanford, the University of Southern California (USC), and the University of Utah. The age of computer networks had arrived! By the early 1970s, ARPANET was reaching beyond its Cold War origins. More and more users were going online; nonmilitary researchers were developing competing systems of communications.

New computer languages were created that made communication among the proliferating networks difficult if not impossible. In 1974, Robert Kahn and Vincent Cerf, two ARPA computer scientists, developed the transmission control protocol/Internet protocol (TCP/IP), a uniform communications language (or protocol), which allowed all the existing communication networks to function and communicate as a single meta-network. The creation of TCP/IP was an extraordinary achievement that set the stage for the rapid expansion of the Internet.

When inexpensive personal computers came online in the 1980s, which were capable of linking to the worldwide telecommunications network, the number of people entering cyberspace increased exponentially. Commercial providers such as CompuServe began making ARPANET accessible to people who were outside the university–military research nexus.

The creation of the World Wide Web (Internet) and the development of inexpensive browser technologies in the early 1990s made the information superhighway accessible to millions. The World Wide Web was the creation of Tim Berners-Lee, who invented a computer language called hypertext, which made possible the interactive exchange of text and graphic images; it also made it possible to link instantaneously with any site on the Internet. By the end of the twentieth century, more than half of all U.S. households had at least one computer, and most public schools were online. These new information technologies created a media community that transcended national boundaries. Telecommunications were an essential part of the global economy, which required instant access to the information superhighway.

CULTURE WARRIORS

Conservative culture warriors advanced two theses: America was in decline, and liberals caused the culture wars that were rending the nation. These conservatives, many of them on the religious Right, felt marginalized by liberalizing cultural changes, and they were outraged by what appeared to them to be an ever-expanding list of evils such as sexual immorality, violent crime, pornography, and drug and alcohol abuse.

Not all the critiques of cultural trends during the 1990s emanated from the Right. Liberals and Centrists identified different indicators of decline: conspicuous consumption, rising inquality, and a loss of community. These liberal critics feared that unbridled individualism was undermining Americans' grassroots activism. Affluent Americans were retreating into gated communities. People were becoming more isolated and detached from community concerns.

Culture wars over art in the 1990s, which got extensive media coverage, were particularly nasty. The National Endowment for the Arts (NEA) funded two photographic exhibits that touched off fierce controversy. One of these exhibits featured a photograph of a crucifix in a jar of the photographer's urine. The other showed an image of the Virgin Mary that had been turned into a tie rack.

Art critics and museum curators defended the exhibits either as imaginative creations or as free expression that must never be censored. Many powerful congressmen, mostly Republicans, but also some liberal Democrats, denounced the exhibits as a misuse of public funds to support trash masquerading as art. Congressional conservatives tried to eliminate the NEA, but it managed to survive on much-reduced funding.

Two other cultural battles during the 1990s were over the way American history was remembered. Conservative culture warriors attacked what they called the "politically correct" or "pc" approaches to U.S. history advanced by liberal elites out of touch with mainstream Americans. The first involved a museum exhibit entitled "The West as America: Reinterpreting Images of the Frontier, 1820–1920" staged at the Smithsonian Institution's National Museum of Art. It represented a modest effort to present more realistic images of how Euro-Americans exploited Native Americans during the exploration and settlement of the West. It was too much for many people to accept, and they protested. A few GOP senators threatened to cut the museum's budget.

The second controversy erupted when the National Air and Space Museum planned a major exhibit that would feature the *Enola Gay*, the B-29 that dropped the atomic bomb that destroyed Hiroshima in 1945. Conservative political leaders, joined by veterans groups, protested the planned exhibit when they learned that it would question the decision to drop the bomb. The project director was forced out, and the exhibit was drastically redesigned. When it opened, the exibit featured the aircraft with no interpretive commentary.

Conservative culture warriors also protested the spread of "political correctness" to many elite college and university campuses. At some institutions of higher learning, in an effort to promote tolerance, liberal administrators promulgated detailed codes of speech and conduct. Some of these codes targeted "hate speech" that students were accused of using toward women, gays and lesbians, and minorities of color. Some professors expressed dismay at working in repressive environments in which newly empowered champions of multiculturalism and "politically correct" speech imposed a new bureaucratic orthodoxy that stifled academic freedom and encouraged an aggressively litigious culture of victimization.

Some of these cultural battles exposed intense regional and class divisions within the nation. Cultural conservatism appealed most notably to working-class white people inhabiting the South, the Plains states, and the Rocky Mountain states. Liberal cultural ideas mostly appealed to well-educated professionals on the east and west coasts and to the elites who inhabited the metropolitan centers of the East and Midwest.

The culture wars, waged fiercely in the early and mid-1990s, always exaggerated by the media, abated somewhat in the later years of the decade. The influence of the Religious Right diminished, although it remained a cultural and political force, especially in the South. These conflicts had always been waged by engaged partisans of the Left and Right with the great mass of ordinary Americans who occupied a vast middle ground paying scant attention to the controversies.

As the 1990s wound down, it appeared that liberals were winning many of the culture wars. More Americans, particularly younger Americans, had become more accepting of changing mores in clothes, hairstyling, and piercing and tattooing bodies. They also became more tolerant of a range of personal behaviors, including sexual practices, marriage and divorce, and family life. The permissiveness that had first manifested itself in the 1960s had permeated the culture by the 1990s. Conservative culture warriors ultimately failed to reverse these long-term cultural trends.

This was surely the case for ongoing family trends. High divorce rates, later-age marriages, and cohabitation combined to render the traditional nuclear family—married couples with children—just one of a variety of family styles. There were no longer any cultural norms. Statistical data from the 2000 census confirmed these trends. Almost a quarter of America's adult population had never married. Married couples headed approximately half of American households. Households headed by a single female with children under age 18 accounted for 22 percent of all families with children of that age.

Liberal and conservative critics of popular culture agreed that there had been an egregious decline in standards and taste during the 1990s. Commercialized sex was rampant, and often very profitable. Surveys showed that two-thirds of late-night television shows had some sexual content including simulated intercourse. The "adult entertainment industry" took in billions of dollars annually during the decade. The "gross-out" capacity of popular culture made a quantum leap. Rappers vied with one another in the use of offensive language and misogyny. The *Jerry Springer Show*, a popular afternoon television talk show, featured a succession of guests who humiliated themselves before large audiences. Fights between enraged guests, whether staged or not, enlivened the action and significantly increased the number of viewers.

Sex and violence increasingly dominated television programs and movies. The violent world of televised professional wrestling attracted massive audiences. Huge, powerful men, often amped on steroids, engaged in nonstop mayhem for the amusement of crowds who knew that the matches were scripted. *Cops*, featuring police videos of real chases, fights, wrecks, and arrests, was a long-running popular television show of the era. Local television news focused on live-action coverage of car wrecks, crime scenes, raging fires, and storm damage. News directors instructed their staffs: "If it bleeds, it leads." Hollywood released films saturated with computerized special effects, blaring sound tracks, violent action, profanity, nudity, and "gross-out" humor. (Scatalogical jokes were the favorites of adolescent boys who made up the largest part of the film-going audience.)

Even as pundits of both Left and Right continued to characterize television as a cultural wasteland and corrupter of young people, it was evident in the nineties, as in earlier eras, that discerning viewers could find many well-crafted shows such as *The Cosby Show* and *Frasier* to watch. Sports coverage improved, and significant annual events such as the NCAA College Basketball Tournament, the World Series, and the Super Bowl attracted large audiences and generated billions of dollars of advertising revenue.

Hollywood produced a large number of films enjoyed by moviegoers of all ages: historical epics, spy thrillers, and romantic comedies with the inevitable happy endings. Hollywood also brought out numerous serious films such as *Rain Man*, a well-crafted story starring Dustin Hoffman and Tom Cruise about an autistic man with extraordinary cognitive abilities and a materialistic striver who find their common humanity. Steven Spielberg directed *Schindler's List*, a film about a German businessman who employed Jews in his factory in Poland to save hundreds of people who would otherwise have perished in Nazi death camps during World War II. Woody Allen, the quirky, angst-ridden independent filmmaker, produced a solid body of work throughout the 1990s, the best of which was *Bullets Over Broadway*, a comedic treatment of the Jazz Age. Art cinemas survived in New York, Chicago, Los Angeles, and San Francisco, showing mostly foreign films that appealed to sophisticated *cinephiles*.

High culture was alive and well in America in the 1990s. American corporations, foundations, and wealthy individuals lavishly funded the world's most extensive cultural infrastructure. Museums, art galleries, opera companies, repertory theaters, and symphony orchestras flourished mostly in the large urban centers. Millions of well-educated affluent Americans made up the large appreciative audiences for accomplished artistic and literary performers.

MULTICULTURALISM

Driven mainly by the rights-conscious efforts of second-generation immigrants, particularly middle-class Hispanic Americans and Asian Americans, increasing numbers of ethnic groups organized to protest against what they perceived to be their marginalization in American life and against the negative stereotyping of their cultures they saw in films, television, and advertisements.

High school and college course offerings became contested arenas. Newly empowered advocates for women, African Americans, Hispanic Americans, Asian Americans, Native Americans, gays and lesbians, and fundamentalist religious groups demanded that high schools and colleges revise their curricula. Multiculturalists challenged Anglocentric course reading lists. Literary scholars revised reading lists to include works by women, persons of color, and Third World writers. Historians hastened to rewrite textbooks to include previously neglected or excluded groups.

Historically dispossessed and disadvantaged groups celebrated their unique cultural identities. In 1999, more than two million people identified themselves as Native Americans, more than twice the 1970 total. This figure reflected not only a natural increase in the Amerindian population but also the growing numbers of people of mixed-race ancestry eager to affirm their ethnic roots. A network of tribal-controlled colleges and universities provided Native Americans with relevant educations and cultural sustenance. Many tribes energetically pursued various business ventures, from growing wild rice to operating gambling casinos. In August 1998, near New London, Connecticut, on Mashantucket Pequot Tribal Nation land, the 550 surviving Pequots, grown rich on profits from their Foxwood Casino complex, proudly unveiled a magnificent museum and research center.

Multiculturalist reforms provoked a backlash. For many conservatives, multiculturalism replaced Communism as the nation's most dangerous enemy. They insisted that these efforts at more inclusive scholarship eroded any sense of a shared national identity. Critics feared that all the counting by race, ethnicity, gender, sexual preference, age, and religious affiliation could lead to a Balkanization of American society. They worried lest identity politics destroy the basic unity of the most successful pluralistic society in world history.

Another multicultural controversy flared in the 1990s over the legal recognition of marriage for same-sex couples. In May 1993, the Supreme Court of Hawaii ruled that the laws barring marriages between same-sex couples were unconstitutional. Responding to the court's decision, Republican congressmen, fearing that if any state recognized same-sex marriages, all the other states would be forced to recognize these marriages as legal, sponsored federal legislation that would deny recognition of these unions. In 1996, President Clinton signed the Defense of Marriage Act, which specified that gay couples would be ineligible for spousal benefits. Over thirty states, including Hawaii, enacted similar legislation. Vermont, alone of the fifty states, recognized "civil unions" between same-sex couples, allowing them to receive most of the legal benefits of marriage.

Like many other struggles over cultural change, multicultural battles subsided during the late 1990s. Surveys revealed that most middle-class Americans, regardless of race or ethnicity, embraced a set of core values: maintaining a democratic political culture, working hard, and an emphasis on individual achievement. As the century drew to a close, they appeared to accept the diversity that defined the American multicultural society.

BLACK AND WHITE, BUT NOT TOGETHER

In the mid-1990s, African Americans remained divided along class lines. At one end of the social spectrum, a large and growing class of black professionals and businesspeople enjoyed affluent lifestyles. In 1998, 12 percent of college students were black, roughly equal to their ratio of the general population. In 1998, nearly half of African Americans in the workforce held white-collar, middle-class jobs. At the other end of the spectrum could be found the impoverished inner-city blacks, representing one-third of the African American population of approximately 30 million. The poorest of the poor, representing perhaps 10 percent of the African American population in 1998, comprised the "underclass."

Although intact families, thriving churches, and other strong institutions could be found in the inner city, this culture of decency often was overwhelmed by a staggering array of social pathologies. As factory jobs once open to urban workers disappeared, inner-city unemployment rates soared. With good jobs no longer available locally, young people faced life on mean streets or held marginal service-sector jobs in car washes or fast-food restaurants. Inner-city pathologies such as high crime rates, drug abuse, welfare dependency, and teenage pregnancies derived from more fundamental problems: lack of good educational and job opportunities.

Festering ethnic antagonisms exploded in May 1992, when a California jury acquitted four white police officers charged with savagely beating an African American suspect, Rodney King. A bystander had videotaped the incident, and portions of the tape were repeatedly broadcast. To nearly all who observed the gruesome sequences, the television camera presented compelling images of police brutality. The verdict to acquit the four policemen, rendered by a politically conservative suburban jury containing no African American members, ignited the most violent race riot in the nation's history, which swept through South Central Los Angeles. Thousands of businesses were looted, and many of them were burned. Fifty-four people were killed, and thousands were injured. Property losses reached $850 million.

The Los Angeles police, poorly led and confused, were initially slow to respond to the riot, and events spun out of control. National Guard troops were rushed to Los Angeles to quell the rioters. Before order was restored and peace returned, approximately 12,000 people were arrested for looting and arson, most of them young black and Hispanic males.

The riot was reminiscent of the 1965 Watts upheaval, but there were significant differences. The 1965 riot had pitted blacks against whites. The 1992 riot had much more complex ethnic dynamics, reflecting the ethno-racial diversity of the nation's second-largest city. One observer called it the nation's first "multicultural riot." Blacks attacked other blacks as well as whites. Hispanics attacked whites. Blacks and Hispanics both attacked Asians. Gangs of African American and Hispanic thugs also engaged in violence and looting. These violent actions exposed the deep divisions and animosities among various groups. The division was sharpest between whites and various minorities. An affluent West Side white woman stated, "We don't know and don't care about the problems of the inner cities . . . most of us don't even know where South Central is. . . ." The King verdict obviously triggered the riot, but the underlying causes appeared to be a potent mix of ethno-racial antagonisms, poverty, and neglect, all exacerbated by a severe economic recession that hit poor people, working-class people, and small business owners especially hard.

In 1995, an ironic sequel to the Rodney King case occurred. From January to October, a former star athlete turned TV sportscaster, film actor, and rent-a-car pitchman, O. J. Simpson, stood trial for the murder of his former wife, Nicole Brown Simpson, and her friend, Ronald Goldman. After a lengthy trial, a jury acquitted Simpson of all charges.

Because of the political and cultural contexts in which the trial occurred, it acquired a significance that far transcended the guilt or innocence of one prominent individual. All of the major media provided constant coverage of the trial for months. Cable TV watchers could catch analyses and perspectives on the trial from ex-prosecutors and ex-defense lawyers. Millions of Americans became personally involved in the "trial of the century." Attorneys for both sides and the judge, Lance Ito, often played to the ever-present television cameras. Due process became judicial theater and Hollywood showbiz. A brutal double murder became sensational prime-time entertainment.

In the eyes of a substantial majority of viewers and expert commentators, prosecutors presented a strong case based on physical evidence that implicated Simpson beyond a reasonable

FIGURE 16.1   A city police officer holds a shotgun on two young suspects as a California state police officer puts handcuffs on them during the riot in South Central Los Angeles.   *Source:* AP/Wide World Photos. Photo by John Gaps III.

doubt in the two murders. The fact that Simpson, whose resources matched those that Los Angeles County could allocate for the trial, could afford a battery of high-priced attorneys to mount a successful defense proved to many Americans that he was immune to the justice system. Simpson's acquittal also reinforced the widely held notion that there was one standard of justice for the rich and another, harsher standard for the poor. The antics of the attorneys on both sides, the often erratic behavior of Judge Ito, and most of all the outcome of the trial suggested to many observers that the U.S. system of criminal justice had produced a farcical miscarriage of justice. The trial also raised an ominous question: Maybe the traditional jury system did not work in a racially polarized society?

Looming over the trial was the ugly reality of racism. Because the murder victims, Nicole Brown Simpson and Ronald Goldman, were white, and because Simpson was a black celebrity, racial attitudes in this country became central to the outcome of the trial and the way people viewed that outcome. The jury, consisting of nine African Americans, eight of them women; a Hispanic male; and two white women, reached a verdict of acquittal within four hours. The jurors rushed to judgment without seriously considering the evidence, much of it quite complex and technical, presented by 133 witnesses who testified during the long trial.

The black–white racial chasm that existed in this country was highlighted on October 4, 1995, when the clerk of the court read the jury's verdict. Around the country, wherever crowds of black Americans had gathered to hear the verdict, they cheered loudly and hugged each other at what appeared to them to be a triumphal deliverance. Wherever crowds of whites had gathered to hear the verdict, they stared in disbelief at what appeared to them to be an awful miscarriage of justice. Polls showed that 87 percent of black Americans agreed with the jury's verdict; 65 percent of whites believed Simpson to be guilty as charged. These numbers dramatically revealed that white and black Americans stared uncomprehendingly at each other from across a vast cultural divide.

The publicity generated by the arrest of Rodney King, the riot, and O. J. Simpson's trial, all highlighted the continuing ethno-racial divide and also called attention to some troubling aspects of the American criminal justice system. More than 6 million people were either on probation or serving time in prisons in 1999, triple the number in 1980. Ethnic and racial minorities accounted for more than two-thirds of the inmates, even though they made up 25 percent of the total population. The huge increase in the number of people on probation and in prison was attributed mainly to the stepped-up war on drugs. Even though studies showed that approximately 80 percent of cocaine users were white and blacks constituted perhaps 12 percent of drug users, African Americans made up over 50 percent of all people arrested for drug possession.

Despite the high rates of arrests and incarcerations of African Americans, experts assessing the status of black people during the nineties identified several indicators of progress. Polls showed that many white people expressed more liberal racial attitudes. Middle-class African Americans were also gratified that affirmative action policies had survived the backlash and were in place in major corporations and elite universities. Black people took pride in the successful military careers achieved by many black people who took advantages of opportunities available to them in America's most integrated institution. African American political leaders won mayoralty elections in several major cities that did not have black-majority populations, including New York, Minneapolis, and Denver.

Most important, black people made economic gains during the 1990s. Median household income rose more rapidly for blacks than for whites. Income for African American married couples, which had been about two-thirds of income for white married couples, rose to nearly 90 percent during the 1990s. At the other end of the income spectrum, black poverty declined rapidly during the decade. One-third of black families were officially defined as poor in 1990. By the end of the era, it had declined to about a fifth of all black families.

However, persisting conditions ensured that black–white relations remained the nations most profound socioeconomic problem. The greatest obstacle to progress was the enduring power of social class, more powerful than race. While middle-class blacks made significant progress in the 1990s, and the number of poor black families living in poverty was much reduced; the average net worth of African American families declined relative to that of whites. The poverty rate for blacks in 2000 was nearly three times what it was for whites. Unemployment rates for black people remained more than twice as high for whites. African Americans were far more likely than whites to lack health insurance and far more likely to not know that they were eligible for means-tested programs such as food stamps or medicaid. Life expectancy of blacks lagged well behind that of whites in 2000. It was 71.2 years for African Americans, 77.4 years for white people.

The most serious of the many problems afflicting poor black families was the worrisome issue of child poverty. In 2000, nearly one-third of African American children under the age of eighteen resided in a poor household. Like the children in low-income white families, poor black children had serious health problems including high rates of asthma, diabetes, and learning disabilities.

Inner-city public schools continued to face formidable obstacles. Continuing residential segregation combined with Supreme Court decisions to resegregate public education during the 1990s. Far fewer black students attended public schools that were 50 percent or more white in 2000 than in the early 1970s. Because of the high concentration of African Americans in many large cities of the North and Midwest, segregated schools were more common in the North than in the South. Similar trends for greater school segregation also separated Hispanic Americans from whites.

The education most Latino and black youngsters received in these segregated schools was generally inferior. Per-pupil funding for predominantly black and Latino inner-city schools was usually much lower than for the mostly white schools in the suburbs. Substantial black–white and Hispanic–white gaps in achievement test scores persisted, and they widened in the 1990s. Two long-standing trends also persisted during the decade: The lower the social class of the student, the lower the test score, and African American and Hispanic students had considerably lower median test scores than whites at every level of social class. How to close or at least narrow these class and ethnoracial gaps in test scores continued to challenge the best efforts of reformers, educators, psychologists, and parents as the twentieth century drew to a close.

HISPANIC AMERICANS AND ASIAN AMERICANS

In 1998, the nation's 23 million Hispanics represented America's fastest-growing minority. Hispanic Americans are themselves a diverse group. They include 16 million Mexican Americans concentrated in California and in the American Southwest; one million Cuban Americans, living mostly in south Florida; and between one and two million immigrants from the Caribbean region and Central America, living mostly on the East Coast or in California. The Hispanic American population also included two million Puerto Ricans, who are American citizens by birth.

Most Hispanics, regardless of their national origins, emigrated to America in search of a better life for themselves and their families. Millions have found success. Family, church, and cultural institutions have sustained hard-working people making it in America. But life remained harsh for millions of Hispanic families. In 1998, 20 percent of Mexican Americans and one-third of Puerto Ricans lived in poverty. Hispanic communities often were devastated by alcohol and drug abuse, soaring crime rates, and high rates of school dropouts and teenage pregnancies.

Fed by continuing high rates of immigration, the Asian American and Pacific Islander populations continued to grow rapidly during the decade of the 1990s. People from Korea, the Philippines, Vietnam, and China continued to come to the United States in large numbers. In 1998, 11 percent of Los Angeles's 3.5 million residents were Asians. Strengthened by family cultures and prizing academic success, Asian Americans showed high rates of college attendance and upward mobility. However, Asian American communities experienced generational tensions as young people got caught between the tug of traditional ways and the lure of American popular culture.

WOMEN AND WORK

By the late-1990s, women had smashed through many sexist barriers in higher education and in the workplace. In many fields that had long been virtually closed to women, such as medicine, law, engineering, and business management, large numbers of women energetically pursued productive careers. There were also large increases in the number of women holding public office in the 1980s and 1990s. In 1996, the number of working mothers with children exceeded the number of mothers with children not working outside of the home. In 1998, one-fourth of all doctors and lawyers were women. By 1999, women constituted almost half of the total workforce.

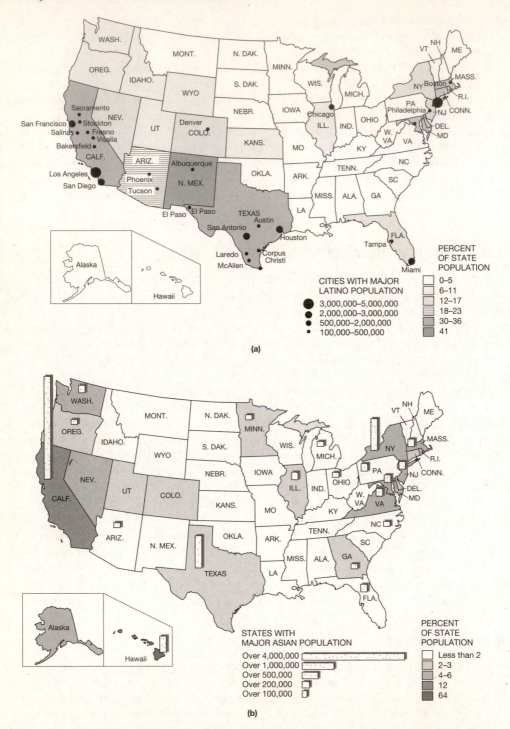

FIGURE 16.2 **(a)** Distribution of Hispanic population in the United States. **(b)** Distribution of Asian population in the United States. *Source:* Public Domain Map.

But as increasing numbers of women moved into formerly male-dominated occupations and professions, disparities continued in the pay women received for performing comparable work. Women who worked full-time in 1999 earned about 73¢ for every dollar a man earned. Many working-class women still confronted a segregated job market in the late 1990s. Sixty percent of working women held "pink-collar" jobs. Many women who had reached managerial positions in business in the late 1990s felt that they were paying too high a personal price for their professional successes. Others complained that they could not fulfill family obligations at home and perform their jobs at the highest levels.

Long-term structural changes in the economy adversely affected working women. The rise of service industries and the implementation of new technologies created millions of new jobs for women but also created new limits and liabilities. Automated offices became the sweatshops of the 1990s. Many businesses, to cut costs, hired part-time and temporary clerical workers. These contingent workers typically received lower pay and fewer benefits than full-timers.

Cultural changes also have accompanied the advent of women into the workplaces of America. Most notable was the change in women's consciousness. Many women in the late 1990s felt that they were equal to men in the market place and had greater ambitions and expectations than

FIGURE 16.3 Workers on the rooftop of a construction project overlooking Oakland, California.   *Source:* AP/Wide World Photos. Photo by Olga Shalygin.

previous generations of women. But traditional values and stereotypes also exhibited strong staying powers. Advertisers no longer celebrated domesticity as a woman's only appropriate realm, but they still advised the successful career woman to keep her weight down and be attractive. Women spent far more of their incomes on clothes, beauty aids, and diet and exercise programs than men.

Brief Bibliographic Essay

Haynes Johnson, *The Best of Times: America in the Clinton Years*, vividly describes the major events and social trends of the 1990s. James T. Patterson, *Restless Giant*, Chapters 8 and 9 are concerned with culture wars, multiculturalism, and black–white race relations. James Davison Hunter, *Culture Wars: The Struggle to Define America* is the best study of those cultural battles. David Hollinger, *Postethnic America: Beyond Multiculturalism* makes the case that most middle-class Americans embrace common core values and have accepted the diversity multiculturalism is promoting without undermining our basic cultural unity. Ellis Cose's *The Rage of a Privileged Class: Why Are Middle-Class Blacks Angry?* is an important and disturbing book. See William Wei's *The Asian American Movement* for study of a large, diverse group of Americans who are making rapid gains in education, wealth, and influence. For the matter of women's pay issues, see Sara M. Evans and Barbara J. Nelson's, *Wage Justice: Comparable Worth and the Paradox of Technocratic Reform*. On contemporary drug problems plaguing Americans, see Erich Goode's *Drugs in American Society*.

CHAPTER

17

Going Global

The opening of the Berlin Wall on November 9, 1989, was the first in a series of stunning events that culminated in the collapse of the Soviet Union and the end of the Cold War that had been the focus of American foreign policy for more than forty years. As the world's only remaining superpower, the United States suddenly found itself incontestably the most powerful nation on the planet. But Americans quickly learned that living in the richest, most powerful, and freest nation in the history of the planet did not insulate them from the dangers of an increasingly unstable world order or even allow them to feel safe and secure within their own country.

At the same time Americans sought new strategic roles in the post–Cold War world, they also had to adapt to the rapidly evolving world economy. The contagion of bankruptcies and currency devaluations that collapsed the booming economies of Thailand and Korea during the summer of 1997 spread to other Pacific Rim countries, and then engulfed Russia and Brazil, highlighting not only the interconnectedness of economic relations but also the volatility of the new global economy in which loan money could be quickly put into and then pulled out of markets around the world.

THE ELECTION OF 1988

As candidates geared up for the 1988 elections, the race for the presidency appeared to be wide open. For both parties, there were several major contenders. When the lengthy primary process finally ran its course in June, the survivors were Reagan's sixty-four-year-old vice president George Bush and Massachusett's governor Michael Dukakis, who was a liberal on most issues. For the vice presidency, Dukakis chose an elderly conservative senator from Texas, Lloyd Bentsen. Bush chose youthful Senator J. Danforth Quayle of Indiana as his vice presidential running mate.

The Republicans conducted a richly financed and efficient campaign. The Bush campaign easily won what media analysts have called the "battle of the sound bites"—that is, the vivid ten-to twenty-second pronouncements uttered daily by the candidates as they campaigned across the nation that would be picked up on the evening television news programs and beamed into millions of living rooms nightly until election day. Bush conducted a predominantly negative campaign, relentlessly attacking Dukakis for being "soft" on crime and defense, and for not supporting the social and cultural issues of the Christian Right. He shored up his conservative support by pledging "no new taxes." Bush also benefited from a strong economy and for having been Ronald Reagan's loyal vice president during a time of national revival.

Dukakis tried to focus his campaign on the issues, but never found one that worked or a rousing theme that resonated among the voters. His campaign was handicapped by divisions within the Democratic Party as centrists fought with liberals, and liberals quarreled with one another. The Democratic Party had become a tangle of contentious constituencies, each pushing its own narrow agenda. Dukakis also hurt his candidacy by his reluctance to either defend himself against Bush's attacks or to take the offensive and fight back.

On election day, the Bush–Quayle ticket buried Dukakis and Bentsen, winning 54 percent of the popular vote to 46 percent, forty-eight million votes for the Republicans to forty-one million for the Democrats. Bush carried 40 of the 50 states and had a 426 to 112 advantage in the electoral vote. Dukakis's defeat could be attributed in part to the continued flight of white voters, who made up over 80 percent of the electorate. Dukakis garnered only about 38 percent of the white vote in 1988. The South was now solidly Republican, as was most of the Midwest and West. Millions of blue-collar workers voted for Bush. However, the Democrats retained control of both houses of Congress.

A KINDER NATION

Foreign policy issues always claimed most of President George H. W. Bush's time and energy, but he devoted attention periodically to domestic issues. In his inaugural address, he promised "to make kinder the face of the nation." But, he also told the American people that the federal government could not do it alone. Americans needed to rely on a "thousand points of light," the voluntary local associations that made up civil society, to improve the nation.

Early in his presidency, Bush had to confront two financial crises, the savings and loan debacle and the huge federal deficits. Bush proposed a rescue plan to either close or sell the bankrupt S&Ls and repay depositors. Congress created a new agency, the Resolution Trust Corporation (RTC), to sell off the assets of the failed thrifts to solvent banks. At the same time, the Federal Savings and Loan Insurance Corporation (FSLIC) was folded into the Federal Deposit Insurance Corporation (FDIC) to provide the billions needed to bail out depositors.

In the spring of 1991, Bush, a fiscal conservative, under heavy pressure from Congress to reduce the federal debt, conceded the need to accept some new taxes. His concession outraged conservatives who had voted in good faith for Bush and his promised "no new taxes." He and the Democratic-controlled Congress eventually agreed on a combination of tax hikes and budget cuts that promised modest reductions in the budget deficits over the next four years. Meanwhile, the economy slipped into a recession, the first in nearly a decade.

Bush also responded to developing concern over the deteriorating performance of public schools. A controversial report, *A Nation at Risk*, published in 1983, had called national attention to a broken system of education that was failing to meet the needs of its students. Bush proposed that schools adopt higher performance standards in core academic subjects and develop more rigorous testing procedures. Liberal Democrats in Congress opposed Bush's proposed remedies, and none were implemented.

Bush's proposals for educational reform reflected a growing conviction that schools must do a better job of educating the nation's young people if America were to remain competitive in a rapidly globalizing economy. In future debates over education policy, there would be a greater focus placed on ensuring academic results as measured by rigorous tests. These debates set the stage for passage of the No Child Left Behind Act in 2002, promoted by Bush's son, the forty-third president, George W. Bush.

The Democratic-controlled Congress enacted some important environmental and social legislation, which Bush usually accepted. Bush signed an important Clean Air Act that toughened enforcement of national air quality standards. Congress also enacted a landmark measure, the Americans with Disabilities Act (ADA) in 1990, which Bush supported. The ADA prohibited private employers from discriminating against disabled people in employment, public services, public accommodations, and telecommunications.

Bush also inherited a host of serious social problems. The most feared pathology was the ongoing AIDS epidemic. By 1990, the disease had claimed over 110,000 lives, and an estimated 1.5 million people had tested HIV-positive. Most of the AIDS-infected cases involved gay males, but in the early 1990s, the proportion of AIDS cases among African American and Hispanic American intravenous drug users grew rapidly. The number of women infected with the AIDS virus was also increasing. Despite the huge sums of money spent on research, there appeared to be no prospect for an early cure or even the development of an effective vaccine. However, some progress occurred in the development of drugs and therapies, which, when taken in combination, suppressed or delayed the onset of AIDS symptoms.

Bush continued the war on drugs begun during Reagan's years. He pushed for more stringent drug testing in the workplaces of America, better enforcement of existing drug laws, and additional measures to interdict the flood of illicit drugs pouring into the country from Mexico, Peru, and Colombia. Despite stepped-up efforts on all three fronts, drugs, especially "crack" cocaine, remained widely available within the United States. Even though the Bush administration spent billions of dollars on its war on drugs, it failed to curb the great American appetite for drugs or significantly slow the illicit traffic.

THE REHNQUIST COURT

By the time of the Bush presidency, the Supreme Court, under the leadership of Chief Justice William Rehnquist, had taken a conservative turn; it was more receptive to challenges to affirmative action and lawsuits aimed at restricting women's access to abortions. Bush also continued Reagan's policy of appointing conservative judges to the federal bench. By the end of Bush's presidency all thirteen federal appeals courts had conservative majorities. In *Webster v. Reproductive Health Care Services* (1989), the Supreme Court, by a five-to-four vote, sustained a Missouri statute that restricted abortions. In *Planned Parenthood v. Casey* (1992), the Court, by a five-to-four decision, upheld a Pennsylvania law requiring a twenty-four-hour waiting period and "informed consent" before an abortion could be performed.

With the retirement from the Court in 1990 and 1991 of two elderly liberal associate justices, William Brennan and Thurgood Marshall, Bush had opportunities to add additional conservative jurists to the Supreme Court. His first appointment, David Souter, an obscure federal judge from New Hampshire, was quickly confirmed by the Senate with little opposition. Bush's second appointee, Clarence Thomas, a conservative African American jurist, was narrowly confirmed by the Senate in October 1991 by a fifty-two to forty-eight vote.

Judge Thomas had to survive challenges from many senators who were dissatisfied with his evasive answers to their questions concerning his views on affirmative action, abortion, and other issues. In dramatic televised hearings before the Senate Judiciary Committee, Thomas also had to refute charges brought by an Oklahoma University law professor, Anita Hill, that he had sexually harassed her when she had worked for him at two federal agencies in 1982 and 1983. The close Senate vote to confirm Thomas was not appreciably affected by the hearings; nearly all of the negative votes were cast by senators who would have voted against Thomas, even if Hill had never made her charges.

The controversy attending Thomas's confirmation made a public issue of the sexual harassment of women in the workforce and political system. Lawsuits filed by women charging sexual harassment in the workplaces of America multiplied in the 1990s.

The insensitive treatment accorded Hill by some male senators bent on discrediting her testimony revived the feminist political movement. Using as their rallying cry, "they still don't get it," woman entered electoral politics in unprecedented numbers during the 1992 elections.

THE END OF THE COLD WAR

The advent of the Bush presidency coincided with dramatic developments that brought about the most fundamental changes in international relations since World War II. In rapid succession, the Soviet empire in Eastern Europe collapsed, the Soviet Union itself disintegrated, and Communism as an ideological alternative to Western liberal capitalism disappeared into the ash heap of history. The Cold War, which had been the dominant reality of international life for nearly a half-century, suddenly ended. Since the collapse of Communism and the disintegration of the Soviet Union occurred during the years after President Reagan left office, it is difficult to establish precisely what role his policies played in the epochal events of 1989–1991. Hard-liners in Washington insisted that the rapid U.S. military buildup in the 1980s, along with the Reagan Doctrine and Reagan's bold rhetorical attacks on Communism, brought about the demise of the Soviet Union. However, it appeared to most observers that the Soviet Union had simply imploded. Mikhail Gorbachev hastened its internal collapse by his bumbling efforts to reform its sclerotic and corrupt system of political economy. Gorbachev inadvertently destroyed the Soviet Union while trying to save it. Neither the CIA nor any of the myriad of Sovietologists inhabiting prestigious U.S. strategic institutes had any indication that the Soviet system was on the verge of collapse until it disintegrated. The sudden collapse of Communism in eastern Europe and the Soviet Union with the resultant American victory in the Cold War was the most significant historical event of modern times.

The most dramatic event heralding the collapse of the Soviet empire in eastern Europe occurred on November 9, 1989, when the Berlin Wall that had so long served as a hated symbol of the *impasse* between East and West was breached. Hundreds of thousands of East Germans rushed into West Berlin. With the borders between East and West Germany fully open, the Communist government of East Germany collapsed. A democratic government quickly replaced it, and on October 3, 1990, East Germany reunited with West Germany. The reunited Germany remained in NATO, and the Warsaw Pact disintegrated.

President Bush forged a working relationship with Gorbachev and supported his reformist efforts. On August 19, 1991, Stalinist reactionaries among the Red Army, the KGB, and the bureaucrats who controlled the Soviet economy attempted a military coup against Gorbachev. It failed because 40,000 citizens of Moscow defied the *putschists* and rallied around the courageous leadership of Mayor Boris Yeltsin. In December 1991, the Soviet Union disintegrated and Gorbachev, presiding over nothing, resigned. President Bush switched his support to Yeltsin. The death of the Soviet Union was officially proclaimed on December 21, 1991, by Yeltsin and several other leaders who announced the formation of a new federation of sovereign states. The former USSR had mutated into an eleven-republic Commonwealth of Independent States, three independent Baltic nations, and an independent Georgia. On December 26, 1991, major European powers and the United States officially recognized the Russian republic under Yeltsin's leadership as the *de facto* successor to the defunct Soviet Union.

During Gorbachev's final days in power, Bush concluded another arms control agreement with the Soviets, the Strategic Arms Reduction Treaty (START I) that further reduced the size of both nations' nuclear arsenals. Bush and Yeltsin negotiated START II in 1992, which placed top limits for each side in the future at 3,000 to 3,500 nuclear warheads. From 1987 through 1992, during a time of fundamental transformations in international relations, the leaders of the world's two superpowers had managed through it all to negotiate a series of treaties that massively reduced the size and cost of their nuclear arsenals thereby significantly reducing the possibility of a nuclear holocaust.

THE POST–COLD WAR WORLD

As the Soviet Union receded from the world stage, Europe, led by a reunified Germany, moved to form the European Community, free of tariffs, travel restrictions, and monetary impediments. Eleven nations with a population of about 350 million promised to transform the transatlantic relationship for good by placing Europe on an equal economic footing with the United States.

While the most prosperous European nations were forming the European Community, Yugoslavia imploded in 1991–1992 as savage fighting erupted among Eastern Orthodox Serbs, Catholic Croats, and Bosnian Muslims. The fighting was especially vicious in Bosnia where Bosnian Serbs, supported by the Serbian regime, slaughtered thousands of Bosnian Muslims, committed a wide range of atrocities against civilians, and drove nearly two million Muslim refugees into neighboring nations. The Bush administration, preoccupied with domestic concerns and wishing to retain friendly relations with the Russians, historically supporters of Serbia, abstained from military intervention into the Yugoslav civil wars.

U.S. foreign policy in Latin America also benefited from the end of the Cold War. Gorbachev announced that Soviet aid to prop up the Cuban economy, which had been running at $5 billion per annum, would be drastically curtailed. In Nicaragua, the *Sandinistas* also felt the impact of the end of the Cold War. The Soviet Union, which had subsidized the *Sandinistas* to the tune of $500 million a year, turned off the aid spigot. In early 1990, the *Sandinistas* permitted free elections to take place in Nicaragua. They were defeated at the polls by a coalition of anti-*Sandinista* forces, led by Violetta Chamorro, who became Nicaragua's first freely elected president in more than sixty years.

The United States sent military forces into Panama in December 1989 to overthrow dictator Manuel Noriega, a supporter of the *Sandinistas* who had grown rich as a drug trafficker for the Colombian Medellin cartel. Noriega's refusal to allow Guillermo Endara, who had been elected president by the citizens of Panama, to assume office provoked the U.S. military intervention. After some bloody street fighting, the U.S. forces secured Panama City. Noriega was taken into custody and brought to the United States. He was tried and convicted on eight felony counts, including drug trafffficking, racketeering, and money laundering. After ridding Panama of Noriega, U.S. officials helped Endara take power.

China also felt the impact of rising anti-Communism. In April 1989, thousands of Chinese students and intellectuals gathered in Beijing's Tiananmen Square to demand democracy for China. The prodemocracy movement spread rapidly, and soon demonstrations sprouted in Nanjing, Shanghai, and other Chinese cities.

FIGURE 17.1   Post–Cold War Europe, 1992.   *Source*: U.S. State Department.

On the morning of June 4, 1989, premier Deng Xiaoping ordered the Chinese army to crush the drive for democracy. A brutal massacre ensued that claimed the lives of at least 1,000 people. Dissident democrats were hunted down and jailed *en masse*. President Bush publicly condemned the Chinese regime's repression of its own people, but he would take no actions that might jeopardize the friendly relations carefully cultivated between the Chinese and Americans at a time when trade between the two nations was expanding rapidly.

While Communist regimes were collapsing in eastern Europe, Rightist authoritarian regimes also were succumbing to the world democratic revival. In Chile, in 1989, General Pinochet's regime gave way to a democratically elected government. In South Africa, Frederick DeKlerk became prime minister in August 1989. Within a few months, he released African National Conference leader Nelson Mandela from prison, where he had languished for more than twenty-five years. In 1991, as DeKlerk began dismantling *apartheid*, President Bush lifted American sanctions against South Africa. In April 1994, there occurred one of the most extraordinary moments in modern world history: South Africa held its first elections in which all South Africans could vote. Mandela was elected president, and a multiracial parliament was chosen.

Elsewhere in Africa, famine threatened millions of people, especially in Somalia, where years of civil war had destroyed any semblance of government. In December 1992, when warring Somali factions diverted UN-sanctioned food relief shipments to black markets, Washington sent in 30,000 U.S. troops to protect food deliveries. U.S. forces were still serving in Somalia when Bush left office. Under President Clinton, the U.S. mission expanded to include restoring order and nation-building activities. Eighteen U.S. Special Forces soldiers were killed in fighting the forces of Somali warlord Mohammed Farah Aidid. Yielding to public pressure to bring the troops home, Clinton withdrew all U.S. forces from Somalia in 1994.

THE GULF WAR

During January and February 1991, America and its allies fought a war in the Persian Gulf against Iraq. The war derived in part from previous U.S. Middle Eastern diplomacy. During the Iraqi–Iranian War, America often aided Iraq to prevent an Iranian victory, which Washington feared could threaten the oil-rich Saudis. During the late 1980s, America sent the Iraqis nearly a billion dollars' worth of agricultural, economic, and technical aid.

Soon after Iraq's war with Iran ended, Kuwait, which, along with Saudi Arabia, had bankrolled Iraq's war with the Iranians, increased its production of oil. World oil prices dropped, hurting Saddam Hussein's government, already deeply in debt and dependent on oil revenues for sustaining the Iraqi economy. Hussein also was angered by the Kuwaitis and the Saudis over their refusal to forgive Iraq's huge indebtedness to them.

Washington's policies in the Gulf region still turned on the notion that Iraq was the major counterweight to Iranian revolutionary aggression. On the eve of Iraq's invasion of Kuwait, the U.S. ambassador to Baghdad, April Glaspie, told Saddam Hussein that the United States would not become involved in regional disputes, although America would defend its vital interests. Hussein apparently interpreted Glaspie's remark as a green light for aggression against Kuwait.

On August 2, 1990, Iraqi forces occupied Kuwait and threatened neighboring Saudi Arabia. Bush, determined to protect the Saudis and to force Saddam Hussein to withdraw his forces from Kuwait, forged an international coalition under United Nations's auspices to thwart Iraqi aggression. Bush also persuaded Soviet leader Mikhail Gorbachev to abandon his former Iraqi clients and support the UN initiative.

The UN promptly enacted Resolution 661, authorizing a trade embargo against Iraq. The international community clamped a tight economic boycott on Iraq and deployed a military force of some 250,000 troops to defend Saudi Arabia from possible attack. Coalition forces included a sizable representation from Great Britain, France, and five Arab countries, including Egypt and the United Emirates.

Initially, Bush appeared willing to use military force defensively, to protect Saudi Arabia and other possible Iraqi targets from attack and to let economic pressures force Saddam Hussein out of Kuwait. However, Bush soon became convinced that the boycott would not work. During November, 580,000 soldiers representing some twenty countries gathered in and near Saudi Arabia.

Many liberal Democrats opposed military action against Iraq. They believed that the economic boycott ought to be given a chance to work, and they also did not want America to go to war without congressional approval. The UN enacted Resolution 629 on November 29, which set

January 15, 1991, as a deadline for Iraqi withdrawal from Kuwait and authorized the use of force to drive the Iraqis from Kuwait if they did not leave by that date. On January 12, both the House and the Senate narrowly enacted resolutions formally approving the use of U.S. military force in the Gulf pursuant to UN Resolution 629.

Having become increasingly dependent on imported oil, much of which came from the Persian Gulf region, Americans understood that Iraq's conquest threatened U.S. and European oil interests. Iraq and Kuwait together produced about 20 percent of the world's daily supply of petroleum. Saudi Arabia accounted for another 25 percent. However, when President Bush made the case for war against Iraq, he stressed Iraq's conquest of Kuwait and Saddam Hussein's tyrannical rule. U.S. officials also expressed concern about Iraq's efforts to develop nuclear weapons.

Operation Desert Storm, the war in the Persian Gulf, began January 16, 1991, when President Bush ordered an Allied air assault on Iraqi positions in Kuwait and on targets in Iraq. For thirty-eight days, America and its allies waged a destructive air war against the Iraqis. On February 23, 1991, 200,000 American, British, and French armored forces roared across the undefended Iraqi border with Saudi Arabia at a point 200 miles to the west of Kuwait. Within four days, Allied forces had overwhelmed the Iraqis, whose fighting capabilities had been seriously eroded by the air attacks that preceded the invasion. President Bush offered a cease-fire, and the Iraqis quickly accepted it. At war's end, coalition forces occupied Kuwait and controlled southern Iraq.

During the short war, 148 (35 from friendly fire) Americans were killed and 467 wounded. A congressional committee estimated that the Gulf War cost $61 billion. Coalition partners, mainly Kuwait and Saudi Arabia, paid an estimated $42 billion of the costs.

Americans joyously celebrated a military victory that had been achieved so quickly and at such a low cost. Parades and celebrations, the likes of which had not been seen since 1945, welcomed home the conquering heroes. President Bush's approval ratings soared beyond 90 percent. In the first major crisis of the post–Cold War era, America had asserted its leadership, and the Soviets had followed the U.S. lead.

For the first time, American home audiences could watch a war around the clock on the Cable News Network (CNN). But the U.S. military tightly controlled television reportage, and American TV viewers saw only a sanitized version of the war. Reporters were allowed in the field only with military escorts who limited what they saw and whom they interviewed. Focusing on the marvels of U.S. high-tech warfare, reporters dubbed the conflict the "Nintendo War."

Although the Allied coalition succeeded in driving the Iraqis out of Kuwait, it failed to bring down Saddam Hussein. Bush encouraged ethnic Kurds and Shiite Muslims within Iraq to rebel, but when they did, Washington allowed Hussein to crush them. Bush's reluctance to destroy Hussein's murderous regime derived from several considerations. Some of America's coalition partners, particularly Egypt and Saudi Arabia, feared that if Saddam were removed, Iraq would disintegrate. They preferred a defanged Saddam Hussein presiding over a stable Iraq than chaos and civil war that could disrupt the balance of power in the Middle East. They also feared Iranian hegemony in the region in the wake of an Iraqi collapse.

U.S. officials also believed that the war had seriously damaged Iraq's military capabilities, and they imposed restrictions on postwar Iraq designed to keep Iraq militarily weak. Iraq was forbidden to import any military assets. Saddam Hussein was also forbidden to rearm or to develop weapons of mass destruction (WMD). UN inspectors were empowered to remain in Iraq to ensure that he complied with the UN prohibitions. The UN also established "no fly" zones over the Shiite and Kurdish regions of Iraq.

FIGURE 17.2 President George H. W. Bush surrounded by American soldiers. *Source:* Photo by Luc Delahayae.

Initially, all Iraqi exports, including oil, were embargoed. UN Resolution 986, adopted April 14, 1995, established an "oil-for-food" arrangement that allowed Iraqis to sell a limited amount of oil to purchasers of their choice; the proceeds from these sales were to fund imports of food and medical supplies. In time, the United Nations' lax oversight of the "oil-for-food" program enabled Hussein to implement a corrupt system in which favored purchasers of the oil at discount prices paid the dictator huge bribes in return. Over the years, much of the money from oil sales found its way into Hussein's bank accounts rather than going for food and medicine for the Iraqi people.

The coalition victory in the Gulf War did not endear Americans to other Middle Eastern peoples. Arab leaders, all of them authoritarian, nervously worried that the battering of Hussein might cause some democratic stirrings among their own people. Muslims also resented the expanded U.S. military presence in the Gulf states and Saudi Arabia, which had served as staging areas for Operation Desert Storm. The close relations that the United States maintained with Israel, which Bush persuaded to stay out of the war, continuously generated furious anti-American sentiment in the Gulf region.

Because of the Soviet collapse and the smashing Iraqi defeat, Israel felt more secure than at any other time since the Jewish state was founded. Responding to American pressures, Israeli leaders agreed to participate in an international conference convened in Madrid in December 1991 to try to resolve the Palestinian issue and to achieve a comprehensive Middle East peace treaty. Delegates from several Arab nations and representatives of the Palestinians engaged in dialogues with Israeli envoys.

THE ELECTION OF 1992

In the summer of 1990, the economy slid into a recession. Millions of people lost their jobs, including many middle-class "white-collar" employees. The state of the economy and jobs for the people became the dominant issues in the 1992 elections.

Reminiscent of Jimmy Carter in 1976, a political unknown captured the Democratic presidential nomination. Bill Clinton, the young, energetic governor of Arkansas emerged from a crowded field of contenders to win his party's nomination. Clinton survived several scandals that threatened to derail his candidacy at its outset. During the New Hampshire primary, his first major test, the media had a field day with three stories—that Clinton had manipulated the Selective Service system to avoid military service during the Vietnam War, that he had smoked marijuana, and that he was a serial womanizer. His efforts to explain away all of these scandals were only partially successful. He probably survived because cultural norms and mores had been evolving in the United States. Clinton's generation, the baby boomers, having grown up in the more permissive sixties, were more tolerant of deviant behaviors than previous generations.

In a crisp acceptance speech, Clinton pronounced an end to spendthrift liberalism and special-interest politics. He called for welfare reform, affordable health care for all Americans, tax cuts for the middle class, tax increases for the very rich, large reductions in budget deficits, and sharp reductions in military spending. In an effort to attract younger and southern voters, he chose Al Gore to be his vice presidential running mate.

In April, a third-party candidate, billionaire populist H. Ross Perot, entered the campaign. While Bush and Clinton had battled their way through the primaries, Perot's electronic grass-roots campaign was fueled by voter outrage at a political system that could not address the real problems facing ordinary Americans. Within weeks, Perot was outpolling both Clinton and Bush in some national surveys.

During the fall campaign, Clinton attacked the policies of the Reagan and Bush administrations, which he charged had compiled "the worst economic record since the Great Depression." He portrayed himself as "an agent of change" to appeal to "Perotistas." Clinton called for welfare reform to obtain the votes of Reagan Democrats. A sign hanging in his campaign headquarters clearly highlighted his main strategy: *It's the economy stupid!*

President Bush, buoyed by his 90 percent approval ratings following the Gulf War, had expected to ride easily into a second term. Two factors helped defeat his reelection bid: the recession and splits within the Republican Party between conservatives and moderates like himself. At the Republican convention, religious conservatives dominated. Pat Buchanan, a right-wing populist, delivered an emotional speech carried on national television in which he declared cultural war on feminists, abortion rights advocates, and gay-lesbian rights advocates. Although it rallied the faithful, Buchanan's reckless rhetoric alienated a broad swatch of independent voters.

On election day, Clinton received 43.7 million votes to 38.1 million for Bush and 19.2 million for Perot. He carried thirty-two states and the District of Columbia, with a total of 370 electoral votes to 168 for Bush and 0 for Perot. For the first time since 1977, the Democrats had won control of both the White House and Congress.

Clinton's moderate campaign partially restored the old Democratic coalition that had been ripped to shreds by Nixon and Reagan. Clinton retained the African American vote. Hard times brought many Reagan Democrats home to Clinton, especially in the Midwestern industrial states. Clinton probably won the election by carrying Ohio, Illinois, Michigan, and Pennsylvania—all of which had gone to Bush in 1988. Clinton also received a majority of the women's vote and the youth vote.

The year 1992 represented upheaval in congressional voting. Elections for the House were held for the first time under the reapportionment brought about by the 1990 census. Demographic trends underway since World War II continued to prevail. Sunbelt states like California, Arizona, Texas, and Florida gained many additional seats. The Northeastern states and the old industrial states of the upper Midwest continued to lose the seats that the Southern Rim states gained. Women, African Americans, Asian Americans, and Hispanics were elected to the House in record numbers. In the Senate, women scored a major breakthrough; five women, all of them Democrats, won seats. Carol Moseley Braun, from Illinois, became the first African American woman to serve in the Senate. California sent two women to the Senate, and Colorado sent a Native American, Ben Nighthorse Campbell.

THE RETURN OF THE DEMOCRATS

With Clinton and Gore in office, and over 100 new members of Congress in place, the baby boomers assumed national leadership. Clinton appointed many women to top-level positions. Women headed the Environmental Protection Agency and the Council of Economic Advisers. Janet Reno was picked to be the first woman attorney general. Clinton's determination to select women for important offices also reflected the influence of his wife, Hillary Rodham Clinton, who became the most powerful First Lady since Eleanor Roosevelt.

The new president quickly got embroiled in a controversy with the Pentagon over his proposal to allow openly gay and lesbian people to serve in the armed forces. In July 1993, Clinton announced a compromise policy that had the support of the Joint Chiefs of Staff: The military would no longer ask prospective recruits questions about their sexual orientation and would no longer employ security forces to hound suspected gays and lesbians out of the armed forces. But gays and lesbians serving in the military could not engage in overt homosexual behavior on or off military duty stations. This "don't ask, don't tell, don't pursue" compromise failed to satisfy gay and lesbian activists. Military security forces for years continued to harass suspected gay and lesbian personnel despite the new policy.

CLINTONOMICS

Although the recession was over by the spring of 1993 and the economy was growing again, unemployment remained fixed at the relatively high rate of 7 percent. In the post–Cold War era, cuts in military and aerospace spending brought massive layoffs at prime defense contractors such as Boeing and McDonnell–Douglas. American businesses were forced to become more efficient to meet the rigors of global competition in the 1990s. They laid off workers and mid-level managers to become more cost-effective operations. Companies replaced human workers with computers and computer-driven machines.

Millions who continued to work had to work harder and longer than ever before. Pressures on workers to be more productive intensified. Record numbers of workers filed disability claims in the 1990s, their disabilities linked to stress or to disabling injuries caused by spending too many hours on computer terminals. Millions of younger workers in the cutthroat 1990s worked harder than their parents, endured more stress, and were less well compensated.

The continued decline of trade unions also contributed to the deteriorating status of working people. In 1999, scarcely 12 percent of American workers belonged to unions, down from a high of 35 percent reached during World War II. Beset by corporate downsizing, the wholesale transfer of jobs overseas, harsh union-busting tactics, and increasingly conservative Congresses that were indifferent or hostile to trade union interests, unions were powerless to lift the wages of most workers or even to protect their jobs. As of 2000, adjusted for inflation, wage levels in unionized industries had been stagnant for over twenty years; meanwhile, corporate profits had soared.

In August 1993, a Democratic Congress raised the top marginal income tax rates from 31 percent to 36 percent, eased taxes on low-income families, and provided funding for education, retraining, and apprenticeship programs aimed at upgrading workers' skills. Deficits, which continued to exceed $200 billion annually in 1994 and 1995, were modestly reduced.

Clinton signed the North American Free Trade Agreement (NAFTA). Negotiated by the Bush administration, NAFTA incorporated Mexico into a free-trade zone already created by Canada and the United States during Reagan's presidency. NAFTA aroused both strong support and fierce opposition. Liberal Democrats and trade union leaders led the opposition. With strong support from Republicans, NAFTA carried Congress, giving Clinton a narrow political victory over the liberal wing of his own party.

Congress also approved a new round of tariff reductions on manufactured goods under the General Agreement on Tariffs and Trade (GATT), which had been in place since the end of World War II. In 1994, Clinton followed these victories by reducing trade barriers with major Pacific Rim nations. In 1995, he became embroiled in a nasty trade dispute with Tokyo over its refusal to allow American companies to sell automotive spare parts to the Japanese. Only after Clinton threatened to impose sanctions that would have severely hurt sales of Japanese luxury automobiles to the United States did the Japanese make concessions.

Polls taken during the 1992 election showed that public concern about the rising tide of violent crime was second only to economic worries. Congress, in 1993, enacted the Handgun Violence Prevention Act. In 1994, it enacted the most costly, far-reaching crime bill in American history. It provided $30 billion to fund increased law enforcement, crime prevention, and prison construction. It extended the death penalty to fifty additional federal crimes, and it banned the sale of certain kinds of assault rifles.

In October 1993, following the lead of Hillary Rodham Clinton, the Clinton administration moved to implement major health care reform. The Clintons' complex plan had three main goals: to provide coverage for the forty-five million Americans who had no health insurance, to hold down costs, and to preserve the high quality of available health care for all Americans. The plan would have drastically restructured the existing health care system. All Americans would be enrolled into large regional health alliances. Individuals could enroll in either a fee-for-service plan, enabling them to choose their own physicians, or in less expensive health maintenance organizations (HMOs), where they would see doctors on the HMO staffs. Employers would pay 80 percent of workers' insurance costs. Self-employed workers would buy their own insurance, and Medicaid would continue to cover the poor. To cover the plan's estimated $100 billion in added costs, Congress would enact large tax increases on tobacco products.

The administration's health care reform proposal instantly attracted legions of critics but had relatively little support. After six months of hearings, the administration conceded defeat on health care reform and settled for some token reforms to contain costs.

THE REPUBLICAN EARTHQUAKE

The 1994 midterm elections amounted to a referendum on Clinton's personal character as well as his performance during his first two years in office. During the spring and summer of 1994, his conservative Republican opponents seized on media accounts that implicated Clinton, and often his wife, in a series of financial, political, and personal improprieties reaching as far back as the 1970s when he served as Arkansas' governor. The most sensational of these scandals was known as "Troopergate." Paula Jones, a former Arkansas state employee, accused a state trooper of bringing her to a hotel room where, she alleged, Clinton made a crude request for sex.

By the summer of 1994, a panel of federal judges had appointed Kenneth Starr, who had been the solicitor general for the United States during Bush's presidency, as an independent counsel to investigate these activities. Starr, with a broad mandate, a large staff, and virtually unlimited funding, investigated all of the scandals as the midterm election campaigns were getting underway. All of the legal and political skirmishing associated with the various scandals received extensive coverage on the three television networks.

Republicans went after Clinton and the Democrats. They were led by a young conservative congressman from Georgia, Newt Gingrich. He composed what he called a "Contract with America" and succeeded in getting most Republican congressional candidates to endorse it. The document was a concise statement of conservative positions on major domestic and foreign policies. It highlighted a series of broad goals including tax cuts, balanced budgets, welfare reform, legal and tort reform, and increased defense spending.

Clinton, sensing the gathering conservative storm, had moved toward the center and had distanced himself from liberals within his own party. He portrayed himself as a budget-balancing, deficit-reducing, welfare-reforming, and crime-fighting Centrist. However, Republicans and the right-wing media relentlessly portrayed Clinton and the Democratically controlled congress as "tax and spend" liberals. The intense Republican campaigns and media coverage of "Troopergate" and other scandals seriously damaged the Democrats. Polls showed Clinton's approval rating falling rapidly. Voters expressed concerns about rising crime rates, unresolved social issues, cultural conflicts, and continuing economic insecurities.

The 1994 midterm elections completed the political transition that had begun with Ronald Reagan's electoral victory in 1980. The elections brought a Republican Congress to power, the first since 1954. The shock troops leading this Republican political "earthquake" were a group of seventy-three mostly young conservative reformers, many of whom had strong ties to the religious Right. Newt Gingrich, the leader of the Republican revolt, was elected Speaker of the House of Representatives. The Republicans also regained control of the Senate for the first time since 1986.

Gingrich read the election results as a mandate for implementing his "Contract with America." Following Gingrich's lead, the 104th Congress set out to downsize the federal government and to dismantle the welfare state. In 1995, the most activist Congress in decades enacted legislation that weakened affirmative action programs, cut foreign aid, cut Medicare, cut taxes, and reduced budget deficits.

As the Republicans seized the legislative initiative, Clinton was forced to adopt a defensive political strategy. He fended off Republican efforts to cut or kill liberal programs whenever he sensed that he had public opinion on his side. Twice in the fall of 1995, Clinton vetoed Republican budget proposals that would have cut social programs. Because these budget resolutions also provided the necessary funds to operate government agencies, Clinton's vetoes forced the federal government to partially shut down. Federal employees went without paychecks, national parks were forced to close, and some citizens failed to receive their Social Security checks.

Public anger focused mainly on Republicans. They were viewed as ideologues whose refusal to compromise created problems for ordinary American citizens. Clinton had outmaneuvered the Republicans. Gingrich was forced to retreat. In early 1996, the Republican-controlled Congress accepted Clinton's budgetary proposals, which retained all entitlement programs at current levels of funding as well as proposed a plan to achieve a balanced budget within seven years. Gingrich and his conservative cohorts discovered that citizens who denounced the welfare state could also resist efforts to curtail middle-class entitlements.

In 1996, both President Clinton and the Republican-controlled Congress sought a Centrist middle ground that produced several important new programs and policies. The minimum wage was increased. A major telecommunications bill replaced government regulation of the industry with open competition among telephone and cable TV companies, which benefited consumers. Congress also transformed federal agricultural policy; it established a program that over seven years would gradually remove restrictions on farmers and phase out subsidy payments going back to the New Deal era of the 1930s.

THE ELECTION OF 1996

Robert "Bob" Dole, the moderately conservative Senate majority leader, emerged as the Republican Party's nominee. He ran on a platform intended to attract all Republican factions: deep tax cuts, a balanced budget, increased defense spending, and opposition to abortion rights. He selected Congressman Jack Kemp, a moderate on most issues who was also a strong prolife advocate, as his running mate.

Bill Clinton conducted a well-funded, smoothly orchestrated Centrist campaign, which he had foreshadowed in his 1996 State of the Union address, when he announced that "the era of Big Government is over." He went after the "soccer mom" vote, suburban women whose political concerns focused on families and children. Clinton championed a Defense of Marriage Act, which he signed in 1996, that defined marriage as a union between a man and a woman. Clinton also attracted support from segments of the business community—particularly Silicon Valley, Hollywood, telecommunication, and multimedia companies. Clinton and Vice President Gore promoted education, job training, and computer literacy as building bridges to the twenty-first century "Information Age."

As the presidential race heated up, Clinton signed the Personal Responsibility and Work Opportunity Reconciliation Act, which terminated the Aid to Families with Dependent Children (AFDC). It ended a federal-state program that had been providing funds since the New Deal era for low-income families, most of which were headed by single mothers with children younger than eighteen. The defederalizing of welfare was the most significant downsizing of the federal government in modern times and further attenuated the social contract that was at the heart of what remained of the federal welfare state. After the new law was enacted, Clinton's lead over Dole widened.

Clinton was the most successful Democratic fundraiser of modern times. Scandals surfaced in the final weeks of the campaign in connection with Clinton's and other Democratic Party fund raisers' activities. Democrats acquired contributions of dubious legality from persons connected to foreign governments, including China. Contributions earmarked for party-building activities, so-called "soft money," often ended up helping to reelect the Clinton-Gore ticket.

Clinton and Gore coasted to easy victories on election day. They got 49 percent of the vote to 41 percent for Dole and only 8 percent for maverick Ross Perot, back for another run. The Democrats accrued 379 electoral votes to 159 for Dole-Kemp. Clinton did especially well among women voters, getting 54 percent of their vote compared with only 38 percent for Dole. The Republicans retained control of both branches of Congress, even gaining a few seats in the Senate. Republicans showed considerable strength in defeat. The Dole-Kemp ticket received a majority of the men's vote. The South, Great Plains, and Rocky Mountain states remained solidly Republican. Pundits interpreted Election 1996 as a personal victory for President Clinton, who had made a remarkable comeback from the Republican "earthquake" of 1994. Dole's ineffective challenge and a surging economy also contributed to Clinton's resounding electoral victory.

The election took place within a generally conservative climate of opinion, reminiscent of the 1920s. Citizen apathy about politics prevailed, especially among younger citizens, who viewed the political process with a mixture of amused contempt and horror. Despite saturation multimedia coverage, scarcely half of the people eligible to vote bothered to do so on election day. It simply did not matter to many millions of American citizens whether Bill Clinton was reelected or replaced by Bob Dole.

A PRESIDENT IMPEACHED

Political gridlock characterized the first two years of Bill Clinton's second term of office. The Republican reformers, outmaneuvered politically by the president, who co-opted many of their "wedge" issues, lost momentum. Clinton proposed modest poll-tested programs to help the middle classes, none of which Congress enacted. The one significant achievement of both Congress and the White House came in May 1997, when they reached a historic agreement on a balanced budget. The federal government produced a balanced budget for the fiscal year 1998, the first in nearly thirty years.

Clinton's second term was marked by scandals, which at times implicated him, several Cabinet members, and Vice President Al Gore. Many of the scandals stemmed from illegal fundraising practices during the 1996 presidential campaign. In July 1997, the Senate convened a special investigating committee, chaired by Republican Senator Fred Thompson of Tennessee, to hold hearings into potentially illegal fund-raising practices relating to both the 1994 and 1996 electoral campaigns.

In January 1998, the fund-raising scandals were displaced by the sensational discovery that President Clinton had had an eighteen-month-long sexual relationship with Monica Lewinsky, a young White House intern from Beverly Hills. The affair attracted the attention of Kenneth Starr, who for three years had been conducting investigations into possible illegal activity by both Bill Clinton and Hillary Rodham Clinton.

On January 27, Starr formally convened a grand jury inquiry into "Monicagate."

President Clinton went on television to deny that he had had a sexual liaison with Lewinsky. Looking the American people squarely in the eye and wagging his right index finger, he emphatically stated, "I did not have sexual relations with that woman, Ms. Lewinsky." Thereafter, he stonewalled the matter, refusing to answer questions or to discuss it further in public.

While Starr's team of experienced prosecutors methodically subpoenaed witnesses and compiled evidence, the President ostentatiously went about conducting the public's business as usual. Behind the scenes, Clinton's legal advisers and political operatives did everything they could to deflect and discredit Starr's investigation. Clinton's lawyers repeatedly tried to find legal grounds to prevent Secret Service agents and senior aides from testifying before the grand jury. The courts kept quashing the legal arguments, and witnesses continued to be compelled to testify. Clinton's power and room for maneuver steadily eroded.

As the investigation moved forward, polls showed that Clinton's approval rating remained high. The economy prospered, the stock market was surging, and the nation was at peace. The same polls also showed that Kenneth Starr remained unpopular with a majority of voters. They did not think having a sexual relationship with an intern and lying about it, even if proven true, were grounds for impeachment. Citizens also indicated that they were bored and disgusted by the matter. They wanted the politicians to put it behind them and get on with conducting the nation's business.

On July 17, prosecutors issued a subpoena compelling the president to testify before the grand jury pursuant to a criminal investigation in which he was a suspect. Starr withdrew the subpoena on July 29 when the president agreed to testify from the White House with his lawyers present. On August 6, Lewinsky, granted immunity from prosecution, testified before the grand jury. She told prosecutors that she had had a sexual relationship with the president.

Clinton testified on August 17. Later that evening, he spoke briefly to the American people. During his four-minute speech, he admitted that he had had "a relationship that was inappropriate" with Lewinsky. He insisted that he had not committed perjury when he denied under oath that he had had sexual relations with Lewinsky, although he acknowledged that his testimony was misleading. But half his speech was devoted to an angry attack on Kenneth Starr. The speech not only failed to end the matter, it ensured its indefinite perpetuation. In the wake of his speech, mainstream media editorialists and leading Democratic senators condemned the president's behavior and his attempts over the past seven months to deceive both Congress and the American people about it.

On September 9, Starr delivered his report to the House of Representatives. He had gathered evidence showing that Clinton may have committed perjury, tampered with witnesses, obstructed justice, and abused the power of his office. Starr's report set the stage for high political drama reminiscent of the days of Watergate when a Senate committee discovered that President Nixon had secretly taped recorded White House conversations. Starr's report posed a real threat that President Clinton could be removed from office.

On September 11, Congress voted upon the recommendation of the House Rules Committee to release the report in full over the Internet. The report outlined Starr's allegations of presidential wrongdoing and set forth the reasons Clinton was liable to impeachment. But it also included accounts of Lewinski's sexual liaisons with Clinton rendered in graphic detail, which she had provided Starr's investigators. Millions of Americans and people in other nations downloaded the report to learn about the sexual behavior of the president of the United States! The next day both the electronic and print media presented the Starr report to the public in its entirety or in edited form with extensive commentary. On September 21, a videotape of the president's testimony to the grand jury was broadcast to the nation. Clinton's political fate now rested in the hands of Congress and public opinion.

After the release of the Starr report, polls showed that two-thirds of Americans still thought Clinton was doing a good job as president and did not want him to be impeached; however, his personal ratings had sunk to all-time lows. Clinton the president was praised for doing a good job; Clinton the fallible human was condemned for immorality and for degrading the revered office of the presidency.

To live television coverage by all major networks and CNN, the Republican Party leadership in the House set the impeachment process in motion. On October 8, Congress voted 258 to 176 to authorize a formal impeachment inquiry. Thirty-one Democrats joined with the Republican majority in authorizing the impeachment inquiry. In an atmosphere poisoned by intense partisan acrimony, for only the third time in American history, the House Judiciary Committee began hearings to see if there were grounds for impeaching a president.

On November 3, as the House Judiciary Committee prepared to hold its historic hearings, the 1998 midterm elections were held. Given the dramatic contexts in which these elections occurred, they amounted to a referendum on the impeachment process. The fate of a presidency hung in the balance. The results surprised the experts and confounded the Republican Right that was determined to destroy the Clinton presidency. After almost a year dominated by scandals that put the White House in jeopardy and the Democrats on the defensive, the Democrats made unexpected gains on election day. They picked up five seats in the House and broke even in the Senate. The Republicans retained control of Congress, but by a smaller majority. In contested House districts, where Republicans made Clinton's alleged immoral and criminal behavior the chief issue, Democratic candidates won more often than they lost.

Revealing of the disconnect between the American people and the Washington political culture was the fact that only 36 percent of those eligible to vote turned out on election day. In many states, the turnout was less than 20 percent. The percentage of young people (ages eighteen to twenty-nine) voting was even smaller. Democrats were particularly successful in persuading African Americans, union members, and women to vote. Despite the fact that there were six news stories about the scandal for every news story about electoral politics, exit polls revealed that most voters claimed that they were not interested in the scandal and that it was not a factor in determining how they voted.

The elections represented a victory for incumbents and the status quo. The nation was prosperous and at peace. What hurt Republicans the most was their capitulation to Clinton on federal spending priorities. Fearful of being blamed if another governmental shutdown occurred, the Republican Congress had enacted all of Clinton's budget proposals during the congressional session that had ended three weeks before the election. Lacking bold leaders and alternative issues, many Republican voters stayed home on election day. In the immediate aftermath of the election, Newt Gingrich, who had rocketed to national prominence with the Republican "earthquake" in 1994, was forced to resign the Speakership of the House. The man who had orchestrated the attacks on Clinton was himself consumed by the fires that he had ignited.

Electoral setbacks did not deter the Republican majority on the House Judiciary Committee; they were determined to destroy their political nemesis. On November 18, the House Judiciary Committee formally convened the impeachment inquiry. On December 11 and 12, the House Judiciary Committee approved four articles of impeachment. The first two articles charged Clinton with perjury, the third article charged Clinton with obstruction of justice, and the fourth article charged Clinton with abuse of power.

The drama built as the full House of Representatives opened formal impeachment hearings on December 18. The next day, William Jefferson Clinton became only the second president in American history to be impeached. The House passed two articles of impeachment: Article 1 charged that Clinton had committed perjury in his grand jury testimony of August 17. It passed by a vote of 228 to 206. Article 2 charged that the president obstructed justice. It passed by a vote of 221 to 212.

On January 7, 1999, the Senate impeachment trial of President Clinton convened, presided over by Chief Justice William Rehnquist, with the senators themselves impaneled as a 100-person jury to hear the case and render a verdict. From January 14 to 16, the impeachment managers from the House presented their cases. From January 19 to 21, a battery of lawyers representing the president presented their defenses. The impeachment managers argued that Clinton should be convicted on both articles and removed from office. Clinton's defense team presented a dual line of defense: The president was not guilty of either charge, and even if he were, they did not rise to the level of impeachable offenses under the Constitution.

As the five-week long trial in the Senate ran its course, polls consistently showed that two-thirds of Americans did not want President Clinton convicted and removed from office. An even larger percentage consistently showed that they approved of the way he performed his job. Virtually all of the nation's most influential newspapers, led by the *New York Times, Washington Post*, and *Los Angeles Times*, opposed convicting the president and removing him from office. All Democratic senators and several moderate Republican senators indicated that they would vote to acquit Clinton.

On February 12, 1999, the Senate voted to acquit the president. The Senate rejected the perjury charge, fifty-five to forty-five, and it split fifty to fifty on the obstruction of justice charge. Many moderate Republican and Democratic senators were clearly uncomfortable with their votes for acquittal, because they believed that there was considerable evidence to substantiate the charges of perjury and obstruction of justice against President Clinton brought by the House, and by their votes, they were acquitting him of all charges. However, they had no choice because they did not want him removed from office. They were voting to save the presidency, not the man whom many of them despised.

Public opinion probably saved Clinton's presidency. Most Americans believed that he was guilty of both the perjury and obstruction of justice charges as did many of the senators who voted for acquittal. Clinton would probably have been removed from office had public opinion been running two-to-one for conviction as it had against Richard Nixon in 1974 just before he resigned the presidency. Once the threat of removal had passed, Clinton's popularity and job approval ratings both dropped sharply.

The impeachment scandals amounted to a prolonged constitutional crisis that seemed to have no impact outside the cocooned world of Washington politics. While the president and the Republican majority in Congress were locked in mortal political combat, most Americans happily went about their business. The news media gave the crisis saturation coverage from start to finish, yet most Americans could not care less, or so they said, and denounced the news media for their obsessive devotion to tabloid politics.

If anything positive could be gleaned from the year-long political train wreck, it was the sustained display of civic discipline by ordinary American citizens. A large majority quickly concluded that a capable president should not be removed from office for matters pertaining to his private life, even though they were reprehensible.

CLINTON AND THE POST–COLD WAR WORLD

For Clinton, domestic affairs took priority over foreign policy issues. Although clearly committed to maintaining American primacy in world affairs, he was handicapped by his lack of foreign policy experience. The Clinton administration also faced the daunting task of developing effective foreign policies in a rapidly evolving global context without precedents and without guidelines to follow. A disorderly and dangerous world had quickly replaced the comparatively stable bipolar world of the vanished Cold War era.

Because Clinton and his senior foreign policy advisers lacked clear objectives and did not have a consistent set of criteria to apply, they could never decide when or how much U.S. power and prestige to commit in situations that did not involve vital national interests. In the early years of his presidency, Clinton's approach to foreign policy amounted to little more than a series of *ad hoc* responses to crises as they arose. Absent the Cold War and no more Soviet Union to worry about, Clinton downplayed international power politics and the use of military force. He strongly supported economic globalization. In the area of foreign economic policy, he had major achievements. He supported the NAFTA, normalized relations with Vietnam, and negotiated significant trade agreements with Pacific Rim nations.

THE BALKAN WARS

The shortcomings of the Clinton approach to foreign affairs were evident in Bosnia and Herzegovina, where the largest war in Europe since World War II raged on. Vicious ethnic fighting among the Serbs, Bosnian Muslims, and Croats had killed over 100,000 people and generated over 3.5 million refugees. The Bosnian Muslims were clearly the victims of aggression and atrocities, and they were hindered in their efforts at self-defense by an arms embargo. Even so, Washington appeared more concerned with avoiding significant military involvement and confining the conflict to the petty successor states of the now-defunct Yugoslav federation than with aiding the struggling Bosnians.

In the fall of 1995, Washington finally took action. The initiative was taken by Assistant Secretary of State Richard Holbrooke. Knowing that the United Nations and the Europeans were incapable of effective action in Bosnia, he brought the leaders of the three warring factions to Dayton, Ohio, in December, brokered a cease-fire, and worked out a complex political settlement to be implemented gradually. The settlement involved sending a NATO force of 60,000 troops, 20,000 of which were U.S. combat soldiers, to police the cease-fire and allow the political settlement to gradually take hold. A vocal majority in Congress and among the American public opposed sending U.S. forces to Bosnia. Military leaders were reluctant to place U.S. forces in a dangerous and violent region where they could incur casualties.

The intervention succeeded in maintaining the cease-fire; however, one year later, the date that Clinton had scheduled for the withdrawal of all U.S. troops, the political settlement had not been implemented. Bosnia-Herzegovina had, in effect, been partitioned, and the U.S. forces settled in for a long campaign.

While Bosnia-Herzegovina endured an uneasy peace, ethnic conflict erupted into war in nearby Kosovo, a Yugoslav province inhabited by 1.8 million ethnic Albanians, who comprised 90 percent of the region's population. The conflict had been building for years. In 1989, the Yugoslav leader, Slobodan Milosevic, revoked the autonomy that the Kosavars had enjoyed since 1974. As the Belgrade regime became more repressive, the Kosovars, following the moderate leadership of Ibrahim Rugova, attempted to create a parallel government that would permit at least a semblance of autonomy within the Yugoslav federation.

In 1991, militant Kosovars founded the Kosovo Liberation Army (KLA); its leaders were committed to achieving independence from Yugoslavia and one day uniting with Albania. KLA terrorists sporadically attacked Serbian soldiers and police stationed in Kosovo. The Serbs retaliated brutally, trying unsuccessfully to eliminate the KLA and its supporters. In the spring of 1998, the KLA began a full-scale rebellion against Serbian authority. Milosevic responded by escalating the violence against the Kosovars. NATO, led by the United States, attempted unsuccessfuly to impose a settlement along the lines of the Dayton Accords.

On March 24, 1999, NATO, commanded by U.S. Army General Wesley Clark, began an aerial war against the Milosevic government to induce him to sign the agreement that he had rejected. Clark had assumed that a few days of precision bombing with high-tech cruise missiles and laser-guided "smart bombs" would quickly return Milosevic to the bargaining table. Instead, Milosevic escalated his campaign of "ethnic cleansing" against the hapless Kosovars.

Within a few weeks, NATO confronted a humanitarian catastrophe. An estimated 800,000 Kosovars were forced into exile in neighboring Macedonia, Albania, and the Yugoslav province of Montenegro. The presence of these refugees threatened to destabilize these small multiethnic countries and draw them into the conflict. Another 600,000 Kosovars were driven from their homes and villages, but remained inside the province, hiding in mountain forests and canyons. Thousands of Kosovars, mostly young men, had been slaughtered. Thousands more were unaccounted for. Hundreds of villages, towns, and cities had been razed. NATO, the United Nations, and numerous international aid agencies rushed to provide food, clothing, shelter, and medicines to the Kosovars.

NATO's gradually escalating air war, *Operation Allied Force*, seriously degraded the Serbian infrastructure and industrial capacity. But it also allowed Milosevic to consolidate his control over Serbia. Further, the bombing could not stop the ethnic cleansing. Hawkish critics of the air war, such as Senator John McCain, doubted that bombing alone could defeat Milosevic. He called for sending U.S. ground combat forces to Kosovo. However, President Clinton ruled out sending in ground forces.

The American public, horrified by televised images of pathetic Kosovars streaming into squalid refugee camps, initially supported the war. But support for the war was lukewarm from

FIGURE 17.3 Ethnic Albanian Kosovar refugees wait to be placed in a tent after crossing into Macedonia at a refugee camp near the village of Blace, 25 km northwest from Skopje, Saturday, April 24, 1999. *Source*: AP/Wide World Photos.

the outset and the American people gradually disengaged from the conflict despite mostly favorable media coverage. On April 30, six weeks into the war, and with the plight of the Kosovars worse than ever, the Republican-controlled Congress defeated a resolution of support for the air war. Within the nation, there were signs of growing antiwar sentiment.

After seventy-eight days of bombing, the war in Kosovo ended when Milosevic signed an agreement that differed little from the one that he had previously rejected. Diplomatic isolation and the increasingly effective bombing campaign convinced him that the NATO offer was the best he was likely to get. Besides, he had accomplished his major goals: He had consolidated his power in Serbia, and he had rid Kosovo, at least temporarily, of much of its Albanian population.

NATO troops, including 7,000 U.S. soldiers, were deployed as peacekeepers in Kosovo as the Serbian troops exited that ravaged land. NATO's postwar goals were to assist the Kosovars as they returned. But a lot of these traumatized people did not want to return to Kosovo; they did not feel safe. Others discovered that they had no homes, farms, or businesses to return to. Many Kosovars, radicalized by their experiences, turned to the KLA. These people would accept nothing less than independence for Kosovo. But the agreement in place did not support independence for Kosovo, even as a distant goal. NATO leaders consistently rejected an independent Kosovo because they saw it as a prescription for perpetual political instability in the Balkans.

President Clinton and Secretary of State Madeleine Albright characterized the Balkan interventions as humanitarian and strategic victories. But the price was steep: an estimated 300,000 people killed, three million more displaced, and countries *de facto* partitioned. Western protectorates of indefinite duration involving thousands of U.S. forces had been created at a cost of $30 billion. Slobodan Milosevic also paid a high price for his ruthless policies. His country lay in ruins, and he was voted out of office. He became the first former head of state to be tried for war crimes and crimes against humanity when he was extradited to the custody of the UN's International War Crimes Tribunal in The Hague, the Netherlands, in 2002. Milosevic died in April 2006, apparently of heart disease, during the fourth year of his trial.

TERRORISM ABROAD AND AT HOME

The war against terrorism reached back into the 1970s and continued during the 1980s and 1990s. In 1988, Pam AM Flight 103 en route to New York exploded over Lockerbie, Scotland, killing all 259 people on board. Years later, a Libyan terrorist was convicted of having planted a powerful plastic explosive on the plane.

In February 1993, terrorism struck the United States when a small group associated with Osama bin Laden bombed the World Trade Center in New York City, killing five people and injuring scores of others. Undertaken in retaliation for U.S. policies in the Middle East, the bombing was the most destructive act of terrorism ever committed in the United States. In 1995, following a dramatic trial, a militant sheikh and four of his Shiite fundamentalist followers were convicted of the bombing. Despite increased surveillance of terrorist groups by the FBI and CIA, Osama bin Laden's group struck again. On August 7, 1998, two powerful car bombs exploded within minutes of each other outside U.S. embassies in Nairobi, Kenya, and Dar es Salaam, Tanzania, killing 225 people and injuring more than 5,000.

On April 19, 1995, a car bomb of tremendous explosive power demolished a nine-story federal office building in Oklahoma City, killing 168 people, many of whom were children. The FBI soon arrested Timothy McVeigh and Terry Nichols, who were charged with the crime. Both men had loose ties with the militia movement, a right-wing fringe group that viewed efforts to impose a measure of gun control as part of a conspiracy by the federal government to extinguish freedom in America. Both were convicted of mass murder. McVeigh was executed by lethal injection, and Nichols was given a life sentence without the possibility of parole.

Previously, on February 28, 1993, FBI agents, working with agents of the Federal Bureau of Alcohol, Tobacco, and Firearms (ATF), had conducted a raid on the compound of the Branch Davidians, an obscure religious sect led by David Koresh. The federal agents suspected Koresh of stockpiling illegal weapons and ammunition in the compound located near Waco, Texas. A short battle ensued in which four ATF agents and six members of the Branch Davidian sect were killed. On April 19, federal agents assaulted the compound where the Branch Davidians had barricaded themselves. A fire, either deliberately or accidentally set, quickly consumed the buildings, killing seventy-six members of the sect, including twenty-one children.

Both the FBI and ATF were criticized from many quarters for what appeared to be a lethal operation carried out against a small group of religious sectarians. Groups such as the National Rifle Association (NRA) were outraged, likening the federal agents to "Hitler's storm troopers." Spokesmen for the militia movement vowed revenge. Two years later to the day, April 19, McVeigh and Nichols bombed the federal building in Oklahoma City.

Acts of domestic terrorism continued. Medical clinics that provided legal abortion services to women became a prime target of terrorists. Several abortion providers were murdered outside their clinics. There were nineteen bombings and burnings of abortion clinics in 1992.

In March 1996, FBI agents, acting on a tip from his brother, arrested fifty-three-year-old Theodore Kaczynski as the suspected "Unabomber," a serial killer who had waged a campaign of terror-bombing since 1979 that had killed three people and injured twenty-three others in sixteen separate attacks. In 1998, after a trial in federal court held in Sacramento, California, Kaczynski, who admitted that he was the Unabomber, was sentenced to life imprisonment without the possibility of parole.

Homegrown terrorist assaults reached new levels of horror in 1998 and 1999, when angry and troubled schoolboys gunned down fellow students and teachers in a rash of schoolboy massacres that took place in various cities across the country. The worst slaughter occurred at Columbine High School in Littleton, Colorado, a prosperous suburb of Denver. On Tuesday morning, April 20, 1999, Eric Harris and Dylan Klebold arrived on campus armed with an arsenal of high-powered weaponry consisting of automatic pistols, automatic rifles, sawed-off twelve-gauge shotguns, and dozens of pipe bombs. They murdered twelve students and a teacher in cold blood and wounded dozens more of their classmates. Then they took their own lives. In the aftermath of the worst school massacre in U.S. history, frightened and grieving survivors struggled to cope with the inexplicable events.

While Islamic terrorists recruited from various Middle Eastern countries bombed the World Trade Center, President Clinton urged Israeli and Palestinian leaders to continue the dialogue begun at Madrid in the wake of the Persian Gulf War. In September 1993, following secret talks, there occurred a historic breakthrough. According to the Oslo Accords, the Palestinian Liberation Organization (PLO) gained limited autonomy in the Gaza Strip and in areas of the West Bank. In return, Yassir Arafat, the leader of the PLO, recognized Israel and renounced terrorism. Despite sporadic efforts by Palestinian militants to disrupt the peace process, it remained in place. But progress stalled in 1996 when the Israelis elected a conservative prime minister Benjamin Netanyahu and the PLO security forces could not suppress terrorist activity.

On October 1998, Clinton helped both sides forge a new agreement at the Wye Conference Center in Queenstown, Maryland. Israel agreed to turn over additional West Bank lands to the

Palestinians, who agreed to eliminate language from their charter calling for the destruction of Israel. Militants in Israel and in lands under the control of the Palestinian authority protested strongly. Sporadic violence continued. Netanyahu's government fell in the wake of the Wye agreement.

The new Israeli prime minister, Ehud Barak, was committed to completing the peace process with the Palestinians. However, Clinton and Barak were unsuccessful in fashioning additional agreements with the PLO. Arafat demanded that Barak acknowledge a Palestinian "right of return" to homes and lands in Israel that were lost during the first Arab–Israeli war in 1948–1949. When Barak refused to grant this concession, Arafat broke off negotiations. Another, more violent *intifada* ensued, this one aided by terrorist organizations and featuring suicide bombers.

Over the next four years, over 4,000 people would die, many of them Palestinian civilians. Clinton's failure to resolve the Israeli–Palestinian conflict has been attributed mainly to Arafat's unwillingness to compromise, but it is better understood as a reminder of how intractable this conflict is. For over fifty years, it has resisted the best efforts of capable political leaders of goodwill to achieve a peaceful resolution of what may be an unresolvable problem.

Brief Bibliographic Essay

Alfred Eckes Jr. and Thomas Zeiler, *Globalization and the American Century* is an important book about the development of the global economy and how it impacts the U.S. economy in multiple ways. Richard Clarke, *Against All Enemies: Inside America's War on Terror*, is a best-selling, highly critical account of U.S. efforts against terrorism in the Clinton and George W. Bush administrations. John Greene, *The Presidency of George Bush*, is the best study to date of the administration of the forty-first president. For the 1991 Gulf War, see Michael Gordon and Bernard Trainor, *The Generals' War: The Inside Story of the War in the Gulf*. Bill Clinton, *My Life*, is a lengthy, rambling, and very readable autobiography. Two American Sovietologists, Robert Jervis and Seweryn Bailer, eds., present diverse looks at the post–Cold War world in *Soviet-American Relations After the Cold War*. For American–Japanese relations, see Akira Iriye and Warren I. Cohen, eds., *The United States and Japan in the Postwar World*. For recent developments in Central America, consult John A. Booth and Thomas W. Walker, *Understanding Central America*. Judith Miller and Laurie Mylorie's *Saddam Hussein* is an informative study that sheds light on the motivations of the Iraqi leader and the genesis of the Persian Gulf crisis.

America in a New Millennium

The United States entered the new millennium as the most powerful nation on earth. In addition to the "hard" economic and strategic power that the American colossus could project around the globe, U.S. "soft" cultural power in the form of fast foods, fashions, television programing, movies, computer games, and pop music also had a global reach. High-tech telecommunication systems and a global economy plugged Americans and the rest of the inhabitants of the global village into an intricate web of economic, social, political, and cultural relations. A new transnational world order was emerging, which had the potential in time of eroding national identities.

The new service-oriented high-tech economy transformed the way most Americans lived and worked. That economy, which had sustained an astonishing decade-long boom during the 1990s, suddenly went slack as the new millennium opened. The Silicon Valley bubble burst, the stock market crashed, unemployment shot up, and bankruptcies multiplied, while millions of Americans struggled to climb out of a recession.

After three years of recession and stagnation, the economy rebounded in the latter half of 2003. Through 2006, all important macroeconomic indicators remained in positive territory. However, even during these three relatively strong years, two ominous economic trends were evident—the steadily shrinking middle classes and a growing inequality of wealth between the rich and the vast majority of Americans who were not rich. During the summer of 2006, the housing boom showed signs of failing, and within a year the housing bubble had burst, triggering a chain of events that plunged the nation, indeed the world, into full-blown financial crisis and economic decline.

In the first years of the twenty-first century, U.S. officials discovered that they could not unilaterally impose American solutions upon the world's vast array of dire problems. AIDS pandemics ravaged the countries of sub-Saharan Africa and threatened to spread to China and India. The Palestinian–Israeli conflict raged on with no peaceful resolution of their fundamental differences in sight. North Korea appeared determined to build nuclear weapons and develop long-range missiles that could strike targets in North America. Iran also strived to develop its own nuclear arsenal. India and Pakistan, both of which possessed weapons of mass destruction (WMD), threatened to go to war with each other over the Kashmir Valley. International terrorism was a persistent threat, culminating in the horrors of September 11, 2001.

By the fall of 2008, the United States was locked into an apparently interminable War against Terror, which involved fighting wars in Afghanistan and Iraq, while also warily observing the actions of leaders in Iran, North Korea, and other countries, regarded as posing current or future threats to American security.

In January 2009, a relatively young and inexperienced political leader, Barack Obama, assumed the presidency to confront the most challenging array of problems to face any American leader since the Great Depression of the early 1930s.

Simultaneously, during the first decade of the new century, Americans struggled to cope with social pressures they scarcely comprehended. The only constant appeared to be ceaseless change. The velocity of history accelerated, and many Americans had the sense of living in a society in perpetual motion, a social order without solid institutional foundations or any clear direction. An ever-changing, ever more diverse social and cultural order raised fundamental questions about individual and national identities.

THE DEMOGRAPHICS OF DIVERSITY

According to the 2000 census, 281,421,906 people inhabited the fifty states comprising the United States of America. For the first time ever, the population increased in all fifty states. The populations of both the largest cities and rural America also showed increases, reversing long-running trends. The South and the West showed the greatest population growth, continuing trends established during World War II.

The 2000 census also revealed the growing diversity of household living arrangements in the United States. For the first time ever, fewer than 25 percent of all households were made up of nuclear families, married couples with children. During the 1990s, the number of single-parent families headed by women who had children grew five times faster than the number of married couples with children. The number of unmarried couples doubled in the 1990s, from three million in 1990 to just under six million in 2000. The decades-long decline in the number of households with children continued into the new millennium. The number of nonfamily households, which consisted of either people living alone or with people who were not related, made up 35 percent of all households, the largest proportion ever.

The new census also showed that people were marrying later, if they married at all. The median age for the first marriage for men reached twenty-seven, and for women it increased to twenty-five. While 14.1 percent of non-Hispanic whites were age sixty-five or older, only 7.9 percent of African Americans fell into that group. In 2000, there were about twenty-one million women age sixty-five or older compared with 14.5 million men, or seventy men for every 100 women.

The median age of the country increased to 35.3, the highest it has ever been. The median age for non-Hispanic whites, who comprised about 70 percent of the nation's population, reached 37.3 in 2000. However, the median age for African Americans was 29.5 and for Hispanics it was 25.8. Census data also showed that there were six million more women than men comprising the national population.

Men narrowed the median life expectancy gap. In 1990, women could expect to live 78.8 years and men could expect to live 71.8 years, a seven-year differential favoring women. In 2000, women could expect to live 79.5 years and men could expect to live 73.8 years, a differential of 5.7 years.

YOUNG PEOPLE OF THE NEW MILLENNIUM

Parents have often made great personal sacrifices to ensure that their children received the best educations possible and had the best opportunities to develop any special talents, skills, or interests they may have. Many parents tried hard to function as positive role models for their children to help prepare them for entering the adult world as confident, responsible and productive citizens. Every year tens of thousands of young Americans graduated from some of the finest colleges and universities in the world.

But the numbers from the 2000 census often told a different story. They revealed how America's children were doing relative to U.S. history and to young people in other lands. U.S. child poverty rates were the highest in the world for developed countries. Child poverty in America was linked to the prevalence of single-parent households invariably headed by women, which are poorer than other households.

Americans spent proportionately less money for primary and secondary education than did most other developed nations. In 2000, Americans spent approximately 3 percent of the U.S. GDP on public schooling. Sweden, Israel, Canada, and France spent almost twice as much proportionately as the United States. Child mortality rates were higher in the United States than in any other developed nation.

In 2008, according to a survey, nearly 40 percent of young people were overweight. Public health officials linked the increasing numbers of obese children to an alarming increase in the number of new asthma cases and a similar increase in the number of people afflicted with adult-onset diabetes. The rapid increase in the number of obese American youngster connected to the public schools many of them attended. Many schools, in order to cut costs and to provide greater choices, have signed contracts with corporate fast-food providers. Youngsters, offered a choice between fresh vegetables and french fries, in 90 percent of the cases, chose the french fries. Young people were eating ever-larger portions of foods high in saturated fats and drinking ever-larger amounts of soft drinks loaded with sweeteners.

Most young people did not get adequate physical exercise. A major cause of this was the sharp decline in high school offerings of physical education classes. Nearly three-fourths of the nation's high schools no longer offered physical education courses in 2008, having either dropped them to save money or replaced them with academic subjects.

Reflecting the growing diversity of the U.S. population, dramatic changes have occurred in public school enrollment in the first years of the twenty-first century. Hispanic and African Americans constituted approximately one-fourth of the total population; however, Hispanic and African American students accounted for over 40 percent of the public school population. Nationally, about two-thirds of all students who entered the ninth grade graduated with regular diplomas four years later. However, only about half of all blacks and Latinos who started high school ever received a diploma. At a time when a college education had become a virtual prerequisite for achieving or maintaining a middle-class lifestyle, only about 10 percent of Hispanic and 15 percent of African American youngsters were earning college degrees.

A MULTICULTURAL SOCIETY

Because of its history as a haven for diasporic populations and because of the upsurge in immigration in recent decades, the United States was home to the most diverse population on the planet. According to the census of 2000, America contained thirty-one ethnic groups with at least one million members each. Multicultural diversity reached virtually into every town and county of the country, but it was in the great cities that America's diverse peoples were concentrated. New York, Chicago, and Los Angeles, America's largest metropolitan centers, attracted large numbers of people from virtually every nation on earth.

According to the 2000 census, the number of foreign-born residents and children of immigrants in the United States had reached 56 million, the highest level in history. One country, Mexico, accounted for more than one quarter of the foreign born. The foreign-born population was heavily concentrated in a few populous states—California, New York, Florida, and Texas. California, with 26 percent, had the highest percentage of foreign-born residents. Los Angeles, with 30 percent of its residents foreign born, led all U.S. cities.

In 2008, the majority of Americans descended from non-Hispanic white Europeans; however, this majority decreased every year in percentage and is expected to become a plurality by 2050. By mid-twenty-first century, the number of Hispanic Americans will probably exceed 100,000,000; they will comprise 25 percent (compared with 15 percent in 2008) of the total population, which is expected to exceed 400 million. The African American population is projected to reach sixty-one million by 2050, which will be about 15 percent (compared with 12 percent in 2008) of the total. The rapidly growing Asian American population will increase to about thirty-three million by 2050, representing about 8 percent (compared with 4 percent in 2008) of the total.

In many important ways, African Americans were flourishing in the early years of the new millennium. Millions of well-educated middle-class black professionals were thriving. Black home ownership and employment both were up. More young African Americans were attending America's finest colleges and universities than ever before. The percentage of black families living below the poverty line was at its lowest point since the federal government began keeping black poverty statistics. Once desolate inner cities such as Chicago's North Lawndale area have become vibrant neighborhoods. Thousands of black political leaders were elected to office at all levels of government. Two African American leaders, Condoleezza Rice and Colin Powell, held powerful positions in President George W. Bush's administration. Clarence Thomas sat as an associate justice on the Supreme Court. In November 2008, Americans elected Barack Obama president of the United States, the most powerful political office on earth.

However, millions of black families continued to struggle to survive and to overcome serious obstacles. If millions of blacks were thriving, millions of others were not. Many inner-city neighborhoods offered neither good jobs nor good schools, and did not foster hope in young people. Among many African American students from middle- and upper-middle-class families, there remained a persistent achievement gap compared with white and Asian students. Shaker Heights, an affluent suburb of Cleveland, was noted for its integrated public high school that consistently ranked as one of the nation's finest. African American students comprised about half of the school's population; however, they accounted for less than 10 percent of those ranked at the top of their class and for 90 percent of those at the bottom. Black students who took the College Board Scholastic Aptitude Tests (SAT), when class and cultural factors were controlled, consistently scored about 100 points lower on both the verbal and math parts of the test than did white and Asian students. Black–white relations remained America's most profound and enduring class and ethnoracial division.

Since the 1980s, Hispanic people have been the fastest-growing ethnic group within the United States. In 2008, Hispanic people, over forty million of them, made up the nation's largest minority group. Hispanics, who could be of any race, were placed into four main groups. By far the largest of these groupings were people of Mexican descent. They accounted for 62 percent of Latinos living in the United States. The second largest group consisted of people who came from Central and South American countries. The other two major Hispanic groups included 3.7 million Americans of Puerto Rican descent and 1.3 million people of Cuban descent.

The booming Hispanic population carried significant political consequences, especially for the states in which Hispanic populations were concentrated: Florida, New Mexico, Arizona, Nevada, Colorado, New Jersey, and particularly Texas and California. In 2008, over half the Hispanic population within the United States lived in Texas and California. In California and Texas, Hispanic political leaders have won election to important city and state offices. On May 17, 2005, Antonio Villaraigosa, the former speaker of the California Assembly, was elected mayor of Los Angeles.

A large majority of politically active Latinos were Democrats. The only Hispanics by group who leaned toward the Republican Party were the Cuban Americans clustered in south Florida. At least one-third of Hispanic voters declined to identify with either party. Many middle-class Hispanics are religious, and tend to have traditional social and family values. Polls also show that Hispanic immigrants and their children are more optimistic about their new country and their prospects within it than native-born non-Hispanic whites.

A NATION OF IMMIGRANTS

According to calculations by the Office of Immigration Statistics in the Department of Homeland Security (DHS), approximately eleven million illegal immigrants were residing in the United States in January 2005. Conservative Republican members of Congress took a hard-line approach focusing on securing the borders against possible terrorists infiltrating America. President Bush, along with Senate Democratic and Republican leaders, called for more comprehensive legislation based on three concerns: securing the borders and staunching the inflow of illegals, regularizing immigration from Mexico by establishing a temporary worker program admitting up to 200,000 immigrants a year, and installing an assimilational system offering illegal immigrants living in the United States an opportunity to earn citizenship over a period of time.

During the spring and summer of 2006, immigrant rights activists organized rallies and demonstrations across the country. Hundreds of thousands of previously marginalized people participated in what was a combination protest against the narrow law-and-order approach to the immigration crisis taken by Congress and an outpouring of Hispanic American patriotic feelings for their adopted country.

Undocumented workers living in the United States formed an integral part of the American labor force. An undocumented immigrant population held one in seven construction jobs, one in five cleaning jobs, one in four agricultural jobs, and one in four restaurant jobs. It is not practicable to expel such a large population. The only way to avoid these immigrants becoming a permanently disenfranchised class was to find a way to bring them into the political order.

Neither the Mexican nor the U.S. government focused on the most crucial goal: facilitating trade and investment to promote greater economic growth for both countries. The immigration crisis that the United States experienced was a consequence of the lack of economic opportunity in Mexico for the mass of its citizens. As long as Mexico remained poor and the lure of opportunity across its border with *Los Estados Unidos* remained powerful, workers will continue to head north. Augmenting border patrols, using the National Guard to police the border, and building fences could not stop the flow. But as the financial crisis and severe economic downturn within the United States worsened in 2007 and 2008, there occurred a noticeable drop-off in undocumented immigrants entering the United States from Mexico. There was also evidence that some immigrants, both legal and illegal, were returning to their homeland because they had lost their jobs.

The Asian American population has changed dramatically in the past decade to include more people from all over Asia, not just East Asians, who for much of the twentieth century made up the bulk of that demographic group within the United States. The immigration explosion of Asian Indians has fueled most of the change. The Asian Indian population more than doubled during the 1990s, from less than one million to nearly two million, becoming the third-largest Asian ethnic nationality within the United States. Asian Indians also constituted the largest group who immigrated to America with H-1B visas, which identified high-tech workers.

The large influx of Asian Indians has forced Americans to reconceptualize what the label "Asian American" represents. Historically, for most Americans, "Asian" has meant people of Chinese, Filipino, Korean, and Japanese descent. However, with the advent of Asian Indians, and with the prospect of millions more South Asians from India, Pakistan, Bangladesh, and Sri Lanka coming to America in the twenty-first century, a broader definition of "Asian American" will be required.

Approximately half of the ten million people of Asian descent inhabiting the United States lived mostly in cities along the West Coast. The number of Chinese, Vietnamese, and Asian Indians doubled or more than doubled during the decade of the 1990s. America's two largest Asian groups, the Chinese and Filipinos, also posted large population gains during that time. The Asian population within the United States grew almost 50 percent during the 1990s and continued to increase rapidly during the first years of the twenty-first century. In 2008, approximately fourteen million Asian Americans lived in the United States, representing 4 percent of the national population.

American Muslims are another important group that is internally very diverse. Approximately one-third of American Muslims are African Americans. On average they generally report lower levels of education and income than other Americans. But Asian American Muslims, principally from India and Pakistan, generally see themselves as thriving. American Muslim women, contrary to stereotypes, are more likely than Muslim men to have college and postgraduate degrees. Muslim women attend mosque as frequently as Muslim men. According to a Gallup poll, 80 percent of Muslims say religion is an important part of their daily life. By political ideology, Muslims are spread across the American spectrum, with about half of them identifying themselves as moderates or centrists. About half of American Muslims are registered Democrats, one-third describe themselves as Independents, and a small minority say they are Republicans.

As a consequence of the revival of massive immigration during the 1970s, America is approaching a profound demographic tipping point. All of those groups that the U.S. Census Bureau categorizes as racial minorities—blacks, Hispanics, and Asians—will account for a majority of the American population by the year 2040. Among young Americans (eighteen and under), this shift will occur by 2023, which means that every child born in the United States from 2005 on will belong to the first postwhite generation.

While America undergoes its demographic makeover, the culture likewise is going through a profound transformation:

> The long-standing model of assimilation toward a common center is being remade in the image of white America's multiethnic, multicolored heirs.[1]

This new multicolored American cultural identity is most evident in the many facets of contemporary popular culture. A multicultural inclusiveness appears to value every identity except "whiteness." Sociologists have noted a whole generation of urban, college-educated liberal whites

---

[1] Hua Hsu, "The End of White America," *The Atlantic* (January/February), 2009, 45–55.

who were engaged in a "flight from whiteness." Perhaps the few white rappers are an extreme example of this escapist syndrome.

Other scholars suggested that the coming demographic shifts will not likely invert the traditional racial hierarchy that has prevailed for centuries, replacing it with a multicultural majority that disdains a white minority. The new cultural order will more likely diminish the power of ethnoracial categories over everyone's lives. It will be flat rather than hierarchical, a more inclusive order that prizes diversity and will treat its inhabitants as individuals rather than as members of a particular racial group. Advertisers and political candidates have already developed versatile images and messages, which can be tailored to meet particular interests, beliefs, preferences, and tastes. Visionaries see a future "beige" American population in which, as a result of racial intermarriage, all discernible racial differences and any cultural preferences based on them, will have disappeared.

ELECTION 2000

Voters were not given much of a choice between the major party presidential candidates during the 2000 election. Democratic Party candidate Al Gore, a Harvard graduate, was the son of a former leader of the Senate; Republican Party candidate George W. Bush was a Yale graduate and the son of a former president. Within the prevailing conservative political climate, both men campaigned as moderate Centrists, Bush from the Right side and Gore from the Left side of a narrow political spectrum. For the increasing factions of voters unhappy with the ideologically neutered campaigns conducted by the mainstream candidates, they could choose between the Green Party candidate Ralph Nader, who ran as an "Old Liberal" critic of money-driven politics, and the Reform Party candidate Pat Buchanan, who ran as an unreconstructed nativist vowing to close down America's relatively open immigration policy. Most Americans, better-off economically than ever before, and living in peace, paid scant attention to national politics or to the presidential campaigns.

Perhaps the most unusual aspect of the rather dull 2000 election was that Al Gore lost an election that he could have won. According to the conventional wisdom, pocketbook issues determined who has won and who has lost presidential elections. Al Gore entered the campaign with apparently overwhelming advantages. As Clinton's capable high-profile vice president for eight years, he was the heir-apparent of the 1990s prosperity binge. He was much better known to the American public than the relatively obscure governor of Texas who bore a famous name. Polls consistently showed that most Americans regarded the economy and their own prospects as "excellent" or "good." For fiscal 2000, the federal budget showed a hefty surplus of $400 billion. Polls also demonstrated that Bill Clinton, despite the impeachment scandal, remained popular.

According to many of the journalists who covered the presidential campaign from start to finish, Al Gore and his cadre of advisers lost Election 2000 because they chose not to exploit Clinton's popularity or to take credit for the good times. Gore would not even allow the popular incumbent to campaign for him lest he provoke some kind of moralistic backlash. Apparently Gore did not understand that the only voters likely to react that way were already committed to voting for Bush. According to historian Douglas Brinkley, had Al Gore campaigned all-out for prosperity and embraced Clinton's administration with no apologies for any personal failings the president may have exhibited, he would have reached the White House. After his election, George W. Bush said that he was surprised that he won given that he was running against "peace, prosperity, and a popular incumbency."

When the campaign opened with the New Hampshire primaries in February 2000, Al Gore defeated his one serious challenger, former senator Bill Bradley. On the Republican side, maverick Arizona senator John McCain won some of the other early primaries, running on his single issue of campaign finance reform. McCain's sudden emergence as a serious presidential candidate was the major surprise of election 2000. McCain quickly became the darling of political reporters covering his campaign because of his open, personal style. But Bush, by shoring up his standing with conservative Republicans, quickly stopped McCain's challenge. Gore and Bush had the major party nominations sewed up by the end of March.

Bush and his running mate Dick Cheney also carefully distanced themselves from some of the pet issues of social conservatives, reinforcing the moderately conservative image, which they consistently projected. Bush spoke of a "compassionate conservatism" and made improving public schools his top domestic priority. Bush and Cheney virtually ignored the Religious Right. Bush refused to agree to appoint only antiabortion jurists. Cheney did not rule out same-sex marriages, leaving that issue to the states to decide.

There were three televised debates during the campaign. Going into the debates, the Gore camp confidently assumed that their candidate would win them all. Gore was a policy wonk, much more cerebral and articulate than Bush. He was the author of many articles and a book about environmental issues. Bush, on the other hand, had provided comedians with many hilarious examples of mangled syntax. Some observers wondered if George W. Bush might be dyslectic or perhaps suffered from a brain disorder. He appeared to be surprisingly uninformed about major international issues, and was not much interested in learning about them.

But Gore managed to lose all three debates. In the first one, he came across as arrogant and rude. In the second, trying to correct the impression he had created in the first debate, he came across as smarmy and insincere. In the third debate, Gore made a serious error when he invaded Bush's physical space. Bush, sensing an advantage, gave Gore a little nod of derision. The debates significantly influenced the campaign. Gore did not overwhelm Bush. Bush came across as knowledgeable enough to do the job and as a "regular guy." Gore came across as something of a bully, who was not as smart as he thought he was.

As election day approached, all the polls gave Gore a tiny, shrinking lead. It was going to be close. The 49 percent of eligible voters who voted on election day produced one of the closest elections in U.S. history. Gore won the popular vote, 50,996,064 to Bush's 50,456,167, even though Bush carried thirty states. Gore also led in the electoral votes 266 to 249, not counting Florida (the winner required 270). Ralph Nader garnered 2,882,897 votes, and may have siphoned off enough potential Gore votes in four states, including Florida, to give those states' electoral votes to Bush. Many Gore supporters bitterly accused the Nader camp of costing them the election, overlooking the inconvenient fact that Gore's inept campaign more likely cost him an election that he could have won. Republicans lost seats in both the Senate and the House of Representatives. Their majority in the House shrank to twelve, and the new Senate had fifty Democrats and fifty Republicans.

THIRTY-SIX DAYS

The closeness of the presidential election created serious problems for the TV networks. The spotlight was on Florida, where the outcome of the election was going to be decided. Early Tuesday evening, on election night, all of the TV news anchors declared Al Gore the winner in Florida. By 2:15 A.M. on Wednesday morning, they had reversed themselves and declared Bush the likely winner. Two hours later, they reversed themselves again, declaring Florida "too close to call," even though Bush was leading by about 1,700 votes.

Network confusion about the outcome of election 2000 set the stage for the most extraordinary thirty-six days in the history of U.S. presidential elections. The American political classes went to war over who would win Florida's twenty-five electoral votes and with them the presidency of the United States. While the politicians and their lawyers battled furiously, most Americans, and much of the rest of the world, watched from the sidelines.

The thirty-six-day political war, which unfolded in Florida following the inconclusive election, raised a plethora of significant issues. Civil rights leaders accused Florida election officials of deliberately disfranchising black voters. The controversy also exposed the antiquated voting technologies and the patchwork of local practices in place for recording and counting votes. To many observers, the election also exposed the electoral college for the eighteenth-century anachronism that it was. They demanded that America elect presidents directly as did all the other modern democracies. Above all, the dispute raised questions about to what extent, if at all, should state and federal courts involve themselves in elections.

The most immediate issues involved recounting votes, and which ones to recount. There were two main categories of votes to be recounted. Some ballots had apparently misled some Gore voters into voting for Pat Buchanan. The larger category of disputed votes were "under votes," votes that the voting machines did not tabulate because voters had not punched their choices completely through on the punch card ballots. Some of the nation's top legal talents argued with one another over if and how they would evaluate dimpled chads, hanging chads, and pregnant chads. (Chads were the bits of cardboard punched out of the cards by voters, or, as in the case of the "under votes," the bits of cardboard not completely punched out.) Gore, trailing in the vote, demanded recounts in those counties where he calculated they would gain him enough votes to win. The Bush people, narrowly ahead in the vote, insisted that there be no recounts. Florida's secretary of state Katherine Harris, an appointee of Governor Jeb Bush, the Republican presidential candidate's brother, halted the recount process on November 27 and declared George W. Bush the winner by 537 votes. Harris insisted that her actions were dictated by the Florida electoral codes. Gore then appealed to the Florida State Supreme Court, comprising mostly Democratic appointees, who overruled Harris and ordered the recounts to continue.

The Bush camp appealed to the U.S. Supreme Court. Late on the night of December 12, the Supreme Court, deeply divided along partisan and ideological lines, in *Bush v. Gore*, decided by a five-to-four decision, that the equal protection clause of the Fourteenth Amendment required that all ballots must be counted the same way, and since Florida did not have a uniform standard for recounting ballots in different counties, all recounts must cease immediately. But no court had ever before imposed any kind of constitutional rule of uniformity in the counting of ballots. Most states, in addition to Florida, used different voting technologies in a single election. By blocking a recount, the Court preserved and endorsed a less accurate count of the ballots. They also declared that their ruling regarding uniformity in ballot counting applied only to the Florida vote for the plaintiff, George W. Bush. The disputed election of 2000 was resolved when five Supreme Court justices, by ordering all recounts to cease while Bush still retained his 537-vote lead, awarded Florida's 25 disputed electoral votes to him.

The four dissenting justices all filed strongly worded opinions. One of them, Justice Stephen Breyer, a Clinton appointee, wrote that the Court's majority opinion was clearly a political one that "runs the risk of undermining the public's confidence in the Court itself."

The next day, an embittered Al Gore conceded the election; George W. Bush became the forty-third president of the United States.

COMPASSIONATE CONSERVATISM

Mindful of the close, controversial election that had brought him to the White House via a 5 to 4 decision of the Supreme Court and of the partisan acrimony that had characterized Washington politics in recent years, President George W. Bush's brief inaugural address focused on the themes of civility, tolerance, and what he called "compassionate conservatism." He promised to consult with Democratic leaders of Congress and to work with them to solve the myriad of problems facing the American people. The new president observed that America's grandest ideal is that "everyone belongs, that everyone deserves a chance, that no insignificant person was ever born."

Concerned to shed the Republican Party's image as the party of, by, and for white men, Bush appointed the most diverse cabinet in U.S. history. Spencer Abraham, a Lebanese American, became Secretary of Energy; Norman Mineta, a Japanese American, became Secretary of Transportation; Elaine Chao, a Taiwanese immigrant, became Secretary of Labor; and Mel Martinez, a Cuban immigrant, became Secretary of Housing and Urban Development. In addition to Chao, two other women were appointed to cabinet positions—Gale Norton as Secretary of the Interior and Ann Veneman as Secretary of Agriculture. Two African Americans were also appointed to the new Cabinet—Roderick Page as Secretary of Education and Colin Powell as Secretary of State.

Although the new president received only 6 percent of the black vote, he appointed two African Americans to two powerful foreign policy advisory positions—the aforementioned Colin Powell at State and Condoleezza Rice as his National Security Adviser. Powell and Rice became the two most powerful black political leaders in the nation's history.

During the first months of the Bush presidency, the White House pushed its top priorities through Congress—educational reform and tax cuts. The No Child Left Behind Act, the new administration's most important education reform, was noteworthy mainly for establishing a larger federal presence in the nation's public schools, and for implementing a testing regimen whereby schools would be held accountable for what they taught, or failed to teach, their pupils.

On May 26, 2001, Congress approved a $1.35 trillion tax cut spread over ten years. One provision of the tax bill provided for immediate tax relief in the form of $300.00 rebates to all single workers and $600.00 to those filing joint returns. The new law also provided for lowering every tax bracket except the 15 percent bracket in stages until 2006. The new law gradually reduced the estate tax and then phased it out altogether after ten years. It also raised the child credit in stages and allowed increased contributions to Individual Retirement Accounts (IRAs) and 401(k)-type pension plans. Taxes for couples would be adjusted downward to eliminate the so-called marriage penalty.

Democratic critics of the Bush tax cuts claimed that most of the tax savings went to rich people, while the middle classes and working classes received only token reductions in their taxes. They also insisted that significantly reducing taxes while the U.S. economy was weak was fiscally irresponsible because it risked rising deficits and imperiled the solvency of the Social Security system. The debate over the tax cuts highlighted a fiscal reality that neither conservative Republicans nor liberal Democrats acknowledged—the federal government was increasingly dependent on income taxes collected from taxpayers in the upper-income brackets.

President Bush's prospects for getting most of his agenda enacted by Congress suddenly were reduced significantly when Republican senator Jim Jeffords of Vermont announced that henceforth he would be an Independent. Jeffords' defection from the Republican Party gave the Democratic Party a 50 to 49 majority in the Senate and thus control of that branch of the federal legislature. Democrat Tom Daschle became the new Senate majority leader replacing Trent Lott.

The Bush presidency also made a series of decisions that provoked criticism from many environmentalists. On March 13, President Bush announced that he would not regulate carbon dioxide emissions from power plants. On March 27, Bush removed the United States from the Kyoto Protocol, the 1997 Treaty negotiated during the Clinton presidency, which required the United States to cut greenhouse gas emissions by one-third over a fifteen-year period.

Since American industries were responsible for the production of more than 25 percent of the emissions, Bush's unilateralist decision to pull the United States out of the Kyoto agreement nullified international efforts to control greenhouse gas emissions. Most environmental scientists believed that greenhouse gases such as carbon dioxide were a major cause of global warming. To all the critics of his antienvironmentalist actions, President Bush had the same rejoinder: He would take no actions that harmed the American economy.

TERRORIST ATTACK!

On the morning of September 11, 2001, at 8:45 A. M. local time, American Airlines Flight 11, a Boeing 767, ripped into the North Tower of the World Trade Center (WTC). Twenty minutes later, United Airlines Flight 175, also a Boeing 767, slammed into the South Tower. Ninety minutes later, both of the 110-story structures had collapsed into gigantic mounds of burning rubble. Buried among the wreckage were over 2,700 people, dead and dying, including 350 firefighters and police officers who had rushed into the buildings just before they collapsed. Located at the southern end of Manhattan, the twin towers of the WTC, the financial nerve center of the global economy, had been potent symbols of America's wealth and of its dominant role in international financial relations. The millions of people who saw the televised images of the second plane crashing into the tower must have felt as if they were witnessing a nightmare from which there could be no awakening.

At almost the same time the WTC was destroyed, a third airliner, probably aiming for the White House, slammed into the Pentagon. A fourth aircraft, diverted from its intended target by a band of courageous passengers, crashed into a field outside of Pittsburgh, Pennsylvania. Informed observers speculated that the fourth airliner was probably headed for the Capitol building in Washington, D.C. All 246 people on board the four aircraft perished. The four planes had been hijacked by members of the *al Qaeda* terrorist network, organized and led by Osama bin Laden.

What made the horror worse on that dreadful day, and for many days afterward, was the fear that more attacks were imminent. How many other planes might have been turned into flying bombs? What other WMD would terrorists unleash on vulnerable Americans—chemical, biological, and even crude nuclear weapons? What other symbolic or strategic targets would be hit? How many more Americans would die? National Guardsmen were hastily mobilized and assigned to guard duties all over the country. The skies over America's great cities and other potential targets were filled with Air Force fighters and refueling aircraft. A nation, which had been attacked, braced itself for possibly many more attacks.

On September 18, four letters containing the lethal anthrax organism were mailed to NBC and other news organizations. On October 9, anthrax-bearing letters were delivered to the offices of two U.S. senators. These letters killed five people and infected twenty-three others. Thirty-one congressional staffers tested positive for exposure to anthrax, forcing the closing of congressional offices for decontamination. A post office in the nation's capital, which had processed some of the letters, was closed for over a year. These frightening and mysterious biological attacks, coming a

FIGURE 18.1 A hijacked jet airliner is caught on camera an instant before it crashed into the South Tower of the World Trade Center. *Source:* AP/Wide World Photos. AP photo/Carmen Taylor.

week after the destruction of the WTCs and the slaughter of nearly 3,000 people, heightened national anxieties and reinforced the strong "what's next?" kind of paranoia felt by millions of Americans.

Searching for historical parallels, media pundits were quick to compare the terrorist attacks with Pearl Harbor. But the surprise attacks at Pearl Harbor had been carried out by Japanese naval aviators, who attacked only U.S. military targets and personnel. The terrorist attacks of September 11 were carried out by members of a shadowy, decentralized terrorist network that represented no nation or state, that deliberately targeted civilians.

The 9/11 attacks were best understood as the most destructive terrorist assaults on the United States yet. They represented escalations of ongoing terrorist campaigns waged against U.S. interests at home and abroad that had originated in the late 1970s.

A surge of old-fashioned patriotism swept across the nation. American flags were proudly flown from front porches and vehicles. Money, commodities, and people poured into New York to aid the victims and to help with the massive cleanup operations. Prayer vigils were held in churches, synagogues, and mosques as well as in public parks and buildings. Rudolph Giuliani provided inspired leadership and became a national hero in his final days as mayor of New York. Ground Zero, the site of the ruined towers, became the scene of the most massive cleanup job in the nation's history. Ground Zero also became sacred ground, consecrated by the blood of heroes who died doing their jobs in the prime of their lives.

Beyond the instant loss of life and property, the deadly assaults inflicted considerable fiscal, financial, and economic pain on America. An official report, issued a year after the fiery destruction of the WTC towers, placed the overall cost to New York City at $95 billion. A sluggish economy, declining tax revenues, plunging stock prices, and increased spending for national defense combined to transform a federal budget surplus of $127 billion for fiscal 2001 into a deficit of $157 billion for fiscal 2002.

Federal tax revenues suffered their largest one-year percentage drop in over fifty years, and expenditures showed their most rapid increase since the early 1980s. Wall Street, already reeling in the wake of the collapse of the Silicon Valley dot-com bubble, suffered its worst one-week loss since the Great Crash of 1929. Forty-six of the fifty states reported budget shortfalls for fiscal 2002. In the wake of the attacks, over a million workers lost their jobs. By the end of the year, the unemployment rate had reached 5.8 percent, the highest in seven years. The attacks helped push a teetering economy into its first recession in a decade.

The attacks also triggered an unprecedented shutdown of all airports in the United States, stranding thousands of travelers around the world. Service started again after a six-day hiatus, but at much-reduced levels and with greatly enhanced security. But fear and uncertainty kept many people away from airports for months. Many airlines, already operating in the red, faced bankruptcy in the aftermath of the attacks and a ruinous falloff in business. Only a quick $15 billion bailout from Congress temporarily halted the disastrous decline of the airline industry.

The federal government made $40 billion available to help New York clear out the rubble, aid the survivors of the victims, and rebuild the area. Nearly all Americans closed ranks to wage the war on terrorism. Extremists on the far Left and far Right dissented. From the Right, Reverend Jerry Falwell, founder and leader of the Moral Majority, called the attacks God's punishment for Americans' sins of liberalism, secularism, abortion, and homosexuality. From the Left, Noam Chomsky wrote a short book, *9/11*, in which he argued that Islamic fundamentalists like Osama bin Laden were retaliating only for numerous terrorist acts committed by the United States against Islamic peoples.

It soon became evident that the government had failed to anticipate or adequately prepare for the terrorist attacks on September 11. The FBI and CIA failed to heed numerous warning signs. One missed opportunity occurred when an FBI field agent noted that a large number of young males of Middle Eastern descent were enrolling in flight schools to learn to fly jet airliners. The report was filed in the FBI's Central Office and not read until after the attacks had occurred. According to Coleen Rowley, a lawyer working out of the Minneapolis, Minnesota FBI office, who testified before a congressional investigating committee, another missed opportunity occurred when FBI agents from Washington, D.C., refused to allow Minnesota agents to search the computer of Zacarias Moussani, an alleged co-conspirator arrested in August 2001, three weeks before the 9/11 attacks occurred. Congressional investigators concluded that there had been enough warning signs for the federal agencies charged with protecting the security of the United States to believe that a terrorist attack was imminent and to take aggressive steps to heighten security at airports.

There were also systemic failures. The CIA and FBI did not coordinate counter-terrorist activities nor exchange intelligence. The FBI had a policy of not sharing intelligence data with CIA operatives in order to protect its bureaucratic turf. It had failed for nearly ten years to penetrate the *al Qaeda* network. Few CIA operatives were fluent in Arabic languages or knew anything about Islamic cultures or traditions. Most CIA field officers assigned to Middle Eastern countries appeared to be more comfortable working within U.S. embassies. They rarely traveled into the countryside or met with people. So they learned nothing about the impending attacks.

THE TRANSFORMATION OF U.S. FOREIGN POLICY

The terrorist attacks transformed George W. Bush's presidency and transformed American foreign policy. The president called the deadly attacks "acts of war" and vowed to hunt down and bring to justice all those found responsible for them. Armed with a UN Security Council resolution, Bush ordered the *Taliban* rulers of Afghanistan, who had long protected bin Laden, to turn him over to U.S. authorities or face military attack. The president warned any nation that harbored terrorists to expect an American response. Secretary of State Colin Powell bluntly announced to all nations, "You're either with us or against us." Congress, with one dissenting vote, granted the president the power to take whatever actions he found necessary to protect the security of the American nation and its people.

There was also a domestic front in the war on terror. Congress created a new cabinet-level agency, the Department of Homeland Security (DHS), to coordinate the activities of over forty state and federal agencies charged with protecting U.S. internal security. Critics of the new unwieldy federal bureaucracy doubted that it could protect all of the nation's ports, rail systems, chemical factories, nuclear plants, water supplies, and a myriad of other vulnerable sites from terrorist attacks.

Civil libertarians worried that some of the security measures taken by the federal government in the wake of the 9/11 terrorist attacks to protect the American people might involve unacceptable invasions of the privacy of individual citizens. Of particular concern was the USA Patriot Act, passed by Congress and signed by President Bush on October 26, 2001. The Patriot Act gave local police added powers to wiretap telephones, monitor Internet and e-mail use, and to search the homes of suspected terrorists without having to first obtain search warrants. The new law also permitted authorities to detain any foreigner suspected of terrorism for seven days without formally charging him with any crime.

Federal agencies secretly collected vast amounts of communication and financial data as they sought to detect and degrade terrorist networks. The National Security Agency (NSA) monitored international phone calls and e-mails. The FBI was allowed to access data on credit and debit card transactions, and wire transfers of funds. The Treasury Department and the CIA shared data provided by Swift, a worldwide banking cooperative.

Critics charged that these activities represented unwarranted extensions of the powers of the executive branch. Members of Congress demanded that they be granted more oversight of intelligence-gathering operations. Guardians of civil liberties asserted that the Bush administration was creating an Orwellian state in which no one could elude the eyes and ears of Big Brother. However, the large majority of Americans appeared to be untroubled by the new security measures, which they regarded as necessary to protect Americans against further terrorist attacks.

After quickly forging an alliance that included NATO countries, Russia, China, India, Egypt, Saudi Arabia, and Pakistan, the U.S. launched a retaliatory war against the *Taliban* and the *al Qaeda* terrorist networks within Afghanistan. President Bush provided strong leadership in a time of crisis. Most Americans responded positively to the defining moment of Bush's presidency. His public approval ratings soared. Eighty-eight percent of Americans said that they supported the war against terrorism in Afghanistan.

The air war and limited ground war that the United States waged against the *Taliban* and *al Qaeda* networks in Afghanistan in the wake of the 9/11 attacks once again reshuffled the world's diplomatic deck. Not only had the Cold War era ended, so had the post–Cold War era, which lasted scarcely a decade.

The Muslim members of the U.S.-led coalition were ambivalent about their roles. The leader who was most ambivalent was also the most essential. Pakistan, led by General Pervez

Musharraf, allowed Americans to mount attacks on the *Taliban* from bases in Pakistan after the United States provided billions of dollars of aid and canceled an embargo that had been clamped on Pakistan after it had exploded a nuclear weapon.

Egypt and Saudi Arabia were even more reluctant allies. The Saudis had contributed millions of dollars to support the *Taliban* and Osama bin Laden, while they were driving the Soviets out of Afghanistan in the 1980s. bin Laden, who was a Saudi citizen of Yemeni descent, the son of one of the richest men in Saudi Arabia, was himself enormously wealthy and used his personal wealth to fund many of *al Qaeda*'s anti-Soviet operations. The CIA had also funneled weapons and money into Afghanistan to aid the *Taliban* and *al Qaeda* in the war against the Soviets. The United States and bin Laden had been *de facto* allies in the war against the Soviet occupation of Afghanistan.

On October 7, 2001, the United States and Great Britain launched a powerful assault against Afghanistan using bombers, fighter planes, and cruise missiles. The U.S.-led coalition quickly established control of the air. They pounded *al Qaeda* training camps and *Taliban* military strongholds. The Americans also provided aid to the opposition Northern Alliance within Afghanistan, which quickly went on the offensive.

The Islamic fundamentalist *Taliban* regime led by Mullah Muhammad Omar, which had sheltered bin Laden and his *al Qaeda* network, quickly collapsed under the pressure of U.S. bombs and attacks by the armies of the Northern Alliance. On November 13, Northern Alliance forces rolled into Kabul, the capital of Afghanistan, where they were enthusiastically greeted by the people, most of whom were delighted to be liberated from the severe *Taliban* regime. Within a month, most of the country was under the control of the Northern Alliance and other anti-*Taliban* forces. Mullah Omar abdicated on December 6 and fled to the mountainous eastern region bordering Pakistan.

On December 22, an interim government headed by Hamid Karzai was installed in Kabul. On June 10, 2002, delegates to a *loya jirga* (grand council) assembled in Kabul to create a constitutional framework for a permanent government. The interim coalition leader Hamid Karzai was elected president, and a new cabinet was sworn in.

As Afghan leaders worked to establish a functioning government for Afghanistan, U.S. and British commandos searched for the elusive bin Laden and his top lieutenants in a cave complex called Tora Bora near the Pakistani border. Although the Allied forces killed or captured hundreds of *al Qaeda* fighters, bin Laden and most of his top aides eluded them, and hundreds of *al Qaeda* fighters survived.

Almost six hundred *Taliban* and *al Qaeda* fighters captured during the war in Afghanistan were flown to the U.S. naval base at Guantanamo Bay, Cuba. The first contingents arrived January 11, 2002. Many were interrogated intensively. The attorney general's office developed a legal rationale for detaining prisoners indefinitely without charging them with any crime, and for using extraordinary measures to elicit actionable intelligence from them. U.S. secretary of defense Donald Rumsfeld designated the detainees "unlawful combatants," not entitled to prisoner-of-war status under the Geneva Conventions.

Lawyers working in the State Department, alarmed by the new policy, stated that the U.S. military had scrupulously observed the Geneva Conventions in previous wars. To stop observing the conventions now risked the mistreatment of U.S. soldiers captured by terrorists. The State Department attorneys also insisted that the United States could not abandon the moral high ground in the ongoing war.

As the war in Afghanistan subsided temporarily and the Karzai government struggled to take hold, Americans went to the polls in November 2002 to elect a new Congress. Few issues separated the parties, and nearly all incumbents were reelected. Republicans, as the party associated with patriotism and national defense, benefited from an agenda that put foreign policy issues in the fore-front. The war on terrorism upstaged social spending issues such as Medicare and Social Security where the Democrats could have had an advantage. In a time of war, the Democrats also failed to get much political traction out of criticizing President Bush's failure to restore prosperity.

Republicans regained control of the Senate and widened their majority in the House of Representatives. Additionally, Republicans won control of a majority of state governorships, including four of the six most populous states. President Bush strengthened his power with Congress by involving himself extensively in various campaigns. He worked hard for Republican candidates for the Senate and the House, and for several gubernatorial candidates. Nearly all of the candidates for whom President Bush campaigned emerged victorious.

The Republican sweep strengthened President Bush and gave his party control of both the Congress and the White House for the first time since 1954. The Republican party appeared to have consolidated its status as the majority party. Republican candidates clearly benefited from the personal popularity of President Bush (polls showed his approval rating in the 65 percent to 70 percent range) and the post-9/11 environment.

THE INVASION OF IRAQ

The Bush administration also broadened the war on terror to incorporate what the president termed "rogue nations" and other terrorist organizations, some with links to *al Qaeda*. President Bush spoke of an "axis of evil" running from Iraq through Iran to North Korea. In September 2002, the Bush administration presented a new national security strategy premised on the doctrine of preemption. If senior officials had access to intelligence data indicating an attack on U.S. interests was imminent, they would order attacks to take out the threat. Hit them before they strike at us. Henceforth preemption would be the main component of U.S. strategic policy in its war on terror.

Iraq was the chosen country where Bush's doctrine of preemption was first applied. Senior officials in the Bush administration apparently had wanted to remove the Iraqi dictator Saddam Hussein from power for a long time. Vice President Dick Cheney and Secretary of Defense Donald Rumsfeld advised President Bush to incorporate "regime change" in Iraq into the expanding war on terrorism for several reasons: (1) It would eliminate the security threat Saddam posed to his neighbors, to core U.S. allies, and ultimately to the United States itself. It would simultaneously enable the United States to establish military bases in a strategically and economically important Arab nation, whose people would welcome American soldiers as liberators. (2) It would provide an opportunity to bring liberal democracy to an important Arab country, which in time could spread to other Middle Eastern countries. (3) It would increase the chances of a peaceful resolution of the interminable Arab–Israeli conflict. (4) It could provide U.S. access to Iraqi oil, which could drive down world oil prices and ease American dependency on Saudi Arabian oil. (5) It would signal to terrorists and to nations that sponsored or harbored terrorists that Washington possessed the political will and military power to take preemptive actions to eliminate perceived threats to U.S. interests wherever they were found. (6) The invasion of Iraq would also demonstrate that the United States was prepared to undertake decisive actions unilaterally if necessary.

Sanctions imposed on Iraq in 1991 in the wake of the Gulf War had required Iraq to destroy all of its WMD, including any chemical, biological, or nuclear weapons that it retained or was developing. The sanctions regime also required Saddam Hussein to allow UN inspectors unfettered access to all the sites where WMDs might be manufactured or stored. U.S. officials maintained that Saddam Hussein had failed to cooperate with UN weapons inspectors and that Iraqi scientists continued to develop and stockpile WMD.

In a speech that he delivered to the UN General Assembly on September 12, 2002, President Bush promised to work with the Security Council to meet the challenge posed by Iraq's defiance, but he also stressed that the international community must act decisively to end the threat posed by Iraq's possession of WMD. On October 10, both houses of Congress by large bipartisan majorities enacted a measure backing President Bush's use of military force against Iraq if it did not comply fully with the UN inspectors. Two weeks later, the UN Security Council enacted Resolution 1441 giving Iraq "a final opportunity" to comply with all the previous UN disarmament resolutions and established a strict timetable for compliance. A few days later, acceding to the threat of force, Iraq agreed to allow UN inspections to resume, while insisting that it did not possess any WMD. The first cadre of UN weapons inspectors led by Hans Blix arrived in Baghdad on November 25.

UN inspectors searched sites throughout Iraq, but could find no WMD. However, inspectors did find evidence that indicated WMD had been previously stored at some sites. Iraqi documents also failed to account for large numbers of WMD that had been discovered during past inspections and had supposedly been destroyed. On December 19, Secretary of State Colin Powell declared that Iraq was in "material breach" of UN resolutions and risked war if it continued its pattern of lying, deception, and noncompliance. On January 7, 2003, Hans Blix issued a report in which he accused Iraq of failure to cooperate with UN weapons inspectors in accounting for and removing chemical and biological weapons. The United States moved closer to war with Iraq a few days later when Secretary of Defense Donald Rumsfeld signed orders deploying 62,000 U.S. troops to the Persian Gulf region. Joining the U.S. military buildup, Great Britain announced that it was sending an aircraft carrier and 26,000 troops to the Gulf.

As the United States and Great Britain ratcheted up the military pressure on Iraq, a worldwide debate on the merits of the impending war intensified. Colin Powell appeared before the UN Security Council on February 5 to make his case for a UN endorsement of a war against Iraq. Citing various intelligence sources, Powell accused Saddam Hussein's regime of removing evidence from various sites and intimidating Iraqi scientists in efforts to deceive UN weapons inspectors. He also accused the Iraqi leaders of maintaining ties with *al Qaeda* and harboring their own terrorist cells.

Following his presentation, ten East European countries, led by Poland, voiced their strong support for the United States; however, France, Russia, and China, all members of the Security Council, opposed taking any military action against Iraq. Their leaders all insisted that Powell had failed to prove conclusively that Iraq retained WMD, had ties with *al Qaeda*, or posed an imminent threat to U.S. security. They demanded that the UN inspections should be given more time. They also maintained that UN sanctions regime against Iraq had worked well enough to contain Saddam Hussein's aggressive tendencies.

As the United States and Great Britain positioned their forces for an invasion of Iraq, millions of people opposed to the war demonstrated in cities around the world. In London an estimated 750,000 people and in Rome an estimated 600,000 people protested the impending war. There were huge antiwar rallies in New York and San Francisco.

On March 5, Hans Blix stated that the weapons inspectors needed more time. China issued a statement declaring that the inspections required more time. France, Germany, and Russia announced that they would oppose a draft resolution submitted to the UN Security Council by the United States, Great Britain, and Spain declaring that Iraq had missed its last chance to disarm peacefully.

In defiance of all the protests and calls for more diplomacy, Colin Powell stated that the United States would lead a "coalition of the willing nations" that would disarm Iraq with or without UN authority. On March 17, President Bush told Saddam Hussein that he and his two

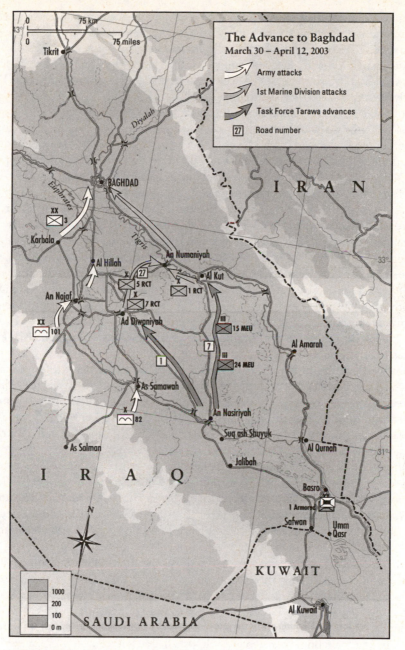

FIGURE 18.2 The Advance to Baghdad, March 30–April 12, 2003. *Source:* U.S. Army map.

sons must leave Iraq within forty-eight hours. Saddam ignored Bush's ultimatum. The U.S.-led military offensive to oust the regime of Saddam Hussein began the evening of March 19, 2003, when U.S. aircraft and Tomahawk cruise missiles attacked targets located in Baghdad. In a television address to the nation, President Bush announced the onset of a military campaign named *Operation Iraqi Freedom.* The Iraq war had begun.

Units of the Army's 3rd Infantry Division and elements of the 1st Marine Expeditionary Force quickly moved northward from staging areas in Kuwait toward Baghdad. In an aerial bombardment, which the Pentagon dubbed its "shock and awe" campaign, coordinated with ground combat elements, U.S. aircraft and cruise missiles rained lethal punishment on selected targets in Baghdad and various Iraqi military units. The aerial campaign was covered live by the U.S. media, particularly the major television all-news channels—CNN, CNBC, and Fox News. Television coverage of the war was supplemented by reports from journalists, many of them veterans, "embedded" with the advancing ground forces.

Within a week, during which U.S. forces continuously surprised, outmaneuvered, and destroyed the Iraqi troops trying to fight back, the Americans had reached the approaches to Baghdad. Never had a large military force combined the elements of movement, flexibility, and lethality of precision weapons so effectively in combat. Never had an invading army moved so quickly and so deeply into enemy territory. While the U.S. forces moved rapidly toward Baghdad, British forces in the south moved more slowly toward Basra, Iraq's second largest city.

Then the lightning U.S. advance hit several snags simultaneously. Fierce sandstorms called *shamals*, that raged for days, impeded progress. Attacks by *fedayeen*, Iraqi irregulars, who made up for their lack of military skills with a willingness to martyr themselves for a cause in which they devoutly believed, threatened to slow the U.S. advance by attacking overextended supply lines. Another complicating factor was the refusal of the Turkish government to allow coalition forces to invade Iraq from the north as had been planned.

After a few days of delay, coalition forces consisting almost entirely of U.S. and British troops crushed the Iraqi military in two weeks of hard fighting. On April 4, U.S. Army and Marine forces met on the outskirts of Baghdad after both had to quash some last-ditch resistance by elite Republican Guard units and the *fedayeen*. The next day, elements of the third Infantry Division reached the city center. On April 8, the regime of Saddam Hussein simply melted away. In the north, fighting continued for a few more days. On April 10, Kurdish forces captured Kirkuk, a large city near the northern oil fields. The next day, Marines occupied Tikrit, Saddam Hussein's hometown.

Coalition forces suffered few casualties. Because of their use of precision weapons, particularly global positioning system (GPS) ordnance and laser-guided bombs (LGBs), there was comparatively light collateral damage inflicted on the hapless Iraqis. On May 1, on board the attack carrier *USS Abraham Lincoln*, standing beneath a large banner that proclaimed "Mission Accomplished," President Bush declared, "In the battle of Iraq, the United States and our allies have prevailed."

As the invasion morphed into an occupation, the high-tech coalition military forces discovered that they could much more easily destroy a weakly defended tyrannical regime than create a stable, democratic nation-state in its stead. The Coalition Provisional Authority (CPA), led by Proconsul Paul Bremer III, created a governing council, which served as an interim government for the new Iraq. Almost immediately, conditions deteriorated for ordinary Iraqis and the occupying coalition forces who were almost all U.S. soldiers.

Many factors contributed to the rapidly worsening situation. The occupiers lacked sufficient troops, military police, and civil affairs officials to establish order. A submerged population that had been oppressed for decades reacted to its sudden liberation by going on a rampage of vandalism, looting, and killing. CPA officials compounded the problem of maintaining order amidst anarchic conditions by disbanding the Iraqi army, thereby eliminating a force which, purged of its most notorious *Baathist* elements, could have functioned to preserve order. In many cities, no U.S. troops were available for occupation duties. The CPA was slow to restore essential services in many provinces. People lacked basic food supplies, cooking oil, electricity, and fresh water.

As UN relief workers and employees of governmental and private agencies rushed to Iraq to begin the challenging tasks of reconstruction and nation-building, an insurgency was building in the cities and regions where Sunnis predominated. They were joined by hundreds of foreign *jihadists*, many of them affiliated with or allies of *al Qaeda*, crossing the porous borders of Iraq from Jordan, Saudi Arabia, Iran, and Syria. By summer 2003, a violent campaign of suicide bombings, assassinations, kidnappings, roadside bombings, and sabotage, although focused in the Sunni Muslim triangle region of western Iraq, spread across the country.

During 2004, the insurgency gained strength and became more sophisticated in its tactics. It recruited from various sources—*Baathist* supporters of the deposed dictator, alienated former soldiers, foreign *jihadists*, Sunni Muslims who understood that any new Iraqi government would probably be dominated by Shiite Muslims who comprised 60 percent of the Iraqi population, criminal gangs, and an assortment of local community and tribal leaders who sensed they might fare better if they aligned themselves with the insurgents. The rebels comprised decentralized, continually shifting coalitions whose particular mix of forces and tactics varied from region to region and from situation to situation.

U.S. officials had not done much advance planning for the occupation regime nor had they anticipated the legion of problems they quickly encountered. They had assumed that the mass of ordinary Iraqis would welcome the coalition forces as liberators and cooperate with them to rebuild Iraq and create a new democratic nation-state. CPA officials were dismayed to find themselves amidst an angry populace that resented the death and destruction incurred during the war to remove Saddam Hussein, the deteriorating conditions of daily life, the slow pace of restoring vital services, and the even slower pace of establishing a new sovereign state. It was not until the summer of 2004 that the CPA dissolved itself and formally transferred sovereignty to an interim Iraqi government headed by Prime Minister Dyad Allawi.

The undermanned U.S. forces, which now included National Guard and Army Reserve units, often engaged in fierce firefights with insurgent forces in rebel strongholds such as Falluja and Najaf. As the violence escalated and U.S. casualties mounted, polls showed that within the United States popular support for the war and President Bush's personal popularity were declining. Senator Ted Kennedy charged that America had become involved in "another Vietnam."

As support for the war declined and criticisms of the administration's Iraq policy increased during 2004, David Kay, the former chief weapons inspector for the Bush administration, appeared before a congressional committee. Kay, whose team of experts had combed Iraq in the aftermath of Saddam Hussein's downfall searching for WMD, told the committee members that he could find nothing. Any stockpiles of chemical or biological weapons that Iraq might have possessed in the early 1990s had been destroyed, either by previous weapons inspection teams or by the Iraqis themselves. Kay admitted that "we were all wrong."

In July 2004, the Senate Intelligence Committee severely criticized the Bush administration's use of intelligence, particularly their reliance on a controversial National Intelligence Estimate prepared in 2002, which made the case for Saddam Hussein's possession of WMD. President Bush had told the American people that the principal reason the United States had sought regime change in Iraq was because of Saddam's possession of WMD, and his history of using them against Iranians and even his own people. These previous actions made him an "imminent threat" to U.S. national security interests. Senators on the Intelligence Committee accused Bush and other senior officials in his administration of either overstating estimates about

Saddam Hussein's WMD or relying on estimates not supported by underlying evidence. The senators also discovered that the CIA never provided any analyses that supported the administration's claims that Saddam Hussein and *al Qaeda* had formed an alliance. The senators concluded that there was no evidence of a "collaborative relationship" between Saddam's regime and *al Qaeda* terrorists.

As the insurgency grew and Senate critics undermined the Bush administration's rationale for war, graphic images of American guards humiliating and torturing Iraqi prisoners in the Abu Ghraib prison were broadcast around the world. These images provided terrorist groups and other anti-American elements within the Muslim world with a propaganda harvest that threatened to derail the fundamental legal and policy pillars upon which the United States rested its conduct of the War on Terror. Critics of the U.S. war suggested that there could be a moral equivalency between the systemic tactics of the terrorists and the U.S. treatment of detainees at Abu Ghraib. Military correspondent Thomas Ricks claimed that these revelations dealt a mortal blow to the moral justifications for the occupation in the eyes of many Iraqis.

President Bush condemned the cruel mistreatment of the prisoners at Abu Ghraib prison, but White House memos revealed that the president's legal counsel Alberto Gonzales had urged the president to exempt *al Qaeda* and *Taliban* prisoners from the protections of the Geneva Convention to prevent U.S. officials from being prosecuted for committing war crimes. In an open letter to President Bush, a distinguished group of 150 American jurists denounced the memos for seeking to circumvent long-established principals of law and common decency.

In the fall of 2004, the number and scale of insurgent assaults were still expanding. An intense program to train Iraqi security forces was operational, but these new soldiers were not ready to battle the insurgents. There was some progress in economic sectors, but the pace was glacial. Oil production was increasing, but it was still below prewar levels. There had been some improvements in the conditions of daily living for many Iraqi families, and they were enjoying their new freedom even amidst chaotic conditions. But only 40 percent of the Iraqi population said the country was better off since the war.

President Bush cast himself as a wartime president and appealed to patriotism and national unity as he launched his reelection campaign in the fall of 2004. By doing so, he could largely ignore domestic issues, which did not play well for the incumbent. Although the economy had recovered from the recession of 2000, economic growth was sluggish and job creation was slow. Tax cuts implemented while the United States waged an expensive foreign war combined with increased congressional domestic spending to erase the budget surpluses of the Clinton years and bring back spiraling federal deficits. The U.S. dollar weakened against the euro and the Chinese yuan because of the growing budget deficits and international trade deficits, plus the mountain of corporate and consumer debt.

The Democrats entered the 2004 election campaign optimistic that they could regain the White House and retake control of at least one branch of Congress. However, they were handicapped by the continuing factional warfare between neoliberals and paleoliberals. The Democrats were also hindered by 9/11 and its aftermath. The Bush administration's focus on the war on terror and the invasion of Iraq shifted the emphasis in the campaign away from domestic issues, the traditional sources of Democratic voter appeal.

Senator John Kerry rather easily won the Democratic Party nomination. He validated his wartime candidacy by calling attention to his heroic military service in Vietnam. He also appealed to the liberal antiwar elements within his party because after his Vietnam service, he had made a televised speech before Congress critical of the war, which he characterized as a mistake that had cost tens of thousands of American lives.

When both candidates hit the campaign trails, Bush proved to be the more effective campaigner. His West-Texas-accented speaking style and his informal manner appealed to ordinary voters, whereas the patrician Kerry came across as aloof and uncomfortable amidst crowds of average folks. He could never articulate a vision of where he wanted to take the nation. On the war, his stance was inconsistent. He had voted to authorize the use of force, but he had criticized Bush's conduct of the war. Later in the campaign, he stated that even if he had known that Saddam Hussein possessed no WMD and had no links to *al Qaeda* or the 9/11 attacks, he still would have voted for the war. But Kerry also voted against a bill providing funds for the war. His own words reflected the contradictions in Kerry's efforts to appeal to both pro- and antiwar constituents: "I actually voted for the $87 billion before I voted against it."

The Republican campaign succeeded in portraying Kerry as a "flip flopper" on the war and other issues. Organizations supporting Republican candidates also attacked his war record. His accusers claimed that some of his medals were undeserved and that he had misrepresented some of his actions in Vietnam. Kerry refused to rebut what he considered false and scurrilous charges, thus allowing them to damage his campaign.

President Bush won reelection in another close election. He obtained a clear majority of voters, with 51 percent of the vote and a three-million-vote margin of victory. He carried 31 states with 286 electoral votes to Kerry's 252. Republicans also increased their majorities in both the House and the Senate. Although not as close as the 2000 presidential election, the 2004 election revealed a nation that was as politically divided as any time since the Civil War.

Bush's victory was attributed to his earnest, folksy style of campaigning. He rolled up his sleeves, waded into crowds, shook a lot of hands, and stayed on message. The Republican party victories were attributed to Karl Rove, Bush's chief political adviser, who orchestrated a well-financed, efficient get-out-the vote operation, especially in small-town and rural America. In addition to the war and national security issues, Republicans also appealed effectively to many heartland voters on "values issues" such as opposition to gay marriage and abortion rights. Probably the main reason Bush was reelected was because a narrow majority of voters decided that the War on Terror and national security in the wake of 9/11 were the most important issues confronting the nation, and they preferred to retain the incumbent in office rather than turn the job over to an uninspiring candidate who did not offer clear or compelling alternative policies.

As President Bush began his second term, he focused on the war in Iraq, the issue that most clearly defined his presidency. On January 30, 2005, the Iraqis held an election to choose a constituent assembly charged with creating the infrastructure for a new government. Shiite Muslims and Kurdish turnouts were high. Sunni Muslim turnout was low because many of them boycotted the election. The election confirmed the displacement of the former Sunni ruling class and the emergence of both a dominant Shiite Muslim majority and a strong Kurdish minority. An alliance of Shiite Muslims led by two religious parties and backed by Grand Ayatollah Ali al-Sistani won 48 percent of the vote. An alliance of the two major Kurdish parties won 26 percent of the vote. A Shiite–Kurd alliance gave them more than the two-thirds majority in the assembly required to approve a new constitution.

As the insurgency expanded and politicians maneuvered in Iraq, within the U.S. House of Representatives Congressman Walter Jones, a Republican from North Carolina, introduced legislation calling on President Bush to set a timetable for the withdrawal of the approximately 138,000 American troops serving in Iraq. General John Abizaid, the U.S. commander in Iraq and the most senior U.S. military officer of direct Arab descent, told members of the Senate Armed Services Committee that the insurgency was growing and more foreign fighters were entering the country. At the time General Abizaid made his remarks, public opinion polls showed that popular support for the Iraq war and the personal popularity of President Bush had for the first time dipped below 50 percent.

President Bush, in a nationally televised speech, rejected all proposals to set any timetable for withdrawal of U.S. forces. He emphatically reaffirmed the U.S. commitment to "stay the course" until a national unity government in control of its own security forces able to maintain order was in place. He called the Iraq war vital to U.S. national security.

During the summer of 2005, the insurgency expanded, and the violence escalated. The number of American casualties increased sharply. Coalition forces also discovered that the insurgency had widened and deepened. At the most obvious level, Sunni refusal to surrender its historic status as the ruling group in Iraq to the majority Shiites drove the insurgency. The Sunni irredentists were joined by a group of foreign *jihadists*, who relished the opportunity to kill U.S. soldiers as well as Iraqis whom they perceived to be collaborating with the Americans. Ominously, a layer of sectarian violence developed, as roving Sunni and Shiite militias kidnapped and killed numbers of their rival sectarians. In Baghdad, a city inhabited by large numbers of both Shiites and Sunnis, containing more than one quarter of the entire Iraqi population, many neighborhoods became engulfed in sectarian warfare. At other levels, local clan rivalries, competing criminal gangs, and even personal vendettas all fed the rising stream of violence that destabilized Baghdad and other regions of Iraq.

In an environment of escalating sectarian conflict, a referendum on the new constitution was held on October 15, 2005. Amidst heavy security, nearly ten million Iraqi citizens voted, an estimated 63 percent of the electorate. Ten days later an electoral commission certified the results. The constitution had been approved. While 79 percent of voters backed the charter, 21 percent opposed it. Of the eighteen Iraqi provinces, it failed of passage in only two, both of which contained Sunni Arab majorities. In Baghdad province, which included the city and surrounding areas, the new constitution received 78 percent of the vote. In the three Kurdish provinces, the charter passed overwhelmingly, obtaining 99 percent of the votes.

However, the new constitution could not resolve many deeply divisive issues or provide the blueprint for a functioning government. Would Iraq be a unitary state containing an autonomous Kurdish region or would it be instead a federation of many autonomous regions? The charter did not define what civil and political rights Iraqi citizens would have. There were many other unresolved issues, of which the most important was how oil wealth would be distributed among the many provinces that contained no producing oil wells.

The new Iraqi government was dominated by the two Shiite religious parties. In the Parliament, their power was reinforced by the two Kurdish separatist parties. The Shiite parties were backed in Baghdad and southern Iraq by armed militias, some with ties to Iran. The Kurdish parties also retained their own militias, which ran northeastern Iraq like an independent state within a state. Several Sunni political parties participated in the government but lacked any real policy-making power. The authority of the Iraqi government did not reach beyond the Shiite and Kurdish-controlled areas. In the lawless regions, Sunni insurgents sporadically fought and killed U.S. soldiers.

During the first half of 2006, the ambiguities inherent in Iraqi nation-state-building continued to prevail. Amidst an increasingly violent and unstable environment, a coalition government led by Prime Minister Nouri al-Maliki struggled to assert its authority. The insurgency, rooted in the refusal of the Sunnis to accept the empowerment of the Shiite majority, supported by the Kurds, had evolved into a multilevel, many-faceted communal war. Basra, Iraq's second-largest city, was controlled by Shiite militias with ties to Iran. In Baghdad, the security forces of the national government itself had been infiltrated by Shiite sectarians, which Nouri could not control. In Baghdad and elsewhere, thousands of Iraqis, mostly civilians, were dying every month, victims of sectarian civil war between Shiite and Sunni militias who enforced their own brand of vigilante justice. Iraqis were killed by suicide bombers as they worshipped in mosques or attended funerals. Neither the U.S. forces nor the security forces of the fledgling Iraqi government could suppress the violence or protect the civilian population.

During fall 2006, U.S. forces made a concerted effort to suppress the sectarian violence raging within and around Baghdad. They failed. October was the bloodiest month since the occupation of Iraq by coalition forces began. U.S. casualties soared, and nearly four thousand Iraqis died as the violence spiraled out of control. On the eve of the 2006 midterm elections within the United States, the American project of helping the Iraqis to achieve a modern democratic nation-state had stalled. The specter of a full-blown civil war, which could lead to a collapse of the government, result in the disintegration of the nation, and draw in neighboring states to protect their interests, loomed menacingly. Polls showed that large majorities of Americans had turned against the Iraq war. Polls also indicated that President Bush and the Republican-controlled Congress were even more unpopular than the stalled Iraq campaign.

The midterm elections occurred amidst a country in turmoil. The election amounted to a referendum on the Iraq occupation, the performance of President George W. Bush, and the performance of the Republican-controlled Congress. Republicans were further damaged by revelations of scandals and widespread corruption, which forced three Republican congressmen to resign their seats. Fiscal conservatives were angered by the extravagant spending of the Bush administration while it simultaneously pushed through substantial tax cuts that ensured years of budget deficits and an accumulating national indebtedness that had reached $7,000,000,000,000 by the fiscal year 2006.

Lingering outrage and bitterness over the way the Bush administration responded to a natural disaster of cataclysmic proportions contributed to the sullen antiadminstration, anti-Republican mood that had settled on the electorate. On August 29, 2005, Katrina, a Category 5 tropical storm roaring in from the Gulf of Mexico, slammed into the Louisiana and Mississippi coastal regions. In New Orleans, several parishes were destroyed, including the Lower Ninth Ward, home to poor African Americans. Canal levees failed, and within forty-eight hours much of New Orleans lay under water.

Compounding the tragedy, rescue and relief operations stalled because of bureaucratic bumbling. The Federal Emergency Management Agency (FEMA), whose mission was to provide assistance to state and local governments in the event of disaster, was not only slow to get its resources to the stricken areas, it actually hampered local relief efforts. Initially, President Bush appeared to be unconcerned about the disaster. Only on the sixth day after the hurricane had struck did the president visit the disaster area, and even then he made no effort to contact the people who had lost loved ones, their homes, and most of their possessions. Bush was villified in the media. *The New York Times* called his performance "a national disgrace."

The racial and class dimensions of the calamity were most disturbing. Two-thirds of New Orleans' population was black, with a poverty rate twice the national average. More than 1,600 people died in New Orleans, 75 percent of whom were black. Polls revealed that two-thirds of New Orleans' African American residents believed that antiblack racism accounted for the federal government's slow and inept response to their plight.

Across the nation on election day, angry voters threw out Republican state legislators, governors, congressional representatives, and senators. Out of the political wreckage emerged an energized Democratic Party, which gained twenty-eight seats in the House of Representatives and six in the Senate, which gave them control of the new Congress. Harry Reid of Nevada was the new Senate majority leader; and for the first time in American history, a woman, a liberal from

California, Nancy Pelosi, became the speaker of the House of Representatives. Democrats also controlled the legislatures of a majority of the states and twenty-eight governorships, the most since the Republican "earthquake" of 1994.

Democratic party leaders understood that they were the beneficiaries of a national backlash against Republican policies and performance, not of an endorsement of Democratic programs, policies, and philosophy. Many of the new Democrats elected to Congress who defeated incumbent Republicans ran as moderates or conservatives. The Republican majority, carefully built over twenty years, had temporarily been destroyed. The Republican Party had been virtually eliminated in the northeastern parts of the country, and Democrats made serious inroads into former Republican strongholds in the Midwest and the Interior West. Only in the South were Republicans still entrenched.

With the Democrats in control of the new Congress and its leaders committed to pressuring his administration to establish a timetable for withdrawing all U.S. forces from a war that many of them considered lost, and knowing that the Iraqi people verged on all-out sectarian civil warfare, President Bush decided to try a new strategy. In his State of the Union address delivered January 23, 2007, he announced that he was "deploying reinforcements of more than 20,000 additional soldiers and Marines to Iraq." On February 10, the president appointed General David Patraeus commander of the multinational force in Iraq. Patraeus oversaw all coalition forces and used them to implement the new "Surge" strategy, which he had had a major role in developing.

Within eight months, coalition forces had turned the Iraq war around. Levels of violence and casualties on both sides were down. It was not only the increase in force size brought about by the surge but also the change in tactics that made it effective. The surge was a sophisticated counterinsurgency strategy that focused on population security. Soldiers and Marines not only cleared terrorists from neighborhoods in order to make them safe for the civilian residents, but they remained in the neighborhoods after securing them. They intermingled with the people and were a daily presence in their lives, providing protection, help, and services.

Other factors contributed to the improvement in security in Baghdad and elsewhere. Sectarian warfare subsided in Baghdad primarily because the Shia defeated the Sunni, and by the fall of 2008, they controlled most of the capital. The Sunnis were not beaten by coalition forces; they were defeated by the Shia-controlled Iraqi government and by Shia militia. Ethnic cleansing resulting in permanent demographic changes helped restore peace to many Baghdad neighborhoods.

As the Surge took hold and the Shia drove the Sunnis out of Baghdad, Sunni tribal sheiks in western provinces, where the Sunnis were in control, contacted coalition commanders and offered to switch sides. They were weary of the brutality and puritanism of *al-Qaeda*-affiliated militants. The "Anbar Awakening" spread. During 2007 and 2008, the U.S. Army employed more than 100,000 Sunni militiamen to provide security in towns and villages. Many were former insurgents. More than any other development, the Anbar Awakening brought relative peace and security to regions that had formerly been the epicenter of the insurgency.

GLOBAL FINANCIAL CRISIS AND RECESSION

In the fall of 2008, as the U.S. elections approached because of significant reductions in casualties and the establishing of a functioning central government in Iraq, the threat of civil war that could have destabilized that country and perhaps much of the Middle East had diminished. The war in Iraq was no longer an important issue to most Americans. They focused on domestic issues—mainly turmoil in the financial sector and a deepening recession.

The financial and economic decline originated in the collapse of housing markets. Problems had developed over the years in the industry, but as long as housing prices kept climbing, fueled by ever-rising levels of debt, the problems remained hidden. But home prices peaked in 2006 and then began to fall. By 2007, the result was a cascade of foreclosures that glutted housing markets and drove down home prices. Las Vegas, Phoenix, and Miami, cities where lenders had granted subprime mortgages to many home buyers with questionable credit ratings, were hit hardest. Blighted neighborhoods, in which many houses stood vacant, because the owners either had lost their homes via foreclosure or had walked away from properties whose mortgages exceeded their value, had become common features of the national landscape.

The intricate interconnectivity of financial markets exacerbated the problem of gluts in regional housing markets where subprime mortgages had been overused and triggered a developing global financial crisis. The local banks and mortgage brokers who granted the subprime mortgages had borrowed the money they were loaning to homebuyers. The banks then sold these mortgages to investment banks who had also borrowed money to purchase them. These banks would then bundle together thousands of mortgages, packaging prime and subprime mortgages together. These mortgage-backed securities would be sliced into smaller pieces and sold on global markets. Giant equity firms and hedge funds purchased billions of dollars of these securities, always using borrowed money.

All these various levels of market players treated these subprime mortgage-backed securities as if they were normal mortgages, which were regarded as safe investments. Investors assumed that home prices would continue to rise; there had never been massive foreclosures or sustained declines in real estate prices in modern U.S. history. Giant insurance companies fueled the investment frenzy by guaranteeing to assume any losses incurred by investors from defaults. Investors also assumed that the global financial infrastructure had developed new instrumentalities for spreading and managing the levels of risk involved in buying and selling these securitized mortgage packages. Rating agencies contributed to the mounting problem by routinely giving high ratings to these securities backed or partially backed by subprime mortgages. It was as if time bombs had been hardwired into these bundles of tradable mortgages that had spread throughout the global financial system.

In 2007, as foreclosures mounted and housing prices skidded down, investors holding these devalued mortgage-backed securities found that they held toxic assets that they could not sell. Nor could they borrow money because lenders refused to accept the mortgage-backed securities as collateral. Investors confronted a credit crunch, a "liquidity crisis." The liquidity crisis also had a psychological dimension, a crisis of confidence. Because banks did not trust other banks, they would not loan them money nor would they buy their mortgage-backed assets. Major investment houses and banks, facing a double-barrelled liquidity crisis and confidence crisis, collapsed. Bear Stearns was absorbed by J. P. Morgan Chase for a fraction of its value; Lehman Brothers went bankrupt. Wachovia, a banking giant, was taken over by Wells Fargo. Facing bankruptcy, Merrill Lynch let Bank of America buy it for less than half its precrash value.

Most of the banks that were major players in the mortgage markets had been borrowing heavily relative to their deposit bases, and plowing the proceeds from these loans into subprime mortgages, which went into free fall in the wake of the bursting of the housing bubble. In 2008, the ratio of total loans to deposits in United States banks hit 3.5 to 1, making the U.S. banking system the most overleveraged in the developed world. Overleveraging exposed many banks to ruinous losses. The collapse of Washington Mutual (WaMu), the largest bank failure in U.S. history, was directly tied to their extreme overleveraging in the subprime mortgage markets. The remnants of WaMu were acquired by J. P. Morgan Chase for the bargain-basement price of $1.9 billion.

Two of the most prominent casualties were the Federal National Mortgage Association (Fannie Mae) and the Federal Home Loan Mortgage Corporation (Freddie Mac). These companies were government-sponsored home mortgage finance giants, whose primary function was to keep mortgage markets liquid, that is, to ensure that mortgage funds would always be available to lower- and middle-income home buyers. When the credit crunch struck, these two giant combines owned or guaranteed almost half of all the home loans in the United States.

When the mortgage crisis caused a precipitous rise in home foreclosures and sharp declines in home prices, concerns about the solvency of Fannie Mae and Freddie Mac drove the value of their stocks sharply down. Although they received no bailout money and the government did not nationalize them, the U.S. Treasury Department took over the management of the two combines and committed itself to maintaining the value of their debt and their holdings. The treasury also retained the option of loaning or granting them funds in the future if that was deemed necessary for their continued operation.

The global financial crisis produced a national and international economic crisis because so many of the nation's largest banks and banks in many other countries got caught up in the crisis of liquidity. These banks had to write down billions of dollars of their devalued assets because of the collapse of the markets for mortgage-backed securities. American banks and foreign banks with operations in the United States, in order to rebuild their reserves as required by the Treasury Department, chose not to loan money but to hoard their income. The result in 2007 and 2008 was a massive reduction in available credit for everyone across the entire economy.

Because the U.S. economy depended on credit-fueled consumer purchases for 70 percent of its annual GDP, the reduction in available credit brought on the deepest recession since the early 1930s. Prospective home buyers with good credit could not obtain mortgages; people wishing to purchase new cars, vans, SUVs, and trucks could not get credit. U.S. companies could not borrow to cover normal operations or to fund expansions. Developers could not borrow money even if they had wanted to build more houses and malls. Two giants of the American auto industry, General Motors and Chrysler, troubled for years by a plethora of serious dysfunctions, verged on bankruptcy. Unemployment skyrocketed, reaching 8.5 percent by the fall of 2008. International trade shrank. China's and Japan's economies suffered because Americans reduced sharply their purchases of imported commodities. A crisis of liquidity that had nearly brought Wall Street to its knees had created a global economic crisis.

U.S. treasury secretary Henry Paulson developed a $700 billion bailout plan, modified by Congress, to attack the key problem at its source, the crisis in liquidity of the mortgage-backed securities, which had caused the global credit system to seize up. The government proposed to purchase these toxic securities with cash, which would enable the banks to rid themselves of these untradable assets of unknowable (if any) value and simultaneously recapitalize their reserves. Political leaders assumed that the banks, rid of their toxic assets, flush with cash and healthy balance sheets, would start lending again and stimulate an economic revival.

The first few months the bailout plan was in place did not yield the hoped-for results. Banks used the bailout money to avoid bankruptcy and stay in business. Most made no effort to make loans to creditworthy businesses and individuals. Some large investment banks incurred populist wrath for paying bonuses to employees whose risky investment practices had nearly brought down the global financial system. American International Group (AIG), a giant insurance company, which had incurred liabilities they could not cover when the mortgage-backed securities markets collapsed, received $180 billion, most of which they promptly transferred to their creditors. Billions of dollars of bailout money went to General Motors and Chrysler, which only delayed their seemingly inevitable march toward bankruptcy and downsizing. In many instances, the government accepted shares of stock in the companies in exchange for the bailout money, making the American people major stakeholders in some of the nation's largest investment banks, insurance companies, and automakers. Such transactions provoked Newt Gingrich, a conservative Republican leader, to complain that the U.S. government was importing European socialism.

ELECTION 2008

The 2008 presidential election took place amidst the backdrop of the severest financial and economic crises to afflict the American people since the Great Depression of the early 1930s. It was the longest and costliest electoral contest in the nation's history. It ran for almost two years and cost in excess of $1 billion, two-thirds of which was raised and spent by the major contenders for the Democratic Party's nomination, Barack Obama and Hillary Clinton. Both Obama, as the first African American, and Clinton, as the first woman, to have realistic opportunities to attain the American presidency, conducted history-making campaigns.

When the primaries and caucuses began in January 2008, senator and former first lady Hillary Clinton was the clear front-runner for the Democratic Party nomination. She led in the polls and enjoyed a big advantage in fund-raising. She had assembled a formidable staff of experienced political operatives to direct her campaign. Many of them had helped Clinton's husband, former president Bill Clinton, win two presidential elections. Most of all, she offered herself as the candidate who had the strength and experience "to make change happen." She had been battle tested, had stood up to the attack dogs of the hard Right, and "was ready to lead on day one." Trailing her were a young, relatively inexperienced junior senator from Illinois, Barack Obama, and the photogenic economic populist John Edwards, who had been John Kerry's vice presidential running mate in 2004. Trailing them were several other candidates who had also entered the Democratic lists.

Party leaders had restructured the schedule to create "Super Tuesday," February 5, the date when twenty-four states would hold either primaries or caucuses that would choose over half the total delegates for the nominating convention. Only Clinton was believed to have the resources to campaign simultaneously in most of these states, and she was expected to harvest enough delegates to virtually secure the nomination on Super Tuesday.

The first contests were the Iowa caucuses staged on January 3, which Clinton was favored to win. But Obama won the Iowa caucuses, and Clinton finished third behind him and John Edwards! Analysts of the 2008 election agree that Obama's dramatic upset victory in the Iowa caucuses changed everything. It shattered the myth of Clinton's inevitable candidacy and transformed Obama's candidacy. Overnight he became the rising political star. The Iowa caucuses set up an epic battle for the Democratic Party presidential nomination between two political trailblazers, a white woman and a black man, that energized the Democratic Party electorate and generated record voter turnouts.

Super Tuesday's results left the two candidates in a virtual tie, with Obama counting 847 delegates to Clinton's 834. Obama then reeled off eleven consecutive victories in primaries and the Maine caucus, which gave him a substantial delegate lead. As his campaign gained momentum, millions of Americans came to appreciate Obama's extraordinary political talents. He was a brilliant orator with a charismatic personality. Reminiscent of John F. Kennedy, Obama possessed the remarkable ability to excite young people and to get them involved in politics and public service. Winning in Iowa, a "white" state, he convinced the nation's African American population that a black man could capture the Democratic Party nomination. He proved adept at raising the huge sums of money needed to finance his sophisticated and costly campaign. He put together an effective campaign organization that registered millions of new voters and turned them out on election days. He and his staffers made innovative use of Internet resources, the "netroots," for fund-raising, networking, and getting his message across. Most of all, he offered his candidacy as proof that the promise of American democracy was open to all who were willing to work hard and contribute to the common good regardless of class or racial background. Barack Obama was the avatar of a new politics, whose slogan "Yes We Can!" expressed the hopes of millions of citizens that he could lead a national renewal and transform the Washington political culture.

But Clinton refused to yield, and she battled on. She presented herself as the scrappy champion of hard-working, blue-collar Democrats. Her focus on bread-and-butter issues during hard times kept her in the race. She scored major victories in Ohio and Pennsylvania, two populous industrial states battered by recession. But with a big win on May 6 in North Carolina, aided by a record turnout of black voters, Obama virtually wrapped up the nomination. Determined to stay in the race until the last primary, Clinton refused to concede the nomination to Obama, even though Democratic Party leaders, fearful that she could damage Obama's chances of winning the presidency in November, pressured her to drop out. On June 7, only after Obama had secured the nomination, did she accept defeat and withdraw.

On the Republican side, a large field of candidates initially entered the primaries and caucuses. The front-runners included Rudy Giuliani, former mayor of New York City whose intrepid leadership during the horrendous events of 9/11 had rallied the people, and Mitt Romney, a wealthy businessman and former governor of Massachusetts. John McCain, the man who would win the Republican nomination, had been trailing badly in the polls less than a month before the primaries began. At one point his campaign had been so strapped for funds that he was forced to reduce his staff and even considered suspending his campaign. However, his campaign quickly caught fire when he won primaries in New Hampshire, South Carolina, and Florida. He followed these victories with a near-sweep of the Republican primaries held on Super Tuesday. Giuliani and Romney dropped out. By winning primaries in Texas and Ohio, John McCain had secured his party's nomination by mid-March.

When the general election campaign between Obama and McCain got underway in September, the controversial war in Iraq was still a major issue. Obama had opposed the Iraq war from the outset, and he had also opposed the Surge. McCain had supported the war and the Surge, which was one of the major factors credited with improving the security situation in Iraq. The war probably bolstered McCain's candidacy initially, and polls showed him and Obama in a virtual tie. Pundits all predicted a close election just as the 2000 and 2004 elections had been.

The unpopularity of the incumbent George W. Bush worked to the advantage of Obama and the Democrats. Although he had supported the war and the Surge, McCain tried to separate himself from Bush on other issues such as climate change and campaign finance reform. However, in numerous TV commercials and at rallies, the Obama campaign demonstrated that Senator McCain's voting record coincided with the president 90 percent of the time. Most analysts believe that Obama's relentless efforts to tie McCain to the unpopular Bush contributed significantly to his electoral victory in November.

Perhaps the most important campaign issue was the matter of change versus experience. Obama offered himself as a fresh new face in politics; he would be the candidate most able to bring change to Washington. The seventy-two-year-old McCain, a Vietnam War hero, contrasted his experience and expertise, especially in foreign policy and military affairs, with the inexperience of Obama.

Obama added some foreign policy heft to the Democratic ticket when he chose Senator Joseph Biden Jr., the chairman of the Senate Foreign Relations Committee, to be his vice presidential running mate. McCain partially undercut his own line of attack by picking the young Alaska governor Sarah Palin to be his running mate. Two media interviews suggested that Palin lacked understanding and even basic knowledge of key foreign policy issues, casting doubt about her qualifications to be vice president or president.

A series of debates among the candidates did not significantly influence the outcome of the election. No one made any big gaffes or breakthroughs; however, the three presidential debates probably did subtly favor Obama over McCain because they enabled the Democratic candidate to display his intelligence, equipoise, and civility. He appeared to enjoy the give and take of the debates. He came across as calm, articulate, thoughtful, and well informed on all the major issues. He appeared to be at ease with himself and prepared to lead the nation if the people chose him.

As election day approached, the financial crisis and deepening recession clearly damaged McCain and the Republicans, and greatly helped Obama and the Democrats. Polls taken in the final weeks of the campaign showed that 60 percent to 75 percent of respondents listed economic concerns as the top issue. Republican congressional candidates braced themselves for the electoral *tsunami* that they knew was coming. Obama's campaign gained strength while McCain's declined.

Obama enjoyed significant advantages during the final days—in fund-raising, in media advertising, and in organizing get-out-the-vote campaigns. Having secured all the states that John Kerry had carried in 2004, Obama poured his considerable remaining resources into key battleground states and several states normally carried by Republican presidential candidates such as Virginia, North Carolina, and Colorado. Obama's media blitz forced McCain on the defensive and made him deploy his limited assets just to try to hold onto his Republican base. Polls showed Obama opening a steadily growing lead. The only questions remaining on election eve were how big his margin of victory would be and how large the Democratic majorities in the next Congress would be.

As election returns poured in on the evening of November 4, it quickly became obvious that Barack Obama would become the first African American president in the history of the republic and that the Democratic Party would add significantly to its majorities in both houses of Congress. The Republican Party suffered its worst electoral defeat since the Goldwater debacle of 1964. The Democrats controlled both the White House and the Congress for the first time since 1994. All the networks declared Obama the winner at 11:00 P.M., eastern standard time (EST). About half an hour later, McCain gave a gracious concession speech in which he congratulated Obama on his historic victory and offered him his full support. President-elect Obama appeared at midnight in Grant Park, Chicago, to deliver his victory speech before a celebrating crowd of 250,000 people. Following his speech, spontaneous block parties broke out in cities all across the land and around the world—in London, Berlin, Tokyo, Rio de Janeiro, and Nairobi.

A record 131,200,000 votes were cast. Sixty-three percent of eligible voters trooped to the polls. Barack Obama received 69,456,897 votes (53 percent); McCain polled 59,934,814 (45.7 percent). After close elections in several states were decided over the next few months, Obama received 366 electoral college votes to 172 for McCain. Democrats acquired large majorities in both houses of the new Congress, 60 senators and 256 congresspersons.

As analysts probed the deeper meanings of the historic election, they examined the troubling legacy of race relations. Race had been the most enduring divide in American politics.

Much progress had been made since the 1950s, primarily as a consequence of the Civil Rights movement and federal policy. Contemporary Americans inhabited a diverse, multicultural society, and nearly all citizens condemned the explicit racism that had confined most African Americans for so long to second-class citizenship.

However, many white Americans still harbored conscious or unconscious resentments against African Americans. These resentments were found most often among men, especially older men, among those who lacked college degrees, among those who worked at blue-collar rather than white-collar jobs, and among those who resided in rural areas of the Midwest and South.

Many thoughtful people expected a white backlash; they worried that enough voters would vote their resentments to deny Obama the presidency. John McCain and Sarah Palin, aware of these voters, while avoiding explicit racial appeals, used coded phrases to attract their votes—McCain played on the contrast between himself as "the American President Americans have been waiting for" and Obama's African roots. Palin addressed crowds of her supporters as "real Americans," implying Obama lacked "real American" *bona fides*.

Obama's race was a plus for him in some states, a minus in others, and probably not a factor in many. His race may have helped him win key battleground states where record turnouts of black voters were decisive. Exit polls revealed that about 10 percent of voters stated that race "was the single most important factor" or "one of the most important factors" in making their choice. These voters backed Obama 53 percent to 46 percent. A sizeable number of these voters probably were white people who liked the idea of having an African American president. In some states, white backlashers voted for Obama because the economy trumped race.

However, Obama also lost votes because of his race. Most obviously in Deep South states such as Mississippi and Alabama, where he ran much worse among white voters than John Kerry had in 2004. He also lost votes in counties of several other states including Texas, Tennessee, Kentucky, and West Virginia. These counties were all predominantly white, rural, and downscale. But Obama probably lost no states because of the backlash vote that he might otherwise have won.

Obama won the 2008 election because of many factors—his extraordinarily successful campaign; the unpopularity of the incumbent; the underfunded, poorly organized campaign conducted by John McCain; and most of all, a sinking economy; but his victory also showed the extent to which race was no longer the great dividing line in American politics.

Because of the historic candidacy of Hillary Clinton, the 2008 election highlighted the powerful roles women increasingly played in American political life. It also highlighted some enduring gender inequalities that limited women's political achievements, even though women comprised 52 percent of the American population and more women than men have voted in every presidential election since 1964. At least ten million more women than men voted in the 2008 elections. Of the estimated ten million new voters in 2008, over 60 percent were women. The percentage of eligible women who voted has consistently been higher than the percentage of eligible men who have turned out on election days for decades.

Women strongly preferred Obama to McCain despite McCain's having chosen Sarah Palin as his vice presidential running mate. Obama received 56 percent of the women's vote to 43 percent for McCain, whereas men split 49 percent for Obama and 48 percent for McCain. A major reason for Obama's success among women voters was their perception that he was better prepared to deal with the nation's financial and economic crises. Obama also directly addressed women's issues like pay equity, maternity leave, and early childhood development. The McCain campaign chose Palin primarily to energize the Republican Party's conservative base, which she did. She was less successful in engaging working-class women, especially millions of working-class black women and Latinas, who voted for Obama by large majorities. Economic issues probably mattered more to most working-class women voters than did the fact that the Republican Party chose a woman to run for vice president who campaigned as a family values and free-market conservative.

The Latino vote was another force reshaping the 2008 political map. The approximately eleven million Hispanic voters who trooped to the polls on election day comprised between 8 percent and 9 percent of all voters. It was by far the largest turnout of Latino voters in American history. Hispanics voted for Obama by a two-to-one margin, and they helped to decide the outcome of several battleground states—Colorado, Florida, New Mexico, and Nevada. Bush had won all of these states in 2004; they all ended up in the win column for Obama in 2008. These states will be critical in 2012 election strategies when there will likely be millions more Hispanic voters, recruited from the ranks of the nation's fastest growing minority. In 2012, probably no candidate will be able to win the electoral votes of Texas and California, the two most populous states, without winning a majority of the large and growing Hispanic vote in both.

Demographic factors contributed significantly to Obama's victory. The ethnic composition of the majority coalition that his campaign organization assembled was a reflection of the multicultural society America had become. About two-thirds of his supporters were white and a third were minorities. The Republican coalition was predominantly white, male, and aging. Obama received over 90 percent of the African American vote. He won both the Hispanic vote and the Asian vote by two-to-one margins. Young voters, ages eighteen to twenty-nine, overwhelmingly backed Obama, approximately 69 percent to 30 percent. Metropolitan voters, the voters who lived in cities, suburbs, and exurbs voted Democratic. Rural voters overwhelmingly voted Republican, but they were a relatively small and declining population. Suburbs and exurbs were the dynamic, fastest growing places in the country. In 2004, Bush had scored well in the suburbs and exurbs, especially in the Sunbelt region. In 2008, many of these suburban and exurban voters abandoned the Republicans and voted for Obama, contributing to his decisive victory.

The Republican brand has been severely degraded. With few moderates remaining in office, the GOP has been reduced mainly to its hard Right base with strength only in the Deep South and some states in Appalachia, the Midwest, and Intramontane West. Demographic and cultural trends suggested the Republican Party faced a bleak electoral future.

THE NEW FACE OF AMERICA

On January 20, 2009, at 12:00 noon local time, Barack Hussein Obama took the oath of office administered by Chief Justice John Roberts to become the forty-fourth president of the United States of America. With his inauguration, which set an attendance record for any event held in Washington, D.C., Obama became the first African American to hold the office of president. People all across America and around the world paid unequalled attention to the inaugural event.

Obama's inaugural address was an understated affair, filled with plain speech. It was devoid of rhetorical flourishes, and there were no memorable sound bites. It was filled with traditional references; Obama located his presidency solidly within American political traditions. His speech was above all a sober call to restore responsibility, both to hold politicians accountable for their actions and to ordinary citizens to get involved in community affairs. He showed his understanding that the nation, indeed the world, confronted many difficult challenges, but he also

FIGURE 18.3   Barack Obama takes the oath of office from Chief Justice John Roberts to become the forty-fourth president of the United States.   *Source:* Magnum Photos, Inc./Eliott Erwitt.

confidently asserted, a la John Kennedy, that he and his nation were prepared to face those challenges and ultimately prevail.

After a day and night of ceremonies, parades, balls, and other social activities, the new administration went to work. Not since 1933 had any president and his senior staff confronted so many challenges nor been under such pressure to act.

The two fronts of the War on Terror, Iraq and Afghanistan, required immediate attention. Although the security situation in Iraq had improved and Iraq had a functioning government, the emerging political order was fragile. Violence continually flared, and U.S. soldiers and Iraqis continued to die. Several issues remained unresolved. The dominant Shia refused meaningful power-sharing with the Sunni. A workable plan for distributing oil revenues from the provinces with oil to those provinces without oil had yet to be devised. It remained an open question whether Iraqi security forces and police could provide order as U.S. troops were pulled out. At best, the "handoff," as the responsibility for maintaining order was passed from the departing Americans to the Iraqis, would be a delicate operation. And even if all went well, thousands of U.S. troops were destined to remain in Iraq for years.

If the situation in Iraq were improving, the situation in Afghanistan was deteriorating. Obama was committed to increasing the number of U.S. forces operating in Afghanistan in an effort to suppress the *Taliban* who had revived their insurgency. The *Taliban* and *al Qaeda* operated out of havens in the lawless borderlands of western Pakistan. American raids in these border areas threatened to extend the war to Pakistan, whose weak government was equipped with nuclear weapons.

The United States confronted other challenges in the Middle East and elsewhere. Although Obama and his Secretary of State Hillary Clinton were committed to trying to resolve the interminable conflict between Israelis and the Palestinians, there were no solutions remotely in sight. Hamas ruled in the Gaza strip, and they refused to recognize Israel as a legitimate entity. The Israeli government refused to even curtail Jewish settlements in the West Bank, much less pressure any of the settlers to leave. The Iranian government remained implacably hostile to the United States and appeared determined to build a nuclear weapon, or at least acquire the capability to build one. North Korea, enigmatic and dangerous, resumed nuclear testing and continued to work on developing long-range missles in defiance of U.S. and world opinion. Obama's options in dealing with a nation whose erratic leaders did not play by the established rules remained severely limited.

Climate change because of global warming was another problem requiring immediate action. The new president had committed his administration to supporting international efforts to curb the release of greenhouse gases (principally carbon dioxide) into the atmosphere and to develop renewable sources of energy. Meanwhile, the United States and all other industrialized nations continue to pump carbon dioxide into the atmosphere and their economies remained dependent on petroleum as their primary energy source.

As a consequence of America's invasion of Iraq, which most of the world did not regard as an imminent security threat to the United States, world opinion strongly condemned America for its unprovoked aggression. Repairing America's degraded international reputation was one of President Obama's most urgent and necessary tasks. Absent trust and respect, America, the one nation with the resources and the will, working in tandem with others to find lasting solutions to at least some of the serious global problems, will probably fail.

At home, the new president had to deal immediately with a deepening recession, rising unemployment, and waves of home foreclosures. Two major automakers, General Motors and Chrysler, approached bankruptcy. The banking industry struggled to stabilize itself. Bankers also lobbied Congress to prevent Obama from fulfilling his campaign pledge to regulate banking operations. Banks, working to rebuild their reserves and liquidate their toxic assets, did not resume lending, and the recession worsened. Stock markets remained far below levels attained in the recent past. The national debt continued to rise; many state governments struggled to provide essential services because of declining tax revenues and mounting indebtedness. California, the most populous state and possessing the world's seventh largest economy, verged on insolvency. Consumer indebtedness reached record levels, and millions of families had debts that exceeded their assets. Government and balance of payments deficits drove the value of the dollar down. International trade shrank in tandem with the global recession.

In addition to shoring up the financial system, trying to stem the rash of home foreclosures, and reviving an economy mired in a deep recession, President Obama has committed his administration to fixing a broken health care system and providing health insurance for the more than 45,000,000 Americans who have none. He has also promised to deal with complex immigration problems, the most urgent of which are securing the long border with Mexico and establishing a path to citizenship for the millions of undocumented workers living in the United States.

As the relatively young and inexperienced president and his staffers went to work, they enjoyed the support and goodwill of most Americans and much of the global population. Capable and confident, Barack Obama was fully engaged with the historic moment. The only certainty in an uncertain world: The president and the American people would be tested.

Brief Bibliographic Essay

A sizeable literature covering the major events occurring in the first years of the new millennium has already accumulated. Sam Roberts, *Who We Are Now: The Changing Face of America in the Twenty-First Century*, is a vast storehouse of important information about the American people. *2000 Presidential Election Crisis* is a collection of articles written by correspondents of the *New York Times*, with an introduction by Douglas Brinkley. *The Cell*, by John Miller, Michael Stone, and Chris Mitchell, explains why the FBI and CIA failed to thwart the 9/11 plot. The National Commission on Terrorist Attacks upon the United States, *The 9/11 Commission Report (2004)*, is a best-selling bipartisan inquiry into the events surrounding the 9/11 attacks. *The Threatening Storm: The Case for Invading Iraq* by Kenneth M. Pollack makes a carefully qualified case for an invasion of Iraq. In *Against All Enemies: Inside America's War on Terror*, Richard Clark, a diplomat and counterterrorism expert, forcibly argues that invading Iraq was a strategic blunder. An excellent brief history of the Iraq war is Williamson Murray and Major General Robert H. Scales Jr., *The Iraq War: A Military History*. Thomas E. Ricks, *The Gamble: General David Patraeus and the American Military Adventure in Iraq, 2006–2008*, is a recent account of the Surge that helped turn the war in Iraq around. Our account of the collapse of the housing markets that triggered the financial and economic crises of 2007–2009 and our account of the 2008 election were constructed from a variety of sources, mostly newspaper and magazine articles. We also relied on Internet sources.

INDEX

Meredith, James, 103, 140

Mexican Americans, 5, 14

Mexico, 135, 206, 227, 241, 290

Microsoft, 251

Middle East, 19, 90–92, 179–181, 195–196, 269–272

"Military-industrial complex," 16

Milliken v. Bradley, 156

Milken, Michael, 228

Mills, C. Wright, 76–77

Milosevic, Slobodan, 281–283

Mineta, Norman, 295

Miranda v. Arizona, 124

Missile Crisis, the, 109–112

Mississippi "Freedom Summer" (1964), 134

Mitchell, John, 164, 166

Mondale, Walter, 193, 225–226

Montenegro, 282

Moral Majority, 201

Mossadegh, Mohammed, 89

Muhammad Ali, 141

Mulroney, Brian, 239

Multiculturalism, 254–255

Mundt, Karl, 82

Murphy, Frank, 5

Murray, Philip, 52

Musharraf, Pervis, 299–300

Muskie, Edmund, 148, 161

Mutually assured destruction, 236

My Lai massacre, 177

N

NAACP. *See* National Association for the Advancement of Colored People

Nader, Ralph, 123, 161, 292–293

NAFTA. *See* North American Free Trade Agreement

Nagasaki, 22

Nasser, Gamal Abdul, 90–91, 125–126, 179

National Air Quality Standards Act, 160

National Association for the Advancement of Colored People, 12, 46, 85

National Defense Education Act, 93

National Endowment for the Arts, 252–253

National Housing Act, 49

National Interstate and Defense Highways Act, 59, 81

National Organization for Women, 145

National Rifle Association, 284

National Security Act, 29

National Security Agency, 191, 299

National Security Council, 29, 178

National Security Council Document Number 68, 34, 37

National Wilderness Preservation Act, 123

Native Americans, 5, 14–15, 142–143, 159, 255

NATO. *See* North Atlantic Treaty Organization

NDEA. *See* National Defense Education Act

NEA. *See* National Endowment for the Arts

Netanyahu, Benjamin, 284–285

Netherlands, 19

New Look, 85–86

New Zealand, 87

Ngo Dinh Diem, 87, 112

Ngo Dinh Nhu, 112

Nguyen Van Thieu, 128, 176, 179

Nicaragua, 196, 239–240, 267

Nichols, Terry, 283–284

Nigeria, 187

Nixon, Richard. 44

　HUAC and, 51–53

　Elected vice-president, 80

　And 1960 election, 98–100

　Wins 1968 election, 149–151

　Southern Strategy of, 156–158

　And 1972 election, 161–162

　Involvement in Watergate scandals, 163–169

　Détente with the Soviet Union, 171–173

　And the Opening to China, 174–175

　And the Vietnam War, 175–179

Nixon Doctrine, the, 172

No Child Left Behind Act, 295

Noriega, Manuel, 267

North, Oliver, 243–245, 246–247

North American Free Trade Agreement, 274, 281

North Atlantic Treaty Organization, 30–33, 91, 94, 125, 182–183, 235, 281–283, 299

North Korea, 35–39

North Vietnam, 87, 127–128, 129, 175–176, 178–179

Northern Alliance, the, 300

Norton, Gale, 295

NOW. *See* National Organization for Women

NRA. *See* National Rifle Association

NSA. *See* National Security Agency

NSC. *See* National Security Council

NSC-68. *See* National Security Council Document Number 68